M O D E R N

Business English

MODERN

Business English

Price R. Voiles

GLENCOE

Macmillan/McGraw–Hill

Lake Forest, Illinois   Columbus, Ohio   Mission Hills, California   Peoria, Illinois

Modern Business English, Eighth Edition
Instructor's Edition

Send all inquiries to:
GLENCOE DIVISION
Macmillan/McGraw-Hill
936 Eastwind Drive
Westerville, OH 43081

ISBN 0-02-803009-5 (student edition)
ISBN 0-02-803010-9 (instructor's edition)

Printed in the United States of America.

1 2 3 4 5 6 7 8 9 BANT 00 99 98 97 96 95 94 93

CONTENTS

CONTENTS

CONTENTS

Part 8
Words and Word References   235

Instructor's Manual

Financial, clerical, administrative, managerial—all types and all levels of jobs in business, industry, and government consist largely of activities that require a thorough knowledge of language and the ability to use language effectively. Skill in using language to communicate is essential for entering, performing in, and advancing in your chosen career or profession.

Modern Business English, Eighth Edition, provides the study, practice, and evaluation resources you need to develop competence in using language effectively and appropriately. Specifically, this Eighth Edition concentrates on both giving you a thorough, practical grasp of the principles of English grammar, usage, and style that help you build the framework for effective business communication and developing your proficiency in applying those principles.

THE STUDENT'S MATERIALS

Modern Business English, Eighth Edition, guides you through a carefully planned series of instructional units organized in a developmental sequence. The units are grouped into eight parts with a survey lesson beginning and a review lesson ending each part. By completing and analyzing the survey, you can identify areas of emphasis for your study. By performing and checking the review, you can evaluate your progress.

Each unit is broken into smaller "instruction/practice" segments in which you study a segment of a unit—usually a half-page to a page—and then work through a "Spot Check" exercise to reinforce what you just studied. At the end of each unit is a two-page worksheet covering all parts of that unit. Both the spot checks and the worksheets offer several types of exercises and self-checking applications to help you develop your language skills.

New to this edition is the use of a second color to highlight certain text features. The content has been expanded slightly to demonstrate additional refinements in selected applications.

Surveys. The Eighth Edition text-workbook is divided into eight parts. Each part opens with a two-page survey, or pretest, that you should complete before studying the principles covered in the units comprising that part. You are encouraged to use the survey results to identify those principles of language usage or style which may require special attention as you study the units in that part.

Units. The eight parts of the text-workbook are divided into thirty-five units, each covering principles related to a particular topic. Every principle is fully explained and immediately followed by a number of example applications.

Spot Checks. Many of the units in the program include spot-check exercises for immediate practice in applying principles a few at a time. These frequent spot checks provide a means of immediately confirming that you have correctly interpreted and applied the principles and examples just studied.

Study Guides. Every unit ends with a study guide that consists of examples that show the correct application of rules presented in the unit. In most cases superscript numbers in these examples cite rule numbers found in the unit instructional material. Besides providing a summary, each study guide is designed to help you apply the principles easily and accurately in the accompanying worksheet.

Worksheets. After finishing the end-of-unit study guide, you complete a worksheet containing practice exercises correlated with that unit. In some instances, the two-page worksheet may contain exercises related to principles covered in previous units as well as rules and principles in the unit just studied. This cumulative application ensures that you can integrate material from previous units with the material in the present units.

Reviews. Each part ends with a two-page review containing practice exercises related to the various principles covered in the particular part. This activity gives you an opportunity to discover and restudy problem topics before taking an end-of-part test.

THE INSTRUCTOR'S MATERIALS

A special Instructor's Edition of *Modern Business English, Eighth Edition,* is available to instructors. The Instructor's Edition contains the following materials.

The Student's Text-Workbook. The Instructor's Edition includes a page-for-page version of the student's text-workbook. Answers to the surveys, spot checks, worksheets, and reviews appear on the same page as in the student edition and are displayed in a second color for easy reference. To make locating material easier, part and unit numbers and titles are listed at the bottom of the page along with the page number.

Additional Exercises. Included in the Instructor's Edition are several supplemental exercises dealing with word choice, spelling, grammar, and usage. These exercises may be given orally or reproduced and distributed to students for extra practice.

Objective Tests. Also provided in the Instructor's Edition is a set of objective tests that the instructor may either duplicate as shown or modify in any way that she or he wishes. The set of masters includes a course pretest, an end-of-part test for each of the eight parts, and a course posttest. Also included is a facsimile key to the tests.

Other Materials. The Instructor's Edition includes a special supplement with comments and suggestions related to use of the program, as well as a list of course activities and a course schedule.

ACKNOWLEDGMENTS

The author is particularly indebted to Mary Alice Wittenberg and the late Kate M. Monro, coauthors of several previous editions of *Modern Business English*. In addition, the author and the publisher extend their sincere thanks to the many instructors and students who assisted in developing and publishing the Eighth Edition.

PART 1

Nouns and Noun Usage

Before you study Units 1 through 3, complete this survey of nouns and noun usage. These exercises will help you identify principles that you may wish to give special attention.

SURVEY

 A **In the space provided, write the plural form of each noun shown in parentheses.**

1. Both (company) have their headquarters here.
2. You may need more (shelf) in your office.
3. The (document) are ready for your signature.
4. To which of the (Colby) did you speak?
5. The firm has survived a number of (crisis).
6. Both she and he are well-known (attorney).
7. Most people respect the (belief) of others.
8. The departmental staff includes two (CPA).
9. What is the price of a 10-pound bag of (potato)?
10. You may want to consider (certificate of deposit).
11. This list includes a few (don't).
12. Each of the (plaintiff) must appear in person.
13. The city owns and operates two sports (complex).
14. The company was founded in the early (1900).
15. One of their (son-in-law) is self-employed.
16. Was the letter sent to all (alumnus) of the college?
17. The company has (studio) in Orlando and Hollywood.
18. What are the most effective advertising (medium)?
19. Some ranchers use public land to graze their (sheep).
20. The counter was covered with (brush) of all kinds.
21. Remember that the word *vacuum* contains two (u).
22. Those new TV (series) received favorable reviews.
23. This area has attracted many new (business).
24. How many (grandchild) do they have?
25. Some publications contain many (footnote).

1. companies
2. shelves
3. documents
4. Colbys
5. crises
6. attorneys
7. beliefs
8. CPAs
9. potatoes
10. certificates of deposit
11. don'ts
12. plaintiffs
13. complexes
14. 1900s
15. sons-in-law
16. alumni
17. studios
18. media
19. sheep
20. brushes
21. u's
22. series
23. businesses
24. grandchildren
25. footnotes

In the spaces provided, write the possessive forms for the following phrases. Be sure to place the apostrophe correctly. Note the example.

0. liabilities of a firm   **0.** _a firm's liabilities_

1. article by Fay R. Wells, Ph.D.   **1.** _Fay R. Wells, Ph.D.'s article_

2. shoes for men and women   **2.** _men's and women's shoes_

3. salary for three weeks   **3.** _three weeks' salary_

4. employer of Bonnie and Brad   **4.** _Bonnie and Brad's employer_

5. assets of both companies   **5.** _both companies' assets_

 In the spaces provided, write the singular possessive, plural, and plural possessive forms of the following nouns. If a noun should not be used as a singular or plural possessive, write _None_ in each appropriate column.

Singular	Singular Possessive	Plural	Plural Possessive
0. agency	agency's	agencies	agencies'
1. manufacturer	manufacturer's	manufacturers	manufacturers'
2. child	child's	children	children's
3. employee	employee's	employees	employees'
4. strawberry	None	strawberries	None
5. board of trustees	board of trustees'	boards of trustees	boards of trustees'
6. chef	chef's	chefs	chefs'
7. gentleman	gentleman's	gentlemen	gentlemen's
8. branch manager	branch manager's	branch managers	branch managers'
9. daughter-in-law	daughter-in-law's	daughters-in-law	daughters-in-law's
10. wife	wife's	wives	wives'

 If a sentence contains an incorrect plural or possessive, underline the error and write the necessary correction in the space provided. If no correction is necessary, write _OK_. Note the examples.

0. How do you spell the <u>street's</u> name?   **0.** _name of the street_

00. <u>George's</u> and Herman's employer gave them bonuses.   **00.** _George_

1. Federal, state, and local governments collect <u>taxs</u>.   **1.** _taxes_

2. We should discuss the <u>proes</u> and cons of both plans.   **2.** _pros_

3. Most customers expect to get their <u>moneys</u> worth.   **3.** _money's_

4. Baldwin <u>Associate's</u> ads are usually humorous.   **4.** _Associates'_

5. <u>Alicia's</u> and Victor's brother owns those buildings.   **5.** _Alicia_

6. Both directories list hundreds of <u>Jones</u> and Smiths.   **6.** _Joneses_

7. What are the bank's <u>criterions</u> for approving loan applications?   **7.** _criteria_

8. Both plaintiffs' <u>attornies</u> met with the reporters.   **8.** _attorneys_

9. Some summer programs are reruns of various series.   **9.** _OK_

10. Were you aware of <u>Ms. Reed</u> planning to resign?   **10.** _Ms. Reed's_

Nouns—Plural Forms

NOUNS

General Definition. *Nouns* are words that name persons, animals, places, objects, ideas, qualities, and activities.

PERSONS:	citizen Jeffrey	executive Margaret	resident Nelson
ANIMALS:	dolphin oyster	parrot donkey	alligator poultry
PLACES:	state Maryland	country Spain	city Cleveland
OBJECTS:	invoice boulder	aluminum machine	statue carpet
IDEAS:	justice freedom	democracy socialism	communism security
QUALITIES:	honesty loyalty	sincerity efficiency	generosity integrity
ACTIVITIES:	golf exercise	tennis study	work travel

As illustrated by the word *travel* in the following sentences, many words may be used as more than one part of speech.

> *Travel* enables us to enrich our lives. (*Travel* functions as a noun—it names an activity.)
>
> Many people *travel* by train every day. (*Travel* functions as a verb—it indicates action.)

Uses of Nouns. The following sentences illustrate some—not all—of the ways in which nouns are used in relation to other words.

> My *supervisor* outlined the procedure in detail. (*Supervisor* is the subject of the verb *outlined*. It tells who took the action expressed by the verb.)
>
> Carole told her *assistant* about the changes. (*Assistant* is the direct object of the verb *told*. It identifies the receiver of the action expressed by the verb.)
>
> The company gives every *customer* excellent *service*. (*Customer* is the indirect object of the verb *gives*. It tells to whom the service is given.)
>
> Harold was in the *office* yesterday. (*Office* is the object of the preposition *in*.)
>
> Joyce is the *owner* of the company. (*Owner* is the complement of the verb *is*. It renames or further identifies *Joyce*, the subject of the verb.)

Noun and Other Functional Labels in Dictionaries. One of the elements of the entry for each word in the main listing of a dictionary is the label indicating the part of speech of the word: noun, pronoun, verb, adjective, adverb, preposition, conjunction, or interjection. For example, before giving the definition of the word, your dictionary may show *n* (for "noun"), *pron* (for "pronoun"), *vb* (for "verb"), or a similar abbreviation to indicate the appropriate part of speech.

Noting the part-of-speech label is especially important if the same word form may be used as more than one part of speech. In such instances, as illustrated previously by the word *travel*, the parts of speech obviously have different meanings and different uses in sentences. Further, in some cases, the parts of speech have additional differences—differences that sometimes result in pronunciation, word division, or other usage errors. These differences are the focus of the Spot Check exercises below.

Spot Check 1

In each group of sentences below, the first sentence illustrates the use of the italicized word as a noun and the other sentence or sentences illustrate the use of the same word as a different part of speech. In the space at the right of each sentence, indicate the part of speech of the italicized word. Then answer the question below the group of sentences by writing *Yes* or *No*. If necessary, use your dictionary to determine the correct answers. (Parts of speech are abbreviated; students may write them in full.)

1. Bill is an *associate* of ours.   n
They seldom *associate* with others.   v
Sue applied for *associate* membership.   adj

Does the pronunciation of *associate* depend upon how it is used as a part of speech?   Yes

2. We have a complete *record* of it.   _____ n
Do you *record* phone messages?   _____ v
The company reported *record*
profits.   _____ adj

Does the pronunciation of *record*
depend upon how it is used as a
part of speech?   _____ Yes

3. The divers found one metal *object*.   _____ n
They *object* to our leaving early.   _____ v

Does the pronunciation of *object*
depend upon how it is used as a
part of speech?   _____ Yes

4. Has the *schedule* been changed?   _____ n
Schedule the meeting for 9 a.m.   _____ v

Does the pronunciation of *schedule*
depend upon how it is used as a
part of speech?   _____ No

CLASSES OF NOUNS

Nouns may be divided into various classes according to the kinds of things they name.

Common Nouns. A *common noun* is a general name—one that may be used to refer to any person, place, or thing or to any member of a large group or class of persons, places, or things.

man	citizen	country	river	invoice
woman	candidate	village	animal	lumber

Proper Nouns. A *proper noun* is a particular name—one that identifies a specific person, place, or thing. Unlike common nouns, proper nouns are always capitalized.

Thomas Joyce Houston Canada Lake Michigan Chrysler
Marilyn George Collins Africa North Dakota Sears

Collective Nouns. A *collective noun* is one that denotes a group of persons, places, or things.

choir	quartet	orchestra	herd	jury
family	audience	committee	flock	team

Concrete Nouns. Nouns that identify things that can be seen, heard, touched, tasted, or smelled are *concrete nouns.*

computer	television	whistle	vanilla	perfume
forest	tractor	gasoline	carpet	coffee

Abstract Nouns. *Abstract nouns* identify things that cannot be seen, heard, touched, tasted, or smelled.

democracy	logic	honesty	luck	stability
integrity	wisdom	success	faith	aspiration

PLURALS OF NOUNS

Many nouns have both a singular form (denoting one person, place, thing, or group) and a plural form (denoting two or more persons, places, things, or groups). In general, however, dictionaries do not show the plural of every noun that has one. For example, *Webster's Ninth New Collegiate Dictionary,* (Merriam-Webster Inc., Springfield, Massachusetts, 1991), the source for spellings here, usually does not show a plural that is spelled simply by adding *s* or *es* to the singular form. In addition to studying the following rules for spelling the plurals of nouns, read the explanatory notes in your dictionary to determine for which types of nouns it indicates plural forms.

Note: Like most rules, some spelling rules presented here have exceptions—and the exceptions are not always indicated.

1. Most Nouns. To form the plural of most nouns, add *s* to the singular noun.

department	crew	carton	idea	garage
departments	crews	cartons	ideas	garages

2. Nouns Ending in *ch, sh, ss, x,* or *z*. If the singular noun ends in *ch, sh, ss, x,* or *z,* add *es* to form the plural.

watch	dish	business	tax	buzz
watches	dishes	businesses	taxes	buzzes

Some singular nouns ending in a single *s* or *z* require that the final *s* or *z* be doubled before adding *es*. Some of them have two acceptable plural forms: *ALSO* indicates that the first form is more common; *OR* indicates that the forms are equally acceptable.

plus	whiz	bus
pluses ALSO plusses	whizzes	buses OR busses

Spot Check 2

In the space provided, add the plural ending to each of the following nouns.

1. alias _es_   **5.** guess _es_   **9.** size _s_

2. church _es_   **6.** mix _es_   **10.** shop _s_

3. file _s_   **7.** minus _es_   **11.** quiz _zes_

4. award _s_   **8.** myth _s_   **12.** crash _es_

3. Nouns Ending in *f, fe,* or *ff*. For most singular nouns ending in *f, fe,* or *ff,* add *s* to the singular form.

roof	belief	safe	staff	cliff
roofs	beliefs	safes	staffs	cliffs

For some singular nouns ending in *f* or *fe,* change the *f* or *fe* to *v* and add *es.*

loaf	half	thief	knife	life
loaves	halves	thieves	knives	lives

A few nouns with these endings have two acceptable plural forms.

dwarf	scarf	calf
dwarfs OR dwarves	scarves OR scarfs	calves ALSO calfs

4. Nouns Ending in *y.*
If the *y* follows a vowel (*a, e, i, o,* or *u*), add *s* to form the plural.

delay	alley	decoy	attorney	guy
delays	alleys	decoys	attorneys	guys

If the *y* follows a consonant, change the *y* to *i* and add *es.*

candy	jury	party	entry	family
candies	juries	parties	entries	families

5. Nouns Ending in *o.*
When the *o* follows a vowel, form the plural by adding *s.*

stereo	studio	trio	duo	folio
stereos	studios	trios	duos	folios

For some nouns ending in *o* preceded by a consonant, the plural is formed by adding *s;* for others, it is formed by adding *es.*

logo	silo	piano	veto	tomato
logos	silos	pianos	vetoes	tomatoes

A number of nouns ending in *o* have two acceptable plural forms.

zero	motto	tornado
zeros	mottoes	tornadoes
ALSO zeroes	ALSO mottos	OR tornados

Spot Check 3

In the space provided, write the plural form of each of the following nouns.

1. itinerary   *itineraries*
2. chief   *chiefs*
3. roof   *roofs*
4. tariff   *tariffs*
5. wife   *wives*
6. family   *families*
7. delay   *delays*
8. memo   *memos*
9. echo   *echoes*
10. casualty   *casualties*

6. Nouns With Irregular Plural Endings.
The plurals of some nouns are formed irregularly, such as by changing one or more internal vowels.

child	tooth	man	mouse	woman
children	teeth	men	mice	women

7. Foreign Nouns.
Many nouns of foreign origin have both an English plural and a foreign plural; some have only one plural form. The English plurals are formed in the same manner as the plurals of other English nouns. The foreign plurals of nouns with the same ending letter or letters are formed in a consistent manner (note that the following nouns are grouped according to their ending letter or letters).

In informal writing, when the English plural and the foreign plural have the same meaning, the English plural is used more often than the foreign plural. Sometimes, as noted in the following list, the plurals are used with different meanings.

Singular Nouns	Foreign Plurals	English Plurals
Ending in *um:*		
addendum	addenda	—
agendum	agenda*	agendums
curriculum	curricula	curriculums
datum	data*	datums
medium	media *(advertising)*	mediums *(people)*
memorandum	memoranda	memorandums
Ending in *a:*		
alumna (fem.)	alumnae (fem.)	—
antenna	antennae *(insect)*	antennas *(TV)*
Ending in *us:*		
alumnus (mas.)	alumni** (mas.)	—
cactus	cacti	cactuses OR cactus
census	—	censuses
terminus	termini	terminuses
Ending in *is:*		
analysis	analyses	—
basis	bases	—
emphasis	emphases	—
parenthesis	parentheses	—
Ending in *on:*		
criterion	criteria	—
phenomenon	phenomena	phenomenons
Ending in *ex* or *ix:*		
appendix	appendices	appendixes
index	indices *(mathematical)*	indexes *(books)*

Agenda and *data* are commonly used as singular nouns.

**Alumni* is used to refer to a group composed of men and women.

8. Nouns That Are Usually Singular. Some nouns that end in *s* are plural in form but are usually singular in usage.

> measles   mathematics   politics   news
>
> The *news is* very encouraging.
> *Measles* sometimes *strikes* adults.

9. Nouns That Are Always Plural. Some nouns that are plural in form are always (or almost always) plural in usage because they have no singular form that conveys the same meaning or, in some cases, because they have no singular form at all.

> annals   clothes   proceeds   scissors
>
> The *scissors were* in the desk drawer.

10. Nouns With One Form for Singular and Plural. The plural and singular forms of some nouns are the same.

> chassis   trout   salmon   sheep
> deer   corps   series   swine
>
> The new *series was* a disappointment to some.
> Several new *series are* in the planning stages.

Words ending in a silent *s* do not change for the plural; however, the plural may be indicated by pro-

nouncing the *s*. For example, the singular of *corps* is pronounced "core"; the plural is pronounced "cores."

Write the plurals of the following nouns in the spaces provided. If necessary, consult your dictionary.

1. series		series
2. diagnosis		diagnoses
3. mouse		mice
4. woman		women
5. medium (communications)		media
6. antenna *(TV)*		antennas
7. criterion		criteria
8. sheep		sheep
9. child		children
10. alumnus		alumni

Study Guide 1

The italicized nouns in the following sentences illustrate the rules you have just studied. The rule numbers are shown, in case you wish to refer to any of the rules.

1. The *managers*[1] agree that the *territories*[4] of some *representatives*[1] are too large.
2. Several *attorneys*[4] and their *clients*[1] were waiting for the *judges*[1] and the *members*[1] of the *juries*[4] to return from lunch.
3. The *trustees*[1], administrative *officials*[1], faculty *members*[1], and *students*[1] were happy to receive the *news*[8] concerning the *donations*[1] of several *alumni*[7].
4. Several local *businesses*[2] manufacture *clothes*[9] for *men*[6], *women*[6], and *children*[6].
5. Some of the *data*[7] on those *disks*[1] was accidentally erased.
6. Many *corporations*[1] and their *employees*[1] make *donations*[1] during fund-raising *campaigns*[1], and the campaign *organizers*[1] distribute the *proceeds*[9] among *hospitals*[1], *schools*[1], *charities*[4], and other *organizations*[1].
7. Some *communities*[4] levy *taxes*[2] on everything from *tomatoes*[5] to *watches*[2] and *pianos*[5].
8. The *plaintiffs*[3] were unable to identify the *thieves*[3].
9. The *chassis*[10] of those *buses*[2] seem to be in good repair.
10. The *interviewers*[1] were especially interested in *candidates*[1] with a strong academic background in *mathematics*[8].

ASSIGNMENT: Complete the Unit 1 Worksheet on pages 7–8.

NAME _____ DATE _____

UNIT 1

Nouns—Plural Forms

WORKSHEET

A In the spaces provided, write the plurals of the following nouns. For each noun that has both an English and a foreign plural, give both plural forms. Note the example.

0. synopsis — 0. synopses
1. reference — 1. references
2. display — 2. displays
3. quiz — 3. quizzes
4. mix — 4. mixes
5. bench — 5. benches
6. meter — 6. meters
7. stereo — 7. stereos
8. convention — 8. conventions
9. cloth — 9. cloths
10. medium — 10. media mediums
11. speech — 11. speeches
12. motto — 12. mottoes ALSO mottos

13. antenna — 13. antennas antennae
14. facility — 14. facilities
15. tooth — 15. teeth
16. height — 16. heights
17. address — 17. addresses
18. lens — 18. lenses
19. mechanic — 19. mechanics
20. waltz — 20. waltzes
21. engineer — 21. engineers
22. critic — 22. critics
23. phenomenon — 23. phenomena phenomenons
24. wish — 24. wishes
25. council — 25. councils

B For each sentence below, determine whether the italicized noun subject is singular or plural in form and in meaning. If the noun is singular, circle the *S* and the verb that goes with it. If the noun is plural, circle the *P* and the verb accompanying it. Note the example.

0. *Pliers* usually (?) only a few dollars.   0. S—costs   (P—cost)
1. The *articles* (?) very informative.   1. S—is   (P—are)
2. The *merchandise* (?) shipped yesterday.   2. (S—was)   P—were
3. Your *analysis* (?) correct to me.   3. (S—seems)   P—seem
4. The *premises* (?) been inspected.   4. S—has   (P—have)
5. The *company* (?) about a thousand people.   5. (S—employs)   P—employ
6. Which *parenthesis* (?) omitted?   6. (S—was)   P—were
7. The *proceeds* of the sale (?) to $748.   7. S—amounts   (P—amount)
8. The *agenda* (?) ready for distribution.   8. (S—is)   P—are
9. Such *media* (?) radio and TV.   9. S—includes   (P—include)

Copyright © by Glencoe.

Unit 1: Nouns—Plural Forms   **7**

10. Our *alumni* (?) regular contributions.   **10.** S—makes   (P—make)

11. The *sheep* (?) a bell on its collar.   **11.** (S—has)   P—have

12. *Cacti* (?) in the desert.   **12.** S—thrives   (P—thrive)

13. The *formula* (?) a secret.   **13.** (S—remains)   P—remain

14. Some say that *clothes* (?) the person.   **14.** S—makes   (P—make)

15. What *criteria* (?) considered?   **15.** S—was   (P—were)

16. The *silos* (?) many tons of wheat.   **16.** S—holds   (P—hold)

17. *Glass* (?) very easily.   **17.** (S—chips)   P—chip

18. *Policies* (?) from company to company.   **18.** S—varies   (P—vary)

19. *Checkers* (?) a popular board game.   **19.** (S—is)   P—are

20. *Steel* (?) a long time.   **20.** (S—lasts)   P—last

21. Our *sales* (?) during the summer months.   **21.** S—increases   (P—increase)

22. *Salmon* (?) upstream to spawn.   **22.** S—swims   (P—swim)

23. The *odds* (?) in your favor.   **23.** S—is   (P—are)

24. The *trio* often (?) at weddings.   **24.** (S—sings)   P—sing

25. All the *fuss* (?) for nothing.   **25.** (S—was)   P—were

C **Underline each error in noun usage in the following sentences, and write the correction in the space provided. If a sentence is correct, write *OK*.**

1. Some firms pay their employees on a weekly bases.   **1.** basis

2. Discount stores sell clothes for children at bargain price.   **2.** prices

3. Many companies develop manuals that summarize various policys and procedures.   **3.** policies

4. Members of the accounting and marketing staves are reviewing sales and expense budgets for next year.   **4.** staffs

5. Sales personnels prepared questionnaires to obtain information about the attitudes of customers toward various brands of products.   **5.** personnel

6. All entries in those indexs should be arranged alphabetically.   **6.** indexes

7. The financial advisors recommended that the investors put their moneys in municipal bonds.   **7.** money

8. Dennis and Kevin, alumnae of Oak Creek College, spent the holidays with their families.   **8.** alumni

9. The speakers thanked the audience for giving them their full attention.   **9.** OK

10. Attorneys sometimes spend hundreds of hours working on each of many legal brieves.   **10.** briefs

Compound and Other Nouns— Plural Forms

PLURALS OF COMPOUND NOUNS

A *compound noun* consists of two or more words used together as one name. Compound nouns are formed in several ways; for example:

TWO NOUNS:

airport	cash register
bookcase	clock-watcher
hallway	stock exchange

ADJECTIVE PLUS NOUN:

half-truth	real estate
shorthand	special delivery
highway	freeway

NOUN PLUS DESCRIPTIVE PHRASE:

attorney-at-law	board of directors
editor in chief	jack-of-all-trades
sister-in-law	point of view

WORDS OTHER THAN NOUNS:

write-up	layoff
get-together	takeover
output	trade-in

Note that there is no consistent pattern for writing compound nouns. Some are written without a space or a hyphen between the words; others are written with a space between the words; and still others are written with a hyphen between the words. When in doubt as to how to write a particular compound noun, consult an up-to-date dictionary and note the part-of-speech label for the particular entry. As illustrated below, a compound may be written one way as a noun and another way as a verb. For example:

NOUN:	double check	markup	write-off
VERB:	double-check	mark up	write off

1. Compound Nouns Written as One Word. To form the plural of most compound nouns written as one word, change the last element of the compound to its plural form by following the rules presented in Unit 1. Remember that the last element may be an irregular noun.

payday	sandwich	takeover	grandchild
paydays	sandwiches	takeovers	grandchildren

2. Compound Nouns Written With Spaces or Hyphens. If a compound noun consists of two nouns written with a space between them, pluralize the second noun.

carbon copy	money order	car wash	coffee break
carbon copies	money orders	car washes	coffee breaks

If the compound noun consists of a noun plus another part of speech or a phrase, change the main element to its plural form. Note that some compound nouns of this type are written with spaces and some are written with hyphens.

account payable	letter of credit	sister-in-law
accounts payable	letters of credit	sisters-in-law

To form the plural of a compound noun that does not contain a noun element, change the last element to its plural form.

get-together	hang-up	write-off	drive-in
get-togethers	hang-ups	write-offs	drive-ins

As illustrated below, some compound nouns have more than one acceptable plural form.

attorney general	court-martial
attorneys general	courts-martial
OR attorney generals	ALSO court-martials

Spot Check 1

Write the plural of each compound noun below in the space provided.

1. footnote		1.	footnotes
2. credit card		2.	credit cards
3. counteroffer		3.	counteroffers
4. brother-in-law		4.	brothers-in-law
5. wristwatch		5.	wristwatches
6. board foot		6.	board feet

7. aftershock	7. _aftershocks_
8. cross-reference	8. _cross-references_
9. account receivable	9. _accounts receivable_
10. mainstay	10. _mainstays_
11. printout	11. _printouts_
12. thunderstorm	12. _thunderstorms_
13. mix-up	13. _mix-ups_
14. coffee break	14. _coffee breaks_
15. bookshelf	15. _bookshelves_
16. letter of credit	16. _letters of credit_
17. money-maker	17. _money-makers_
18. side effect	18. _side effects_
19. sideline	19. _sidelines_
20. lead-in	20. _lead-ins_
21. standby	21. _standbys_
22. tax shelter	22. _tax shelters_
23. team player	23. _team players_
24. editor in chief	24. _editors in chief_
25. half-truth	25. _half-truths_

PLURALS OF ABBREVIATIONS, NUMBERS, LETTERS, SYMBOLS, AND OTHER WORDS

3. Most Abbreviations. For most abbreviations, form the plural by adding *s* to the singular abbreviation.

apt.	dept.	mo.	yr.	hwy.	pkg.	mgr.	No.
apts.	depts.	mos.	yrs.	hwys.	pkgs.	mgrs.	Nos.

4. Abbreviations Ending With a Capital Letter. Preferably, form the plural of an abbreviation that consists of capital letters or that ends with a capital letter by adding only an *s* to the singular abbreviation. Note that many abbreviations consisting entirely of capital letters are commonly written without periods.

CPA	Ph.D.	YWCA	M.D.	VIP	VCR
CPAs	Ph.D.s	YWCAs	M.D.s	VIPs	VCRs

5. Abbreviations Ending With an Uncapitalized Letter. To form the plural of an abbreviation that consists of uncapitalized letters followed by periods or that ends with an uncapitalized letter followed by a period, add an apostrophe and *s* to the singular abbreviation.

c.o.d.	f.o.b.	M.Ed.
c.o.d.'s (BUT: CODs)	f.o.b.'s	M.Ed.'s

6. Letters, Numbers, and Symbols. Form the plurals of uncapitalized letters by adding an apostrophe and *s,* but add only an *s* to form the plurals of most capital letters.

cross t's	dot i's	u's or v's
a few Cs	some Ds	Ps and Qs

For the sake of clarity, use an apostrophe and *s* to form the plural of each of the following capital letters:

A's (to avoid confusion with the word *As*)
I's (to avoid confusion with the word *Is*)
M's (to avoid confusion with the abbreviation *Ms.*)
U's (to avoid confusion with the word *Us*)

Also, for the sake of consistency of style within a letter or other document, express the plurals of capital letters in the same manner.

Some students' report cards contain nothing but A's and B's. (NOT: Some students' report cards contain nothing but A's and Bs.)

For symbols and for numbers written in figures, add only an *s* to form the plural.

&s	#s	5s	20s	1900s

Following the rules for other nouns, add *s* or *es* to form the plurals of numbers written in words.

fives	sixes	twenties	nineteen hundreds

7. Words Referred to as Words. In most instances, form the plural of a word referred to as a word by adding *s* or *es*.

ifs, ands, or buts	yeses and noes
ins and outs	whys and wherefores

However, use an apostrophe and *s* if the plural form is unfamiliar or is likely to be misread.

or's or nor's	that's and which's

If a word already contains an apostrophe, add only an *s* to form the plural.

can'ts	don'ts	haven'ts	shouldn'ts

8. Units of Weight and Measure. For an abbreviation of a metric unit of weight or measure, use the same form for the singular and the plural. Also note that abbreviations of metric terms are always written without periods.

m (meter OR meters)	1 m	3 m
L (liter OR liters)	1 L	5 L
g (gram OR grams)	1 g	7 g
km (kilometer OR kilometers)	1 km	2 km
kg (kilogram OR kilograms)	1 kg	6 kg
cm (centimeter OR centimeters)	1 cm	4 cm
dam (dekameter OR dekameters)	1 dam	8 dam

The abbreviations of many customary terms of weight and measure are also the same for singular and plural, and the trend is to write them without periods.

ft (foot or feet)	1 ft	6 ft
in (inch or inches)	1 in	3 in
oz (ounce or ounces)	1 oz	12 oz

Other customary units have two widely used plural forms, but the trend is to use the form without the *s*. Also note the trend toward omitting periods.

lb or lbs	7 lb or 7 lbs
qt or qts	4 qt or 4 qts
yd or yds	3 yd or 3 yds

9. Single-Letter Abbreviations. For a few single-letter abbreviations, form the plural by doubling the letter that represents the singular.

p. (page)	p. 25
pp. (pages)	pp. 25-30
f. (and the following page)	pp. 18 f.
ff. (and the following pages)	pp. 12 ff.

10. Nouns With Numbers. When accompanied by numbers, certain nouns use the same form for singular and plural. These terms include *hundred, thousand, dozen,* and *gross.*

five hundred	16 dozen	one million
four score	12 gross	one dozen
three thousand	$10 million	one hundred

Although abbreviations are frequently used in technical writing, tabulations, and business forms, most terms are written in full in letters, memos, and other documents. Such abbreviations as *Mr., Mrs., Ms., Jr., c.o.d., a.m.,* and *FBI* are customarily abbreviated in all types of communications.

Spot Check 2

Write the plural of each of the following items in the space provided.

1. Fig. *(figure)* — 1. Figs.
2. YWCA — 2. YWCAs
3. col. *(column)* — 3. cols.
4. Ed.D. — 4. Ed.D.s
5. cm *(centimeter)* — 5. cm
6. 10 — 6. 10s
7. yd *(yard)* — 7. yd OR yds
8. won't — 8. won'ts
9. km *(kilometer)* — 9. km
10. I *(the letter)* — 10. I's
11. l. *(line)* — 11. ll.
12. v. *(verse)* — 12. vv.
13. *one* million — 13. two million
14. yes — 14. yeses
15. A and B — 15. A's and B's
16. p. *(page)* — 16. pp.
17. L *(the letter)* — 17. Ls
18. Form 1040 — 18. Form 1040s
19. RN *(Registered Nurse)* — 19. RNs
20. bbl *(barrel)* — 20. bbl
21. u *(the letter)* — 21. u's
22. in *(inch)* — 22. in
23. five — 23. fives
24. no — 24. noes
25. why — 25. whys

PLURALS OF PROPER NOUNS

11. Proper Nouns Ending in *ch, sh, s, x,* or *z*. If a proper noun ends in *ch, sh, s, x,* or *z,* form the plural by adding *es* to the singular noun.

| Lynch | Walsh | Willis | Max | Hertz |
| Lynches | Walshes | Willises | Maxes | Hertzes |

Exceptions: If a proper noun ending in *ch* is pronounced as though the *ch* were a *k,* add only an *s;* for example, the plural of *Dietrich* is *Dietrichs.*

Also, note that a proper noun such as *French* or *Dutch* is plural when it refers to the people of a country. However, if it is the name of a person, form the plural by adding *es: Frenches* or *Dutches,* for example.

For the following names, change the *y* to *i* and add *es* if the word *Mountains* is omitted:

| Rocky Mountains | Smoky Mountains | Allegheny Mountains |
| the Rockies | the Smokies | the Alleghenies |

12. Other Proper Nouns. For most other proper nouns, form the plural by adding *s* to the singular noun.

| Barbara | German | Dakota | Kelly | Riley |
| Barbaras | Germans | Dakotas | Kellys | Rileys |

13. Courtesy and Other Titles With Names of Persons. Titles are most frequently used in the singular form. However, when a title precedes a personal name, the formal style is to pluralize the title; the informal style is to pluralize the name.

Singular	Formal Plural	Informal Plural
Ms. Burton	(the) Mses. Burton OR: (the) Mss. Burton	(the) Ms. Burtons
Miss Colby	(the) Misses Colby	(the) Miss Colbys
Mr. Blake	(the) Messrs. Blake	(the) Mr. Blakes
Mrs. Welsh	(the) Mesdames Welsh OR: (the) Mmes. Welsh	(the) Mrs. Welshes
Dr. Wang	(the) Drs. Wang	(the) Dr. Wangs

14. Titles in Addresses. Plurals of titles in addresses are used as follows:

Mesdames or *Mmes.,* the plural of *Mrs.,* is used frequently in listing the names of married women with different surnames: *Mesdames* (or *Mmes.*) *Barnes, Carlson,* and *Davis. Mrs.* is more often used when married women have the same surname: *the Mrs. Edsons.*

Either *Mses.* or *Mss.* may be used as the plural of *Ms.* This title, in either its singular or its plural form, may be used with names of women, regardless of their marital status. However, if a married woman uses her husband's first name or initials instead of her own, the title *Mrs.* should be used (for example, *Mrs. David Suarez,* not *Ms. David Suarez*).

Misses, the plural of *Miss,* is not an abbreviation and therefore is not followed by a period.

Messrs., the plural of *Mr.,* is the abbreviation of *Messieurs* and is followed by a period. This title is correctly used in addressing a professional partnership composed entirely of men (for example, *Messrs. James Hubbard and Robert Shannon, Attorneys-at-Law*). However, if a company or corporate name includes the names of persons, do not use *Messrs.* before the personal names.

INCORRECT:	Messrs. Boyd and Warren, Inc. Messrs. R. K. Lloyd & Co.
CORRECT:	Boyd and Warren, Inc. R. K. Lloyd & Co.

Avoid the plural forms of titles in addresses that involve the names of several people; however, plural forms may be necessary in certain cases. For example, rather than write *Messrs. J. R. Collins and W. L. McCormick* as the first line of the address, write the name of each person on a separate line and use the appropriate courtesy title before each name.

Mr. J. R. Collins
Mr. W. L. McCormick
90 West Waters Avenue
Tampa, FL 33615

Spot Check 3

In the spaces provided, write the plurals of the following nouns.

1.	Carolina	1.	Carolinas
2.	Koch	2.	Kochs
3.	Riley	3.	Rileys
4.	Miss Davis *(formal)*	4.	(the) Misses Davis
5.	Murdoch	5.	Murdochs
6.	French *(family name)*	6.	Frenches
7.	Japanese	7.	Japanese
8.	Ms. Mallory *(informal)*	8.	(the) Ms. Mallorys
9.	Mrs.	9.	Mesdames OR Mmes.
10.	Mr.	10.	Messrs.
11.	Ms.	11.	Mses. OR Mss.
12.	Welch	12.	Welches
13.	Wirtz	13.	Wirtzes
14.	Bendix	14.	Bendixes
15.	Foley	15.	Foleys
16.	Standish	16.	Standishes
17.	Dr.	17.	Drs.
18.	Miss West *(informal)*	18.	Miss Wests
19.	Mr. Perez *(formal)*	19.	Messrs. Perez
20.	Mrs. Jones *(informal)*	20.	Mrs. Joneses

Study Guide 2

A. The following sentences show applications of the rules for forming plurals of compound nouns. As you read each sentence, give particular attention to the italicized nouns. The numbers following them refer to the rules presented in this unit.

1. The *regional managers*[2] are working on their *sales budgets*[2].
2. *Sky marshals*[2] have been assigned to prevent *skyjackings*[1].
3. Those *flashlights*[1] will be needed in case of *blackouts*[1].
4. My *brothers-in-law*[2] are enrolled in different *junior colleges*[2].
5. Some *drugstores*[1] sell everything from *toothbrushes*[1] to *lawn chairs*[2].
6. Do *book clubs*[2] offer publications at lower prices than *bookstores?*[1]
7. Both their *daughters-in-law*[2] and their *grandchildren*[1] spent the day at an amusement park.
8. Economic *slowdowns*[1] may result in temporary *layoffs*[1] of workers in government, business, and industry.
9. The *sales representatives*[2] gave new *price lists*[2] to customers.
10. Most *stockbrokers*[1] paid no attention to the rumors concerning possible *takeovers*[1] of companies by *corporate raiders*[2].
11. One of the *stagehands*[1] has written several *short stories*[2].
12. The *teenagers*[1] were given an opportunity to express their *points of view*[2].
13. *Directors of marketing*[2] may request *field tests*[2] of products.
14. I bought two *stepladders*[1] and some *paintbrushes*[1] at neighborhood *garage sales*[2] last week.
15. During recent *news conferences*[2], *spokespersons*[1] for the companies denounced unidentified *rumormongers*[1].
16. They deposited their *paychecks*[1] in their *checking accounts*[2] and rented *safe-deposit boxes*[2].
17. What do you think of the *life-styles*[2] of those *officeholders*[1]?
18. Both *lieutenant governors*[2] claimed they had paid their *income taxes*[2] on time.
19. We saw several *grand pianos*[2] in their *showrooms*[1].
20. These *guidelines*[1] were developed for *freelancers*[2].

B. The following sentences illustrate rules for forming the plurals of abbreviations, letters, numbers, symbols, words referred to as words, and proper nouns. The numbers following the italicized terms refer to rules given in this unit.

1. Only one of the *Mses. Cason*[13] works in the personnel department.
2. I wonder what the following items will cost a decade from now:
   5 *lb* potatoes[8]
   1 *L* gasoline[8]
   2 *pkgs.* of chewing gum[3]
3. Please see the organization chart on *pp.* 8-10[9].
4. The word *withhold* contains two *h's*[6].
5. This handwritten draft contains too many *howevers*[7] and some *7s*[6] that could be misread as *4s* or *9s*[6].
6. As a graduate student, she received nothing but *A's* and *B's*[6].
7. Over *10 million*[10] people live and work in the metropolitan area.
8. How many *Blisses*[11] and *Wirtzes*[11] do you know?
9. Several *Germans*[12] visited the *Frenches*[11], *McClintochs*[11], and *Murphys*[12] a week or so ago.
10. The article is of special interest to *CPAs*[4].
11. We handle many *c.o.d.'s*[5] every day.
12. The address on the envelope was as follows:
    Messrs.[14] Edgar Martinez and L. C. Sheahan, Attorneys-at-Law.

13. Charles and Barbara are among the *RNs*[4] at Memorial Hospital.

14. This carton contains *two dozen*[10] eggs.

15. The register contains several *tens*[6] and a few *twenties*[6].

16. These instructions contain a great many *don'ts*[7].

17. Note the rules on *pp. 20 ff*[9].

18. The *Helmses*[11] stayed at a resort in the *Rockies*[11].

19. We counted four *yeses*[7] and six *noes*[7].

20. Those *VCRs*[4] were manufactured during the *1980s*[6].

ASSIGNMENT: Complete the Unit 2 Worksheet on pages 15–16.

UNIT 2

Compound and Other Nouns—
Plural Forms

WORKSHEET

The following compound nouns are written as separate words—some incorrectly. Write the plural of each compound noun, indicating whether it should be hyphenated (*cross-purposes*) or written with a space between the words (*lieutenant colonels*) or written without a space or a hyphen between the words (*shortcuts*). Use the dictionary if necessary. Note the examples.

0.	super market	supermarkets	**10.**	standby	standbys
00.	do gooder	do-gooders	**11.**	trade mark	trademarks
1.	week end	weekends	**12.**	letter head	letterheads
2.	stock broker	stockbrokers	**13.**	brief case	briefcases
3.	print out	printouts	**14.**	note book	notebooks
4.	major general	major generals	**15.**	work load	workloads
5.	work station	workstations	**16.**	trade in	trade-ins
6.	bill of sale	bills of sale	**17.**	time card	time cards
7.	deputy sheriff	deputy sheriffs	**18.**	air port	airports
8.	ware house	warehouses	**19.**	sister-in-law	sisters-in-law
9.	check book	checkbooks	**20.**	dairy farm	dairy farms

Note the abbreviations in the sentences below. If the abbreviations are correct and would normally be used in a sentence appearing in a business letter or memo, write *OK* in the space provided. If an abbreviated term should be written in full or replaced by some other expression, underline it and write the necessary correction in the space provided.

1. The meeting scheduled for Tues. has been postponed.   1. _Tuesday_

2. Marion Stephens is pres. of Benson, Inc.   2. _president_

3. He will leave early tomorrow a.m., not afternoon.   3. _morning_

4. She works for the FBI in Washington, D.C.   4. _OK_

5. Ms. Richards and Mr. Quayle were in Ariz. last week.   5. _Arizona_

6. I paid $10 a gal for paint at Olsten Bros.   6. _gallon_

7. Sharon and Tom are alumni of Michigan State Univ.   7. _University_

8. Please send the statement of account to this address:
Carlson & Warner
200 Northern Boulevard
East Lansing, MI 48820.

8. _____ OK

9. Several <u>c.o.d.s</u> were delivered to local YMCAs.

9. _____ c.o.d.'s OR CODs

10. They received their <u>Ph.D.'s</u> from UCLA last June.

10. _____ Ph.D.s

C In the space provided, write the plural form of each of the following nouns. Use the informal plurals for personal names with titles. Note the examples.

0. lb *(pound)*	**0.** ___ lb OR lbs	**25.** Miss	**25.** ___ Misses
00. James	**00.** ___ Jameses	**26.** Stanley	**26.** ___ Stanleys
1. 1990	**1.** ___ 1990s	**27.** if	**27.** ___ ifs
2. Ms. Ellis	**2.** ___ Ms. Ellises	**28.** Mrs. Ryan	**28.** ___ Mrs. Ryans
3. Mr. Jones	**3.** ___ Mr. Joneses	**29.** Miss Stein	**29.** ___ Miss Steins
4. German	**4.** ___ Germans	**30.** Parrish	**30.** ___ Parrishes
5. oz *(ounce)*	**5.** ___ oz	**31.** p. *(page)*	**31.** ___ pp.
6. can't	**6.** ___ can'ts	**32.** CPA	**32.** ___ CPAs
7. TV	**7.** ___ TVs	**33.** no	**33.** ___ noes
8. yes	**8.** ___ yeses	**34.** IOU	**34.** ___ IOUs
9. A	**9.** ___ A's	**35.** pro and con	**35.** ___ pros and cons
10. Mallory	**10.** ___ Mallorys	**36.** m *(meter)*	**36.** ___ m
11. Mr.	**11.** ___ Messrs.	**37.** m *(letter)*	**37.** ___ m's
12. Ed.D.	**12.** ___ Ed.D.s	**38.** yr. *(year)*	**38.** ___ yrs.
13. St. *(Street)*	**13.** ___ Sts.	**39.** 2 × 4	**39.** ___ 2 × 4s
14. mo. *(month)*	**14.** ___ mos.	**40.** gal *(gallon)*	**40.** ___ gal
15. OK	**15.** ___ OKs	**41.** Wilcox	**41.** ___ Wilcoxes
16. Antonio	**16.** ___ Antonios	**42.** Fish	**42.** ___ Fishes
17. &	**17.** ___ &s	**43.** No. *(Number)*	**43.** ___ Nos.
18. 1 million	**18.** ___ 5 million	**44.** eighth	**44.** ___ eighths
19. g *(gram)*	**19.** ___ g	**45.** wk. *(week)*	**45.** ___ wks.
20. Dr. Swartz	**20.** ___ Dr. Swartzes	**46.** YWCA	**46.** ___ YWCAs
21. CPU	**21.** ___ CPUs	**47.** km *(kilometer)*	**47.** ___ km
22. T *(letter)*	**22.** ___ Ts	**48.** 10	**48.** ___ 10s OR 10's
23. five	**23.** ___ fives	**49.** L *(liter)*	**49.** ___ L
24. qt *(quart)*	**24.** ___ qt	**50.** third	**50.** ___ thirds

Nouns—Possessive Case

CASES OF NOUNS

The term **case** refers to the form of a noun (or pronoun) that indicates the relation of the noun to other words in a sentence. Nouns have three cases, or forms: **nominative case, objective case,** and **possessive case.**

Nominative Case. The **nominative case** indicates the noun is the subject or the complement of a verb.

> The *receptionist* volunteered to proofread the report. (*Receptionist* is the subject of the verb *volunteered.*)
>
> Patrick Ward is the *receptionist.* (*Receptionist* is the complement of the linking verb *is;* it renames or further identifies *Patrick Ward,* the subject.)

Objective Case. The **objective case** indicates that the noun is the object of a verb, the object of a preposition, the object of an infinitive, the subject of an infinitive, or the complement of the infinitive *to be.* As illustrated by the noun *receptionist* in the preceding and following example sentences, the nominative and objective cases of nouns are the same in form.

> Several customers complimented the *receptionist.* (*Receptionist* is the object of the verb *complimented;* it names the receiver of the action expressed by the verb *complimented.*)
>
> Do you know the name of the *receptionist?* (*Receptionist* is the object of the preposition *of.* The prepositional phrase *of the receptionist* modifies the noun *name.*)
>
> The clinic plans to hire another *receptionist.* (*Receptionist* is the object of the infinitive *to hire.*)
>
> The manager asked the *receptionist* to attend the meeting. (*Receptionist* is the subject of the infinitive *to attend.*)
>
> Another employee would like to be a *receptionist.* (*Receptionist* is the complement of the infinitive *to be.*)

Possessive Case. The **possessive case** of a noun indicates ownership or possession of something named by another noun. As illustrated below, the possessive case of a noun differs from the nominative case and the objective case.

> The *receptionist's* desk is in front of the main entrance. (*Receptionist's* indicates ownership or possession of the desk.)

The possessive case can also show a family or other relationship, identification, origin, or authorship rather than actual possession or ownership.

> The *supervisor's* nephew applied for the job. (A supervisor obviously cannot own a person.)
>
> How many of *Faulkner's* novels have you read? (*Faulkner's* indicates authorship of the novels.)

USE OF THE POSSESSIVE CASE

The appropriateness of using the possessive case of a noun depends mainly upon what the noun identifies. Sometimes, however, it also depends upon whether or not the possessive form clearly conveys the intended meaning of the writer or speaker.

Nouns Naming Animate Things. The possessive case is used most often for nouns that name people and animals.

client's address	Kay's office	mayor's comments
chicken's wings	dog's leash	committee's report

A possessive noun is a substitute for an *of* phrase. The use of possessive nouns contributes to both fluency and conciseness of expression. Note that the following sentence is smoother and shorter when *interviewer's* is substituted for *of the interviewer.*

> The questions *of the interviewer* were easy to answer.
>
> The *interviewer's* questions were easy to answer.

To determine whether the possessive form of a noun should be used in a particular situation, substitute an *of* phrase for it. If the phrase clearly conveys the proper meaning, use the possessive form of the noun. In the preceding example sentence, *of the interviewer* clearly conveys the proper meaning; therefore, using *interviewer's* is appropriate.

To avoid ambiguity, however, it is sometimes necessary to use an *of* phrase or some other expression instead of the possessive form of a noun. For example, the meaning of *Louise's photograph* is not clear. It can be interpreted to mean a photograph *of Louise* that was taken by someone else, a photograph of something or someone else that was taken *by Louise,* a photograph that was taken by someone *for Louise,* or a photograph that is owned *by Louise.*

Nouns Naming Inanimate Things. For a noun naming an inanimate object, using an *of* phrase is generally preferable to using the possessive form of the noun.

> Be sure to study the terms *of the contract.* (NOT: Be sure to study the *contract's* terms.)
>
> Who is the owner *of the car.* (NOT: Who is the *car's* owner?)

However, when the noun refers to time or measurement, the possessive form is frequently used.

> Miss McNair paid a *month's* rent in advance.
> What is the property worth in *today's* market?
> One motorcyclist bought a *dollar's* worth of gasoline.

Similarly, when such nouns as *company, firm,* and *store* are used in a manner that indicates they have characteristics of persons, the possessive forms are commonly used.

> What is your *company's* policy regarding discounts?
> The *store's* new catalog will be available next month.

Nouns Providing Description Only. In some instances, a noun is used only to provide identification or description of another noun. When a noun is used in this way, do not use the possessive form.

> sales tax   United States embassy   Idaho potatoes
> sports complex   Las Vegas casinos   Illinois farmland

FORMING THE POSSESSIVE CASE OF NOUNS

The possessive case of a noun is formed by adding an apostrophe (') or an apostrophe and *s* (*'s*) to the noun. It is important to remember that the spelling of the singular or plural noun itself does not change when the possessive is formed.

1. Singular Nouns. For most singular nouns, form the possessive by adding *'s* to the singular noun.

> corporation   dog   secretary   Ed   mayor
> corporation's   dog's   secretary's   Ed's   mayor's

If a singular noun ends in an *s* or *z* sound (*ch, s, sh, ss, x,* or *z*), form the possessive by adding *'s* to the singular noun unless doing so makes the possessive difficult to pronounce. Note that the *'s* adds a syllable to the pronunciation of the singular noun itself.

> Dr. Birch's office   Mr. Weiss's account
> Ms. Walsh's check   witness's testimony
> Mrs. Fox's check   Miss Mendez's report

If adding *'s* would make the possessive noun difficult to pronounce, add only an apostrophe to a singular noun ending in an *s* or *z* sound.

> Moses' journey   Mr. Hodges' assistant

When writing the possessive form of a noun, remember that the apostrophe always comes *after* the last letter of the noun—regardless of whether or not the last letter is *s.* To avoid the mistake of inserting the apostrophe before an *s* that is part of a singular noun, write the complete noun before adding the apostrophe or the apostrophe and *s.* For the possessive form of *Mr. Haynes,* for example, write *Mr. Haynes's* (not *Mr. Hayne's*).

2. Plural Nouns. To form the possessive of a plural noun ending with the letter *s,* add only an apostrophe after the *s.* To avoid a mistake, first write the plural noun; then add the apostrophe.

> bosses   two weeks   the Hollises
> bosses' plans   two weeks' pay   the Hollises' house

If the plural noun does not end with the letter *s,* write the plural form and then add *'s.*

> children   women   mice
> children's clothes   women's fashions   mice's feet

3. Compound Nouns. To form the possessive case of a singular or a plural compound noun, add an apostrophe (') or an apostrophe and *s* (*'s*) to the last element of the compound. Follow the rules given for forming the possessives of singular and plural nouns. Add *'s* unless the last element ends with the letter *s.*

> grandchild   grandchild's birthday
> grandchildren   grandchildren's birthdays
>
> district attorney   district attorney's office
> district attorneys   district attorneys' offices
>
> son-in-law   son-in-law's employer
> sons-in-law   sons-in-law's employers

Using an *of* phrase is often preferable to using the possessive of a plural compound noun.

> My *children's playmates' parents* attended.
> BETTER: The *parents of my children's playmates* attended.
>
> The *editors in chief's responsibilities* were discussed.
> BETTER: The *responsibilities of editors in chief* were discussed.

4. Nouns Joined by *and*. When nouns joined by *and* show separate ownership, write each noun in possessive form.

> Macy's and Gimbel's stores (stores owned by two companies)
> men's and women's shoes (two kinds of shoes)

When nouns joined by *and* show joint ownership, change only the last noun to its possessive form.

> Lord and Taylor's store (one store)
> Janet, Raymond, and Diane's nephew (one nephew)

Study each *italicized* noun or combination of nouns below to determine whether it should be written in possessive form. If it should, write the possessive form in the space provided. If it should not, indicate how the noun (or the entire phrase) should be written.

1. *carpenter* hand   1. carpenter's
2. *sales* report   2. sales report
3. *father-in-law* name   3. father-in-law's
4. *brothers-in-law* jobs 4. brothers-in-law's
5. *Dr. Benisch* fee   5. Dr. Benisch's
6. the *Nimitzes* farm   6. (the) Nimitzes'
7. worth of a *dime*   7. a dime's worth
8. *Larry* address   8. Larry's
9. *dog* bark   9. dog's
10. *boy* and *girl* names 10. boy's (and) girl's
11. *Ann* and *Al* mother 11. Ann (and) Al's (mother)
12. all *ladies* garments 12. ladies'
13. *Texas* cattle   13. Texas cattle
14. a *tree* height   14. height of a tree
15. two *months* rent   15. (two) months' rent
16. the *company* plans   16. company's
17. *witnesses* testimony 17. witnesses'
18. *judge* order   18. judge's
19. the *gentleman* remark 19. gentleman's
20. *Archimedes* discovery 20. Archimedes'

5. Nouns in Organization and Other Names. The apostrophe is often omitted in organization names, titles of publications, names of holidays, and other names which appear to require the possessive

form. For example, in the name *American Bankers Association,* the words *American Bankers* identify an association composed of people in the banking industry. When writing the name of a company or other organization, always follow the style of the official name or title.

Sears	*Reader's Digest*
Saks Fifth Avenue	Father's Day
American Bankers Association	*Ladies' Home Journal*
bachelor's degree	*Harper's Bazaar*

6. Abbreviations. To form the possessive of a singular abbreviation, add an apostrophe and *s* (*'s*) at the end of the abbreviation.

Walsh & Co.'s	Joyce Stein, M.D.'s	FBI's
Paul Martinelli Sr.'s	Norton, Inc.'s	CPA's

To form the possessive of a plural abbreviation that ends with the letter *s,* add only an apostrophe.

Harris Bros.' bid	both M.D.s' opinions

7. Other Nouns. If a name consists of several words, form the possessive on the last word.

Department of Water and Power's report
Long Island Railroad Company's plans
the commissioner of consumer affairs' investigation

Sometimes the noun that the possessive modifies is understood rather than expressed.

You can get this at your neighborhood *pharmacist's.*
Randy's was the best entry in the contest.

In some idiomatic expressions, a possessive noun functions as the object of the preposition *of.*

Some friends of *Fred's* helped us for a while.
After leaving the office, we stopped at *Barbara's.*

The *of* phrase and the regular possessive are interchangeable in some situations.

Helen introduced me to *Mrs. Vance's* niece.
Helen introduced me to a niece *of Mrs. Vance.*

8. Nouns With Gerunds and Participles. The possessive case is used before gerunds (also known as **verbal nouns**). A **gerund** is a verb that ends in *ing* (*driving, planning, singing,* or *writing,* for example) and functions as a noun.

Customers were pleased by the *store's lowering* its prices. (Customers were pleased by the *lowering of prices.*)

Some accidents are caused by *drivers' ignoring* traffic signals. (*Ignoring traffic signals* causes some accidents.)

The possessive case is not used before present participles. A *present participle* is a verb that ends in *ing* and functions as an adjective or as part of a verb phrase.

> Customers were pleased by the *store lowering* its prices. (Customers were pleased by the store *that lowered its prices.*)
>
> Some accidents are caused by *drivers ignoring* traffic signals. (Some accidents are caused by drivers *who ignore traffic signals.*)
>
> Our company *is lowering* its prices. (*Lowering* is part of the verb phrase *is lowering.*)
>
> Some drivers *are ignoring* traffic signals. (*Ignoring* is part of the verb phrase *are ignoring.*)

Spot Check 2

Write the possessive of each italicized noun in the space provided.

1. *Ladies* Home Journal   1. <u>Ladies'</u>

2. *Brown & Myers Corp.* stock   2. <u>Brown & Myers Corp.'s</u>

3. *Jason Lee, Jr.* report   3. <u>Jason Lee, Jr.'s</u>

4. *Lisa* cooperating with us   4. <u>Lisa's</u>

5. the *Ellises* inviting them   5. <u>Ellises'</u>

6. *Irene Gardner, D.D.S.*, fee   6. <u>Irene Gardner, D.D.S.'s</u>

7. *NBC* local station   7. <u>NBC's</u>

8. a *CPA* qualifications   8. <u>CPA's</u>

9. the *firms* agreeing on terms   9. <u>firms'</u>

10. get at a neighborhood *grocer*   10. <u>grocer's</u>

Study Guide 3

The following sentences illustrate rules for forming and using possessives. If you are unsure why an italicized noun is or is not in possessive form, refer to the rule indicated and to the "Use of the Possessive Case" section of Unit 3.

1. You are eligible for *three weeks'*[2] vacation.
2. What is the *city's*[1] main industry?
3. The office is an *hour's*[1] drive from my home.
4. What are the *witnesses'*[2] names and addresses?
5. Several *economists'*[2] opinions appeared in the *Investor's*[5] Corner column.
6. The procedures manual includes a description of an *administrative assistant's*[3] duties.
7. Their *daughters-in-law's*[3] degrees are in business administration.
8. *Don's and Martin's*[4] homes are near *Elaine's*[7].
9. The *ASPCA's*[6] purpose is known by everyone.
10. The *speaker's*[8] arriving late made the *group*[8] waiting for the meeting become restless.
11. *Martin and Associates'*[5] recommendations have been implemented.
12. Have *Ohio's*[4] and *Kansas's*[1,4] representatives spoken with the reporters yet?
13. *Laura's*[1] plan is to complete her *master's degree*[5].
14. The insurance claim forms require *Anthony Messina, M.D.'s*[6] signature.
15. The two *suppliers*[8] running out of stock caused problems for us.
16. You can get the prescription filled at your neighborhood *pharmacist's*[7].
17. We received *Wells Bros.'*[6] bid this morning.
18. The Youngs are members of the *group*[8] requesting a change in the zoning regulation.
19. All the *sales representatives'*[3] presentations were excellent.
20. Shirley accepted *Glen and Lois's*[4] invitation.

> **ASSIGNMENT: Complete the Unit 3 Worksheet on pages 21–22 and the Part 1 Review on pages 23–24.**

UNIT 3

Nouns—Possessive Case

WORKSHEET

 A Study each italicized phrase in the following sentences. If the possessive is expressed correctly, write *OK* in the space provided. If the possessive is incorrect, write it correctly. Note the examples.

0. What is the name of *Ms. Day's assistant?*   **0.** OK

00. The *office's doors* are locked.   **00.** doors of the office

1. Are the *tenants' claims* reasonable?   **1.** OK

2. The *account's balance* is overdue.   **2.** balance of the account

3. We bought a *few dollar's worth* of seeds.   **3.** few dollars' worth

4. The annual *sale's meeting* ended last week.   **4.** sales meeting

5. Did you accept the *Rosses's invitation?*   **5.** Rosses' invitation

6. I appreciate *Mr. Ames assisting* me.   **6.** Mr. Ames' assisting

7. Both *boards of directors approval* is needed.   **7.** boards of directors' approval

8. *Fay Li's, M.D. specialty* is pediatrics.   **8.** Fay Li, M.D.'s specialty

9. Is this *Cathy or Walter's copy?*   **9.** Cathy's or Walter's copy

10. It appeared in *The Readers' Digest.*   **10.** The Reader's Digest

11. The *light's flickering* was irritating.   **11.** flickering of the light

12. What is the name of *Ed's and Ann's store?*   **12.** Ed and Ann's store

13. Is a *masters' degree* a prerequisite?   **13.** master's degree

14. Everyone enjoyed the *band playing.*   **14.** band's playing

15. Is it *Lila or Rita's ticket?*   **15.** Lila's or Rita's ticket

16. Roger took a *years' leave of absence.*   **16.** year's leave of absence

17. What is her *son's-in-law occupation?*   **17.** son-in-law's occupation

18. We had two *carpenters' repairing* the roof.   **18.** carpenters repairing

19. Did *Ray accepting* the offer surprise you?   **19.** Ray's accepting

20. Both *manufacturer's products* are reliable.   **20.** manufacturers' products

21. One of the *chair's legs* was broken.   **21.** legs of the chair

22. The store sells *womens' and mens' shoes.*   **22.** women's and men's shoes

23. What is the *committee's recommendation?*   **23.** OK

24. Do you know the *Harnishes's address?*   **24.** Harnishes' address

25. What is the *FDIC's policy* in such cases?   **25.** OK

B If the *of* phrase can correctly be changed to a possessive, write the corresponding possessive form in the space provided. If the *of* phrase should be retained, write *OK*. Note the example.

0.	office of Ryan	**0.**	Ryan's office
1.	address of the publisher	**1.**	publisher's address
2.	balance of the account	**2.**	OK
3.	names of the witnesses	**3.**	witnesses' names
4.	office of Wells & Granger	**4.**	Wells & Granger's office
5.	salary of one month	**5.**	one month's salary
6.	products of Ryan Bros. and of Miller, Inc.	**6.**	Ryan Bros.' and Miller, Inc.'s products
7.	responsibilities of employers	**7.**	employers' responsibilities
8.	needs of people	**8.**	people's needs
9.	cover of the directory	**9.**	OK
10.	fans of the team	**10.**	team's fans
11.	absence of three days	**11.**	three days' absence
12.	landing of the plane	**12.**	OK
13.	news of yesterday	**13.**	yesterday's news
14.	state of the economy	**14.**	OK
15.	report of H. R. Brock Jr.	**15.**	H. R. Brock Jr.'s report
16.	plans of the corporation	**16.**	corporation's plans
17.	worth of a few cents	**17.**	few cents' worth
18.	discount of 10 percent	**18.**	OK OR 10 percent discount
19.	plans of the architects and of the engineer	**19.**	architects' and engineer's plans
20.	wedding of the couple	**20.**	couple's wedding

C In the spaces provided, write the singular possessive, the plural, and the plural possessive forms of the nouns listed below. Note the example.

Singular	*Singular Possessive*	*Plural*	*Plural Possessive*
0. auditor	auditor's	auditors	auditors'
1. owner-manager	owner-manager's	owner-managers	owner-managers'
2. chef	chef's	chefs	chefs'
3. Kelly	Kelly's	Kellys	Kellys'
4. agency	agency's	agencies	agencies'
5. lawyer	lawyer's	lawyers	lawyers'
6. salesclerk	salesclerk's	salesclerks	salesclerks'
7. boss	boss's	bosses	bosses'
8. Stevens	Stevens's	Stevenses	Stevens'
9. publisher	publisher's	publishers	publishers'
10. engineer	engineer's	engineers	engineers'

PART 1

Nouns and Noun Usage

REVIEW

 A Underline each error in the formation or use of nouns in the following sentences, and write the necessary corrections in the spaces provided. If a sentence requires no correction, write *OK*.

1. Perhaps the board's decision will be made public at tomorrows press conference.

   1.   tomorrow's

2. The company's spokes' person refused to answer one reporter's questions.

   2.   spokesperson

3. The driver's speeding drew the police attention.

   3.   police's

4. Designer fashions for woman are featured in this week's sale.

   4.   women

5. Nancy and Betty's husband may campaign for the mayor's reelection.

   5.   Nancy's; husbands

6. Two vice presidents resigning took the president of the company by surprise.

   6.   vice presidents'

7. We have both managers' approval of the procedures outlined in these memorandas.

   7.   memoranda OR memorandums

8. The firm building those condoes is one of the largest housing developers in this area.

   8.   condos

9. Were you aware of Mr. Thomas applying for a job in the agency's downtown office?

   9.   Mr. Thomas's

10. H. L. Ross Jr. promotion was announced today.

  10.   H. L. Ross Jr.'s

11. Morton's & Payne's agency expects a 10 percent increase in sales this month.

  11.   Morton & Payne's

12. Some ranchers plan to ship their cattles to market within the next two or three months.

  12.   cattle

13. Several companies have immediate openings for sale's personnel.

  13.   sales

14. Several scientists reported the same phenomena.

  14.   OK

15. Moss Bros. headquarters building is in Tulsa.

  15.   Moss Bros.'

16. The attornies waiting outside have a 2 o'clock appointment with Dr. Barber.

  16.   attorneys

17. Automobile agencies are eager to deal with customers wanting to make trade ins.

  17.   trade-ins

18. Many French, German, and other foreign business executives have toured the new facilitys.

  18.   facilities

19. The Jones' daughter has been living overseas since the early 1980s.

19. Joneses'

20. A group of investors bought the firm for two millions dollars.

20. two million dollars

21. Marion bought a car exactly like Alex.

21. Alex's

22. Strong winds and falling trees damaged the rooves of several buildings.

22. roofs

23. Both indexes contain several cross references.

23. cross-references

24. The campers reported seeing two wolfs' entering the forest.

24. wolves

25. Several banks have branchs in this and other neighborhoods throughout the city.

25. branches

B In the space provided, write the plural of each noun shown in parentheses. For proper nouns used with titles, use the informal plural forms.

1. The city has added a hundred (acre) to the park.

1. acres

2. Congress overrode two of the President's (veto).

2. vetoes

3. There are four (s) in *Mississippi.*

3. s's

4. Both are in their early (twenty).

4. twenties

5. The industry has survived other (crisis).

5. crises

6. You should keep those (receipt) for tax purposes.

6. receipts

7. Please eliminate some of the (I) in this draft.

7. I's

8. Both (Ms. Kelly) will be at the convention.

8. Ms. Kellys

9. How many honorary (Ph.D.) does Pat have?

9. Ph.D.s

10. Both serve on several (board of directors).

10. boards of directors

11. What (criterion) do you use in measuring success?

11. criteria

12. He and she are retired (lieutenant colonel).

12. lieutenant colonels

13. Please read both (memorandum) carefully.

13. memorandums OR memoranda

14. How many (alumnus) attended the ceremony?

14. alumni

15. Some (standby) were able to board the flight.

15. standbys

16. How many (stockholder) does the company have?

16. stockholders

17. Rents are high in those apartment (complex).

17. complexes

18. She is one of six (senator-elect).

18. senators-elect

19. The company's ads appear in various (medium).

19. media

20. Both (warehouse) are closed for inventory.

20. warehouses

21. Some stores ask people to open (charge account).

21. charge accounts

22. You should obtain two or three (appraisal) before selling those items.

22. appraisals

23. They have devoted most of their (life) to helping others.

23. lives

24. Most households have two or more (radio).

24. radios

25. The two (Dr. Innis) on the staff of this clinic are not related.

25. Dr. Innises

PART 2

Pronouns and Pronoun Usage

Before you study Units 4 through 7, complete this survey of pronouns and pronoun usage. These exercises will help you identify principles that you may wish to give special attention.

SURVEY

 To complete each of the following sentences, decide which of the pronoun forms shown in parentheses is correct. Write your answers in the spaces provided.

1. If you were (he, him), what would you do?
2. Will either of those styles retain (its, their) popularity very long?
3. Did Jeff or (her, she) attend the meeting?
4. We did the work (ourself, ourselfs, ourselves).
5. Is (any one, anyone) of the drafts acceptable?
6. (Them, Those) cartons are empty.
7. To (who, whom) did you address the memo?
8. Doris asked Don and (I, me, myself) for advice.
9. (Us, We) employees deserve a salary increase.
10. Each country has (it's, its, their) own customs.
11. Ron has less experience than (her, she).
12. Which of the offices is (your's, yours)?
13. (It's, Its) a pleasure to work here.
14. Lori and (he, him) were in Dayton last week.
15. Leon repaired the clock (himself, hisself).
16. Connie and (I, me) developed the questionnaire.
17. (Every one, Everyone) of the windows is broken.
18. Maybe (these, this) news will not surprise you.
19. (Who's, Whose) responsibility should it be?
20. Are you certain the signature is (her's, hers)?
21. Everyone did (her, his, her or his, their) part.
22. The copy was sent to Diane or (he, him).
23. (There's, Their's, Theirs) may be a better plan.
24. When you see Ellen, ask (her, she) to call Lynn.
25. (It's, Its) a question that we must answer.

1. he
2. its
3. she
4. ourselves
5. any one
6. Those
7. whom
8. me
9. We
10. its
11. she
12. yours
13. It's
14. he
15. himself
16. I
17. Every one
18. this
19. Whose
20. hers
21. her or his
22. him
23. Theirs
24. her
25. It's

26. She will hire those (who, whom) she thinks have the best qualifications.   26. __who__

27. Everyone but (them, they) had studied the plan.   27. __them__

28. (Them, They) are the ones responsible.   28. __They__

29. Our next manager is likely to be (her, she).   29. __she__

30. Ann and Ray appreciated (our, us) helping them.   30. __our__

31. To (who, whom) was the letter addressed?   31. __whom__

32. Both of you should be proud of (yourself, yourselfs, yourselves).   32. __yourselves__

33. Jean felt she had no one to blame but (her, herself).   33. __herself__

34. I didn't see (anyone, anyone's) leaving early.   34. __anyone__

35. The manual was written for (us, we) new members.   35. __us__

36. (Who, Whom) will be elected governor?   36. __Who__

37. (This, These) kinds of records should be kept.   37. __These__

38. Senator Felton is among (them, those) not seeking reelection.   38. __those__

39. What is the name of (you're, your) supervisor?   39. __your__

40. The baby dropped (her, his, it's, its) bottle.   40. __its__

41. You may want to obtain (someone else, someone else's) advice.   41. __someone else's__

42. Between you and (I, me, myself), I think it would be a good investment.   42. __me__

43. Mr. Bond's son looks exactly like (he, him).   43. __him__

44. Each of the women expressed (her, their) views.   44. __her__

45. Did you read in the newspaper (that, where) trade negotiations are underway?   45. __that__

46. Walter, you should apply for the job (yourself, yourselfs, yourselves).   46. __yourself__

47. Does the manager expect you and (I, me) to work overtime this weekend?   47. __me__

48. Some of the medicine had lost (it's, its, their) potency.   48. __its__

49. Several employees received (her, his, their) vacation pay yesterday.   49. __their__

50. The position requires (some one, someone) with an accounting background.   50. __someone__

 In the following sentences, underline each error in pronoun usage; then write the appropriate correction in the space provided. If no correction is is necessary, write *OK*.

1. It's something you and them will have to do after the office closes today.   1. __they__

2. Everyone who has bought and used these brand of detergent recommends it to others.   2. __this__

3. You and I may need to do that job ourself.   3. __ourselves__

4. We appreciate you giving us your analysis of the situation.   4. __your__

5. I'm not sure whether the package over there is mine or someone else.   5. __someone else's__

6. Whom do you think should assist them?   6. __Who__

7. One of the visitors left their papers on the receptionist's desk.   7. __his or her__

8. Does he or she have any idea who's order it is?   8. __whose__

9. The check is endorsed with your name, but is the signature your's or his?   9. __yours__

10. Our managers seem confident of us being able to meet the deadline.   10. __our__

UNIT 4

Personal Pronouns—Nominative and Objective Case

PRONOUNS

Pronouns are words that take the place of nouns. The use of pronouns eliminates the monotonous repetition of nouns and creates greater fluency of expression.

> When Phyllis called Martin, Phyllis asked Martin to review the marketing plans of Phyllis and to share with Phyllis the suggestions of Martin for improving the marketing plans.

> When Phyllis called Martin, *she* asked *him* to review *her* marketing plans and to share with *her his* suggestions for improving *them*.

CHARACTERISTICS OF PERSONAL PRONOUNS

A ***personal pronoun*** refers to a particular person or thing. Unlike other kinds of pronouns that will be presented in subsequent units, personal pronouns have different forms to indicate person, number, gender, and case. The following chart summarizes the forms and characteristics of personal pronouns covered in this unit.

	NOMINATIVE CASE		OBJECTIVE CASE	
Person	**Singular**	**Plural**	**Singular**	**Plural**
First	I	we	me	us
Second	you	you	you	you
Third	she, he, it	they	her, him, it	them

Person. The term ***person*** is used to indicate whether a particular personal pronoun refers to the person speaking, to the person spoken to, or to the person or thing spoken about.

If the pronoun refers to the person speaking, as in the following sentences, it is ***first person.***

> *I* plan to apply for the job.
> The company may hire *me*.

In each sentence below, the italicized pronoun refers to the person spoken to and is ***second person.***

> *You* may want to apply for the job too.
> The company may decide to hire *you*.

Finally, if a pronoun refers to a person or to a thing about which something is said, it is ***third person.***

> Fred is in Chicago today, but *he* will be back in the office next Monday.
> Ann wanted to leave earlier, but *she* had to attend a staff meeting.
> Mr. McManus received the letter yesterday and answered *it* immediately.

Number. First person and third person personal pronouns have singular and plural forms. The second person pronoun *you* may refer to one person or to two or more persons; however, whether the reference is singular or plural, *you* requires a plural verb when it is the subject.

> When *I* offer suggestions, the manager thanks *me*. (The first person pronouns *I* and *me* are singular.)

> When *we* offer suggestions, the manager thanks *us*. (The first person pronouns *we* and *us* are plural.)

> *You* are a highly valued customer. (In this sentence, the second person pronoun *you* refers to one person but, as the subject, requires the plural verb *are*.)

> *You* are highly valued customers. (In this sentence, the second person pronoun *you* refers to two or more people and, as the subject, requires the plural verb *are*.)

> Joan said *she* referred the inquiry to Alvin and asked *him* if *he* would respond to *it* for *her*. (Each of these third person pronouns is singular.)

> Mr. Baker asked the managers to suggest topics for the sales conference and to submit *them* as quickly as *they* could. (*They* and *them* are third person plural personal pronouns.)

Gender. The third person singular personal pronouns have different forms to indicate gender, or sex: masculine, feminine, or neuter.

MASCULINE GENDER:	*He* asked the manager to advise *him*.
FEMININE GENDER:	*She* asked the manager to advise *her*.
NEUTER GENDER:	The check has no date on *it*.

In some instances, the pronoun *it* refers to a person or to an animal whose sex is not indicated. In such cases, the pronoun *it* is common gender—as are all first and second person personal pronouns and all third person plural personal pronouns. Note the pronouns of common gender in these sentences:

Perhaps the *baby* is crying because *it* is hungry.

I almost forgot that the Wilsons asked *me* to tell *you* that *they* would like for *us* to have dinner with *them* next Saturday if *we* possibly can.

Three cashiers were hired yesterday, but *they* won't start working until next Monday.

In many instances, of course, *they* and *them* refer to things rather than to people or to animals; for example:

Power tools may cause injuries if *they* are misused or have short circuits in *them.*

Case. The term **case** refers to the form of a pronoun or a noun that indicates the relation of the noun or pronoun to one or more other words in a sentence. For example, as discussed in Unit 3, the possessive case of a noun indicates ownership, authorship, or a similar relationship between the possessive noun and whatever is identified by another noun (*Mike's address* or *Dorothy's supervisor,* for example).

Personal pronouns have three cases. The *nominative case* and the *objective case* forms are listed in the preceding chart and discussed in this unit. The *possessive case* is presented in Unit 5.

USES OF THE NOMINATIVE CASE OF PERSONAL PRONOUNS

The nominative case of a personal pronoun is used when the pronoun is the subject of a verb or functions as a predicate nominative. As indicated in the chart, these are the nominative case forms of personal pronouns:

I   we   you   he   she   it   they

1. Subject of a Verb. If the pronoun is the subject of a verb in a sentence or clause, use the nominative case of the pronoun. Note the italicized pronouns and verbs in the following sentences.

I write two or three memos almost every day.

We offer quality merchandise at reasonable prices.

We salesclerks *try* to be helpful and courteous at all times. (*We,* not *salesclerks,* is the subject of the verb *try. Salesclerks* functions as an **appositive,** which is a noun that explains or clarifies a preceding noun or pronoun.)

You have a very heavy workload.

Jack said that *he has* an extra copy of the manual.

Shirley ignores whatever gossip *she hears.*

The car is five years old, but *it is* still in excellent condition.

The Paleys stayed with friends while *they were* in Richmond last month.

2. Predicate Nominative. If the pronoun following a verb explains the subject of the verb, use the nominative case of the pronoun. A pronoun (or a noun) that functions in this way is often called a ***predicate nominative,*** but it may be referred to as a **subject complement** or as a **predicate complement.**

As illustrated below, a form of the verb *be* links the predicate nominative to the subject.

The *receptionist* on duty yesterday was *I.*

Burton & Associates' first *clients* were *we.*

Perhaps the next successful *entrepreneur* will be *you.*

The *winner* is *she.*

The most gracious *loser* may have been *he.*

The company's main *competitors* are *they,* Klein Corporation and Reynolds & Company. (Note that *Klein Corporation* and *Reynolds & Company* explain who *they* are and therefore function as appositives.)

OBJECTIVE CASE OF PERSONAL PRONOUNS

The objective case of personal pronouns has a number of different uses, as indicated in the following discussion. These are objective case forms of personal pronouns:

me   us   you   her   him   it   them

3. Direct Object of a Verb. The ***direct object*** of a verb identifies who or what is the direct receiver of the action expressed by the verb. It may be a noun or, as illustrated below, a pronoun in the objective case.

The storm *caught us* by surprise.

Dr. Thomas interviewed Jan and immediately *hired her.*

If a verb has two or more direct objects and one or more of them is a pronoun, mentally repeating the verb with each pronoun object may help you ensure that you have used the objective case of the pronoun. In such sentences as the one below, some writers and speakers incorrectly use the nominative case instead of the objective case of a pronoun.

Because all seats in the coach section were occupied, the flight attendant *seated Kim, Ralph,* and *me* in the first class section. (NOT: Kim, Ralph, and *I.*)

4. Indirect Object of a Verb. The *indirect object* of a verb is a pronoun or a noun that tells to whom something is given or for whom something is done.

> During a meeting with Ralph, Ms. Tremain *gave him* an important assignment. (The pronoun *him* is the indirect object and the noun *assignment* is the direct object of the verb *gave*.)

> Please *send her* an invitation. (*Her* is the indirect object and *invitation* is the direct object of the verb *send*.)

A sentence containing an indirect object may be reworded so that the indirect object becomes the object of a preposition; for example:

> Alicia sent *me* a copy of the article.
> Alicia sent a copy of the article *to me*.

Thus mentally inserting the word *to* before a pronoun used as an indirect object may help you choose the correct form of the pronoun.

5. Object of a Preposition. The objective case of a pronoun may be used as the object of a preposition. A *preposition* is a joining word (for example, *of, to, from, between,* or *except*) which shows the relation of a noun or pronoun following it (the object of the preposition) to some other word in the sentence.

> Several *of us* have not seen the new machines.
> Two orders *from them* were received late yesterday afternoon.
> The work should be divided *between you and me*. (NOT: you and I.)

Spot Check 1

In the following sentences, decide which of the pronoun forms shown in parentheses is correct and then circle it.

1. Ms. West asked (he, **him**) what (**he**, him) would like to do next.

2. (Us, **We**) secretaries thought the new computers were intended for (**us**, we).

3. You must have given (**her**, she) an excellent recommendation—(her, **she**) got the job!

4. James and (**I**, me) thought you were (her, **she**).

5. The visitors said (them, **they**) would like to meet with Mr. Crews; however, (**he**, him) was unable to see (**them**, they).

6. The managers invited (**us**, we) administrative assistants to have lunch with (they, **them**).

7. Bryan, the receptionist, said (**he**, him) thought (them, **they**) should have invited (he, **him**) too.

8. Perhaps the managers will invite (he, **him**) and (I, **me**) the next time.

9. If (**you**, yous) find any errors, please inform (**us**, we) of (it, **them**, they).

10. (Her, **She**) and (**he**, him) are eligible for promotions, aren't they?

---

6. Subject of an Infinitive. When a pronoun is used as the subject of an infinitive, it must be in the objective case. An *infinitive* usually consists of the word *to* plus a verb, such as *to request, to draft, to call,* or *to send*.

> Miss Olson advised *him to request* a transfer.
> Kurt asked *me to draft* the reply.

When the infinitive appears after the verb *make* or *let,* the word *to* is generally omitted; for example:

> The children's parents sometimes make *them perform* various household chores.

> Ken thinks Ms. Osman will let Roberta and *him transfer* to the San Francisco office. (Note that the infinitive has a compound subject: the noun *Roberta* and the pronoun *him*.)

7. Object of an Infinitive. A pronoun used as either the direct or the indirect object of an infinitive must be in the objective case.

> Mr. Williams asked Pam *to give him* a revised report. (*Him* is the indirect object and *report* is the direct object of the infinitive *to give*.)

> First National Bank seems eager *to interview us*. (*Us* is the direct object of the infinitive *to interview*.)

8. Pronouns With the Infinitive *To Be*. When the infinitive *to be* has a pronoun as its subject, the pronoun must be in the objective case.

> The owners want *us to be* more productive.
> We expect *them to be* more understanding.

Also, since *to be* requires the same case after it as before it, a pronoun that follows *to be* must be in objective case.

> Rita mistook *me* to be *him*. (Note that both pronouns are objective case.)

> I mistook *her* to be the manager. (Note that *to be* is preceded by the objective case pronoun *her* and followed by the noun *manager*.)

> I mistook the manager to be *her*. (Whether *to be* has a pronoun subject or, as here, a noun subject such as *manager*, the pronoun following it must be in the objective case.)

In each of the preceding sentences, notice that the subject of the infinitive *to be* is different from the subject of the verb *mistook* and that both the subject and the complement of *to be* are in the objective case. If the infinitive *to be* is not immediately preceded by a pronoun or a noun, however, a pronoun that follows *to be* must agree with the subject of the verb in the sentence or clause and be in the nominative case, as illustrated below.

> *I* was mistaken to be *she*. (Both *I*, the subject of the verb *was mistaken*, and *she* are nominative case.)

> The owner was thought to be *he*. (Remember that a noun has the same form for the nominative case as it has for the objective case. When used as the subject of a verb, a noun is in the nominative case.)

Spot Check 2

In each of the sentences below, decide which of the pronoun forms shown in parentheses is correct and then circle it.

1. Creditors expect (*us*, we) to make payments on time.

2. Henry wants you and (*her*, she) to help (he, *him*).

3. The attorney asked (I, *me*) to be a witness.

4. I doubt that you would want to be either (he, him) or (her, *she*).

5. The directors may question (he and she, *him and her*) about the proposal.

6. The next governor is expected to be (her, *she*).

7. A few customers wanted (*us*, we) to grant (*them*, they) larger discounts.

8. Would you want (*them*, they) to serve on the committee?

9. They advised (*us*, we) consumers to be wary of offers that seem too good to be true.

10. Mr. McCoy may ask you or (I, *me*) to serve on the committee.

AGREEMENT OF PRONOUNS AND ANTECEDENTS

The **antecedent** of a pronoun identifies the person or thing to which the pronoun refers. The antecedent of a personal pronoun may be another pronoun or a noun.

Although *I, we,* and *you* do not require stated antecedents, *he, it, they,* and other third person personal pronouns must have stated antecedents. As you have noticed, the example sentences in this unit and elsewhere in this book often contain third person pronouns without stated antecedents. The reason is that the sentences are intended to be viewed as excerpts of written and oral messages containing sentences in which the antecedents were stated previously and therefore properly omitted in the sentences here.

9. The Principle of Agreement. The basic principle of pronoun and antecedent agreement is that a pronoun must agree with its antecedent in person, number, and gender. As the following examples illustrate, applying this principle to first and second person personal pronouns is usually easy.

> *I* thought Rose left a message for *me*. (*I* refers to the speaker and never has a stated antecedent. The pronoun *me* agrees with *I*, its antecedent.)

> Darlene asked Bob and *me* whether *we* had consulted *you*. (*We* refers to *Bob* and the speaker; *me* refers to the speaker only. *You* refers to the person spoken to and has no stated antecedent.)

Using third person pronouns requires careful attention, however. The lack of antecedents or the improper placement of antecedents results in ambiguity.

> *He* said *he* paid *him* yesterday. (No definite antecedent for any pronoun makes the meaning unclear.)

> Willis said Harry paid *him* yesterday. (The meaning is clear—the antecedent of *him* is *Willis*.)

When a pronoun might refer to either of two nouns, reword the sentence so that the pronoun clearly refers to the correct noun.

> While Peggy was talking with Maureen, *she* received several telephone calls. (Did Peggy receive the telephone calls—or did Maureen?)

> While *she* was talking with Maureen, Peggy received several telephone calls. (*She* clearly refers to *Peggy*.)

Third person singular pronouns must agree with their antecedents in gender, person, and number.

> *Ms. Belov* wanted to know whether *she* should take an extra copy with *her*.

> *Lloyd* mistakenly thought *he* had the tickets with *him*.

> Leslie endorsed the *check* and cashed *it*.

They and *them* are of common gender and may be used to refer to any third person plural antecedent.

> *Tickets* for the concert are still available, but *they* are very expensive.

> *Otis and Hilda* are in Mobile today; however, *they* will be here tomorrow.

The Harrises made *reservations* at the Plaza but had to cancel *them*.

Oliver and Olivia thought the bouquets were for *them*.

When the antecedent of a pronoun is a singular noun of common gender (*supervisor, doctor, owner,* or *executive,* for example), use *he or she, him or her,* or a similar combination of third person singular pronouns. To avoid the excessive repetition of such combinations of pronouns in your own writing and speech, change the antecedents to their plural forms and use plural pronouns.

> If an *employer* makes too many demands, *he or she* may have disgruntled employees.
>
> If *employers* make too many demands, *they* may have disgruntled employees.
>
> An experienced *accountant* may consider a refresher course to be too elementary for *him or her*.
>
> Experienced *accountants* may consider a refresher course to be too elementary for *them*.

INDEFINITE USE OF *IT* AND *THEY*

10. The Pronoun *It*. The pronoun *it* generally must have a definite antecedent. In certain idiomatic expressions, especially those that relate to weather and time, *it* does not have a stated antecedent.

> Dean read the *memo* and sent *it* to Shirley.
>
> *It* is raining. (*It* relates to weather and has no stated antecedent.)
>
> *It* is 2:30 a.m. (*It* refers to time and does not have a stated antecedent.)

11. The Pronoun *They*. The pronoun *they* must have a definite antecedent. It should not be used to refer to people in general.

> **NOT:** *They* still say the economy will continue to improve.
>
> **BUT:** Some *government officials* say the economy will continue to improve.

Remember, however, that the antecedent of a third person personal pronoun may appear in a sentence preceding the one in which the pronoun appears. For example, the following use is correct.

> We attended a meeting conducted by some *government officials* last week. *They* said, and probably still say, that the economy will continue to improve.

Spot Check 3

In each of the sentences below, decide which of the pronoun forms shown in parentheses is correct and then circle it.

1. Paula thinks Mr. Wilkinson wants (her, she) to help (he, him).

2. If you were (her, she), what would you do?

3. Olivia said the instructor considered (her, she) a good student.

4. Lewis was waiting for Ted and (I, me) to help (he, him).

5. Bob and Ellen checked the reports and found (it, them) to be accurate.

6. We give every customer the personal attention (he, she, he or she) wants and deserves.

7. The package arrived this morning, but I have not opened (it, them).

8. The best-qualified candidate is considered to be (her, she).

9. Every investor knows (he, she, he or she, they) may gain—or lose.

10. Please check the merchandise carefully before you accept (it, them).

Study Guide 4

A. As you read the following sentences, refer to the rules indicated if you are unsure why the italicized pronouns are in the nominative case.

1. Perhaps *you* and *I*[1] should reconsider the offers *we*[1] received.

2. *We*[1] employees need better equipment.

3. The company has indicated *it*[1] may relocate.

4. Some stockholders said *they*[1] would support the plan.

5. J & M's top representatives are *he*[2] and *she*[2].
6. Two potential victims of the scheme are *you*[2] and *I*[2].
7. The leading contender is thought to be *she*[8].
8. *He*[1] or *she*[1] is likely to be a winner.
9. The biggest losers are likely to be *we*[8] consumers.

10. *They*[1], Sheldon and Catherine, own and operate a successful bakery.
11. The price of Model 20 went up last year, but *it*[1] is likely to go down this year.
12. The letters were written yesterday, but *they*[1] were not mailed until this morning.

B. In the following sentences, the italicized pronouns are in the objective case—and the rules indicated explain why.

1. Wesley told *me*[3] about the meeting.
2. Please send *her*[4] a photocopy of the invoice.
3. Maybe Ms. Wolfson will divide the work between *you*[5] and *me*[5].
4. We should ask *him*[6] to find a different supplier.
5. The Nelsons hired a new attorney to represent *them*[7].

6. The secretaries consider *him*[8] and *her*[8] to be good supervisors.
7. Edgar thought the judge to be *her*[8].
8. Did you mistake *her*[8] to be *me*[8]?
9. I placed the order and then canceled *it*[3].
10. Miss Romero glanced at the pamphlets and then threw *them*[3] in the wastebasket.

C. Refer to the rules indicated at the end of each sentence if you cannot explain the choice of pronouns in the following sentences.

1. A sales representative knows that *he* or *she* must be aware of customers' needs.[1,9]
2. The customer, Mrs. Benton, said *she* would like to open an account.[1,9]
3. A baby may cry if *it* is hungry.[1,9]
4. Any new employee may rely on coworkers to help *him* or *her* at the outset.[7,9]

5. The attorneys, Mildred Rodriguez and Walter Vargas, said *they* thought the contract was invalid.[1,9]
6. *It* is unusually warm today.[1,10]
7. Many executives say *they* work far more than 40 hours a week.[1,9,11]
8. *It* is nearly midnight.[1,10]

ASSIGNMENT: Complete the Unit 4 Worksheet on pages 33–34.

UNIT 4

Personal Pronouns—Nominative and Objective Case

WORKSHEET

 A **From the pronouns given in parentheses, select the correct one and write it in the space provided.**

1. Ray thinks you may let (he, him) leave early.

2. Pete mistook (I, me) to be Denise.

3. Would you want to be Lester or (her, she)?

4. Al thinks you and (he, him) should leave now.

5. John thought it was (I, me) who wrote the report.

6. It is (us, we) tenants who should complain.

7. Why do you believe (us, we) to be at fault?

8. Perhaps (we, us) assistants should try again.

9. The manager should promote you and (her, she)

10. The contents weigh less than the package label says (it, they) should weigh.

11. Every employee must carry (her, his, her or his) part of the work load.

12. Barry inspected the premises and found (it, them) uninhabitable.

13. Campers heard the wolf howl but did not see (her, him, it, them).

14. The report was drafted by Lewis and (I, me).

15. It is (her, she) who chairs the committee.

16. The estate was divided among Mabel and (them, they).

17. The sponsors of the contest said (it, they) may be discontinued after this year.

18. (Us, We) dealers have done our best to promote and sell the new machines.

19. Maybe you and (them, they) will find the suggestions helpful.

20. The measure is supported by (us, we) consumers.

21. The alumni said (he, she, they) would contribute more to the scholarship fund.

22. Ms. Watts may let (he, him) use a larger office.

23. The principal stockholders are thought to be (them, they).

24. Ethel's children bought (her, them) diamond earrings.

25. Mrs. Lee bought a set of dishes and gave (it, them) to the newlyweds.

1. him
2. me
3. she
4. he
5. I
6. we
7. us
8. we
9. her
10. they
11. her or his
12. them
13. it
14. me
15. she
16. them
17. it
18. We
19. they
20. us
21. they
22. him
23. they
24. her
25. it

B Underline each incorrect pronoun; then write the correct pronoun in the space provided. If the sentence is correct, write *OK*.

1. The store succeeded because they sold quality merchandise.   1. __it__

2. The changes will not affect we in marketing.   2. __us__

3. I think it was him who solved the problem.   3. __he__

4. The girls' parents always support them.   4. __OK__

5. Is the letter addressed to you or she?   5. __her__

6. Dawn and me found the lecture interesting.   6. __I__

7. We would not want to be they.   7. __OK__

8. Mrs. Flynn spoke to Hilary and he about the job.   8. __him__

9. The TV series were canceled because few people watched it.   9. __them__

10. Every employee wants to do all they can to help the firm succeed.   10. __she or he OR he or she__

11. I thought it was she calling for assistance.   11. __OK__

12. The owners should be pleased with the plans us architects developed.   12. __we__

13. The applicants felt that he or she favorably impressed the interviewer.   13. __they__

14. The change will have no effect on you or I.   14. __me__

15. Mike and me were hired as consultants.   15. __I__

16. If you were her, would you file a claim?   16. __she__

17. Customers hope them will be given prompt, courteous service.   17. __they__

18. We bought used equipment and had to replace them in less than a year.   18. __it__

19. Are Terry and him going to Denver with you?   19. __he__

20. The claim seemed trifling to Beth and I.   20. __me__

C Rewrite the following sentences, keeping in mind the rules about pronouns and antecedents. Supply proper names and other words necessary to make the meaning clear. (Answers will vary.)

1. After she showed her the help-wanted ad, she applied for the position.

   After Peggy showed her the help-wanted ad, Joyce applied for the position.

2. They are already predicting the winner of the election.

   Some political experts are already predicting the winner of the election.

3. Mr. Innis's manager said he thought he would be transferred to the Atlanta office.

   Mr. Innis's manager said he thought Mr. Innis would be transferred to the Atlanta office.

4. Did you read in last night's newspaper that they want to demolish it?

   Did you read in last night's newspaper that the owners of the hotel want to demolish it?

Personal Pronouns—Possessive Case and Compound Forms

POSSESSIVE CASE OF PERSONAL PRONOUNS

The **possessive case** of a personal pronoun, like the possessive case of a noun, indicates ownership, authorship, or a similar relationship. Unlike the possessive forms of nouns, however, the possessive forms of personal pronouns are always written *without* an apostrophe. Note the following chart, which lists all the singular and plural possessive forms of personal pronouns.

PERSONAL PRONOUNS

Possessive Case

Person	Singular	Plural
First	my, mine	our, ours
Second	your, yours	your, yours
Third	his, her, hers, its	their, theirs

Be careful not to confuse the possessive pronoun *its* with the word *it's,* which is a contraction of *it is* or *it has.*

> The company succeeded in reducing *its* costs. (Possessive pronoun.)
>
> Do you think *it's* a wise investment? (Contraction of *it is.*)
>
> *It's* been a pleasure to work with you. (Contraction of *it has.*)

Also avoid confusing the possessive pronoun *their* with *they're,* the contraction of *they are,* or with the adverb *there.*

> Some employers pay *their* employees biweekly. (Possessive pronoun.)
>
> *They're* confident they will be successful. (Contraction of *they are.*)
>
> What did you do while you were *there?* (Adverb.)

Similarly, don't confuse the possessive pronoun *your* with *you're,* the contraction of *you are.*

> If *you're* a sports enthusiast, you will want to have all the books in this new series in *your* library.

Remember that *theirs* is a possessive pronoun and *there's* is a contraction of *there is* or *there has.*

> We kept our copies, but they threw *theirs* away. (Possessive pronoun.)
>
> *There's* a public telephone in the lobby. (Contraction of *there is.*)
>
> *There's* been only one major change this week. (Contraction of *there has.*)

As discussed and illustrated below, some possessive forms of personal pronouns are used only as modifiers. Others are used only as subjects, objects, and predicate nominatives. A few may be used as modifiers, subjects, objects, or predicate nominatives.

Note that a pronoun or a noun that modifies a gerund must always be in the possessive case. A **gerund,** or **verbal noun,** is a verb form ending in *ing* (for example, *calling, ordering, planning,* or *writing*) that functions as a noun.

> I appreciate *your calling* yesterday.
> Marie's *writing* is clear and concise.

1. Possessive Forms Used as Modifiers. The possessive pronouns *my, our, your,* and *their* are always used as modifiers of nouns and gerunds.

> What is the balance of *my account?*
>
> *Our representative* will be happy to assist you.
>
> Some members commented about *our arriving* late.
>
> Do you maintain a record of *your expenses?*
>
> We appreciate *your notifying* us of the price changes.
>
> The officials have not completed *their examination* of the bank's records.
>
> *Their finding* the records in order relieved the anxiety of many people.

Her, his, and *its* sometimes—not always—function as modifiers of nouns and gerunds, as in the following sentences.

> Charlotte finished *her work* ahead of schedule.
> Ann's friends just learned of *her adopting* a child.
> Mr. Andrews told us *his version* of the story.
> Martin completed *his checking* of the copy yesterday.
> The bank is consolidating some of *its operations.*
> The baby's parents spoke about *its sleeping* so much.

2. Possessive Forms Used as Subjects, Objects, and Predicate Nominatives.

The possessive pronouns *mine, ours, yours, hers,* and *theirs* are always used as subjects, objects, and predicate nominatives. They are never used as modifiers.

> One of the briefcases is *mine*. (*Mine* substitutes for "my briefcase" and functions as a predicate nominative.)
>
> The order was shipped to a competitor's warehouse instead of to *ours*. (*Ours* takes the place of "our warehouse" and functions as the object of the preposition *to*.)
>
> My proposal has been rejected, but *yours* is still under consideration. (*Yours* substitutes for "your proposal" and functions as the subject of the verb *is*.)
>
> I brought my copy of the agreement, but she forgot *hers*. (*Hers* takes the place of "her copy of the agreement" and functions as the object of the verb *forgot*.)
>
> I was asked to confirm your reservations and to cancel *theirs*. (*Theirs* substitutes for "their reservations" and functions as the object of the infinitive to *cancel*.)

As discussed in Unit 4, *her* is also the objective case form of the pronoun *she* and may be used in such ways as those indicated below.

> Please remind *her* of our meeting. (*Her* is the direct object of the verb *remind*.)
>
> Did you buy a gift for *her*? (*Her* is the object of the preposition *for*.)
>
> The company offered *her* a much higher salary. (*Her* is the indirect object of the verb *offered*.)
>
> I asked *her* to serve on the committee. (*Her* is the subject of the infinitive to *serve*.)
>
> You may want to consult *her* first. (*Her* is the object of the infinitive *to consult*.)
>
> I intended to send *her* a copy yesterday. (Her is the indirect object of the infinitive *to send*.)

The pronouns *his* and *its* also may be used in ways other than as modifiers of nouns and gerunds. Note the uses in these sentences, for example:

> She canceled her subscription, but he renewed *his*. (*His*, meaning "his subscription," is the direct object of the verb *renewed*.)
>
> I think Janet's office is next to *his*. (*His*, meaning "his office," is the object of the preposition *to*.)
>
> We renewed our contract with McKay, Inc., but a competitor canceled *its*. (*Its*, meaning "its contract," is the direct object of the verb *canceled*.)
>
> I hope to finish my work today, but I am not sure when Frank expects to complete *his*. (*His*, meaning "his work," is the direct object of the infinitive *to complete*.)
>
> Some metals have lost most of their value, but gold has retained most of *its*. (*Its*, meaning "its value," is the object of the preposition *of*.)

The state plans to increase its contribution, but the federal government intends to reduce *its*. (*Its*, meaning "its contribution," is the object of the infinitive *to reduce*.)

Spot Check 1

As you read each sentence, decide which word in the parentheses is correct and underline it.

1. She said the responsibility is (her, her's, <u>hers</u>).

2. The company has lowered (it's, <u>its</u>) prices.

3. Ms. Moore appreciated (<u>our</u>, ours, us, we) working overtime.

4. Jan's work is usually neater than (<u>mine</u>, my).

5. They have sold (<u>their</u>, there, they're) house, and we are thinking of selling (<u>our</u>, our's, ours).

6. Patrick asked us to help (he, <u>him</u>, his).

7. (Your, Your's, <u>Yours</u>) is an excellent suggestion.

8. Were you aware of (<u>her</u>, her's, hers, she) being ill last week?

9. (Their's. Theirs, <u>There's</u>) been another change in the weather.

10. We considered other suggestions but decided to accept (her's, <u>hers</u>).

11. (Mine, <u>My</u>) policy is not to mind other people's business— only (<u>mine</u>, my).

12. We are happy to learn of (he, him, <u>his</u>) receiving a promotion.

13. (Their, There, <u>They're</u>) planning an anniversary celebration.

14. Maybe (you, your, <u>you're</u>) being too cautious.

15. They wish they were able to spend more time (<u>their</u>, there, they're).

16. (Their, <u>There</u>, They're) seems to be too much work left to do.

17. The Wilsons' sons-in-law sold (his, <u>their</u>, there, they're) interests in the company.

18. Every employer should treat (her, his, <u>her or his</u>, their) employees fairly.

19. She and I are friends of (there's, their's, <u>theirs</u>).

20. (Their, There, <u>They're</u>) probably thinking that (your, <u>you're</u>) waiting for (<u>them</u>, they) to make the first move.

COMPOUND PERSONAL PRONOUNS

Compound personal pronouns are formed by adding *self* or *selves* to several of the "simple" forms of personal pronouns presented previously. The chart below lists all the accepted forms of compound personal pronouns. Notice in particular the difference between the second person singular and plural forms.

COMPOUND PERSONAL PRONOUNS

Person	Singular	Plural
First	myself	ourselves
Second	yourself	yourselves
Third	himself, herself, itself	themselves

Like other personal pronouns, compound personal pronouns must agree in person, number, and gender with their antecedents. One of the usage differences, however, is that all compound personal pronouns—except *yourself* and *yourselves*—must have stated, not understood, antecedents in the sentences in which they appear. In many instances, *you* is the understood subject and the understood antecedent of *yourself* or *yourselves*. Whether *you* refers to one person and is or is not used with *yourself,* or whether *you* refers to more than one person and is or is not used with *yourselves, you* requires a plural verb when it is the subject. Note the agreement of the compound personal pronouns with their antecedents in the following sentences.

> Maybe *I* should buy *myself* some new clothes.
>
> All of *us* need to look out for *ourselves.*
>
> Don't blame *yourself* for everything that goes wrong. (The antecedent is the understood subject *you.*)
>
> *You* have every right to be proud of *yourselves.*
>
> *Brenda* bought the ring for *herself.*
> *She* considers *herself* a dedicated employee.
>
> *Mr. Valdez* injured *himself* while skiing.
>
> How well does *he* conduct *himself* in stressful situations?
>
> Computerized equipment gives the *factory* the appearance of operating by *itself.*
>
> Contrary to all the rumors, *Richard himself* is not a suspect in the case.

Compound personal pronouns are used both as *intensive pronouns* and as *reflexive pronouns,* as indicated in the following discussion.

3. Intensive Pronouns. When used solely to emphasize a noun or another pronoun that precedes it, a compound personal pronoun functions as an *intensive pronoun.* As illustrated previously and below, the compound personal pronoun need not immediately follow its antecedent.

> *I* gave the message to Dr. Chung *myself.*
>
> *We ourselves* have no objection to the reorganization.
>
> *Ms. Pierce* decided to make the reservations *herself.*
>
> Try to make the necessary repairs *yourself.*
>
> You may own and operate businesses *yourselves.*
>
> The *owners themselves* have said that the building needs a new heating system.

4. Reflexive Pronouns. As a reflexive pronoun, any compound personal pronoun may be used as either the direct or the indirect object of a verb when the object is the same person or thing as the subject of the verb. Note the italicized subjects and objects of the verbs in the following sentences.

> *Lena* blamed *herself* for the error.
> *Mr. Simmons* gave *himself* a haircut.
> This *software* will destroy *itself* under certain conditions.

A compound personal pronoun also may be used as the object of a preposition or as the subject or object of an infinitive.

> Make a copy for *yourself.* (Object of preposition.)
>
> Nick considers *himself to be* an expert programmer. (Subject of infinitive.)
>
> Members of Congress voted *to give themselves* a raise. (Indirect object of infinitive.)
>
> She took the course *to prepare herself* for a better-paying job. (Object of infinitive.)

Common Usage Errors. Avoid the common error of using a compound personal pronoun without a stated antecedent.

> Our supervisor invited Terry and *me* to attend the conference. (NOT: Terry and myself.)
>
> Raquel and *I* will make the necessary corrections. (NOT: Raquel and myself.)

Except when *you* is understood to be the antecedent, as in the following sentences, a compound personal pronoun must always have a stated antecedent.

> Please try to repair the machine *yourself.*
>
> Prepare *yourselves* for exciting careers in business, industry, and government.

Spot Check 2

In the following sentences, write the correct compound personal pronoun in the space provided.

1. You must endorse the check ___yourself___, Jim.

2. I bought ___myself___ a sweater.

3. We bought the tickets for ___ourselves___.

4. Roland ___himself___ was unable to solve the problem.

5. Wilma considers ___herself___ to be very efficient.

6. Most people like to help ___themselves___.

7. The firm found ___itself___ in a financial bind.

8. She gave ___herself___ a good rating.

9. All of you should be very proud of ___yourselves___.

10. They ___themselves___ were late for the meeting.

11. About the only person he doesn't blame is ___himself___.

12. I'm certain the window did not break ___itself___.

13. My supervisor, Ms. Torrance, usually answers the phone ___herself___.

14. Children quickly learn how to do some things for ___themselves___.

15. I have been in similar situations ___myself___.

Study Guide 5

A. Study the following sentences carefully. Can you explain why the italicized words, rather than the ones shown in parentheses, are correct? If not, refer to the rules indicated.

1. Is the final decision *yours* (your)[2] or *hers* (her)[2]?
2. The company reported *its* (it's)[1] earnings for the second quarter.
3. Harry said we should not be concerned as a result of *his* (him)[1] resigning.
4. Did Ms. Reed say anything about *my* (me)[1] working late?
5. Be sure to sign *your* (you're)[1] name on each copy.
6. We must remember to bring *ours* (our's)[2].
7. The bank has no record of *your* (you, you're)[1] making a deposit last week.
8. *Theirs* (Their's, There's)[2] seem to be the lowest prices.
9. Do you like *yours* (your, you're)[2] better than *hers* (her, hers)[2]?
10. Some flights were delayed, but *theirs* (their's, there's)[2] left at the scheduled time.
11. *Your* (you're)[1] copy looks legible, but *mine* (my)[2] doesn't.
12. *My* (me)[1] wishing it would stop raining won't make it happen.
13. Neighbors complain about *our* (ours)[1] dog, usually saying that *its* (it's)[1] barking disturbs *their* (there, they're)[1] sleep.
14. For some people, gold has lost *its* (it's)[1] luster as an investment.
15. Many businesses extend charge privileges to *their* (there, they're)[1] customers.

B. If you are uncertain of the use of compound personal pronouns in the following sentences, refer to the rules indicated.

1. I would prefer to do the work *myself*[3].
2. He is unlikely to pat *himself*[4] on the back.
3. We gave *ourselves*[4] the benefit of the doubt.
4. Lynn *herself*[3] should be held responsible.
5. He is more certain of *himself*[4] than I am.
6. Mr. Johnson considers *himself*[4] to be a wise consumer.
7. Do doctors treat *themselves*[4] when they are ill?
8. The defendants may represent *themselves*[4] if the case goes to trial.
9. The committee *itself*[3] can do nothing but recommend policies.
10. Elaine was successful in repairing the cart *herself*[3].

ASSIGNMENT: Complete the Unit 5 Worksheet on pages 39–40.

UNIT 5

Personal Pronouns—Possessive Case and Compound Forms

WORKSHEET

 A **In each sentence, which pronoun in the parentheses is correct? Write your answer in the space provided.**

1. (You, Your, You're) work is excellent.
2. I think (him, his) filing a claim is justified.
3. Of the two plans, (their's, theirs) is better.
4. (It's, Its) almost three o'clock.
5. Some orders arrived, but (her, her's, hers) was not among them.
6. We saw (their, them) sitting in your office.
7. The winners may be you and (I, me, myself).
8. (Their, There, They're) helping us.
9. The Kellys are friends of (our, ours) too.
10. (Your, You're) being very generous, aren't you?
11. (Him, His) challenging the results seems proper.
12. Everyone must decide for (herself, himself, herself or himself, theirselves, themselves).
13. The agent suggested (me, my) traveling by plane.
14. Bradford & Company is generous to (it's, its) employees.
15. Leroy did the painting by (himself, hisself).
16. (Their, There, They're) leaving tomorrow.
17. We have never used such tools (ourselfs, ourselves).
18. The owner insisted on (our, us) paying a month's rent in advance.
19. The work of everyone but (her, her's, hers) was praised.
20. The Grangers invited Bruce and (me, myself) to a party last Saturday.
21. They seem capable of helping (theirselves, themselfs, themselves).
22. (Your's, Yours) are OK, but Jill's are not.
23. The Jacksons are friends of (me, my, mine).
24. (Their's, Theirs, There's) a big difference.
25. The trees had lost most of (it's, its, their, there, they're) leaves.

1. Your
2. his
3. theirs
4. It's
5. hers
6. them
7. I
8. They're
9. ours
10. You're
11. His
12. herself or himself
13. my
14. its
15. himself
16. They're
17. ourselves
18. our
19. her
20. me
21. themselves
22. Yours
23. mine
24. There's
25. their

Underline each error in pronoun usage in the following sentences, and write the correction in the space provided. If a sentence is correct, write *OK*.

1. We thanked everyone for his cooperation.

2. Nick said his office will be next to your's.

3. They plan to do most of the work theirself.

4. Why does he always blame hisself?

5. Your the one who deserves credit for its success.

6. The equipment is to be used by yourself and her.

7. When a customer expresses her or his opinion of any products of our's, we listen carefully.

8. You may win the grand prize yourself.

9. We're delighted that your going with us.

10. For myself, the software posed no difficulty.

11. Each of the women expressed their opinions.

12. They believed there's to be winning tickets.

13. If its raining, they're not playing golf.

14. The firm wants to buy some of its stock for it.

15. I heard there moving soon.

16. We gave ourselfs the benefit of the doubt.

17. She and I were grateful for him helping us.

18. Ms. French presented her plan to Millie and myself.

19. Members of the audience showed its appreciation.

20. Sylvia has no one to blame but her.

21. Arlene herself asked Bill and myself to serve on the panel.

22. We didn't allow us enough time, did we?

23. If the two of you are qualified, you should apply yourself.

24. What is the reason for them canceling the order?

25. Customers complained about the service rather than the merchandise themselves.

1. her or his OR his or her
2. yours
3. themselves
4. himself
5. You're
6. you
7. ours
8. OK
9. you're
10. me
11. her
12. theirs
13. it's
14. itself
15. they're
16. ourselves
17. his
18. me
19. their
20. herself
21. me
22. ourselves
23. yourselves
24. their
25. itself

UNIT 6

Indefinite Pronouns

CHARACTERISTICS OF INDEFINITE PRONOUNS

Unlike personal pronouns, **indefinite pronouns** generally refer to persons, places, and things that are unidentifiable or not readily identifiable. Note the difference between the reference of each personal pronoun and that of each indefinite pronoun in these sentences.

> I forgot to ask *someone* to give *you* a key to the office. (The personal pronoun *I* refers to the person speaking, and the personal pronoun *you* refers to the person spoken to. The person to whom the indefinite pronoun *someone* refers is unidentified and is not readily identifiable.)

> Ms. Carson reported the problem to Andrew and asked *him* to do *something* about it. (The personal pronoun *him* refers to *Andrew*, and the personal pronoun *it* refers to *problem*. However, what the indefinite pronoun *something* refers to is unknown.)

Although indefinite pronouns, unlike personal pronouns, do not have stated or readily understood antecedents, they have the characteristics of person, number, gender, and case.

Person. Indefinite pronouns refer to persons, places, and things spoken about and therefore are third person pronouns. Thus if an indefinite pronoun is the antecedent of a personal pronoun, the personal pronoun ordinarily must be third person (*it, he, she,* or *they,* for example).

> John took *everything* out of his desk and put *it* on the windowsill.

> *Most* have renewed *their* subscriptions, but a *few* have canceled *theirs*.

Sometimes, however, an indefinite pronoun is modified in a manner that makes the use of a first or second person personal pronoun more appropriate than a third person personal pronoun.

> *Most* of *us* have *our* names and addresses printed on *our* checks.

> Did *either* of *you* park *your* car next to the fire hydrant?

Number. With very few exceptions, indefinite pronouns do not have different forms to indicate number. Exceptions include the indefinite pronouns *one,*

which has the plural form *ones,* and *other,* which has the plural form *others*.

In meaning and usage, some indefinite pronouns are always singular, others are always plural, and a few may be either singular or plural.

SINGULAR:
Everyone in the office *has* a nameplate on *his or her* desk.

PLURAL:
Several were able to finish *their* work quickly.

SINGULAR OR PLURAL:
Some of the equipment *is* antiquated, and we should replace *it*. (The modifying phrase *of the equipment* makes *some* singular.)

Some memorize *their* social security numbers. (The rest of the sentence makes it clear that *some* is plural.)

Gender. Singular indefinite pronouns that end in *thing (everything, nothing,* and *something)* are neuter gender.

> If there was *anything* in the envelope, I did not see *it*. We try to keep *everything* in *its* place.

Other singular indefinite pronouns and all plural indefinite pronouns are common gender.

> *Each* of us is entitled to *his or her* opinion.

> *Each* of the women stated *her* goals very clearly.

> *Each* of the folders has several papers in *it*.

> *Many* of *us* use public transportation instead of driving *our* cars.

Case. For indefinite pronouns, the nominative case and the objective case are the same form. For example, in the first sentence below, *everyone* is the subject of the verb *ordered* and is therefore in the nominative case. In the second sentence, *everyone* is the object of the verb *introduced* and is therefore in the objective case.

> *Everyone* ordered chocolate cake for dessert.
> The chairperson introduced *everyone* on the panel.

For some indefinite pronouns, the possessive case is formed by adding an apostrophe and *s* or, in a few instances, by adding only an apostrophe.

> *anybody's* guess   *everyone's* wishes   *someone's* jacket
> each *other's* job   the *others'* homes   *one's* ideas

For others, as illustrated below, ownership or authorship is indicated by an *of* phrase.

duty *of each* (NOT: each's duty)
names *of all* (NOT: all's names)

USE OF INDEFINITE PRONOUNS

1. Singular Indefinite Pronouns. The following indefinite pronouns are singular (*one* is the only pronoun listed that has a plural form—*ones*). As illustrated by the sentences below them, they require singular verbs when they are used as subjects.

another   each   everything   no one   somebody
anybody   either   neither   nothing   someone
anyone   everybody nobody   one   something
anything   everyone

Everyone has a copy of the agenda.
Nothing is in the envelope.

When a singular indefinite pronoun refers to a person and there is no indication of the gender, or sex, of the person, use *she or he, his or her,* or a similar pair of feminine and masculine pronouns.

Everyone expects *his or her* paycheck on time.

Each of the managers has said *she or he* would like to attend the convention.

If there is an indication of the sex of the person to whom the indefinite pronoun refers, use the personal pronoun that agrees in gender. As illustrated below, the gender of the person referred to by the indefinite pronoun is sometimes indicated by the noun in an *of* phrase following the indefinite pronoun.

One of the women said *she* drives to *her* office every day.

One of Cynthia's brothers bought *himself* a personal computer.

Each of the bridesmaids made *her* own gown.

Neither of the boys had enough money with *him.*

2. Plural Indefinite Pronouns. The indefinite pronouns *both, few, many,* and *several* are always plural. These pronouns require plural verbs when they are used as subjects. Note the personal pronouns used to refer to them.

Both have *their* copies of the agreement with *them.*

Few of the company's sales representatives submit *their* reports late.

Many of our clients bring wills and other documents *they* have drafted *themselves.*

Mrs. Marcus keeps her jewels in a safe-deposit box, but *several* of her friends keep *theirs* at home.

3. Indefinite Pronouns That Can Be Singular or Plural. *All, any, more, most, none,* and *some* are

sometimes plural and sometimes singular. When one of these pronouns refers to amount or quantity (how much), treat it as singular.

Some of the lumber has knotholes in *it.*

None of the principal *itself* is included in the first payment.

When the pronoun refers to number (how many), treat it as plural.

Some of our employees prefer to cash *their* checks *themselves.*

None of the plaintiff's witnesses have changed *their* original statements about what *they* saw or heard.

Spot Check 1

Underline the expression in parentheses that correctly refers to the indefinite pronoun.

1. Everyone must decide for (himself, herself, himself or herself) which plan is best.

2. All have submitted (her, his, her or his, their) recommendations to us.

3. Everything seems to have (it's, its, their) advantages and disadvantages.

4. All are satisfied with the sports equipment (she or he, they) bought for (her or him, themselves).

5. Many of our clients were surprised by the return on (his or her, their) investments.

6. Please obtain (each's approval, the approval of each).

7. Some of the trees had moss on (it, them).

8. Everyone knows (he, she, he or she) will need to check (his, her, his or her) work (himself, herself, himself or herself).

9. None of the gasoline has water in (it, them).

10. One of her sisters-in-law sublets (her, their) apartment to my boss.

11. Each of the customers gave (her or his, their) evaluation of the new machine.

12. All of us know what (they, we) must do tomorrow.

13. Each of you should be proud of (herself or himself, yourself, yourselves).

14. Few of the tags have correct prices on (it, them).

15. One of the bank's loan officers may be willing to advise us when we talk with (her, him, <u>her or him</u>).

---

4. Compound Indefinite Pronouns. Although *no one* is always written as two separate words, other compound indefinite pronouns formed by combining *no, any, every,* or *some* with *one, body,* or *thing* are written as solid words.

anybody	nobody	everything	someone
anyone	nothing	everybody	something
anything	everyone	somebody	

Do not confuse compound indefinite pronouns with similar expressions in which *no, any, every,* or *some* is a modifier written as a separate word. Note how the meanings of the italicized expressions differ in the following sentences.

Someone on the committee may be able to answer your question.

Some one of the various plans should be acceptable to them.

Everyone in the office is planning to attend the spring conference.

Every one of the inquiries has been answered.

When *else, another,* or *other* is used with an indefinite pronoun, write it as a separate word and consider it part of the indefinite pronoun.

There was *nothing else* anyone could do to change their minds.

We were unaware of the changes, but *everyone else* seemed to know about them.

Use the word *other* with the indefinite pronoun *each* when speaking of two persons or things, and use *another* with the indefinite pronoun *one* when speaking of three or more persons or things.

Two of the firm's subsidiaries compete with *each other.*

You, Gene, and I should help *one another.*

5. Possessive Indefinite Pronouns. Use an apostrophe and *s* to form the possessive form of a singular indefinite pronoun; use just the apostrophe for plural indefinite pronouns formed by adding *s* to the singular (*others,* for example). If the pronoun is a compound, change the last word in the compound to its possessive form.

Everyone's response to the plan was favorable.
Each *one's* name and address was checked carefully.

We don't know what the *others'* travel arrangements are.

Perhaps you and I should check *each other's* spelling and punctuation.

No one else's bid is likely to be lower than ours.

If the pronoun does not have a possessive form, use an *of* phrase.

The plans *of each* of them remain a mystery.

Spot Check 2

In each sentence, underline whichever expression shown in parentheses is correct.

1. (Every one, <u>Everyone</u>) should feel free to express his or her opinions.

2. (<u>Some one</u>, Someone) of them will be appointed to that government post.

3. Does (any body, <u>anybody</u>) need an extra copy?

4. The two winners congratulated (<u>each other</u>, one another).

5. Countries rely on (each other, <u>one another</u>) for various products.

6. Please obtain (each's address, <u>the address of each</u>).

7. (<u>No one</u>, Noone) knows what the outcome will be.

8. Do you and she know (<u>each other's</u>, one another's) parents?

9. (Any one, <u>Anyone</u>) who is interested should contact Leslie.

10. Pat, Fay, and Rachel can wear (one anothers', <u>one another's</u>) clothes.

11. We need many (other's, <u>others'</u>) input before we make a decision.

12. (<u>Any one</u>, Anyone) of those styles would be preferable to this one.

13. Only one (<u>other's</u>, others') suggestions came up during the discussion.

14. The job requires (some one, <u>someone</u>) with a technical background.

15. (Some thing, <u>Something</u>) must have happened to them.

Study Guide 6

Do you understand why the italicized words in these sentences are correct? If not, refer to the rule(s) indicated at the end of each sentence.

1. The *others* usually *send their* payments to the Des Moines office.[2]
2. *Each* of the sales representatives *uses his or her* computer every day.[1]
3. *None* of the customers *were* unhappy with *their* purchases.[3]
4. *Some* of the bread *has* raisins in *it*.[3]
5. *Few* of the speakers *are* likely to use more time than has been scheduled for *them*.[2]
6. *Everyone* in the office *wants* a copy for *her or his* personal use.[1,4]
7. *Each* of the women *plans* to allow the use of *her* name in the ads.[1]
8. I may need to use *someone else's* office manual.[4,5]
9. *Some* of the members *pay their* dues in advance.[3]
10. *Any one* of them *is* satisfactory to *us*.[1,4]
11. *Either* of the two houses *is* suitable for a small family.[1]
12. *Both* of the firms *need* to find ways of reducing *their* expenses.[2]
13. *No one was* able to explain the reason for the change in procedures.[1,4]
14. *None* of the tenants *have paid their* rent for last month.[3]
15. *Neither* of the firms *permits* the use of *its* trademarks without *its* written permission.[1]
16. *One* of the firms *plans* to move *its* headquarters to North Dakota.[1]
17. *Many* appliances *are* available in a wide variety of decorator colors.[2]
18. Do you plan to ask for *anyone else's* suggestions?[4,5]
19. *All* of us *know* what *we* must do to improve *ourselves* and advance in *our* careers.[3]
20. *Neither* of the contractors *agrees* that *any* of the work *was done* in a slipshod manner.[1,3]
21. *Most* of the homeowners *pay their* real estate taxes on time.[3]
22. *Some* of them *want* to obtain *others'* advice before *they decide* upon a course of action.[3,5]
23. *Was* there *anyone else* in the office last Saturday?[1,4]
24. *Do all* competing firms *know* the strengths and weaknesses of *one another's* products and services?[3,5]
25. She and I help *each other* as much as we can.[4]

ASSIGNMENT: Complete the Unit 6 Worksheet on pages 45–46.

UNIT 6

Indefinite Pronouns

WORKSHEET

 A **Decide which expression shown in parentheses is correct; then write your answer in the space provided.**

1. (Few, Some) of the merchandise arrived late.

2. (Some one, Someone) smudged the painting.

3. (Every one, Everyone) of the receipts should be kept for tax purposes.

4. (Many, Much) of the staff seemed shocked by the announcement.

5. The three of them seem to know (each other, one another) very well.

6. Is (any one, anyone) of the accounts overdue?

7. Everyone wanted to tell us about (her, his, her or his, their) recent travel experiences.

8. It's yours—(no one else, no one else's).

9. Everyone said (he, she, he or she, they) successfully solved the puzzle.

10. The security guard inspected (every one's, everyone's) luggage.

11. One of the men expressed (his, their) feelings in a very forceful manner.

12. Both of the women left (her, their) luggage in the taxi.

13. All of us should give the manager (his or her, our, their) support.

14. One of the companies was represented by two of (its, their) top executives.

15. All but one (was an oak, were oaks).

16. Some of the firms reported (its, their) quarterly profits yesteday.

17. (No one, Noone) had the information I needed.

18. (Many, Much) of the cattle will be sold.

19. A few of us were unable to finish (our, their) work before the deadline.

20. All members of the jury cast (its, their) votes in favor of the plaintiff.

21. One of the women forgot (her, his, her or his, their) briefcase.

22. Each of us can do (some thing, something) to help conserve energy.

23. Some use (her or his, their) credit cards for major purchases only.

24. None of the fabric had flaws in (it, them).

25. Our branch managers keep in touch with (each other, one another) on a daily basis.

1. _Some_

2. _Someone_

3. _Every one_

4. _Many_

5. _one another_

6. _any one_

7. _her or his_

8. _no one else's_

9. _he or she_

10. _everyone's_

11. _his_

12. _their_

13. _our_

14. _its_

15. _were oaks_

16. _their_

17. _No one_

18. _Many_

19. _our_

20. _their_

21. _her_

22. _something_

23. _their_

24. _it_

25. _one another_

Underline each error in pronoun usage in the following sentences, and write the correction in the space provided. If a sentence is correct, write *OK*.

1. Everyone has their strengths and weaknesses.
2. Our opinion is the same as everyone else's.
3. All of us left their luggage in the lobby.
4. The work could have been done by anyone of us.
5. Most submitted its applications today.
6. Some of the paint had lead in them.
7. Was he aware of someone canceling the ad?
8. I think each's loss was about $100.
9. Other's bids were being considered.
10. I did not see anybody's using your phone.
11. Everything stayed where they belonged.
12. We very much need everyones' cooperation.
13. Everyone of the accounts is in order.
14. Perhaps you and I should help one another.
15. Should we solicit anyone else advice?
16. We sought the advice of other's.
17. Was anything else missing from your office?
18. Each described their educational background.
19. Noone bothered to inform either of us.
20. The one's being considered are Klein's.
21. Few requested its vacation pay in advance.
22. Each of the pets had their collar on.
23. The ceilings of some need repainting.
24. Someone spilled some thing on the floor.
25. Most of the committee members work well with each other.

1. her or his OR his or her
2. OK
3. our
4. any one
5. their
6. it
7. someone's
8. the loss of each
9. Others'
10. anybody
11. it
12. everyone's
13. Every one
14. each other
15. anyone else's
16. others
17. OK
18. her or his OR his or her
19. No one
20. ones
21. their
22. its
23. OK
24. something
25. one another

UNIT 7

Relative and Interrogative Pronouns

RELATIVE PRONOUNS

A **relative pronoun**—such as *who, that,* or *which*—connects a modifying clause to the antecedent of the relative pronoun. As illustrated below, the relative pronoun is part of the modifying clause.

> The person *who bought the building* intends to renovate it. (The clause modifies *person,* the antecedent of *who.*)
>
> Mr. Raglan plans to interview everyone *who has submitted an application.* (The clause modifies *everyone,* the antecedent of *who.*)
>
> The company *that did the work* experienced some delays. (The clause modifies *company,* the antecedent of *that.*)
>
> The ad contains statements *which some of us consider misleading.* (The clause modifies *statements,* the antecedent of *which.*)

Modifying clauses introduced by relative pronouns function as adjectives and are known as **relative clauses.** A clause of this kind is a **dependent clause,** that is, a group of words that contains a subject (such as *who* in the first example or *some* in the last example) and a predicate (such as *bought the building* or *consider misleading*) but that does not make sense by itself.

Pronouns used to introduce clauses that function as adjectives are also used to introduce clauses that function as nouns; for example:

> Perhaps you know *who will replace him.* (The clause is the object of the verb *know.* Notice that the antecedent of *who* is not stated and is not readily identifiable.)
>
> Alicia believes *that you will apply for the position.* (The clause is the object of the verb *believes. That* functions solely as a connecting word; it isn't a substitute for a noun or a pronoun.)
>
> It's difficult to tell *which are yours and which are mine.* (The two clauses function as the object of the infinitive *to tell.* The antecedents of *which* are not stated and cannot be readily identified.)

Forms of Relative Pronouns. Relative pronouns do not have different forms to indicate person, number, or gender. Note that *who* has different forms to indicate case.

RELATIVE PRONOUNS

NOMINATIVE:	who	that	which
OBJECTIVE:	whom	that	which
POSSESSIVE:	whose		

Use of *Who, Whom,* and *Whose.* The relative pronouns *who, whom,* and *whose* are used to refer to people.

> The *customer who* filed the claim decided to settle out of court.
>
> The *speaker whom* we invited first was unable to accept our invitation.
>
> *Anyone whose* credit history is satisfactory may obtain a charge card.

Use of *That.* The relative pronoun *that* is used to refer to people, animals, and things.

> No *child that* has measles should be in school.
>
> The only *pets that* I have are a Chihuahua and a bird.
>
> Every *computer that* we use has two disk drives.

Modifying clauses introduced by *that* are *restrictive clauses.* Such a clause is essential to the identification of the person or thing the clause modifies and to the meaning of the sentence. Note how omitting the modifying clause affects this sentence:

> Margaret put everything *that she had in her purse* on the table.
>
> Margaret put everything on the table.

Use of *Which.* The relative pronoun *which* is used to refer to animals and things.

> The ASPCA provides shelter for *pets which* have been abandoned.
>
> Our *company, which* was founded in 1982, manufactures office furniture.

Both *which* and *that* are used to introduce restrictive clauses. However, only *which* is used to introduce nonrestrictive clauses. A *nonrestrictive clause* provides information that can be omitted without significantly affecting the meaning of a sentence. As illustrated above, commas are used to set off a nonrestrictive clause—but not a restrictive clause.

For inanimate objects, possession is indicated by the phrase *of which* instead of *whose.*

The incident occurred in the parking lot of a mall, the name *of which* I do not remember. (NOT: a mall whose name I do not remember.)

AGREEMENT WITH ANTECEDENTS

A relative pronoun must agree with its antecedent in person and number.

It is *I who am* at fault. (The first person singular pronoun *I* is the antecedent of *who*. Therefore, the subject *who* requires the first person singular verb *am*.)

I think it is *she who prepares* the monthly sales reports. (The antecedent of *who* is the third person singular pronoun *she*. Therefore, the subject *who* requires the third person singular verb *prepares*.)

Those who prepare for interviews make a good impression. (If the antecedent is a plural noun or pronoun, a relative pronoun subject requires a plural verb.)

You may apply for the *license, which costs* about $15, at any local government office. (The antecedent of *which* is the singular noun *license*. Therefore, the subject *which* requires the third person singular verb *costs*. Remember that all nouns are third person.)

FUNCTIONS OF RELATIVE PRONOUNS IN CLAUSES

It is important to know the function of the relative pronoun in any clause so that the correct form may be used. *Who* requires special attention because it changes form to indicate case *(who, whom, whose)*.

1. Subject of a Verb. A relative pronoun may be the subject of a verb. When it is, remember that the verb must agree in person and number with the antecedent of the relative pronoun.

It is I *who leave* late every day. (The verb *leave* is correct because the antecedent of *who* is the first person singular pronoun *I*.)

It is she *who is* in charge of the project. (The verb *is* agrees with the the antecedent of *who*, the third person singular pronoun *she*.)

Taxpayers *who are* eligible for a refund should file their returns early. (The verb *are* is correct because the antecedent of *who* is the plural noun *taxpayers*, which—like all nouns—is third person.)

Please draft a letter *that answers* all their questions. (The third person singular verb *answers* is correct because the antecedent of *that* is the singular noun *letter*.)

2. Object of a Verb. A relative pronoun may be the object of a verb.

The stationery *that* you *requisitioned* is out of stock.

Jan is the candidate *whom* most members *prefer*.

3. Object of a Preposition. A relative pronoun may be the object of a preposition (*of, for, to, with, by,* or *on,* for example).

The names of those *to whom* we sent questionnaires are confidential.

The accounts *for which* Hilda is responsible average nearly $2000.

4. Subject or Object of an Infinitive. A relative pronoun may be the subject or object of an infinitive. If so, it must be in the objective case.

Please send a copy to Dr. Suarez, *whom* we have invited *to speak* at the June meeting. (Subject.)

Annette Payne is the supervisor *whom* the manager is planning *to promote*. (Object.)

5. Modifier of a Noun or Pronoun. If the antecedent of the relative pronoun is *not* an object, *whose* may be used as a modifier.

Mrs. Larson, whose assistant is ill, asked me to help. *Everyone whose work* is up to date may leave early.

Do not confuse the possessive pronoun *whose* with *who's,* the contraction of *who is* or *who has*.

6. Linking Word Only. Sometimes the relative pronoun functions solely as a linking word. In such instances, the relative pronoun is sometimes omitted.

The house *(that)* Donna bought is very modern.

7. Errors in the Use of *Who* and *Whom*. The use of *who* instead of *whom* is a common error. Here are some suggestions that will help you.

Mentally omit *I believe, I think,* or a similar expression when it appears in a clause introduced by a relative pronoun.

Lee is the candidate who?/whom? (I believe) will endorse our proposal.
Mr. Wang, who?/whom? (I think) you have met, is our new general manager.

Rearrange the clause so that the subject, verb, and object (if any) appear in that order.

who?/whom? will endorse our proposal.
you have met who?/whom?

Substitute *he, she,* or *they* for the relative pronoun. If one of those three pronouns would be correct, use the relative pronoun *who*. If *him, her,* or *them* would be correct, use the relative pronoun *whom*.

She will endorse our proposal is correct; therefore, use *who* in the following sentence:

Lee is the candidate *who,* I believe, will endorse our proposal.

You have met him is correct; therefore, use *whom* in the following sentence:

UNIT 7

Relative and Interrogative Pronouns

WORKSHEET

 A **Which of the pronouns shown in parentheses is correct? Write your answer in the space provided.**

1. The hotel, (that, which) was built at the turn of the century, has been completely modernized.

2. We were among those (who's, whose) luggage was lost.

3. (Whoever, Whomever) is appointed will find the position very challenging.

4. (Who's, Whose) substituting for Mr. Farley?

5. The memo lists the names of those (who, whom) have an employment anniversary this month.

6. Do you know (who, whom) repaired this machine?

7. The car (that, which) we wanted was too expensive.

8. She said (that, which) we can rely on her to help.

9. Do you know to (who, whom) the contract was awarded?

10. The account, (that, which) has a balance of $522.78, is 60 days overdue.

11. Stroms or Caldwell, Inc., (whatever, whichever) offers the lower bid, will get the contract.

12. For (who, whom) was the bouquet intended?

13. Mark, (who, whom) I believe to be highly qualified, may be persuaded to accept the nomination.

14. To (who, whom) was the letter addressed?

15. I have no idea (who's, whose) writing it is.

16. If you could be someone else, (who, whom) would you be?

17. I don't know (who's, whose) making the calls.

18. (Who, Whom) shall we ask to be chairperson?

19. The song is one (that, which) everyone knows.

20. To (who, whom) should I address my inquiry?

21. There is no one (who, whom) deserves a promotion more than you do.

22. We will meet with (whoever, whomever) is their representative.

23. The agency (that, who, whom) represents Ashley Welbourne is R. Carson & Associates.

1. which
2. whose
3. Whoever
4. Who's
5. who
6. who
7. that OR which
8. that
9. whom
10. which
11. whichever
12. whom
13. whom
14. whom
15. whose
16. who
17. who's
18. Whom
19. that OR which
20. whom
21. who
22. whoever
23. that

24. Alvin said he could recommend someone (who's, whose) name we would recognize immediately.

24. _____whose_____

25. (Who, Whom) did the visitors ask to see?

25. _____Whom_____

 B The following sentences contain errors in the use of relative, interrogative, and other pronouns. Underline each error and write the correction in the space provided. If no correction is necessary, write *OK*.

1. It was John and her who arranged the meeting.

1. _____she_____

2. Sue is a person who you can rely on.

2. _____whom_____

3. Whom do you think will oversee the project?

3. _____Who_____

4. Max thinks he deserves a raise hisself.

4. _____himself_____

5. Who's signatures appear on the June 1 contract?

5. _____Whose_____

6. The car, that I bought last year, needs repairs.

6. _____which_____

7. They asked Joyce and I to advise them.

7. _____me_____

8. We sent a sample to every one who wanted one.

8. _____everyone_____

9. Randy and myself are willing to work overtime.

9. _____I_____

10. The dispute is about whom should be held liable.

10. _____who_____

11. Who have you heard will be their representative?

11. _____OK_____

12. That is a company about whom we know very little.

12. _____which_____

13. The speaker said us consumers need to buy fewer imported products.

13. _____we_____

14. The meeting, whose purpose is unknown to us, has been postponed until 2 p.m.

14. ___the purpose of which___

15. The store who sold us the TV is out of business.

15. ___that OR which___

16. They have no one to blame but theirselves.

16. _____themselves_____

17. Nancy is the one who said the ring she found was your's.

17. _____yours_____

18. It's a breed of cattle with whom I am unfamiliar.

18. _____which_____

19. Every one of them is willing to help anyone who needs their assistance.

19. _____his or her_____

20. The owner's manual, that contains many drawings, gives step-by-step operating instructions.

20. _____which_____

21. If its raining, we will have to cancel the picnic.

21. _____it's_____

22. Who's questioning the policy led to its being changed?

22. _____Whose_____

23. Who did you say is likely to be the next president of the National Association of Manufacturers?

23. _____OK_____

24. Who, in your opinion, should the mayor appoint to the commission?

24. _____Whom_____

25. Larry said there would be very little left for himself and me to do.

25. _____him_____

PART 2

Pronouns and Pronoun Usage

REVIEW

To review various principles of correct pronoun usage, select the word or words that correctly complete each sentence. Write your answers in the spaces provided.

1. (Who, Whom) do you think would be a good candidate?

2. Joan is someone (who's, whose) completely reliable.

3. One of the restaurants had (its, their) license revoked.

4. Everyone will have to make (her, his, her or his, their) reservations.

5. No one has more to do than you and (I, me, myself).

6. The twins can wear (each other's, one another's) clothes.

7. My subscription expired, but I don't think (her, her's, hers) has.

8. Helen and (I, me, myself) have been invited.

9. The manager did not object to (our, us) leaving a little early.

10. Some of the furniture had scratches on (it, them).

11. We appreciated (him, his) paying promptly.

12. To (who, whom) was the check issued?

13. Did all the senators (who, whom) you wanted to interview meet with you?

14. Was it (her, she) who placed the order?

15. Did you see (anyone, anyone's) entering the store before 8 a.m.?

16. (Any one, Anyone) of them is satisfactory.

17. The firm prefers (some one, someone) with experience.

18. Some of the containers had different labels on (it, them).

19. Walter seems to prefer staying by (himself, hisself).

20. Some of the oil had water in (it, them).

21. (Us, We) cashiers work very hard.

22. Some of the sheep had shed most of (its, their) wool.

23. No one but you and (I, me) knew about it.

24. One of the men reported that (his, their) car had been stolen.

25. It was (them, they) who received medals.

26. Are both friends of (you, your's, yours)?

1. _____Who_____

2. _____who's_____

3. _____its_____

4. _____her or his_____

5. _____I_____

6. _____each other's_____

7. _____hers_____

8. _____I_____

9. _____our_____

10. _____it_____

11. _____his_____

12. _____whom_____

13. _____whom_____

14. _____she_____

15. _____anyone_____

16. _____Any one_____

17. _____someone_____

18. _____them_____

19. _____himself_____

20. _____it_____

21. _____We_____

22. _____their_____

23. _____I_____

24. _____his_____

25. _____they_____

26. _____yours_____

27. The desk, (that, which) I bought at a garage sale, is solid oak.

28. Neither of the reports had errors in (it, them).

29. The couple celebrated (its, their) tenth wedding anniversary in Hawaii.

30. I think they will wait for you and (I, me, myself) a while longer.

31. The agency has changed (it's, its, their) name several times.

32. I think (their, there, they're) planning to meet in Pittsburgh next week.

33. Would you want to be (he, him)?

34. We asked our guests to serve (themselfs, themselves).

35. We consider (them, they) to be ideal candidates.

36. Both of you will be reimbursed for (their, your) expenses.

37. The operators of the machine said some of (it's, its, their) parts were worn out.

38. We hope the next manager will be (her, she).

39. It is (we, us) who must control expenses.

40. If the roof leaks, we should repair (it, them) immediately.

41. Was there a misunderstanding between Mrs. Wells and (her, she)?

42. We should solicit (someone else, someone else's) advice.

43. The only ones absent were Stanley and (me, I, myself).

44. If you were (he, him), would you accept the company's offer?

45. Try to be less critical of (you, yourself) and your staff.

46. (Who, Whoever) accepts the offer will not regret doing so.

47. Did you read in *Newsweek* (that, where) a trade agreement will be reached?

48. The four of them sometimes edit (each other's, one another's) reports.

49. Is there any excuse for (anybody, anybody's) being inconsiderate of others?

50. Hilda said that you and (her, she) volunteered to work overtime next week.

27. which
28. it
29. their
30. me
31. its
32. they're
33. he
34. themselves
35. them
36. your
37. its
38. she
39. we
40. it
41. her
42. someone else's
43. I
44. he
45. yourself
46. Whoever
47. that
48. one another's
49. anybody's
50. she

PART 3

Verbs and Verb Usage

Before you study Units 8 through 12, complete this survey of verbs and verb usage. These exercises will help you identify principles that you may wish to give special attention.

SURVEY

 A **For each sentence in which the italicized verb or verb phrase is correct, write *OK* in the space provided. If the verb or verb phrase is incorrect, write the correct one in the space provided.**

1. We *should of consulted* you first.

2. I like the new offices, but he *don't*.

3. If you *was* the President, would you have vetoed the last bill passed by Congress?

4. How many times *have* you *wrote* to them?

5. I thought they *was changing* the procedure.

6. Canfield and Associates *have submitted* the lowest bid on the construction project.

7. *Has* she *give* you her recommendations?

8. The package *was setting* in the hall.

9. Neither of the offices *are* vacant.

10. There *was* only two letters in the folder.

11. I *am working* here since 1989.

12. All of us *knowed* it was a mistake.

13. The vice president and general manager *are* also a member of the board of directors.

14. Usually, the proceeds of the fund-raising drive *amounts* to a thousand dollars or less.

15. *Is* either of you *planning* to work late?

16. Sixty miles *are* too far to drive to work.

17. The general manager, as well as the branch managers, *are studying* the proposal.

18. The jury *has been arguing* among themselves since the case came to trial.

19. The finance committee *have approved* the operating budget for the next fiscal year.

1. <u>should have consulted</u>

2. <u>doesn't</u>

3. <u>were</u>

4. <u>have written</u>

5. <u>were changing</u>

6. <u>has submitted</u>

7. <u>Has given</u>

8. <u>was sitting</u>

9. <u>is</u>

10. <u>were</u>

11. <u>have been working</u>

12. <u>knew</u>

13. <u>is</u>

14. <u>amount</u>

15. <u>OK</u>

16. <u>is</u>

17. <u>is studying</u>

18. <u>have been arguing</u>

19. <u>has approved</u>

20. Mr. Metcalf said he *shall be* able to meet with them next Thursday.

20. will be

21. Half of the company's assets *has been sold.*

21. have been sold

22. Some of the information in the letters *are* confidential.

22. is

23. Jane is the only one of the secretaries who *subscribe* to that weekly magazine.

23. subscribes

24. Dr. Kraer is one of those people who *meets* deadlines with little or no difficulty.

24. meet

25. Roger recommended that the repairs *are made* immediately.

25. be made

B In the space provided, write the correct form of each verb shown in parentheses. Note the example.

0. Where (be) you yesterday afternoon?

0. were

1. No one has (apply) for the job.

1. applied

2. She (go) to both meetings last year.

2. went

3. The train (have) left when we arrived at the station.

3. had

4. I have (be) in Indianapolis several times.

4. been

5. Pauline (shall) have informed us, but she did not.

5. should

6. Where was he (sit) when you saw him?

6. sitting

7. We arrived just as Mr. Bullard (begin) to talk about the importance of promptness.

7. began

8. (Do) Keith still need your assistance?

8. Does

9. Someone (throw) away the pamphlet I needed.

9. threw

10. The catalogs (be) now being printed by a firm in Wisconsin.

10. are

11. Steve thought he (will) get a better offer.

11. would

12. Currently, only one of the companies (offer) discounts.

12. offers

13. Several of my friends (see) the play last week.

13. saw

14. I think Janet is one of those people who always (write) legibly.

14. write

15. Miss Rogers has (ask) us to help her.

15. asked

16. The report was (write) by Elvira.

16. written

17. The pilots have (fly) thousands of miles without accidents.

17. flown

18. When we asked her, Ethel (tell) us how to set up the report.

18. told

19. (Have) anyone noticed the error yet?

19. Has

20. I wish that I had (know) much earlier of your interest in the project.

20. known

21. (Be) you aware of the situation when I spoke to you last week?

21. Were

22. Some of the grain (be) being shipped today.

22. is

23. Cecil (say) he would notify them.

23. said

24. The car (speed) past us and hit a tree.

24. sped

25. I wish I (be) able to accept the invitation, but I will be on vacation then.

25. were

UNIT 8

Forms of Verbs

VERBS AND VERB PHRASES

Verbs are words that express action or state of being. As illustrated below, a number of commonly used verbs are compounds—some written with a hyphen, others written with a space between the words, and still others written with neither a hyphen nor a space between the words.

> Some employees *park* their cars in a nearby garage.
>
> Visitors sometimes *double-park* their cars in front of the building.
>
> We immediately *check* our bills when we *check out* of a hotel or motel and *update* our expense records later.
>
> They *seem* nervous because the deadline *is* tomorrow. (Unlike the previous examples, each of these verbs expresses state of being.)

A **verb phrase** is a group of words that consists of one or more *helping,* or *auxiliary,* verbs and a *main* verb, which is always the last word in a verb phrase. As illustrated below, a verb phrase tells what the subject does, what is done to the subject, or what the state of being of the subject is.

> Rick *is demonstrating* the new machine. (The action of the subject, *Rick,* is expressed by the helping verb *is* and the main verb *demonstrating.*)
>
> The new machine *is being demonstrated* by Rick. (What is done to the subject, *machine,* is expressed by the helping verbs *is* and *being* plus the main verb *demonstrated.*)
>
> Your suggestions *have been* very helpful. (The state of being of the subject, *suggestions,* is expressed by the auxiliary verb *have* and the main verb *been.*)
>
> The information *may be* inaccurate. (The helping verb *may* and the main verb *be* form a verb phrase that indicates the state of being of the subject, *information.*)

ACTIVE AND PASSIVE VERBS

Verbs that express action—and only those that express action—may be used as active verbs or as passive verbs.

Active Verbs. When the subject performs the action expressed by a verb or verb phrase, the verb or verb phrase is said to be **active.** If the subject does *not*

direct the action to an object, as in each of the following sentences, the verb or verb phrase is **intransitive.**

> Some of us *walk* to the office every day. (*Walk* expresses the action of *some,* the subject.)
>
> Your *supervisor* always *speaks* very highly of you. (*Speaks* expresses the action of *supervisor,* the subject.)

If the subject directs the action to an object, as in each sentence below, the verb or verb phrase is **transitive.** The person or thing that receives the action is known as the **direct object.**

> Our employees *process* many orders every day. (The subject—*employees*—directs the action—*process*—to the direct object—*orders.*)
>
> One of our representatives *will meet* Mr. Edwards at the airport. (The subject—*one*—directs the action—*will meet*—to the direct object—*Mr. Edwards.*)

In many instances, the subject directs the action to an object and transmits the object to someone or something. The receiver of the object is known as the **indirect object.**

> Bruce LaBarre, one of our local critics, *gave* the new movie an excellent review. (The subject—*Bruce La-Barre*—directs the action—*gave*—to the direct object—*review*—and transmits it to the indirect object—*movie.*)
>
> I *am sending* you another copy immediately. (The subject—*I*—directs the action—*am sending*—to the direct object—*copy*—and transmits it to the indirect object—*you.*)

Passive Verbs. When the subject receives the action expressed by a verb phrase, the verb phrase is **passive** (and always transitive). Note that a passive verb phrase always includes a form of *be (be, am, is, are, was, were, been,* or *being)* as a helping verb and a past participle as the main verb. It may also include one or more other helping verbs, such as *have* or *will;* for example, *have been delayed, will be mailed,* or *has been received.*

> The new movie *was given* an excellent review by Mr. LaBarre.
>
> Another copy *is being sent* to you immediately.

Copyright © by Glencoe.

LINKING VERBS

A *linking verb* indicates a state of being; it is neither active nor passive. Such a verb or verb phrase connects the subject to a modifying word or phrase (called a *predicate adjective*) or to a noun or pronoun that renames or further identifies the subject (called a *predicate nominative*). The verb—or the main verb in a verb phrase—is often a form of the verb *be.* If it is not a form of *be,* it is a verb that could be replaced by a form of *be,* such as *seem, appear,* or *become.* Study each of the following examples carefully.

> Juan *is* very cooperative. (*Is* links the subject *Juan* to the predicate adjective *cooperative.*)
>
> Both of them *seem* nervous. (*Seem,* which could be replaced by *are,* links the subject *both* to the predicate adjective *nervous.*)
>
> Mrs. Milton *will be* our new representative. (*Will be* links the subject *Mrs. Milton* to the predicate nominative *representative.*)
>
> Lucille *has become* the leading candidate. (*Has become* links the subject *Lucille* to the predicate nominative *candidate.*)

TENSES OF VERBS

The *tense* of a verb indicates the time of the action, condition, or state of being. For example, if the time of the action is now, the *present tense* is used.

> The committee *meets* every Tuesday.
> This set of glasses *matches* yours.
> Ms. Olson *is* a senior vice president of the bank.
> Our suppliers *are* reliable.
> Neither plan *appears* to be acceptable.

To indicate that the action or state of being took place in the past, the *past tense* is used.

> The committee *met* only once a month last year.
> Two athletes *matched* the current world record.
> Who *was* in charge of the department yesterday?
> Both houses *were* vacant.
> Everything *seemed* to be in order.

If an action or state of being has not yet happened, the *future tense* is used.

> Pauline *will drive* you to the airport this afternoon.
>
> The next meeting *will be* early next month.
>
> The new postal rates *will become* effective within the near future.

The present, past, future, and other tenses of verbs, which will be discussed in the next unit, require a thorough understanding of the various parts of verbs.

THE PARTS OF MOST VERBS

With the exception of *be* and some helping verbs, which will be discussed later, verbs have five parts: two present tense forms, one past tense form, one past participle form, and one present participle form. Note the following parts of some commonly used verbs.

Present Tense	Past Tense	Past Participle	Present Participle
call, calls	called	called	calling
carry, carries	carried	carried	carrying
enjoy, enjoys	enjoyed	enjoyed	enjoying
find, finds	found	found	finding
save, saves	saved	saved	saving
think, thinks	thought	thought	thinking
write, writes	wrote	written	writing

Verbs that have a past tense and a past participle formed by simply adding *d* or *ed* (sometimes after changing a final *y* to *i*) to the present tense form that would be used with *to* are *regular verbs.* Note the verbs *call, carry, enjoy,* and *save* in the preceding chart, for example.

Such verbs as *find, think,* and *write* are examples of *irregular verbs,* which are those having parts not formed in a consistent manner. Other irregular verbs include *be, do,* and *have.* (A chart showing the parts of a number of troublesome verbs appears later in this unit.)

Present Tense. The present tense form that does not end in *s* or *es,* such as *call* or *write,* is used with the singular pronoun subject *I* and with all plural pronoun and noun subjects (*you, we, they, both, employers,* and so on). This form is the same as the infinitive form without the word *to;* for example, *(to) carry, (to) collect, (to) save, (to) write,* and so forth.

> I *carry* a pen or a pencil with me most of the time.
> Perhaps *you collect* stamps or coins as a hobby.
> *Both* of them *save* time by using public transportation.
> Many *employees write* letters, memos, and reports.

The present tense form that ends in *s* or *es,* such as *carries* or *writes,* is called the *third person singular form* because it is used only with a third person singular subject. Such a subject may be the pronoun *he, it, she, everyone, each,* or *nothing,* for example; or it may be a singular noun such as *Anita, Bob, account, computer,* or *office.*

> *She* usually *carries* a briefcase to work.
> Bob *collects* stamps as a hobby.
> A *computer saves* a great deal of time and effort.
> *Everyone* in the department *writes* memos and letters.

Past Tense. The **past tense** of regular verbs is formed by adding *d* or *ed* (sometimes after changing a final *y* to *i*) to the infinitive form without the word *to;* for example, *carried (carry* plus *ed)* or *saved (save* plus *d).* The past tense of irregular verbs, such as *find* and *write,* is not formed according to any consistent pattern. For example, the past tense of *find* is *found;* the past tense of *write* is *wrote.*

> *Everyone found* the article that *you wrote* to be very interesting.
>
> *I saved* money by using the discount coupons that *others collected* for me.

Past Participle. The **past participle** is the same as the past tense for regular verbs. Irregular verbs, such as *find* and *write,* do not follow any consistent pattern for the past participle, which is often different from the past tense form. As illustrated below, the past participle is used as the main verb (always the last verb) in a verb phrase.

> *We have carried* all the cartons into the stockroom.
> *Both letters were written* by someone else.
> *One* of the copies *was saved.*

Present Participle. The **present participle** is formed by adding *ing* to the infinitive form without the word *to;* for example, *collecting (collect* plus *ing), carrying (carry* plus *ing),* and *writing (write* plus *ing).* As illustrated below, the present participle is used with one or more helping verbs in a verb phrase.

> *Kathy will be writing* a memo to each member of the staff.
>
> *They are saving* more than some of us.
> *Both* of them *have been working* very hard on this project.

Spot Check 1

In the space provided, write the form of the verb indicated in parentheses.

1. Many people (*enjoy*—present tense) such sports as tennis and baseball.

   1. enjoy

2. I (*find*—past tense) the information for him.

   2. found

3. He (*enjoy*—present tense) his work.

   3. enjoys

4. She (*write*—past tense) to you yesterday.

   4. wrote

5. We are (*enjoy*—present participle) our vacation.

   5. enjoying

6. Ray has (*write*—past participle) to them.

   6. written

7. Pat (*save*—present tense) part of every paycheck.

   7. saves

8. Some (*save*—present tense) more than others.

   8. save

9. We (*carry*—past tense) the luggage ourselves.

   9. carried

10. Has anyone (*find*—past participle) the key?

    10. found

THE PARTS OF SOME HELPING VERBS

As indicated below, some helping verbs have only one or two forms each.

will	shall	may	can	ought	must
would	should	might	could	——	——

> *Shall* I *make* the reservations?
> They *could have taken* a later flight.
> We *must order* a new supply this week.

THE PARTS OF THE VERB *BE*

Unlike all other verbs in the English language, the verb *be* has eight different parts.

> be   am   is   are   was   were   been   being

Be is the part that is used in the infinitive form with the word *to* or with such helping verbs as *will* and *may.* As illustrated below, *be* is also used in requests and commands, in motions made at meetings, and following such verbs as *recommend* and *suggest.*

> *Be* sure to check these figures carefully. (Command.)
>
> Please *be* more cautious. (Request.)
>
> I move that the meeting *be* adjourned. (Motion.)
>
> Who *will be* our next mayor? (Main verb in a verb phrase.)
>
> Your flight *may be delayed* an hour. (Helping verb in a verb phrase.)
>
> Would you like *to be* president of a large corporation? (Infinitive.)
>
> We expect the change *to be announced* next week. (Helping verb in an infinitive.)
>
> We recommended that the meeting *be* postponed. (Recommendation or suggestion.)

Present Tense. *Am, are,* and *is* are present tense forms. *Am* is used with the pronoun subject *I*.

> I *am* a member of that organization.
> I *am being* more cautious this time.

Is, the third person singular form, is used with such singular pronoun subjects as *he, it, she, each,* and *everything* as well as with all singular noun subjects (*employer, city,* and *suggestion,* for example). As illustrated below, *is* also is frequently used as a helping verb.

> *Everything* in the store *is* on sale at reduced prices.
> *She is* a highly effective manager.
> The *company is considered* to be the leader in its field.

Are is used when the subject is *you* or any plural pronoun or plural noun.

> You *are* the one most likely to receive a promotion.
> Some of the items *are* out of stock.
> Both buildings *are managed* by a real estate firm.
> We *are* fortunate to have you as our keynote speaker.
> The Rocky Mountains *are* a favorite tourist attraction.

Past Tense. Unlike other verbs, *be* has two past tense forms. *Was* is the singular form, and *were* is the plural form.

> I *was* in Detroit last week.
> *Mr. Ruiz,* our supervisor, *was planning* to take his vacation in July.
> When *we were* in the office last Friday, you were very busy.
> Several *applicants were considered* for the job.

Past Participle and Present Participle. *Been,* the past participle, and *being,* the present participle, have the same uses as the present and past participles of other verbs.

> Mr. Baker *has been* with our company for nearly five years.
> I thought the meeting *had been postponed.*
> Perhaps they *are being* overly critical.
> Fred *is being considered* for a position in their marketing department.

Spot Check 2

In the space provided, write the part of the verb *be* that is indicated in parentheses.

1. I (present tense) eager   1. _____am_____
   to finish the assignment.

2. You (present tense) the   2. _____are_____
   best-qualified candidate.

3. He (present tense) out   3. _____is_____
   of the office today.

4. We (present tense) confi-   4. _____are_____
   dent of your success.

5. Everyone (past tense)   5. _____was_____
   late for the meeting.

6. Both machines (past   6. _____were_____
   tense) out of order.

7. She (present tense) in   7. _____is_____
   the conference room.

8. We have (past participle)   8. _____been_____
   there several times.

9. The witness is (present   9. _____being_____
   participle) evasive.

10. Would you like (infini-   10. _____to be_____
    tive) on the committee?

TROUBLESOME VERBS

The principal parts of a number of troublesome verbs are listed below and on the following page. Because the third person singular form of the present tense and the present participle are formed in such a highly consistent manner, they are not included in the chart.

PRINCIPAL PARTS OF SOME TROUBLESOME VERBS

Present	Past	Past Participle
am, is, are	was, were	been
begin	began	begun
break	broke	broken
bring	brought	brought
buy	bought	bought
catch	caught	caught
choose	chose	chosen
come	came	come
creep	crept	crept
do	did	done
drink	drank	drunk OR drank
drive	drove	driven
eat	ate	eaten
fall	fell	fallen
find	found	found
flow	flowed	flowed
fly	flew	flown
forbid	forbade OR forbad	forbidden
forget	forgot	forgotten OR forgot
get	got	got OR gotten

Present	Past	Past Participle	Present	Past	Past Participle
give	gave	given	see	saw	seen
go	went	gone	sell	sold	sold
grow	grew	grown	set *(to place)*	set	set
have, has*	had	had	show	showed	shown OR showed
hide	hid	hidden OR hid	shrink	shrank ALSO shrunk	shrunk OR shrunken
hold	held	held			
lay *(to place)*	laid	laid	sing	sang OR sung	sung
lie *(to recline)*	lay	lain	sit *(to rest)*	sat	sat
lie *(to tell a falsehood)*	lied	lied	sleep	slept	slept
			speak	spoke	spoken
make	made	made	steal	stole	stolen
pay	paid	paid	sting	stung	stung
prove	proved	proved OR proven	swim	swam	swum
raise *(to lift)*	raised	raised	take	took	taken
ride	rode	ridden	think	thought	thought
ring *(to sound)*	rang	rung	wear	wore	worn
rise *(to move up)*	rose	risen	write	wrote	written
run	ran	run			

Has is third person singular.

Study Guide 8

A. As you read each sentence, decide whether the italicized verb or verb phrase is active or passive. Compare your decision with that shown in parentheses at the end of the sentence. If necessary, review the discussion of active, passive, and linking verbs in this unit.

1. Ms. McFarlane *has been appointed* advertising manager. (Passive.)
2. Many companies *are purchasing* new equipment. (Active.)
3. We *met* for breakfast in the cafeteria (Active.)
4. *Has* he *forgotten* his promise? (Active.)
5. The store *may give* you a refund. (Active.)
6. The payment *is being made* today. (Passive.)
7. Smoking *is prohibited* in many different places. (Passive.)
8. All provisions of the contract *must be enforced*. (Passive.)
9. The storm *caused* very little damage in this area. (Active.)
10. All flights *may be canceled* because of the snowstorm. (Passive.)

B. As you read each sentence, decide which part of a verb the italicized word illustrates. If necessary, review the discussion of the parts of verbs.

1. He *is* a good credit risk. (Present—third person singular.)
2. I *am* unaware of any changes in the procedures. (Present—first person singular.)
3. Have you *made* a commitment to them? (Past participle.)
4. Both speakers *were* a few minutes late. (Past tense—plural.)
5. Your flight will be *leaving* at three this afternoon. (Present participle.)
6. Dr. Benson *was* here yesterday afternoon. (Past tense—singular.)
7. I think you have *shown* excellent judgment. (Past participle.)
8. Mr. Ashburn *went* with us to Moline. (Past tense.)
9. The warehouse has *been* closed for three days. (Past participle.)
10. Our company *has* its headquarters in Duluth. (Present tense—third person singular.)
11. Who *gave* the most interesting talk? (Past tense.)

12. I *forgot* to ask for a receipt. (Past tense.)

13. He *manages* his time wisely. (Present tense—third person singular.)

14. She *has* the ability to get along with everyone. (Present tense—third person singular.)

15. He has *done* more than half of the work. (Past participle.)

16. Those accounts *are* delinquent. (Present tense.)

17. I *have* their telephone number and address. (Present tense.)

18. We *fax* a number of messages every day. (Present tense.)

19. Both companies are *beginning* to make a profit. (Present participle.)

20. The annual report *has* been mailed to all stockholders. (Present tense—third person singular.)

21. Walter *said* that all the information he provided them was correct. (Past tense.)

22. Mrs. Williamson has *recommended* that Margaret, Phyllis, and Steven be appointed to the committee. (Past tense.)

23. According to the article in our local newspaper, Martin and Anderson Inc. has been *awarded* a contract to demolish the old convention center. (Past participle.)

24. If I remember correctly, their account is *being* handled by Richard. (Present participle.)

25. Neither of them *had* any responsibility for what happened. (Past tense.)

ASSIGNMENT: Complete the Unit 8 Worksheet on pages 63–64.

UNIT 8

Forms of Verbs

WORSHEET

 A In the space provided, write the correct form of each verb shown in parentheses.

1. I have (forget) the name of their attorney.

2. The company has (grow) rapidly.

3. He (be) still a member of the finance committee.

4. I thought Lynn (be) with you when you called.

5. The price of the stock (fall) yesterday.

6. Have you (make) your reservations?

7. She has been (live) in Austin for a year.

8. We (go) with them to the game last Sunday.

9. She (drink) two cups of coffee this morning.

10. It (take) me an hour to get to work today.

11. I (see) the movie twice last week.

12. Bob (return) my call around noon yesterday.

13. Perhaps they are (meet) right now.

14. He has (forget) my telephone number.

15. Who was (sit) at the receptionist's desk?

16. The sun (rise) at 5:42 a.m. today.

17. Yes, I had (think) of applying for the job.

18. Arlene (do) not look well right now.

19. We should have (be) more careful.

20. We have (double-check) all the data.

21. If he (rely) on us, he may be disappointed.

22. Willis (have) asked Jill to help him again.

23. Those plants (grow) an inch last night.

24. We (start) the project last month.

25. Has the company (choose) a different site?

1. _____ forgotten

2. _____ grown

3. _____ is

4. _____ was

5. _____ fell

6. _____ made

7. _____ living

8. _____ went

9. _____ drank

10. _____ took

11. _____ saw

12. _____ returned

13. _____ meeting

14. _____ forgotten OR forgot

15. _____ sitting

16. _____ rose

17. _____ thought

18. _____ does

19. _____ been

20. _____ double-checked

21. _____ relies

22. _____ has

23. _____ grew

24. _____ started

25. _____ chosen

B Which of the verbs shown in parentheses is correct—the form of *lie* or the form of *lay?* Write your answer in the space provided.

1. She (laid, lay) her glasses on her desk.   1. __laid__
2. The statue was (laying, lying) on its side.   2. __lying__
3. Do you think they were (laying, lying) to us?   3. __lying__
4. The store's service personnel will (lay, lie) the carpet for us.   4. __lay__
5. The fire marshall said we should have (laid, lain) on the floor.   5. __lain__
6. In which nest did the sparrow (lay, lie) its eggs?   6. __lay__
7. Be sure to use the proper type of adhesive when you (lay, lie) these tiles.   7. __lay__
8. As soon as I (lay, laid) on the couch, I felt better.   8. __lay__
9. We were (laying, lying) bricks yesterday.   9. __laying__
10. Our dog always (lays, lies) near the front door.   10. __lies__

C Which of the verbs shown in parentheses is correct—the form of *set* or the form of *sit?* Write your answer in the space provided.

1. We (sat, set) in the front row.   1. __sat__
2. Would you like to (set, sit) somewhere else?   2. __sit__
3. The Ashes were (setting, sitting) outside.   3. __sitting__
4. Don't forget to (set, sit) the alarm.   4. __set__
5. Both packages (sat, set) there for two days.   5. __sat__
6. Her ring has an expensive (setting, sitting).   6. __setting__
7. All of us were tired of (setting, sitting).   7. __sitting__
8. How long do you think she (sat, set) there?   8. __sat__
9. The sun always (sets, sits) in the west.   9. __sets__
10. Should I (set, sit) the plants outdoors?   10. __set__

D Which of the verbs shown in parentheses is correct—the form of *raise* or the form of *rise?* Write your answer in the space provided.

1. Has the price been (raised, risen)?   1. __raised__
2. I hope the water level (raises, rises).   2. __rises__
3. The demand for electricity (rose, raised) substantially.   3. __rose__
4. Have our costs (raised, risen, rose)?   4. __risen__
5. Salaries may not (raise, rise) as quickly as we would like.   5. __rise__
6. A hundred dollars has been (risen, raised) so far today.   6. __raised__
7. Everyone was asked to (raise, rise).   7. __rise__
8. One of the farmers (raises, rises) chickens.   8. __raises__
9. The taxes were (raised, risen) last year.   9. __raised__
10. Is the price of gold (raising, rising)?   10. __rising__

THE PRESENT TENSE

The **present tense** is used to express a present fact or an unchangeable truth.

> Los Angeles *is* the largest city in California. (Present fact.)
>
> The sun *rises* in the east and *sets* in the west. (Unchangeable truth.)

Sometimes, as in the following sentences, the present tense is also used to imply future action.

> This special sale *ends* tomorrow. (This sale *will end* tomorrow.)
>
> Their flight *arrives* at 6:45 this evening. (Their flight *will arrive* at 6:45 this evening.)

Note that the present tense should *not* be used to relate a past event or to tell of something that began in the past and is continuing at the present time.

> Andy *told* me that he applied for the job. (NOT: Andy *tells* me that he applied for the job.)
>
> Ms. O'Neill *said* that she prefers to use public transportation. (NOT: Ms. O'Neill *says* that she prefers to use public transportation.)
>
> I *have been* with the same company for three years. (NOT: I *am* with the same company for three years.)
>
> Marsha *has known* John since 1988. (NOT: Marsha *knows* John since 1988.)

Present Tenses of the Verb *Be*. The verb *be* has three present tense forms: *am, is,* and *are.*

> I *am* an amateur baseball player.
>
> You *are* an excellent speaker.
>
> She *is* one of the company's top executives.

Present Tenses of Other Verbs. Most verbs other than *be* have two present tense forms; for example, *believe* and *believes, try* and *tries, have* and *has.*

The form that would make sense if it were used with the word *to,* such as *believe* or *try* or *have,* is used with all subjects other than a third person singular pronoun (such as *he, it, she, each,* or *everyone*) or a singular noun.

> *I believe* that *we have* their support. (The subject *I* is first person singular, and the subject *we* is first person plural.)

Perhaps *you believe* that *you have* too much work to do by yourself. (The second person pronoun *you* is always considered plural—even when it clearly refers to one person, as it does in this sentence.)

Perhaps *you believe* that *you have* the necessary information yourselves. (In this sentence, the second person pronoun *you* refers to more than one person.)

Some *retailers believe* that *they have* too much merchandise on hand. (*Retailers,* the subject, is third person plural.)

For regular verbs, such as *believe* and *try,* the third person singular form of the present tense ends in *s* or *es.* For an irregular verb, such as *have,* the third person singular form of the present tense is not constructed in a consistent manner. Whether it is a regular verb or an irregular verb, the present tense form that would *not* make sense if it were used with *to* is used only when the subject is a third person singular pronoun or a singular noun.

> *Bryan believes* that *he has* an excellent credit rating. (The noun *Bryan,* the pronoun *he,* and the verbs *believes* and *has* are third person singular.)
>
> *Everyone* on the staff *believes* that *he or she has* a solution to the problem. (The indefinite pronoun *everyone,* the personal pronouns *he* and *she,* and the verbs *believes* and *has* are third person singular.)

Passive Form of Present Tense. The passive form of the present tense consists of the helping verb *am, is,* or *are* plus the past participle of a verb.

> I *am irritated* by inconsiderate people.
>
> You *are considered* an excellent credit risk.
>
> The company's slogan *is known* by almost everyone.

THE PRESENT PROGRESSIVE TENSE

The **present progressive tense** shows that something is in progress at the present time. The active form of the present progressive tense is composed of *am, is,* or *are* plus a present participle.

> I *am preparing* my expense report.
> Everyone *is listening* to what the instructor *is saying.*
> We *are being* careful, but they *are being* too cautious.

Passive Form of Present Progressive Tense. The passive form of the present progressive tense consists of the helping verbs *am being, is being,* or *are being* plus the past participle of the main verb.

> I *am being considered* for some other assignment.
>
> The new album *is being sent* to radio stations throughout the country.
>
> Our financial records *are being audited* by Gilbert and Associates.

THE PRESENT PERFECT TENSE

The *present perfect tense* shows that the action or state of being occurred in the present time or at some indefinite time before the present. It consists of the helping verb *has* or *have* plus a past participle.

> The building *has been* under construction for nearly a year.
>
> Mrs. Hamilton *has run* for public office several times.
>
> We *have received* many inquiries as a result of the article in last week's issue of *Business Week.*
>
> The Wilcoxes *have been* our neighbors since 1989.

Passive Form of the Present Perfect Tense. The passive form of the present tense consists of *has been* or *have been* plus a past participle.

> Every purchaser of the 1991 model *has been notified* of the mechanical defect.
>
> Both of her novels *have been published* in Spanish and French as well as in English.

THE PRESENT PERFECT PROGRESSIVE TENSE

The *present perfect progressive tense* indicates continuous action in the present time and consists of *has been* or *have been* plus a present participle.

> Dr. Olivea *has been conducting* management seminars since 1986.
>
> Both companies *have been advertising* in our magazines for several years.

Spot Check 1

In the following sentences, decide which of the verb forms shown in parentheses is correct and underline it.

1. Each employee (<u>has</u>, have) a copy of the manual.
2. Jean (is, <u>has been</u>) living in Portland for a year.
3. He (do, <u>does</u>) more than anyone else.
4. The machines (has, <u>have</u>) been repaired.
5. Jerry's request (are, <u>is</u>) being reviewed.
6. Both accounts (<u>are</u>, is) overdue.
7. The warehouse (are, <u>is</u>) temporarily closed.
8. You always (<u>do</u>, does) excellent work.
9. Some software programs (has, <u>have</u>) bugs in them.
10. They (<u>are</u>, is) being very cooperative.
11. I (<u>am</u>, are, is) optimistic about the future.
12. Some of us (has, <u>have</u>) been working overtime.
13. Your flight (are, <u>is</u>) being rerouted to Dallas.
14. She seldom (request, <u>requests</u>) the assistance of others.
15. Two advertising agencies (<u>are</u>, is) vying for our account.
16. Stewart (do, <u>does</u>) his share of the housework.
17. Everything (seem, <u>seems</u>) all right.
18. The Millers (are, <u>have been</u>) our customers for years.
19. The firm is (know, knowed, <u>known</u>) for its quality products and excellent service.
20. Their prices (<u>seem</u>, seems) reasonable.

THE PAST TENSE

The *past tense* shows that a state of being existed in the past or that an action occurred in the past.

> Mr. Keene *ordered* a new supply of stationery last week.
>
> Both newspapers *published* the photographs yesterday.

The past tense of regular verbs is formed by adding *d* or *ed* to the present tense form that would make sense if it were used with *to.*

> | invite | reach | delay | rely | omit |
> |--------|-------|-------|------|------|
> | invited | reached | delayed | relied | omitted |

The verb *be* has the singular past tense form *was* and the plural past tense form *were.*

> While you *were* in Phoenix, I *was* in Raleigh.
>
> Two important visitors *were* in the office this morning.

Other irregular verbs have one past tense form. As indicated in the chart on pages 60–61, the past tense of such verbs is not formed according to a consistent pattern.

have	stand	write	do	speak	fly
had	stood	wrote	did	spoke	flew

Each candidate *spoke* for nearly an hour.
Some *stood* soon after the plane *left* the ground.

Passive Form of the Past Tense. The passive form of the past tense is composed of *was* or *were* plus the past participle of the main verb.

> The check *was cashed* at a local supermarket.
> Both movies *were shown* on TV last night.

THE PAST PROGRESSIVE TENSE

The *past progressive tense* indicates state of being or action begun and continuing in the past. It is expressed by *was* or *were* plus a present participle.

> The factory *was operating* at full capacity until last year.
> We *were planning* to attend the meeting in Toronto.
> When I saw the folders, they *were lying* on your desk.

Passive Form of Past Progressive Tense. The passive form of the past progressive tense is formed by using *was being* or *were being* with a past participle.

> I thought that the contract *was being renegotiated*.
> Counterfeit money *was being circulated* in several metropolitan areas.
> At that time, some financial institutions *were being closed* by government officials.

THE PAST PERFECT TENSE

The *past perfect tense* shows action or state of being that was completed at some definite time in the past. It is expressed by *had* plus a past participle.

> I *had mailed* the letter before I received your telephone call.
> By the time we arrived, most of the others *had gone* home.
> I *had planned* to meet with him last Friday, but he was unavailable.

Passive Form of Past Perfect Tense. The passive form of the past perfect tense consists of *had been* plus a past participle.

> Before the bridge collapsed, all vehicular traffic *had been rerouted*.
> All arrangements *had been made* several weeks before the meeting took place.

THE PAST PERFECT PROGRESSIVE TENSE

The *past perfect progressive tense* shows that the action was being completed at some definite time in the past. This tense is composed of *had been* plus a present participle.

> Until this year, the company *had been leasing* cars for its marketing representatives.
> Until he joined our company, Timothy *had been earning* $400 a week.

Spot Check 2

In the following sentences, decide which of the verb forms shown in parentheses is correct and underline it.

1. She (had, has, have) gone to work when I called her house.

2. Until recently, Lyle (had, has, have) been using his parents' car.

3. We thought the new desks (was, were) being delivered from their local warehouse.

4. I wonder why the call (was, were) transferred to her office.

5. The orders (was, were) being processed when I asked about them.

6. Who (showed, shown) Nick the memo from the personnel manager?

7. The letter from Kay was (wrote, written) on blue stationery.

8. They told me they (was, were) planning to vacation in Hawaii.

9. I think they (did, done) an excellent job.

10. The operation (has, had) been scheduled for today, but it (was, were) postponed early this morning.

11. Irene and Peter (was, were) discussing the pros and cons of moving out of the city.

12. The house was (build, built) in the early 1800s.

13. Until this month, the Martins (have, had) been living in Raleigh.

14. By the time the store closed, most shoppers had (gone, went) home.

15. The window was (broke, broken) by one of the carpenters.

THE FUTURE TENSE

The *future tense* denotes action expected to take place in the future. Except in very formal speech and writing, the future tense is expressed by the helping verb *will* with the present form of the main verb.

> We *will be* among those attending the conference in Trenton next week.
>
> The office *will close* at 2 p.m. next Friday.

In very formal situations, *shall* is used with the subjects *I* and *we*, and *will* is used with all other subjects. This formal use is discussed later in this unit.

Passive Form of the Future Tense. The passive form of the future tense is ordinarily composed of *will be* plus a past participle.

> You *will be notified* by registered mail.
> Several streets *will be repaved* later this year.

THE FUTURE PROGRESSIVE TENSE

The *future progressive tense* indicates a continuing action in the future. It is expressed by *will be* (or *shall be* in formal situations) plus a present participle.

> You *will be receiving* a duplicate copy within a day or two.
>
> Two laboratories *will be testing* the new product in July.

THE FUTURE PERFECT TENSE

The *future perfect tense* indicates action to be completed before a specified time in the future. This tense is expressed by *will have* plus a past participle.

> The owner of the repair shop probably *will have cashed* the check before I have a chance to stop payment on it.
>
> Winter *will have arrived* before most of us are ready for it.

Passive Form of Future Perfect Tense. The passive form of the future perfect tense is composed of *will have been* plus a past participle.

> Your office *will have been repaired* when you return tomorrow.
>
> The customer survey *will have been completed* before July 1.

It is often better to use the simple future tense instead of the future perfect, which may be an awkward way to express a thought.

> Contributions for the United Fund *will have been collected* from every member by Friday.
>
> **BETTER:** Contributions for the United Fund *will be collected* from every member by Friday.

THE FUTURE PERFECT PROGRESSIVE TENSE

The *future perfect progressive tense* indicates action that will be in progress at a specific time in the future. It is composed of *will have been* plus a present participle.

> Next Monday Mr. Ambruster *will have been working* for Benson Brothers six years.
>
> By the time this meeting ends, we *will have been sitting* for two hours or more.

FORMAL USE OF *SHALL* AND *WILL, SHOULD* AND *WOULD*

Some employers still insist on a highly formal style of expression, particularly in written communications. Therefore, you should be familiar with the formal usage of *shall, will, should,* and *would.*

Shall and **Will.** To express the simple future tense, use *shall* with the pronoun *I* and *we* and use *will* with all other pronoun and noun subjects.

> *I shall be* happy to make your reservations for you.
>
> *We shall present* your proposal to our board of directors next month.
>
> *You will have* an opportunity to bid on other projects.
>
> The *winner will appear* on a nationally televised program in August.

To express determination or a promise, use *will* with the subjects *I* and *we* and *shall* with all other pronoun and noun subjects.

> I *will respond* to that complaint myself.
> We *will build* your house to your specifications.
> You *shall be* responsible for the cost of repairs.
> June *shall be* in charge of the office during the manager's absence.
> Each payment *shall be* due and payable on the first of each month.

Use *shall* for all questions in which the subject is *I* or *we.* If the subject is some other pronoun or a noun, use the word that might be expected in the answer.

> *Shall I send* an invitation to Dr. Farnsworth too?
> *Shall we have* dinner at Wilfredo's?
> *Shall you be* ready for the interview?
> *Will he pay* you for the work you did?

Should and **Would.** *Should* and *would* follow the same pattern of usage as *shall* and *will.*

> I *should be* able to meet with them tomorrow.
> We *should appreciate* your returning both copies.
> You *would be* happier if you accepted their offer.

Ms. Stewart *would like* to meet with us at nine o'clock tomorrow morning.

Your report *would answer* most of their questions.

When the intended meaning of *should* is "ought to," it is used with all subjects.

I *should answer* that letter right away.

You *should request* a raise if you think you have earned one.

The store *should give* you a refund.

Everyone *should keep* all important papers in a safe place.

ERRORS IN USE OF TENSES

When the verbs in the main and dependent clauses of a sentence refer to actions or conditions that occur at the same time, they ordinarily should be in the same tense.

She *knew* that the stones *were* imitation diamonds.

However, the idea to be expressed may involve differences in time and therefore require the tense of the verb in the dependent clause to be different from that of the verb in the independent clause. Use the tense that expresses the idea you wish to convey.

I *believe* that Miss Caldwell *is* in Indianapolis.

I *believe* that Miss Caldwell *was* in Indianapolis.

I *believe* that Miss Caldwell *will be* in Indianapolis.

She *left* early so that she *would arrive* by noon.

She *will be* upset if she *arrives* after noon.

She *would be* upset if she *arrived* after noon.

She *would have been* upset if she *had arrived* after noon.

Use *might, could, would,* or *should* in the dependent clause if the past tense is used in the main clause. These words are the past forms of *may, can, will,* and *shall.*

Bert *told* me that he *might attend* the opening session.

Never use the preposition *of* as a substitute for *have*. If the contraction of *should have* is the intended expression, use *should've.*

We *should have gone* with them. (NOT: *should of gone.*)

Spot Check 3

In the following sentences, decide which of the words shown in parentheses is correct and underline it.

1. I should (of, <u>have</u>) told you a few days ago.

2. You (should, <u>would</u>) be surprised if you knew how little we spent.

3. Their flight probably (shall, <u>will</u>) arrive at the scheduled time.

4. All of those items (shall, <u>will</u>) have been shipped before May 1.

5. By tomorrow everyone (shall, <u>will</u>) have heard the rumor.

6. Next Monday Steve (shall, <u>will</u>) have been a CPA for one year.

7. Both invoices (shall, <u>will</u>) be mailed tomorrow.

8. Some of us believe the office (shall, <u>will</u>) be closing early Friday.

9. (Shall, <u>Will</u>) both of you be in San Francisco next week?

10. (<u>Shall</u>, Will) I close the door?

11. (<u>Should</u>, Would) we accept their recommendations?

12. Ben said that he (should, <u>would</u>) ask his associates to contribute.

13. I thought she (may, <u>might</u>) be willing to speak at the seminar if you asked her.

14. I would have been surprised if the flowers (lasted, <u>had lasted</u>) two weeks.

15. If the announcement is made prematurely, many people (shall, <u>will</u>) be upset unnecessarily.

16. Martha (<u>should</u>, would) have been invited, but we did not have her new address or telephone number.

17. Everyone (shall, <u>will</u>) be surprised.

18. He (would of, <u>would've</u>) gone if we had asked him, wouldn't he?

19. She knew that she (will, <u>would</u>) be promoted.

20. If I had known, I (may, <u>might</u>) have gone.

21. We were quite certain that the order (will, <u>would</u>) be delayed.

22. Jack felt that he (is, <u>was</u>) misled by the agent.

23. Are you sure that she (is, was, <u>is OR was</u>) in charge?

24. They plan carefully so that they (<u>will</u>, would) avoid mistakes.

25. She (tells, <u>told</u>) me she bought a new car.

Study Guide 9

A. Study the italicized verbs in the following sentences. Can you identify the tense of each verb and explain its use?

1. I *am* sure that both companies *hire* outside consultants occasionally.
2. *Shall* we *tell* them that this equipment *will be replaced* in July?
3. The distribution center *is* near the airport; the main offices *are* on Queens Boulevard.
4. Where *were* they when we *needed* them last week?
5. Which candidate *is considered* the favorite?
6. Several stores *are having* special sales next week.
7. The procedures manual *is being revised.*
8. Both of them *have made* several attempts to reach a settlement.
9. The contract *has been extended* for two years.
10. Mr. Graham *has been speaking* more than an hour.
11. Marlene and Dan *were waiting* for you when I *saw* them.
12. The rumor *was being circulated* throughout the company.
13. You *had left* before we *arrived.*
14. Until recently the store *had been accepting* all major credit cards.
15. You *will receive* a corrected statement of your account within a few days.
16. I *will give* you the information you *requested,* but I *would appreciate* your giving me a day or two.
17. The temporary personnel *will be arriving* sometime this afternoon.
18. You *will have heard* the news from someone else by the time you *receive* this letter.
19. It *appears* that the building *will have been demolished* before the group *obtains* a temporary restraining order.
20. At noon we *will have been working* five hours without a break.

B. As you read the following sentences, notice how the verbs in parentheses convey different meanings.

1. Perhaps Miriam (filed, should file, will file) a countersuit.
2. I (tried, have tried, may try) to schedule a meeting with them.
3. All customers (receive, will receive, will be receiving) announcements of special sales.
4. The company (is, was) considered the leader.
5. I (could finish, could have finished) the reports if I (had, had been given) more time.
6. If you (consult, had consulted) an expert, you (will receive, would have received) advice on how to reduce your taxes.
7. How much (do, did) you expect to receive?
8. The government (is, has been, should be) attempting to reduce the budget deficit.
9. Where did you say you (live, lived)?
10. The prices of automobiles (are, were, have been, will be, may be, should be) lower.

ASSIGNMENT: Complete the Unit 9 Worksheet on pages 71–72.

NAME _____ DATE _____

UNIT 9

Tenses of Verbs

WORKSHEET

 A **Which of the words shown in parentheses is correct? Write your answer in the space provided.**

1. Your uncle (says, said) you like your new job.
2. We (should of, should've) been notified.
3. Some of the jewelry has been (stole, stolen).
4. Ken (is, has been) a supervisor for two years.
5. I thought that you (may, might) be willing to help.
6. We (can, could) not place the order until we received the manager's approval.
7. Julie thinks she (shall, will) accept their offer.
8. (Shall, Will) I notify Mrs. Larkin?
9. Have they (gone, went) to the meeting in Baltimore?
10. The flight (has, had) departed before we arrived at the airport.

1. _____said_____
2. _____should've_____
3. _____stolen_____
4. _____has been_____
5. _____might_____
6. _____could_____
7. _____will_____
8. _____Shall_____
9. _____gone_____
10. _____had_____

B **In the space provided, write the correct form of the verb shown in parentheses.**

1. The district managers (meet) at noon yesterday.
2. Until recently, the company (be) privately owned.
3. We (buy) a gift for the receptionist last week.
4. I should have (go) with them.
5. I (know) that she would be offered a higher salary.
6. We thought they (leave) yesterday afternoon.
7. Paul said he (take) the examination yesterday.
8. I (shall) have been notified much earlier.
9. It (begin) to rain the minute we walked outside.
10. The notices (be) mailed yesterday.
11. Have you (see) the company's new headquarters?
12. You should have (be) with us.
13. We should have (know) what the outcome would be.

1. _____met_____
2. _____was_____
3. _____bought_____
4. _____gone_____
5. _____knew_____
6. _____left_____
7. _____took_____
8. _____should_____
9. _____began_____
10. _____were_____
11. _____seen_____
12. _____been_____
13. _____known_____

14. The plan is (be) reviewed by several people.

14. _being_

15. Negotiations have been (break) off for some time.

15. _broken_

16. The jury (find) the defendants to be innocent.

16. _found_

17. Have you (write) to those prospective customers?

17. _written_

18. If I had her address, I (will) give it to you.

18. _would_

19. Carl (say) he gave the letter to you.

19. _said_

20. (Be) you in St. Paul or Minneapolis last week?

20. _Were_

21. The warehouse was (build) in 1982.

21. _built_

22. These papers should be (throw) away.

22. _thrown_

23. Have you ever (fly) an airplane yourself?

23. _flown_

24. Helen is (manage) a real estate agency in Portland.

24. _managing_

25. The manufactuer has (deny) responsibility for it.

25. _denied_

C Underline the incorrect verbs in the following sentences, and write the corrections in the spaces provided. If a sentence requires no correction, write *OK*.

1. I would of gone with you if you had asked me.

1. _would have gone_

2. Both of them knowed they were responsible.

2. _knew_

3. We now think that she shall be a candidate.

3. _will be_

4. Mr. Chapman says that he was in Nevada last week.

4. _said_

5. The temperature has rose during the past hour.

5. _has risen_

6. Has Mr. Fox wrote to the company about the delay?

6. _Has written_

7. The tree growed quickly after we transplanted it.

7. _grew_

8. He said that Albany was the capital of New York.

8. _is_

9. If she be nominated, everyone will vote for her.

9. _is nominated_

10. The Walters are planning to leave in the morning.

10. _OK_

11. Jack said he would have told us if we asked him.

11. _had asked_

12. If he continued to break his promises, he will not receive another invitation from us.

12. _continues_

13. They done exactly what they were asked to do.

13. _did_

14. I should have took a vacation before starting a new job.

14. _should have taken_

15. I probably shall be late again.

15. _OK_

16. The water level raised several feet recently.

16. _has risen OR rose_

17. Was Al ask to draft a reply?

17. _Was asked_

18. They eat lunch and then offered to help us.

18. _ate_

19. What time did the sun raise this morning?

19. _did rise_

20. No onc sung better than Lena did.

20. _sang_

Agreement of Subject and Verb

BASIC PRINCIPLE OF AGREEMENT

1. The basic principle of agreement of subject and verb is as follows: ***A verb must agree with its subject in person and number.*** Note how this principle is applied in the following sentences.

I am familiar with their products. (The first person singular verb *am* agrees with the first person singular subject *I*. Note that *be* is the only verb that has a special first person singular form: *am,* which is used with the pronoun subject *I*.)

We are members of several associations. (The plural verb *are* agrees with the first person plural subject *we*. The plural form of a verb agrees with any plural subject, regardless of whether the subject is first, second, or third person.)

You are a conscientious employee. (The second person subject *you* always requires a plural verb. In the example sentence, *you* clearly refers to one person, but *you* clearly refers to more than one person in this sentence: *You are* conscientious employees.)

They are unlikely to replace their equipment because *it is* less than a year old. (The plural verb *are* agrees with the third person plural subject *they*. The third person singular verb *is* agrees with the third person singular subject *it*. As discussed in Unit 8, all verbs except a few helping verbs have a special third person singular form.)

When *she is* out of the office, *he acts* as our manager. (The third person singular verbs *is* and *acts* agree with the third person singular subjects *she* and *he*.)

Mr. Fernandez thinks that other *customers are receiving* larger discounts. (The third person singular verb *thinks* agrees with the third person singular subject *Mr. Fernandez*. In the verb phrase *are receiving,* the plural helping verb *are* agrees with the plural subject *customers*. Remember that all nouns are considered to be third person.)

Both think that *one earns* less than the other. (The plural verb *think* agrees with the third person plural subject *both*. The third person singular verb *earns* agrees with the third person singular subject *one*.)

In sentences such as those just illustrated, it is easy to identify the subject, to tell whether the subject is singular or plural, and to decide whether it requires a singular verb or a plural verb. Errors in agreement of subject and verb often occur, however, when the subject and the verb are separated by a number of words, when the subject is composed of more than one word, and when the verb appears before the subject.

HOW TO IDENTIFY THE SUBJECT

The following suggestions will help you properly identify the subject and therefore help you choose the correct verb to use with it.

2. Subject and Verb Separated by Modifiers. Words and phrases that appear between the subject and the verb ordinarily do not affect the number of the subject and therefore should not be allowed to affect the number of the verb. The verb agrees with its subject, not with a noun or a pronoun placed between the verb and its subject.

The *procedure* for handling requests for donations *appears* on pages 11–12 of the manual.

A few *stores* in the Ridgewood area *are* open 24 hours a day.

If the subject is *all, some,* or another indefinite pronoun that may be either singular or plural, the modifying phrase that follows the subject must be considered.

Some of the information in each of those pamphlets *is* inaccurate. (*Some* is used with reference to the singular noun *information;* therefore, *some* is a singular subject and requires the singular verb *is*.)

Some of their products *are* very similar to ours. (*Some* is used with reference to the plural noun *products;* therefore, *some* is a plural subject and requires the plural verb *are*.)

Some of us *need* more time to review their proposal. (*Some* is used with reference to the plural pronoun *us* and requires the plural verb *need*.)

3. Subject and Verb Separated by Parenthetical Expressions. Parenthetical expressions introduced by such words and phrases as *including, as well as,* and *together with* do not affect the number of the subject or of the verb that should be used with it. These expressions are not necessary to the sense of the sentence.

I, as well as most of my neighbors, *am* happy with the new streetlights.

The *price,* including taxes and dealer preparation charges, *has been reduced* to $11,540.

The regional *managers,* together with the director of marketing, *have been* at a conference in Topeka since Tuesday.

Those *packages,* as well as this letter, *are* ready to mail.

The *ceiling,* in addition to the walls, *needs* to be painted.

She, as well as I, *writes* to them at least two or three times a month.

4. Verb Followed by Subject. When the verb or part of the verb phrase precedes the subject, the best procedure is to mentally place the subject and the verb in their normal order. In normal order, the subject and the modifiers closely connected to it appear before the verb.

Is the *house* next to yours for sale? (The *house* next to yours *is* for sale.)

Does the *amount* of the proposed settlement *surprise* you? (The *amount* of the proposed settlement *does surprise* you.)

Have all *meetings* scheduled for tomorrow *been canceled?* (All *meetings* scheduled for tomorrow *have been canceled.*)

Enclosed are the *documents* you requested. (The *documents* you requested *are enclosed.*)

How *was* their *order shipped?* (Their *order was shipped* how.)

When *were* those *appointments canceled?* (Those *appointments were canceled* when.)

What *are* their *account numbers?* (Their *account numbers are* what.)

Does either of you *know* her address? (*Either* of you *does know* her address.)

5. Verb Preceded by *There* or *Here*. When the word *there* or *here* precedes the verb, as in the following examples, the subject follows the verb.

There *is* a *newsstand* in the lobby of this building.
Perhaps there *are* too many *topics* on the agenda.
Here *is* an *inquiry* from a customer in Dubuque.
Here *are* some *letters* from customers in Wyoming.

6. Verb Followed by a Predicate Nominative. When the verb is followed by a predicate nominative (a noun or pronoun that renames or further identifies the subject), the verb agrees with its subject, not with the predicate nominative.

Expenses are something we must watch carefully.
Something we must watch carefully *is* expenses.
The first *one* to leave the party *was* you.
You were the first one to leave the party.
High *taxes are* the result of many things.

Spot Check 1

Underline the verb in parentheses that agrees with the subject in each of the following sentences.

1. The color of these drapes (match, <u>matches</u>) that of the carpet.

2. The drawers of the cabinet in her office (<u>are</u>, is) usually locked.

3. There (was, <u>were</u>) two foreign visitors today.

4. (Has, <u>Have</u>) the invoices been prepared?

5. Here (are, <u>is</u>) the list of names and addresses.

6. The main subject of discussion (<u>was</u>, were) investments.

7. When (do, <u>does</u>) the meeting begin?

8. Such experiences (<u>are</u>, is) part of almost everyone's life.

9. Some of the property (belong, <u>belongs</u>) to the Martins.

10. Items made of silver (<u>tarnish</u>, tarnishes) easily.

11. The last one to get a raise (<u>was</u>, were) you.

12. I (<u>am</u>, is) one of the new members of the staff.

13. (Has, <u>Have</u>) their promises been kept?

14. The manager, as well as the assistant manager, usually (go, <u>goes</u>) to several conventions every year.

15. Each of the candidates (<u>has</u>, have) appeared on TV.

16. None of the trees (has, <u>have</u>) been transplanted.

17. The report containing those figures (<u>has</u>, have) been sent to Mr. O'Neal.

18. Where (are, <u>is</u>) the nearest service center?

19. Dishes (<u>are</u>, is) an appropriate gift for newlyweds.

20. When (was, <u>were</u>) the invitations mailed?

21. (Was, <u>Were</u>) you surprised?

22. Paul, as well as we, (agree, <u>agrees</u>) with you.

23. Where (are, <u>is</u>) your copy?

24. (<u>Has</u>, Have) anyone told them?

25. None of us (<u>know</u>, knows) them.

SUBJECTS JOINED BY *AND*

7. Two or More Singular Subjects. Singular subjects that are joined by *and* and that identify different persons or things require a plural verb.

> *Friday* and *Saturday are* the two busiest days for us.
> *She* and *Jim have offered* to help us.
> The *owner* and the *manager were* in Fort Worth.

If the subjects indicate one person or thing or closely related ideas, a singular verb is required.

> The *owner* and *manager has met* with us on several occasions. (The absence of a modifier before *manager* indicates that one person has both jobs.)
> The *vice president* and *general manager* of our division *is* a very friendly person. (The two nouns indicate one person with two titles.)
> *Bacon* and *eggs is* the first item on the breakfast menu.

8. Singular Subjects Modified by *Every* or a Similar Expression. When two or more singular subjects connected by *and* are modified by *every, each, many a,* or *many an,* a singular verb is required.

> Every *stove* and *refrigerator* in the store *is* on sale at unbelievably low prices.
> Many a *man, woman,* and *child has visited* this amusement park.

9. Plural or Plural and Singular Subjects. Plural subjects or a plural subject and a singular subject connected by *and* require a plural verb.

> *Drivers* and *pedestrians need* to be very careful at that intersection.
> Two *rings* and a *bracelet were lying* on the counter.

SUBJECTS JOINED BY *OR* OR *NOR*

10. Singular Subjects. Singular subjects connected by *or, either . . . or,* or *neither . . . nor* are singular and require a singular verb. If the subjects differ in person, the verb agrees in person with the subject nearer or nearest the verb.

> *Is* the *owner* or the *manager* willing to meet with the reporters?
> *Does he* or *Vera plan* to join that organization?
> Either a *set* of towels or a portable *mixer is* a practical gift.
> Neither the *taxi* nor the *bus was* badly *damaged.*
> Neither *she* nor *I am scheduled* to work Saturday. (Note that the first person singular pronoun *I* is closer to the verb; therefore, *am*—not *is*—is used.)

11. Singular Subject and a Plural Subject. When *or, either . . . or,* or *neither . . . nor* connects a singular subject and a plural subject, the verb agrees in number with the subject immediately preceding it. If the subjects differ in person as well as in number, the verb agrees in person and number with the subject nearer or nearest to it.

> Neither the *carpet* nor the *drapes need* to be replaced.
> Neither the *walls* nor the *ceiling has been painted* recently.
> Either *they* or *I was* not *listening.*
> *She, he,* or *you are* likely to get the assignment.
> *You* or *she is* likely to get the assignment.

Spot Check 2

Decide which of the verbs shown in parentheses is correct; then underline it.

1. She or Lance (has, *have*) already called Dr. Peter Wilson.

2. Neither she nor I (has, *have*) been with the company a year.

3. Neither you nor he (*was*, were) responsible for the delay.

4. Neither the plaintiff nor the defendants (was, *were*) interested in an out-of-court settlement.

5. Every man and woman (*has*, have) an opportunity to participate.

6. You or I (*am*, is, are) responsible for those changes.

7. The secretary and treasurer (are, *is*) absent today, I believe.

8. Many a peach, pear, and apple (*has*, have) been picked in these orchards.

9. (Am, Is, *Are*) you, Connie, or I supposed to attend that meeting?

10. Ms. Ryan and her assistant (has, *have*) tried to telephone them.

11. Either the manager or I (*am*, are, is) mistaken.

12. Employers and employees (*share*, shares) the cost of group insurance.

13. (Has, *Have*) Sally or you seen Ms. Benton today?

14. How (*was*, were) the issue resolved?

15. (*Are*, Is) the tenants or the owner paying for the repairs?

16. A general manager and a vice president (are, <u>is</u>) on the panel.

17. When (do, <u>does</u>) the board meeting begin?

18. Every disk drive and printer (are, <u>is</u>) on sale at half price.

19. Pie and ice cream (are, <u>is</u>) his favorite dessert.

20. Bridges and tunnels (<u>link</u>, links) the boroughs of the city.

21. I am not sure whether Mr. James or the Innises (<u>own</u>, owns) the building.

Study Guide 10

Study the following sentences, noting the agreement of each verb with its subject. If you are unsure why a particular verb form is used, refer to the rule indicated.

1. The *shoes* on that shelf *are* on sale at half the regular price.[1,2]

2. One *supplier* of those products *has increased* its prices.[1,2]

3. The *windows,* as well as the roof, *need* to be repaired.[1,3]

4. The *letter,* together with several related documents, *was misplaced.*[1,3]

5. *Is* the *payment* overdue?[1,4]

6. *Have* the *members* of the committee *reached* a decision?[1,4]

7. There *is* to be an *announcement* sometime this morning.[1,5]

8. Here *are* three *estimates* for printing the annual report.[1,5]

9. A *prerequisite* for many jobs *is* excellent communication skills.[1,2,6]

10. *Taxes are* the primary source of income for any government.[1,6]

11. Her *house* and *garage have* aluminum siding.[1,7]

12. The *owner* and *operator* of the service station *is* ill.[1,2,7]

13. The *owner* and the *manager* of the apartment building *live* in one of the suburbs.[1,2,7]

14. *Ham* and *cheese was* the only kind of sandwich available.[1,7]

15. Every *toaster* and *microwave oven* in the store *comes* with a warranty.[8]

16. Our new *chairs* and *desks are being delivered* today.[1,9]

17. Some *magazines* and a *newspaper were lying* on your desk.[1,9]

18. Neither *she* nor *I am scheduled* to go with him.[1,10]

19. Either a small *truck* or a *van is needed* for this job.[1,10]

20. *Have* either *you* or *he been invited?*[1,11]

21. *Is she* or *I being considered* for that job?[1,4,10]

22. Neither the *windows* nor the *door was* open.[1,11]

23. *Do you* or *he have* a copy of the May sales report?[1,4,11]

24. *Has he* or *you agreed* to meet with them?[1,4,11]

25. *Does* Bill or *anyone else know* about your plans?[1,4,10]

ASSIGNMENT: Complete the Unit 10 Worksheet on pages 77–78.

UNIT 10

Agreement of Subject and Verb

WORKSHEET

 Decide which of the verbs shown in parentheses correctly completes the sentence; then write your answer in the space provided.

1. Each monthly payment, including finance charges, (are, is) $224.75.
1. _is_

2. When (do, does) Dave and Connie take their vacations?
2. _do_

3. (Was, Were) either they or you planning to work this weekend?
3. _Were_

4. Every letter, memo, and report (need, needs) to be checked carefully.
4. _needs_

5. One of the companies (lease, leases) cars directly from the manufacturer.
5. _leases_

6. All orders received today (has, have) been processed.
6. _have_

7. The sidewalks, as well as the streets, (are, is) being repaired.
7. _are_

8. When (was, were) the adjustments made?
8. _were_

9. Neither coffee nor dessert (come, comes) with the meal.
9. _comes_

10. (Has, Have) either of you read the article?
10. _Has_

11. The pollution of lakes and rivers (concern, concerns) all of us.
11. _concerns_

12. There (are, is) several candidates for that position.
12. _are_

13. The sales and advertising managers (report, reports) to the director of marketing.
13. _report_

14. Ham and eggs (are, is) her usual breakfast.
14. _is_

15. Every man, woman, and child (learn, learns) from experience.
15. _learns_

16. Their one and only goal (are, is) to own their own business.
16. _is_

17. (Are, Is) the owner and manager in the office today?
17. _Is_

18. Some of our customers (pay, pays) cash for all purchases.
18. _pay_

19. The chief executive officer and the senior vice president (like, likes) the plan.
19. _like_

20. Two windows and a door (need, needs) to be replaced.
20. _need_

21. Perhaps each of you (agree, agrees) with us.
21. _agrees_

22. (Do, Does) the other members agree with you?
22. _Do_

23. None of the space (has, have) been rented.
23. _has_

24. Some of them (want, wants) to raise taxes.
24. _want_

25. Enclosed (are, is) the lease and a check.
25. _are_

Underline each incorrect verb or verb phrase and write the necessary correction in the space provided. If a sentence is correct, write _OK_.

1. Neither the owner nor the tenants expects the issue to be resolved immediately.

2. Enclosed is the application form and a check.

3. Some of the topics on the agenda was not discussed at the meeting this morning.

4. Don't he or you have a parking space?

5. The sales tax on these items amount to $1.50.

6. Most of their suggestions makes sense to us.

7. Does either the Browns or the Halls have a financial interest in the company?

8. Are either of the receptionists eligible for promotion this month?

9. A takeover of those companies seem unlikely.

10. Also interested in buying the building is a Canadian company.

11. Our lease on these offices expire in April.

12. The taxes on this property amounts to $2400 a year.

13. All hopes the deficit will shrink rapidly.

14. There is plenty of things to keep us busy.

15. Most disappointed of all was the commission members.

16. The two families usually gets together during the summer for picnics.

17. My gift to her were a pair of earrings.

18. Every sofa and sofabed are on sale now.

19. Brown and yellow makes a nice combination of colors for this office.

20. Is their liabilities more than their assets?

21. Neither he nor she deserve more than you or me.

22. How many of the copies has been distributed?

23. Does the letter and the packages need to be mailed immediately?

24. Secretaries, as well every executive, writes letters and memos.

25. Either Ms. Ryan and Mr. Walker or Miss Wells and I conducts orientation programs for new employees.

1. expect
2. are
3. were discussed
4. Doesn't have
5. amounts
6. make
7. Do have
8. Is
9. seems
10. OK
11. expires
12. amount
13. hope
14. are
15. were
16. get
17. was
18. is
19. make
20. Are
21. deserves
22. have been distributed
23. Do need
24. write
25. conduct

Agreement of Subject and Verb (Continued)

SUBJECTS THAT ARE SINGULAR IN MEANING

1. Quantities and Amounts. A subject that is plural in form but that expresses one quantity or amount requires a singular verb.

> *Seventy-five cents was* all the change I had.
>
> *Thirty minutes seems* like an eternity to anyone waiting for someone else.
>
> *Twelve feet* of copper tubing *was needed* to connect the water heater.
>
> A *hundred tons* of wheat *has been* shipped already.

2. Groups of Words. A name, title, slogan, quotation, phrase, or clause that is used as a subject requires a singular verb.

> *Cypress Gardens is* a well-known tourist attraction.
>
> *Burton & Associates has* an office in this building.
>
> *Economic Policies was published* last year.
>
> *"When it rains, it pours" appears* on every container of Morton's salt.
>
> *What the company's response will be* obviously *is* a matter of conjecture.
>
> *To be president of a large corporation continues* to be Marilyn's goal.
>
> *Displaying the paintings in the conference room was* indeed a good idea.

3. Nouns That Are Plural in Form. Some nouns that are plural in form are singular in meaning and require singular verbs.

> The *news* of a settlement *was broadcast* early this morning.
>
> *Mathematics is* an easy subject for some.

4. Indefinite Pronouns. Some indefinite pronouns, such as *each* and *everyone,* are always singular and require singular verbs.

> *Each* of the apartments *has* a small terrace.
> *Someone has borrowed* the Wilson file.

SUBJECTS THAT ARE PLURAL IN MEANING

5. Nouns That Are Plural in Form and in Meaning. Some nouns are plural in form and in meaning, but each of them refers to a single item; for example, *goods, thanks,* and *earnings.* As subjects, such nouns require plural verbs.

> The *proceeds* of the campaign *amount* to $625.
>
> The *odds are* in your favor.
>
> Our *thanks go* to each of you.
>
> The *earnings* usually exceed our projections.

6. Some Indefinite Pronouns. Some indefinite pronouns, such as *both* and *several,* are always plural and require plural verbs when they are used as subjects.

> *Both* of them *have been hired* as consultants.
>
> *Several are planning* to attend the matinee performance today.
>
> *All* have a stake in the outcome.

Spot Check 1

In each sentence, underline the form of the verb that the subject requires.

1. Fifty dollars (was, were) paid on the account yesterday.

2. Two liters (are, is) all this container will hold.

3. Hot Springs (are, is) a city in Arkansas.

4. "To be or not to be" (open, opens) a well-known soliloquy.

5. That the company will not relocate (please, pleases) us employees.

6. (Was, Were) economics one of the subjects you studied?

7. Everything (seem, seems) to be in order.

8. Their credentials (are, is) impressive.

9. Few (support, supports) the proposed changes.

10. Where the meeting should be held (has, have) not been decided.

7. Collective Nouns. A collective noun that is singular in form may be either singular or plural in usage. If the persons or things in the group it names act as a unit, a singular verb is required. If the members of the group act as individuals, a plural verb is required.

> The *council has adopted* the measure. (The council is acting as a unit, not as separate individuals.)
>
> The *council were* not in agreement on some elements of the measure. (The council is spoken of as a group of separate individuals who did not agree on various issues.)

A collective noun that is plural in form requires a plural verb, of course.

> The *committees have submitted* their reports.
> Large *flocks* of Canadian geese *migrate* every year.

8. Nouns With One Form for Singular and Plural. Some nouns, such as *series* and *deer,* may be either singular or plural in meaning and require either a singular or a plural verb, depending on the intended meaning in a particular sentence.

> Another *deer has been acquired* by the local zoo.
> Several *deer have been acquired* by the local zoo.

9. Fractions and Percentages. A fraction or a percentage used as a subject may be either singular or plural, depending on whether it refers to something as a single unit or as separate units. If the fraction or percentage is followed by an *of* phrase containing a singular noun, use a singular verb. If the *of* phrase contains a plural noun, use a plural verb with the fraction or percentage.

> *Half* of the work *was done* by others.
> *Half* of the dishes *were broken*.
> *Six percent* of the selling price *is added* for sales tax.
> About *30 percent* of the questionnaires *have been returned* so far.
> *One-third* of the expense *is* deductible.
> *One-third* of the expenses *are* deductible.

10. Relative Pronouns. A relative pronoun may be either singular or plural, depending on its antecedent. For example, if the noun or pronoun to which the relative pronoun refers is singular, the relative pronoun subject requires a singular verb.

> The company wants to hire someone *who has* excellent communication skills. (The antecedent of *who* is the singular pronoun *someone;* therefore, *who* requires the singular verb *has*.)

> The company wants to hire graduates *who have* excellent communication skills. (The antecedent of *who* is the plural noun *graduates;* therefore, *who* requires the plural verb *have*.)

When the words *the only one* appear before an *of* phrase preceding a relative pronoun subject, use a singular verb with the relative pronoun subject. In this case, the pronoun *one* is the antecedent of the relative pronoun subject.

> Jack is *the only one* of them *who drives* to work every day. (The singular pronoun *one,* not the plural pronoun *them,* is the antecedent of *who;* therefore, *who* requires the third person singular verb *drives*.)
>
> It is *the only one* of their products *that is* out of stock. (The antecedent of *that* is *one,* not *products*.)

When the word *one* or the words *only one* appear before an *of* phrase preceding a relative pronoun subject, use a plural verb with the relative pronoun subject. In this case, the antecedent of the relative pronoun is the object of the preposition. As illustrated below, mentally rephrasing the sentence helps to isolate the antecedent of the relative pronoun and to select the correct verb for the relative pronoun subject.

> Mike is one of three *applicants who have* the necessary qualifications. (Of three applicants who have the necessary qualifications, Mike is one.)
>
> Maria is only one of the *employees who were considered* for the position. (Of the employees who were considered for the position, Maria is only one.)
>
> Ours is one of several *offices that open* at 8:30 a.m.
>
> Our agency is only one of *several that sell* insurance.

11. Indefinite Pronouns. Such indefinite pronouns as *some* and *all* may be either singular or plural. When one of these pronouns is the subject, it is necessary to consider the noun or pronoun in a modifying phrase or to consider the sense of the sentence as a whole in order to determine whether it requires a singular verb or a plural verb.

> *Some* of the gasoline *has* water in it. (*Some* is used with reference to *gasoline* and requires the singular verb *has*.)
>
> *Some* of the plans seem unrealistic. (*Some* is used with reference to *plans* and requires the plural verb *seem*.)
>
> *Some were* ill for a day or two. (*Ill for a day or two* indicates that *some* is used with reference to people or animals.)
>
> *All need* to obtain passports.
>
> *All* of our expenses *were* reasonable.
>
> *All* of the exhibit space *has been rented*.

Which of the verb forms shown in parentheses agrees with the subject? Underline the one you select.

1. The committee (has, have) accepted your new proposal.

2. The jury (has, have) eaten nothing but snacks.

3. Salmon (swim, swims) upstream to spawn.

4. Twenty percent (are, is) a very high interest rate.

5. Three-fourths of the members (has, have) paid their dues.

6. The plan that (offer, offers) the most benefits will be accepted.

7. Employees who (wish, wishes) to work overtime should see Jim.

8. This printer is one of those that (make, makes) a lot of noise.

9. This inquiry is only one of many that (require, requires) special attention.

10. This is the only one of the machines that (need, needs) to be repaired now.

AGREEMENT IN SOME SPECIAL SITUATIONS

12. A *Number* and *The Number* as Subjects. The expression *a number* is plural and requires a plural verb when used as a subject; *the number* is singular and requires a singular verb.

> A *number* of us *are planning* to attend the ceremony.
>
> A *number have volunteered* to serve on the finance committee.
>
> *The number* of new products *is* almost unbelievable.
>
> *The number* of candidates *continues* to grow.

13. Subjects of Incomplete Verbs. Be careful not to omit a helping verb or a main verb that should be different from one appearing earlier in a sentence or clause.

> INCORRECT:
> A chair *was broken,* and two or three desks *marred.*
>
> CORRECT:
> A chair *was broken,* and two or three desks *were marred.*
>
> INCORRECT:
> The company *has* and still *does dispose* of toxic wastes in a responsible manner.

> CORRECT:
> The company *has disposed* and still *does dispose* of toxic wastes in a responsible manner.

14. Subjunctives. The ***subjunctive*** form of a verb indicates something contrary to fact. The subjunctive frequently appears in clauses beginning with *if, as if,* and *as though.* The most commonly used subjunctive forms are *be* and *were.* Notice the different meanings in the following sentences.

> If this *is* the right key, it *will unlock* the door. (A fact.)
> If this *were* the right key, it *would open* the door. (Contrary to fact—it is not the right key.)
>
> Diane *is receiving* a bonus. (A fact.)
> Diane wishes she *were receiving* a bonus. (Contrary to fact—she is not receiving a bonus.)
>
> Mr. Mills *was* angry. (A fact.)
> Mr. Mills acted as though he *were* angry. (Contrary to fact—he was not angry.)

The subjunctive is also used after such verbs as *request, ask, order,* and *insist.*

> I request that the meeting *be postponed.* (NOT: is postponed.)
>
> Residents insisted that the streets *be repaired.* (NOT: are repaired.)
>
> I asked that your secretary *take* a message for you. (NOT: takes.)

The subjunctive usually refers to present or future time. Note that the subjunctive verb *were* is followed by *would* or *should* rather than by *will* or *shall.*

> If the report *were* available, I *would give* you a copy.
>
> If he *were* here, I *should be* glad to discuss this matter with him. (OR: would be.)

It is now common practice to use the regular form of the verb rather than the subjunctive unless it is definite that the statement is contrary to fact. However, the subjunctive is always used in motions that are made at meetings.

> I *move* that the meeting *be adjourned.*
>
> It *has been moved and seconded* that nominations *be closed.*

Spot Check 3

Which of the verb forms shown in parentheses agrees with the subject? Underline the one you select.

1. A number of stores (charge, charges) for delivering merchandise.

2. The number of new customers (surprise, <u>surprises</u>) us.

3. Frank has been and (continue, <u>continues</u>) to be a good customer.

4. When we entered, the windows (was, <u>were</u>) open and only one of the doors (closed, <u>was closed</u>).

5. If I (was, <u>were</u>) you, I (accept, <u>would accept</u>) their offer.

6. Millicent acts as though she (is, <u>were</u>) Queen Elizabeth's sister.

7. She asked that Paul (notifies, <u>notify</u>) you of the delay.

8. I suggest that the change (<u>be</u>, is) made.

9. If he (be, <u>was</u>, <u>were</u>) there, I did not see him.

10. The number 13 (are, be, <u>is</u>) considered unlucky by some.

11. A number written in figures (<u>are</u>, be, is) easier to spot than one written in words.

12. If that item (was, <u>were</u>) in stock, we (will, <u>would</u>) ship it to you immediately.

Study Guide 11

Note the agreement of the subjects and verbs in the following sentences. If you are unsure why a particular verb is used, refer to the rule indicated.

1. *Thirty minutes has been allowed* for the meeting.[1]
2. A *few cents* sometimes *makes* a big difference.[1]
3. *Beverly Hills is* in California.[2]
4. *Smith Brothers,* a local firm, *does* small construction jobs.[2]
5. *In the afternoon is* when *most* of our meetings *are held*.[2,11]
6. *"Serving people's need for knowledge" is* the company's slogan.[2]
7. *Anyone* with outstanding qualifications *has* an excellent chance of getting that job.[4]
8. The evening *news* usually *includes* a statement or two about the stock market.[3]
9. Most *goods* that we order from them always *arrive* in good condition.[5]
10. The *finance committee has* six members.[7]
11. The *jury* hearing the case probably *disagree* on some of the issues.[7]
12. *Is* the *chassis* of your car in good condition?[8]
13. Both *series attract* a large number of spectators.[8]
14. *All* of us *think* that at least *two-thirds* of the members *support* Lee's candidacy.[11,9]
15. *Half* of the stores *are* open Sundays.[9]
16. About *80 percent* of those *who are registered plan* to vote.[9,10]

17. Eleanor is the only one of our group *who drives* a convertible.[10]
18. Your application is one of those *that are being considered*.[10]
19. Every company prefers customers *who pay* their accounts promptly.[10]
20. You are the candidate *who has* the best chance of winning.[10]
21. *Some* of the roads *need* extensive repairs.[11]
22. *Some* of the information *appears* to be inaccurate.[11]
23. *Both* of the companies *have contributed*—and still *contribute*—to various charities.[6,13]
24. A *number* of firms *have* exhibits at the convention hall.[12]
25. The *number* of companies in this area *increases* every year.[12]
26. Earl wishes *he were* the winner.[14]
27. If *Hilda had been* there, she *would have known* what to do about it.[14]
28. I recommended that *Ann be appointed* to the commission.[14]
29. Did you insist that the *cashier call* the store manager?[14]
30. Lucy moved that the *meeting be adjourned*.[14]

ASSIGNMENT: Complete the Unit 11 Worksheet on pages 83–84.

UNIT 11

Subject and Verb Agreement (Continued)

WORKSHEET

 A Determine which of the verb forms shown in parentheses correctly completes the sentence; then write it in the space provided.

1. A number of homes (are, is) for sale.

2. Five dollars (was, were) all it cost.

3. The majority of the employees (has, have) been notified.

4. She is one of those who (has, have) plenty of self-confidence.

5. The board of directors (do, does) not agree on that particular issue.

6. Two-thirds of the amount (was, were) raised by selling subscriptions.

7. The number of satisfied customers (continue, continues) to increase rapidly.

8. Forest Hills (host, hosts) many tennis tournaments.

9. "All the news that's fit to print" (are, is) the newspaper's slogan.

10. Economics (are, is) one of the courses.

11. Few of them (favor, favors) the changes.

12. His trousers (was, were) spattered with mud.

13. The proceeds of the bake sale usually (exceed, exceeds) everyone's estimate.

14. How many copies will be needed (has, have) not been determined.

15. Model 110 is the only one of the new models that (meet, meets) our needs.

16. I suggested that the price (be, is) reduced.

17. The new series of nature books (was, were) published in June.

18. All of our work (has, have) been done.

19. Several series of games (was, were) scheduled for last Saturday.

20. She is only one of those who (refuse, refuses) to listen to gossip.

21. Norton is one of the employees who (work, works) at home sometimes.

22. These are the orders that (require, requires) special attention.

23. Phillip requested that Peggy (assume, assumes) part of the responsibility.

24. Nearly 80 percent of the work (has, have) been completed.

25. If I (was, were) she, I would request your advice.

1. _____are_____
2. _____was_____
3. _____have_____
4. _____have_____
5. _____do_____
6. _____was_____
7. _____continues_____
8. _____hosts_____
9. _____is_____
10. _____is_____
11. _____favor_____
12. _____were_____
13. _____exceed_____
14. _____has_____
15. _____meets_____
16. _____be_____
17. _____was_____
18. _____has_____
19. _____were_____
20. _____refuse_____
21. _____work_____
22. _____require_____
23. _____assume_____
24. _____has_____
25. _____were_____

B The following sentences contain various kinds of errors involving verbs—not just errors in agreement. Underline all incorrect verbs; then write your corrections in the spaces provided. If a sentence does not contain an error, write *OK*.

1. A number of employees has taken this course.
2. A vice president and a treasurer was to have been elected today.
3. Mars Brothers have a store in that mall.
4. Some of the news that was reported yesterday made everyone happy.
5. Are physics easier than chemistry?
6. Sixty cents were all I had with me.
7. We should of known they would leave early.
8. It don't seem to make any difference to them.
9. He and Hazel usually gets to work on time.
10. Spain is one of the countries that exports olives.
11. The audience was laughing and talking until the speaker arrived.
12. If you was there, you would know.
13. Who has recommended that Alice writes those reports?
14. Walsh & Associates now sell real estate.
15. Both Olson and Stillman offers good service.
16. Only one of them accept personal checks.
17. I wish we had went with you yesterday.
18. Some of the home remedies seems to work.
19. The windows were open, and the door closed.
20. Neither you nor I are to blame.
21. Do either of those jobs appeal to you?
22. John acted as though he is angry.
23. I am living here since 1990.
24. He or one of the others left the cartons setting on your desk.
25. Lower revenues was the cause of the city's budget problems.

1. have taken
2. were
3. has
4. OK
5. Is
6. was
7. should have known
8. doesn't seem
9. get
10. export
11. were laughing and talking
12. were
13. write
14. sells
15. offer
16. accepts
17. had gone
18. seem
19. was closed
20. am
21. Does appeal
22. were
23. have been living
24. sitting
25. were

UNIT 12

Verbals

KINDS OF VERBALS

A *verbal* is a verb form that is not used as a verb in a sentence. The three kinds of verbals are *infinitives, participles,* and *gerunds.* As indicated in the following discussion, infinitives may be used as adjectives, adverbs, or nouns. When participles function as verbals, they modify nouns or pronouns and are classified as adjectives. Gerunds are used only as nouns.

INFINITIVES

An *infinitive* usually consists of the word *to* (often called "the sign of the infinitive") plus a verb: *to be, to meet,* or *to buy,* for example.

> We are planning *to meet* with their representative next Monday.
> Would you like *to be* a contestant on a TV game show?
> She went to the store *to buy* some personal stationery.

After such verbs as *need, see, hear, feel, let,* and *help,* the word *to* is often omitted.

> Please help me *move* this file cabinet.
> Did you hear anyone *open* the door?
> You can help us *be* more efficient and productive.

Like any other verb form, an infinitive may have a subject, an object, or both a subject and an object. Also, because it is a verb form, an infinitive may be modified by an adverb.

> Our manager expects us *to process* customers' orders promptly and correctly. (The infinitive *to process* has the subject *us* and the direct object *orders;* it is modified by the adverbs *promptly* and *correctly.*)
> Ms. Thomas asked me *to give* you a copy of the report. (The infinitive *to give* has the subject *me,* the object *copy,* and the indirect object *you.*)
> It is a good idea *to exercise* daily. (The infinitive *to exercise* is modified by the adverb *daily.*)

Tenses of Infinitives. An infinitive has only two main tenses: the *present* and the *perfect.* Each of these tenses expresses time in relation to that of the main verb in the sentence or clause.

The *present infinitive* may be used with a main verb of any tense. This form of the infinitive may express the same time as the main verb, or it may express future time in relation to that of the main verb.

> I need *to leave* early today.
> I needed *to leave* early yesterday.
> I will need *to leave* early tomorrow.
> For several days I have been needing *to leave* early.
> Everyone will be expecting me *to leave* early.
> We are ready *to circulate* the agenda now.
> The agenda is ready *to be circulated* now. (Note that an infinitive has a passive form.)
> I would have liked *to meet* with them myself. (NOT: to have met.)

The present infinitive is frequently used with such verbs as *expect, plan,* and *intend.*

> Mr. Albertson plans *to be* in the office tomorrow.
> I expected Pat *to call* a few days ago.
> Do you intend *to renew* your subscription?

The *perfect infinitive* denotes action that has been completed *before* the time of the principal verb. It may be used with a verb of any tense.

> I am happy *to have met* with them before the others arrived.
> The order that we received today was *to have been delivered* a week ago. (Note the passive form for the present perfect infinitive.)

In the following example, notice how changing from the present to the perfect form of the infinitive affects the meaning of the sentence.

> We believe him *to be* an honest politician.
> We believe him *to have been* an honest politician.

Uses of Infinitives. An infinitive may be used as a noun, an adjective, or an adverb. In the following sentences, the infinitive is used as a noun.

> *To resign* would be a serious mistake. (*To resign* is the subject.)
> The team's goal is *to win.* (*To win* is a predicate nominative. It further identifies *goal,* the subject of the linking verb *is.*)
> Most of us need *to work.* (*To work* is the object of the verb *need.*)

In the following sentences, the infinitives function as adjectives—modifiers of nouns and pronouns.

> If you want quality merchandise at low prices, our store is the place *to shop*. (*To shop* modifies the noun *place*.)
>
> Who was the last one *to be hired?* (*To be hired* modifies the pronoun *one*.)

As illustrated below, infinitives may also be used as adverbs—modifiers of verbs and adjectives.

> Mr. Olivero called *to reschedule* his appointment. (*To reschedule,* together with *his appointment,* modifies the verb *called*. It tells why Mr. Olivero called.)
>
> We were fortunate *to obtain tickets*. (*To obtain tickets* modifies the adjective *fortunate*.)

Split Infinitives. A ***split infinitive*** has a word placed between *to* and the verb, as in the phrase *to immediately call*. As illustrated below, it is generally better to place the intervening word either before *to* or after the verb.

> I tried *immediately to call you*.
> I tried *to call you immediately*.

Sometimes it is preferable to split the infinitive to avoid an awkward construction, to add emphasis, or to convey the intended meaning.

> The manager asked us *to individually check* the diskettes. (In this position, *individually* modifies and emphasizes *check*.)
>
> The manager asked us *to check* the diskettes *individually*. (The infinitive is no longer split.)
>
> The manager asked us *individually to check* the diskettes. (In this position, *individually* gives a different meaning to the sentence: The manager asked us one at a time—not all of us at the same time.)

An infinitive is not considered split if the word comes before a participle following *to be*.

> Our employees expect *to be fully reimbursed* for business expenses.
>
> Is it realistic to expect every problem *to be completely resolved?*

PARTICIPLES

Participles are verb forms that may be used as adjectives as well as verbs. Note the ***present participles*** used as adjectives in the following sentences.

> What is the name of the person *calling?* (*Calling* modifies the noun *person*.)
>
> Some of those *waiting* will be able to board this flight. (*Waiting* modifies the pronoun *those*.)

Now note the use of ***past participles*** as adjectives in the following sentences.

I am sure that the merchandise *delivered* is not the merchandise *ordered*. (*Delivered* and *ordered* modify the noun *merchandise*.)

Would it be possible to read everything *written?* (*Written* modifies the pronoun *everything*.)

Like other verb forms, participles may be modified by adverbs and have objects or complements. Note the use of participles before, as well as after, the nouns or pronouns they modify.

> A store *losing money* is unlikely to stay in business. (*Money* is the object of the participle *losing*.)
>
> The Customs Service frequently seizes *illegally imported* merchandise. (The adverb *illegally* modifies the past participle *imported*.)
>
> A bank is very unlikely to cash a check *endorsed improperly*.

When used as a verb, as in the following sentences, a participle is used with other verbs to express the action of a subject.

> Who *is writing* the copy for the next series of ads?
> We *are waiting* for them to respond to our letter.
> Perhaps your letter *was delivered* to someone else.
> Ms. Crawford *has ordered* two new printers.

Use of Participles. Which form of the participle to use is determined by the relationship of the participle to the tense, or time, of the main verb or verb phrase in the sentence or clause in which it appears.

The present participle expresses the same time as that of the verb or verb phrase—present, past, or future. Note that the present participle always ends in *ing*.

> The person *speaking* is Dr. Yvonne Garcia. (Present tense.)
>
> Everyone *attending* the orientation session asked questions. (Past tense.)
>
> Those *completing* the course will be eligible for a tuition refund. (Future tense.)

The past participle expresses time before that indicated by the main verb or verb phrase.

> All questionnaires *returned* yesterday *are* on my desk. (Present tense.)
>
> The price *stated* in the catalog *was* incorrect. (Past tense.)
>
> Payments and charges *made* after the 15th of the month *will appear* on next month's statement. (Future tense.)

The perfect participle shows action completed before the time indicated by the main verb.

> Tony, *having read* the report, *sent* it to Ms. Gilson. (Past tense.)

The check, *having been endorsed, is* ready to deposit. (Present tense.)

The changes, *having been approved* by Mrs. Alberts, *will become* effective the first of next month. (Future tense.)

Errors in the Use of Participles. A common error in the use of participles is known as the ***dangling participle,*** which is a participle that has no definite or correct noun or pronoun to modify.

> INCORRECT:
> Exceeding the weight limit, the post office will not accept the packages.
>
> CORRECT:
> The post office will not accept the packages exceeding the weight limit.
>
> CORRECT:
> The post office will not accept the packages that exceed the weight limit. (Rephrasing the sentence is sometimes preferable for clarity.)
>
> CORRECT:
> If the packages exceed the weight limit, the post office will not accept them.

For clarity, the participle should be placed close to the noun or pronoun that it modifies. Frequently it is desirable to use a clause rather than a participial phrase, as shown in the last two examples above.

The noun or pronoun modified by a participle must be in the nominative or objective case, not in the possessive case.

> If you are looking for Paul, I noticed *him sitting* in the conference room. (NOT: his sitting.)
>
> The interviewer questioned *people planning* to vote. (NOT: people's planning.)

GERUNDS

A ***gerund,*** or *verbal noun,* is a verb form ending in *ing* that is used as a noun: *running, singing,* or *writing,* for example. Gerunds always function as nouns, as indicated by the following examples. Also note that a noun or pronoun that modifies a gerund must be in the possessive case.

> *Painting* is a hobby for many. (*Painting* is the subject.)
>
> Until today we were unaware of his *resigning.* (*Resigning* is the object of the preposition *of.* Note that *resigning* is modified by the possessive pronoun *his.*)
>
> Jerry enjoys *skiing.* (*Skiing* is the object of the verb *enjoys.*)
>
> The most welcome news was Marie's *winning.* (*Winning* functions as the predicate nominative—it further explains *news,* the subject of the linking verb *was.* Note the possessive noun *Marie's.*)

A gerund may have an object and be modified by adverbs.

> They did not seem annoyed by my *calling* them almost every day.
>
> *Writing* reports is part of the job. (*Reports* is the object of the gerund *writing.*)
>
> *Driving* carefully makes sense. (The adverb *carefully* modifies the gerund *driving.*)

Tenses of Gerunds. A gerund has two tenses, the present and the perfect. The present tense of a gerund expresses the same time as the main verb or the time following that expressd by the main verb. Note the italicized gerunds and verbs in these sentences.

> Her plans *include taking* a vacation.
>
> *Applying* for a loan *was* fairly easy.
>
> They *will appreciate* our *helping* them.

The perfect tense of a gerund expresses time previous to the time expressed by the main verb. Study these examples carefully.

> Your *having worked* to pay part of your college expenses impressed the interviewer.
>
> They regret *having invested* in those junk bonds.
>
> Your *advising* us will be appreciated.

Study Guide 12

A. Study the italicized infinitives in the following sentences. Can you identify the tense of each infinitive and explain why that particular tense is used?

1. Some consider real estate *to be* a very good investment.
2. Others consider real estate *to have been* a very good investment.
3. Where are they planning *to have* the reception?
4. Are you planning *to go* to the concert?
5. I planned to help him *move* the new furniture into his office.

6. Would you have liked *to hire* someone else?
7. Each of them is pleased *to have received* two or three job offers.
8. Is your goal *to develop* a new marketing plan?

9. The other company is considered *to be* more aggressive.
10. Were they pleased *to have been granted* another interview?

B. Study the following sentences and decide whether the italicized word in each is a gerund or a participle.

1. The company is *relocating* its headquarters.
2. After *notifying* the others, I spoke with Dr. Laura.
3. Thank you for *correcting* those errors.
4. Did you notice anything *missing* this morning?
5. *Saving* regularly is the best way to save money.
6. *Speaking* before a large audience makes some people nervous.

7. Is the person *speaking* a friend of yours?
8. Many people were surprised at the council's *passing* such a controversial resolution.
9. We very much appreciate your *bringing* us up to date.
10. *Rising* costs probably will result in somewhat higher prices.

C. Note the use of the italicized nouns in the following sentences and the gerund or participle that determines which case is used.

1. *Investors* expecting the company to make a profit will not be disappointed.
2. Some have criticized the *government's* handling of the situation.
3. Did you notice a *visitor* waiting in the reception area?
4. Everyone applauded the *banks'* lowering interest rates.
5. We saw *Carl* leaving with some of the sales representatives at noon.

6. I heard *Terry* asking for permission to leave at three o'clock.
7. Have you read anything about the *city's* building a new sports stadium?
8. Most of those surveyed said they liked their *mothers'* cooking better than their *fathers'*.
9. Some *companies'* advertising appeals to very young children.
10. The museum paid over a million dollars for another *Picasso* painting.

ASSIGNMENT: Complete the Unit 12 Worksheet on pages 89–90 and the Part 3 Review on pages 91–92.

UNIT 12

Verbals

WORSHEET

A   In the following sentences, determine whether the words ending in *ing* are gerunds or participles. If the italicized word is incorrect, write the correct form in the space provided. If no change is necessary, write *OK*.

1. Many employers dislike *employees* making personal telephone calls.
2. We visited several *agencies* selling real estate.
3. Do you think the *store* increasing prices is a good idea?
4. Do many parents complain about their *children* eating habits?
5. The *witnesses* lying got them in trouble.
6. I saw the *package* lying in the receptionist's office.
7. Did you see *anyone's* driving recklessly down the highway?
8. Many people are still talking about the *government* firing the air traffic controllers.
9. I overheard *Tom's* telling Ms. Katz about the contract.
10. *Me* complaining to him won't do any good.
11. We were unaware of *them* planning to move.
12. We saw bushels of *apples'* rotting on the ground.
13. The walls are so thin we can hear our *neighbors'* whispering.
14. Dodie said something about *Phyllis* not feeling well.
15. Was it *him* or her complaining that resulted in all these changes?
16. Have you ever seen *his* driving a bus?
17. We saw a painting of *Washington's* crossing the Delaware.
18. I appreciate *you* offering to help me.
19. Do you know *whose* teaching the course?
20. The report named several *cities'* raising taxes.

1. _employees'_
2. _OK_
3. _store's_
4. _children's_
5. _witnesses'_
6. _OK_
7. _anyone_
8. _government's_
9. _Tom_
10. _My_
11. _their_
12. _apples_
13. _neighbors_
14. _Phyllis's_
15. _his_
16. _him_
17. _Washington_
18. _your_
19. _who's OR who is_
20. _cities_

B   In these sentences, if the tense of the infinitive shown in italics is correct, write *OK* in the space provided. Otherwise, write the infinitive correctly.

1. He seems sorry not *to apply* for the job given to Mr. Weems.
2. *To have settled* for less would have been a mistake.

1. _to have applied_
2. _To settle_

3. We had planned *to have sold* our home last spring.

4. You ought *to check* the model number before you placed the order.

5. If you had seen the memo, you would have wanted *to have rewritten* it.

6. We had hoped *to have left* before now.

7. The payment appears *to be credited* to the wrong account.

8. *To solve* the problem, we will need their cooperation.

9. We would like *to be informed* much earlier than we were.

10. I left the letters *to sign* on your desk.

3. _to sell_

4. _to have checked_

5. _to rewrite_

6. _to leave_

7. _to have been credited_

8. _OK_

9. _to have been informed_

10. _to be signed_

C **Rewrite the following sentences, incorporating whatever corrections and additions are necessary to make each sentence grammatically correct and clear in meaning. (Answers will vary.)**

1. We are looking for a place with an outdoor patio to eat.

We are looking for a place to eat that has an outdoor patio.

2. Speaking Japanese, no one could understand the visitors.

No one could understand the visitors speaking Japanese.

3. By taking a shortcut, I thought you would be at the office before me.

I thought that by taking a shortcut, you would be at the office before me.

4. Darting across the road, the driver almost hit a deer.

The driver almost hit a deer darting across the road.

5. A car went down the street pulled by a truck.

A car pulled by a truck went down the street.

PART 3

Verbs and Verb Usage

REVIEW

In the following sentences, underline each incorrectly used verb or verbal; then write the necessary correction in the space provided. If a sentence is correct, write *OK*.

1. There was a number of applicants scheduled for interviews yesterday.

2. I recommended that your agency is hired.

3. It would have been nice to have been with you and the others.

4. How many of the accounts is delinquent?

5. Have either of you seen Ms. Morrison today?

6. If he was there, he probably remembers the name of the speaker.

7. Isn't any of the crops ready to harvest?

8. The supply of fresh fruits and vegetables are still inadequate this winter.

9. The plants growed very little last month.

10. We are living here for nearly two years.

11. Mr. Jeffreys says he bought a new car.

12. Their prices have went down again.

13. Five years are a long time to wait for a settlement.

14. Neither Ms. Davis nor members of her staff has received a copy of the announcement.

15. You are the only one of the candidates who have the necessary training and experience.

16. Some of the land in those counties were sold to speculators.

17. There was papers laying all over the floor.

18. The farmer said if the hens did not start lying soon, they would be sent to market.

19. If I had been at the meeting, I would see them for myself.

20. The cartons set near the entrance most of last week.

21. I wish I was able to help them.

22. Maybe we should have ask someone else.

23. Model 440 is only one of those that is available for $500 or less.

24. Two nickels was all I had in my pocket.

25. What was the guide trying to explain to the tourists?

1. were
2. be
3. to be
4. are
5. Has seen
6. OK
7. Aren't
8. is
9. grew
10. have been living
11. said
12. have gone
13. is
14. have received
15. has
16. was sold
17. were lying
18. laying
19. would have seen
20. sat
21. were
22. should have asked
23. are
24. were
25. OK

26. If either of the men know the answer, he should tell us.

27. This car has been drove only a few thousand miles.

28. Her favorite vegetable are beets.

29. The increase in the number of building permits reflect improved economic conditions.

30. Stillwell Associates do consulting work.

31. Proofreading these reports is one of the things that remains to be done.

32. Has either Miss Rogers or Ms. Wells took charge of the marketing department?

33. There was few people present when the first speaker was introduced.

34. I doubt that either of them would of done the job any better than we did.

35. Who suggested that you and I are appointed to the committee investigating that problem?

36. Had I found them, I would have give them to you immediately.

37. She said she swum every day last week.

38. The band was wearing two different uniforms.

39. We should have payed less for those items.

40. Some of that medicine taste very bitter.

41. A third of the orders was processed before noon.

42. The errors were corrected and the report distributed.

43. Did either of them demonstrate the machine before you use it?

44. About 40 percent of the responses has been tabulated.

45. Every man and woman were given a copy of the company's handbook.

46. In this folder are the list of employees having employment anniversaries this month.

47. Shall either of them be invited?

48. Janice or I usually keeps a record of petty cash expenditures.

49. The secretary and treasurer were not at the meeting this morning.

50. About ten minutes are allowed for each presentation.

26.	knows
27.	has been driven
28.	is
29.	reflects
30.	does
31.	remain
32.	Has taken
33.	were
34.	would have done
35.	be appointed
36.	would have given
37.	swam
38.	were wearing
39.	should have paid
40.	tastes
41.	were processed
42.	was distributed
43.	used
44.	have been tabulated
45.	was given
46.	is
47.	Will be invited
48.	keep
49.	was
50.	is allowed

PART 4

Other Parts of Speech and Their Usage

Before you study Units 13 through 16, complete this survey of other parts of speech and their usage. These exercises will help you identify principles that you may wish to give special attention.

SURVEY

 In the following sentences, underline each error in the use of adjectives, adverbs, prepositions, and conjunctions, and write the necessary corrections in the spaces provided. If no correction is necessary, write *OK*.

1. Both of them have to much work.
2. She was smiling until she walked in to her office.
3. The vase fell off of the cabinet and broke.
4. Neither he or I know what the result will be.
5. This cake tastes very sweetly to us.
6. What is the most tallest building in the world?
7. Have you ever used them diskettes?
8. Most everyone in the office has a computer.
9. You are a better candidate than anyone.
10. The copier works as good as it ever has.
11. That piece of equipment is stationery, but the other one is movable.
12. The clerk spoke so loudly that everybody in the office complained.
13. It would be better to go then to stay here.
14. We would sooner leave before the rush hour.
15. She takes a 3-miles hike every evening.
16. Who is going beside you and Francine?
17. We need someone who can speak convincing.
18. The reward will be divided between several of my coworkers.
19. This report appears to be quiet complete.
20. What is their principle objection?
21. There were far less people in the audience than we had expected.
22. Of all the brands available, which one is requested more often?
23. An announcement is expected eminently.

1. too
2. into
3. off (OMIT of)
4. nor
5. sweet
6. tallest (OMIT most)
7. those
8. Almost
9. anyone else
10. well
11. stationary
12. OK
13. than
14. rather
15. 3-mile
16. besides
17. convincingly
18. among
19. quite
20. principal
21. fewer
22. most
23. imminently

24. Her promotion will be formerly announced by Mr. Velasco.

25. Where are you going to next?

26. Like I told you yesterday, Part 30-1A is not available.

27. Are you on the committee studying the company's personal policies and procedures?

28. His writing is so eligible that he cannot read it himself.

29. There's seeming no reason for such a long delay in responding to that inquiry.

30. This machine is significantly different than the one we had before.

31. Your pay increase will be retroactive from the first of January.

32. The witness had nothing farther to say.

33. Dr. Farnsworth is expecting a honorarium.

34. It is the worse movie of all time.

35. What kind of a job does Mr. Olsen have?

36. Being that the ring was expensive, I decided not to buy it.

37. The reason he left was because he was ill.

38. We will never know how easy the machine is to use without we try it.

39. She went home because she was not feeling good.

40. Neither the windows or the doors close properly.

41. We should try and do the best that we can.

42. I doubt as how the deadline will be met.

43. Did you read in the newspaper where health insurance has become prohibitively expensive for many people?

44. Well made shoes are a good investment.

45. This styles of clothes are fashionable.

46. Which of the file drawers is emptiest?

47. Some of the work was all ready done.

48. Several changes were made when we were out of the office last week.

49. Firstly, we must collect all the data.

50. It seemed all together inappropriate.

24.	formally
25.	OMIT to
26.	As
27.	personnel
28.	illegible
29.	seemingly
30.	from
31.	to
32.	further
33.	an
34.	worst
35.	kind of (OMIT a)
36.	Because OR Since
37.	that
38.	unless
39.	well
40.	nor
41.	to
42.	that OR whether
43.	that
44.	Well-made
45.	These
46.	most nearly empty OR empty
47.	already
48.	while
49.	First
50.	altogether

Adjectives

FUNCTION OF ADJECTIVES

An **adjective** is a word that describes or limits the meaning of a noun or a pronoun. By giving color and distinction to the words they modify, adjectives help to convey thoughts precisely and interestingly. An adjective that describes tells "what kind of," and one that limits tells "which" or "how many."

wide street	*this* magazine	*several* letters
excellent record	*those* folders	*rapid* progress
expensive jewelry	*few* errors	*all* residents
bright light	*many* customers	*friendly* people

Adjectives that modify pronouns generally follow linking verbs. Those that modify nouns may, of course, precede the nouns or follow linking verbs.

Everyone was *courteous* and *helpful.*
He and she seem *happy.*
Accurate records are *important.*
Diamonds are *expensive.*

Some words, such as *statistical* and *extensive,* are always used as adjectives. Many words, however, may be used as two or more different parts of speech; such words are adjectives only when they modify nouns and pronouns.

The *light* at the end of the driveway is always on. (*Light* functions as a noun; it is the subject of the verb *is.*)

Someone should *light* a candle. (In this sentence, *light* is the main verb in the verb phrase *should light.*)

We were carrying several *light* packages. (*Light* functions as an adjective modifying the noun *packages.*)

Would you like to work for a larger *company?* (*Company* is a noun functioning as the object of the preposition *for.*)

Are there exceptions to any *company* policies? (*Company* functions as an adjective modifying *policies.*)

Most grocery stores sell *frozen* desserts. (*Frozen* is a past participle used as an adjective modifying the noun *desserts.*)

The water in that bottle *has frozen.* (The past participle *frozen* is the main verb in the phrase *has frozen.*)

Remember that possessive nouns and pronouns are considered adjectives when they modify nouns and pronouns.

her ideas	*his* statement	*your* staff
mayor's office	*child's* game	*owners'* claims

PROPER ADJECTIVES

A **proper adjective** may be a word derived from a proper noun, such as *Canadian* from the proper noun *Canada,* or it may be a proper noun used as an adjective, such as *Illinois* in the phrase *the Illinois delegation* or *New England* in the phrase *the New England countryside.*

Most proper adjectives are capitalized, but those that have lost their association with the nouns from which they were derived are no longer capitalized. Be sure to consult a dictionary or other authoritative reference when you are uncertain whether to capitalize a particular adjective.

American industry	*venetian* blinds
Victorian era	*india* ink
African heritage	*morocco* binding

COMPOUND ADJECTIVES

A **compound adjective** consists of two or more words used as a unit to modify a noun or a pronoun, as in the phrase an *up-to-date report.* Many compound adjectives are combinations of various parts of speech; others consist of whole phrases.

ADJECTIVE AND NOUN:	*long-range* plans
NOUN AND ADJECTIVE:	*mile-long* hike
ADJECTIVE AND PARTICIPLE:	*friendly-looking* person
ADVERB AND PARTICIPLE:	*well-known* actor
NOUNS:	*labor-management* talks
PHRASE:	*over-the-counter* sales

Although dictionaries list a number of compound adjectives, writers and speakers frequently construct them to suit their particular needs.

The Hyphen in Compound Adjectives. The use of the hyphen in a compound adjective is determined by the position of the adjective in relation to the noun it modifies and by the kinds of words that make up the compound adjective. If the compound adjective comes *before* the noun, it is usually hyphenated. If the compound adjective comes *after* the noun, the hyphen may not be needed if the words are in normal order. Study the following examples and use them as guides.

We obtained *up-to-date* information.
The *information* we obtained is *up to date.*

They constructed a *30-story* building.
Their new building has *30 stories.*

You are eligible for a *three-week* vacation.
You are eligible for *three weeks'* vacation.

A *well-known* authority spoke on investments.
Her views are *well known.*

We found some *unheard-of* bargains.
Such prices are *unheard of.*

You may wish to invest in *tax-exempt* bonds.
The interest will be *tax-exempt.*

The lumber came from a *government-owned* forest.
This property is *government-owned.*

Both of them are *law-abiding* citizens.
Most citizens are *law-abiding.*

Their team has a *left-handed* pitcher.
Lewis is *right-handed.*

They sent two *smooth-talking* representatives.
Both turned out to be anything but *smooth-talking.*

Most of us must file *income tax* returns in April.
Both are *junior college* graduates.
The Wilsons are in the *real estate* business.
You may be eligible for a *10 percent* discount.
The company reported a *$15 million* profit last year.

If the first word of a compound modifier is an adverb ending in *ly,* the modifier is not hyphenated.

Both of them have *clearly defined* goals.
Pat is a *highly successful* real estate agent.

Before using a hyphen, be sure that the words function as a unit in modifying a noun. For example, in the phrase *first-rate company, rate* cannot stand alone as a modifier of *company;* both words are needed to form the adjective. However, in the phrase *new fall fashions, new* could modify *fashions* without *fall;* therefore, *new* and *fall* are separate adjectives.

ARTICLES

The adjectives *a, an,* and *the* are **articles.** The definite article *the* identifies a specific object. *A* and *an* are indefinite articles because they do not designate a specific object or person; for example, *an official* means *any official.*

The use of *a* or *an* is determined by the word that immediately follows the article. If the word begins with a *consonant sound,* use the article *a.* Always remember to think of the sound, not the spelling.

a building	*a* hundred	*a* one-hour meeting
a program	*a* monopoly	*a* formal agreement

Use *an* before a word beginning with any *vowel sound* except long *u.* Note that *an* is used before a word beginning with a silent *h* and that *a* is used before a word beginning with a long *u* sound.

an applicant	*an* opinion	*a* one-way street
an event	*an* uncle	*a* uniform
an idol	*an* honor	*a* European

The use of *a* and *an* before abbreviations and numbers also depends on sound, not spelling.

an FBI agent	*a* UN member	*an* 8-mile hike
an X ray	*a* 6-hour flight	*a* c.o.d. order

Repeat the article to show that two separate objects are modified:

We bought *a* blue and *a* green rug. (Repeating the article *a* shows that two rugs were bought.)

Ms. Mercado has served as *the* secretary and *the* treasurer of the club. (Repeating the article *the* makes it clear that she has held two different positions.)

When only one object is modified, do not repeat the article:

We bought *a* blue and green rug. (The single article *a* shows that only one rug was bought—a rug that is blue and green.)

Ms. Mercado has served as *the* secretary and treasurer of the club. (The single article *the* shows that she has held one position—that of secretary-treasurer.)

The articles *a* and *an* should not be used after such expressions as *kind of, sort of, model of,* and *type of.*

What *kind of* store is it? (NOT: kind of a.)
What *sort of* response did you get? (NOT: sort of a.)
What *model of* car did you buy? (NOT: model of a.)

PREDICATE ADJECTIVES

A **predicate adjective** follows a linking verb and modifies the subject. Remember that linking verbs indicate state of being or condition, not action; for example, *am, is, are, has been,* and *seems.*

Your suggestions were *helpful. (Helpful* modifies *suggestions,* the subject of the linking verb *were.)*

Both of them have been *cooperative. (Cooperative* modifies *both,* the subject.)

The first speaker seemed rather *nervous.*

I am completely *confident* that each of those manuals will be very *useful.*

Verbs referring to the senses (such as *look, sound, smell, taste,* and *feel*) and such verbs as *be, appear,* and *seem* are frequently followed by predicate adjectives.

> Something about the building looks *different*. (NOT: differently)
>
> Your suggestion sounds *good* to me. (NOT: well)
>
> She said that she feels *well*. (NOT: good When referring to health, use *well*)
>
> This coffee tastes *bitter*. (NOT: bitterly)
>
> This milk smells *bad*. (NOT: badly)
>
> Their price seems *reasonable*.

Spot Check 1

In the following sentences, underline whichever expression shown in parentheses is the correct one.

1. All the tables were set with expensive (china, China).

2. Was it a (chinese, Chinese) restaurant?

3. It is a (well managed, well-managed) and successful organization.

4. Both he and she are (junior college, junior-college) students.

5. The dairy sells (Pasteurized, pasteurized) milk.

6. An (oily looking, oily-looking) substance was spilled on the floor.

7. The store gave us a (10 percent, 10-percent) discount.

8. You are eligible for (two weeks', two-weeks') vacation.

9. There was a (30 minute, 30-minute) delay.

10. This machine is (out of order, out-of-order).

11. The station broadcasts (up to the minute, up-to-the-minute) news.

12. Yesterday was an (unusually-clear, unusually clear) day.

13. The land is (government owned, government-owned).

14. Why not invest in a (tax exempt, tax-exempt) fund?

15. Did you find (a, an) error?

16. She was awarded (a, an) unusual prize.

17. He is (a, an) union official.

18. You may be eligible for (a, an) FHA mortgage.

19. What kind (of, of a) machine is that?

20. Those styles are (old fashioned, old-fashioned).

COMPARISON OF ADJECTIVES

Adjectives have different forms to indicate that the nouns they modify are being compared with other nouns. The **positive degree** is the form of the adjective used when no comparison is made. The **comparative degree** is the form used when two persons or things are being compared. The **superlative degree** is the form used when three or more persons or things are being compared.

> The kitchen is *small*. (No comparison is being made; therefore, the positive degree is the form used.)
>
> The kitchen is *smaller* than the living room. (Two rooms are being compared; the comparative degree is the form used.)
>
> The kitchen is the *smallest* room in the house. (The room is being compared with several others; thus the superlative degree is the form used.)

Use of the Endings *er* and *est*. The comparative degree of adjectives of one syllable and some adjectives of two syllables is regularly formed by adding *er* to the positive form. The superlative degree is formed by adding *est* to the positive form. For words ending in *y* preceded by a consonant, change the *y* to *i* before adding *er* or *est*.

POSITIVE	COMPARATIVE	SUPERLATIVE
big	bigger	biggest
clean	cleaner	cleanest
easy	easier	easiest
heavy	heavier	heaviest
pretty	prettier	prettiest
quick	quicker	quickest
short	shorter	shortest
young	younger	youngest

Use of *More* or *Less* and *Most* or *Least*. The comparative degree of many adjectives of two syllables and of most adjectives of more than two syllables is indicated by using *more* or *less* with the positive form. The superlative degree is indicated by using *most* or *least* with the positive form. *Less* and *least* are always used to indicate a decreasing amount or degree.

POSITIVE	COMPARATIVE	SUPERLATIVE
active	more active	most active
	less active	least active
candid	more candid	most candid
	less candid	least candid
discreet	more discreet	most discreet
	less discreet	least discreet
expensive	more expensive	most expensive
	less expensive	least expensive
successful	more successful	most successful
	less successful	least successful

Adjectives With Irregular Degree Forms. Some adjectives have irregular comparative and superlative forms. When in doubt about the forms of an adjective, consult a dictionary, which will give the comparative and superlative forms of irregular adjectives.

POSITIVE	COMPARATIVE	SUPERLATIVE
bad	worse	worst
far *(distance)*	farther	farthest
far *(degree)*	further	furthest
good	better	best
ill	worse	worst
little *(amount)*	less, lesser	least
little *(size)*	littler	littlest
many	more	most
much	more	most
well	better	best

Absolute Adjectives. Certain adjectives cannot be compared. **Absolute adjectives** cannot logically be compared because of their meanings. The following words are commonly used adjectives of this type.

accurate	dead	fiscal	parallel	round	unique
complete	empty	genuine	perfect	square	unanimous
correct	exact	impossible	real	stationary	wrong

However, the degree to which something approaches the full meaning of *some* of these adjectives may be correctly indicated by using the adjective with *more nearly, most nearly, less nearly,* or *least nearly.*

Your assessment is *more nearly accurate* than mine.

Of the various buildings under construction, which one is *most nearly complete?*

Some authorities also accept the use of *almost, more,* and other adverbs with various absolute adjectives.

His writing is *almost impossible* to read.

May we use 3.1416, or would you prefer that we use a *more exact* amount to equal pi?

CORRECT USE OF ADJECTIVES

Adjectives and the nouns they modify must agree in number. For example, *this* and *that* are singular and *these* and *those* are plural. *Them* is never an adjective.

This style of shoes is new. (NOT: These style.)

That type of carpeting will last for years. (NOT: Those type.)

These letters are ready to mail. (NOT: These letter.)

Those kinds of tiles are often used in kitchens. (NOT: Those kind OR Them kinds.)

Those containers are empty. (NOT: Them containers.)

Be careful to use the comparative degree of an adjective when comparing two persons or things and the superlative degree when comparing three or more, as in these examples.

Sears Tower is *taller* than the Empire State Building. (Two buildings are being compared.)

What is the *least expensive* meal on the restaurant's menu? (Several meals are listed on a restaurant menu.)

When a person, place, or thing is compared with others in its own group, the comparative degree is used and the word *other* or *else* is inserted. This addition separates the person or thing being compared from the others within the group and prevents the person or thing from being compared with itself.

The Mississippi is longer than *any other* river in the United States. (NOT: longer than *any* river in the United States.)

You have more patience than *anyone else* I know. (NOT: more patience than *anyone* I know.)

When the person or thing being compared is included within its group, *other* and *else* are not used. Compare the preceding and the following examples.

The Mississippi is the *longest* river in the United States. Of all the people I know, you have the *most* patience.

Always compare like things. A careless omission may result in an apparent comparison of unlike things. Similarly, the use of the incorrect form of a pronoun can lead to an incorrect comparison.

The sales for July were lower *than those* for June. (NOT: The sales for July were lower than June. In this sentence, the comparison is incorrectly made between *sales* and *June.*)

She earns a higher salary than *he*. (NOT: She earns a higher salary than *him*. This sentence compares a salary and a person.)

Avoid double comparisons. For example, do not use *more* or *less* with an adjective formed by adding *er* to the positive degree.

Which of the two routes is *shorter?* (NOT: more shorter OR more short.)

In my opinion, roses are the *prettiest* flowers. (NOT: most prettiest OR most pretty.)

In the following sentences, underline which-ever expression shown in parentheses that correctly completes the sentence.

1. Monday is the (busier, <u>busiest</u>) day of the week for us.

2. Neither of them had anything (farther, <u>further</u>) to say.

3. Who is the (more, <u>most</u>) famous novelist in the country?

4. This room is (squarer, <u>more nearly square</u>) than that one.

5. There were (<u>fewer</u>, lesser) people in the audience than we had expected.

6. We owe (<u>less</u>, littler) than they do.

7. You have more experience than (anybody, <u>anybody else</u>) applying for the position.

8. Of the three reports, yours was the (better, <u>best</u>) one.

9. This is the (most prettiest, most pretty, <u>prettiest</u>) dress in the store.

10. Would you prefer (them, <u>those</u>) pens?

11. Why did she order (these, <u>this</u>) size of envelopes?

12. Your office is (<u>neater</u>, more neater) than mine.

13. Warren is usually (candider, <u>more candid</u>) than Marty.

14. This train is (<u>slow</u>, slower, slowest).

15. This package weighs the (littlest, <u>least</u>) of all that I have handled today.

16. This container holds a (littler, <u>lesser</u>) amount than that one.

Study Guide 13

Study the following groups of words, noting the difference in meaning between those in each group. Also note the example sentences.

1. adverse — an adjective—opposite or unfavorable
   averse — an adjective—disinclined

   The medicine produced an *adverse* reaction.
   Ed may be *averse* to receiving criticism.

2. biannual — an adjective—twice a year
   biennial — an adjective—every other year

   This is the first of the *biannual* reports to be issued this year.

   We attended the *biennial* conference last year, but we do not plan to attend next year.

3. capital — an adjective—main, chief; a noun—wealth, seat of government
   capitol — a noun—building in which a state legislature meets
   Capitol — a noun—building in which the United States Congress meets

   Controlling expenses is of *capital* importance.
   What is the *capital* of Vermont?
   While in Albany, we visited the *capitol*.
   Have you visited the *Capitol* in Washington, D.C.?

4. complementary — an adjective—completing, contrasting
   complimentary — an adjective—favorable, free

   Bill sent me a *complimentary* copy.
   Is green a *complementary* color of red?

5. credible — an adjective—believable
   creditable — an adjective—praiseworthy

   Each of them gave a *credible* report.
   Yours is a *creditable* achievement.

6. elicit — a verb—to draw forth
   illicit — an adjective—illegal

   We were unable to *elicit* a satisfactory response.
   It was considered to be an *illicit* arrangement.

7. eligible — an adjective—qualified
   illegible — an adjective—unreadable

   All *eligible* employees should participate.
   The signature on that letter is *illegible*.

8. eminent — an adjective—prominent
   imminent — an adjective—impending

   Both of them are *eminent* scientists.
   The formal announcement of the merger of the firms is *imminent*.

9. **famous** an adjective—widely and favorably known

   notorious an adjective—widely and unfavorably known

   prominent an adjective—leading, conspicuous

   Albert Einstein was, of course, a *famous* scientist.
   Al Capone was a *notorious* criminal.
   A *prominent* political leader spoke at the dinner.

10. **few** an adjective—refers to number

    less an adjective—refers to amount or quantity

    We have received only a *few* suggestions.
    There is *less* work to do than we thought.

11. **fiscal** an adjective—pertaining to financial matters

    physical an adjective—perceptible to the senses, relating to the body or to material things

    The company's *fiscal* year begins July 1.
    Each must pass a *physical* examination.

12. **human** an adjective—of people

    humane an adjective—benevolent, sympathetic, compassionate, considerate

    Some animals exhibit almost *human* behavior.
    The prisoners received *humane* treatment.

13. **liable** an adjective—responsible, obligated

    libel a verb—to defame; a noun—a written defamatory statement

    likely an adjective—probable

    Which of the drivers will be held *liable*?
    Neither would intentionally *libel* anyone.
    Two mentioned in the article sued for *libel*.
    The prices of those products are *likely* to rise.

14. **miner** a noun—worker in a mine

    minor an adjective—small, unimportant; a noun—person under legal age

    The *miner* entered the shaft of the coal mine.
    I was able to find only one or two *minor* errors.
    No *minor* will be admitted.

15. **passed** a verb—past tense of *pass*

    past an adjective—former, previous; a preposition—after, beyond; a noun—time gone by

    The two weeks *passed* very quickly.
    Were you in Des Moines this *past* month?
    Did you go *past* their store this morning?
    It happened sometime in the *past*.

16. **personal** an adjective—of a person

    personnel a noun—employees

    What is your *personal* opinion of the policy?
    How many sales *personnel* are there?

17. **principal** an adjective—main; a noun—head of a school, sum of money

    principle a noun—rule or truth

    What was his *principal* reason for resigning?
    Who is the *principal* of that school?
    The *principal* of your account will increase.
    She spoke about one *principle* of economics.

18. **quiet** an adjective—still, calm

    quite an adverb—wholly, considerably

    quit a verb—to stop, leave

    Roger needs a *quiet* place to work.
    You are *quite* right about the matter.
    Jim *quit* his job yesterday.

19. **stationary** an adjective—fixed, unchanging

    stationery a noun—materials for writing

    The machine is supposed to remain *stationary*.
    Almost all companies use letterhead *stationery*.

20. **to** a preposition—toward

    too an adverb—more than enough

    two an adjective—one plus one; a noun—a couple

    Take the deposit *to* the bank before noon.
    Some spend *too* much time on little things.
    Two people are needed to do that work.
    The *two* of them will be here this afternoon.

ASSIGNMENT: Complete the Unit 13 Worksheet on pages 101–102.

UNIT 13

Adjectives

WORKSHEET

 A Before each expression write *a* or *an*, whichever is correct.

1. __an__ article
2. __a__ billboard
3. __a__ corporal
4. __an__ idea
5. __an__ expressway

6. __a__ highway
7. __an__ ocean
8. __a__ uniform
9. __an__ hour
10. __a__ hybrid

11. __an__ underwriter
12. __an__ MBA degree
13. __a__ one-time offer
14. __an__ 8 a.m. meeting
15. __a__ CBS reporter

16. __an__ official
17. __an__ account
18. __an__ honor
19. __a__ package
20. __an__ item

 B Supply the adjective that refers to each of the following places. If necessary, consult the dictionary.

1. Mexico __Mexican__ restaurant
2. Italy __Italian__ opera
3. France __French__ perfume
4. Portugal __Portuguese__ language
5. Germany __German__ scientist

6. Norway __Norwegian__ ship
7. Japan __Japanese__ custom
8. Peru __Peruvian__ gold
9. Greece __Greek__ salad
10. Denmark __Danish__ pastry

 C In the space provided, write the correct comparative or superlative form of the adjective shown in parentheses.

1. This machine is (heavy) than that one.
2. You are (tall) than I.
3. She is (competent) than either of them.
4. Is Alaska the (large) of the 50 states?
5. The groom was (nervous) than the bride.
6. It is the (expensive) car made today.
7. Who has the (easy) job in the company?
8. Which of those two machines is (new)?
9. Your report is (complete) than his or mine.
10. Which of the three companies has the (few) employees?

1. heavier
2. taller
3. more competent OR less competent
4. largest
5. less nervous OR more nervous
6. least expensive OR most expensive
7. easiest
8. newer
9. less nearly complete OR more nearly complete
10. fewest

D In these sentences, underline each error in the use of adjectives; then write the correct form in the space provided. If a sentence is correct, write *OK*.

1. Pat would be a better manager than <u>anyone</u>.
2. This chain looks <u>expensiver</u> than that one.
3. It was the <u>worse</u> fire anyone had ever seen.
4. She thinks it was the most difficult decision she has ever made.
5. He has the <u>most</u> neatest desk in the entire office.

1. _anyone else_
2. _more expensive_
3. _worst_
4. _OK_
5. _neatest_

E In each of the following sentences, select whichever term shown in parentheses is correct; then write it in the space provided.

1. She is a (passed, past) president of the association.
2. It is (liable, libel, likely) to rain today.
3. The skaters decided the ice on the lake was (to, too, two) thin.
4. Isn't this machine supposed to be (stationary, stationery)?
5. When does your company's (fiscal, physical) year begin?
6. Which of (them, those) brands of soap is most popular?
7. Whom do you consider to be the most (eminent, imminent) person in the country today?
8. Are you an (eligible, illegible) bachelor?
9. The patient had an (adverse, averse) reaction to the medication.
10. Our (biannual, biennial) reports are issued in January and July.
11. The company hired a new (personal, personnel) manager.
12. The other driver was held (liable, libel, likely) for the accident.
13. It was a very (miner, minor) mistake.
14. There were (fewer, lesser) answers than questions.
15. Pets should be treated in a (human, humane) manner.
16. Everyone seemed to be aware of the (elicit, illicit) arrangement.
17. Each of them had a (credible, creditable) excuse for staying home.
18. Are you (quiet, quite) certain the office will be closed Monday?
19. Patrick Henry was a (famous, notorious) speaker and politician.
20. Their departure is (eminent, imminent).

1. _past_
2. _likely_
3. _too_
4. _stationary_
5. _fiscal_
6. _those_
7. _eminent_
8. _eligible_
9. _adverse_
10. _biannual_
11. _personnel_
12. _liable_
13. _minor_
14. _fewer_
15. _humane_
16. _illicit_
17. _credible_
18. _quite_
19. _famous_
20. _imminent_

F Insert hyphens wherever they should be placed in each of the following phrases.

1. solidly built homes
2. up-to-the-minute news
3. neatly wrapped package
4. quarterly sales report
5. city-owned land

6. well-balanced diet
7. easy-to-understand directions
8. mid-September sale
9. friendly-looking person
10. high-priced merchandise

Adverbs

FUNCTION OF ADVERBS

An **adverb** modifies a verb, an adjective, or another adverb. Adverbs answer these questions: *How? When? Where? Why? To what extent or degree?* Note how the use of adverbs in the following sentences helps to make the meaning of the words they modify more precise.

> She speaks *rapidly.* (*Rapidly* modifies the verb *speaks;* it tells how.)
>
> Your order was shipped *yesterday.* (*Yesterday* modifies *was shipped;* it tells when.)
>
> The visitors were waiting *downstairs.* (*Downstairs* modifies *were waiting;* it tells where.)
>
> Both were *extremely* cooperative. (*Extremely* modifies the adjective *cooperative;* it tells to what extent or degree.)

Phrases and dependent clauses often function as adverbs that tell why.

> Mrs. Lane applied for a loan *because she would like to buy a new car.* (This dependent clause modifies the verb *applied.)*
>
> He resigned *to obtain a better job.* (This infinitive phrase modifies the verb *resigned.)*
>
> We stayed *for several reasons.* (This prepositional phrase modifies the verb *stayed.)*

Adverbs may also modify infinitives, participles, and gerunds; for example:

> We are planning to leave *early.* (*Early* modifies the infinitive *to leave;* it tells when.)
>
> *Carefully* analyzing the data, Miss McBride discovered four errors. (*Carefully* modifies the present participle *analyzing;* it tells how.)
>
> We must follow these *recently* published regulations. (*Recently* modifies the past participle *published,* which functions as an adjective modifying *regulations.)*
>
> Thank you for waiting *patiently.* (*Patiently* modifies the gerund *waiting,* which is the object of the preposition *for.)*

Such words as *too, quite,* and *very* always function as adverbs. However, many adverbs are formed by adding *ly* to adjectives and participles.

ADJECTIVES:	true	sincere	casual
ADVERBS:	truly	sincerely	casually
PARTICIPLES:	convincing	exceeding	supposed
ADVERBS:	convincingly	exceedingly	supposedly

COMPARISON OF ADVERBS

The forms used to show comparison of adverbs are similar to those used to show comparison of adjectives. The **positive degree** is used when no comparison is being made. The **comparative degree** is used when two things are being compared; the **superlative degree,** when three or more things are being compared.

> I left *early.* (No comparison is being made; the positive degree is used.)
>
> You left *earlier* than I. (The time you left is compared with the time I left; therefore, the comparative degree is used. Note that the verb *left* is understood, not stated, with the subject *I.)*
>
> Of the entire staff, Katie left *earliest.* (The time Katie left is compared with the time several people left; therefore, the superlative degree is used.)

Use of the Endings *er* and *est.* The comparative degree of some short words used as adverbs is formed by adding *er* to the positive degree. The superlative degree is formed by adding *est* to the positive degree.

POSITIVE	COMPARATIVE	SUPERLATIVE
fast	faster	fastest
soon	sooner	soonest

Use of *More* or *Less* and *Most* or *Least.* The comparative degree of most adverbs is formed with *more* or *less.* The superlative degree is formed with *most* or *least.*

POSITIVE	COMPARATIVE	SUPERLATIVE
calmly	more calmly less calmly	most calmly least calmly
efficiently	more efficiently less efficiently	most efficiently least efficiently
quickly	more quickly less quickly	most quickly least quickly

Adverbs With Irregular Degree Forms. A number of words used as adverbs have irregular forms in the comparative and the superlative degrees. Many of these words may also be used as adjectives.

POSITIVE	COMPARATIVE	SUPERLATIVE
badly	worse	worst
far *(distance)*	farther	farthest
far *(degree)*	further	furthest
ill	worse	worst
little	less	least
much	more	most
well	better	best

Absolute Adverbs. Like absolute adjectives, ***absolute adverbs*** cannot logically be compared because of their meanings. The following are some examples.

always	forever	sometimes
annually	never	twice
basically	partly	universally

However, some absolute adverbs are commonly used with such adverbs as *more, less, most, least, almost, quite,* and similar words in comparisons.

> Mark *almost always* pays his bills promptly.
> The report is *not quite* complete.

Implied Comparisons. Adverbs such as *very, rather, too,* and *exceedingly* are often used with adjectives or other adverbs to intensify meaning. A comparison is implied in such constructions, but it is not as strong as that conveyed by the superlative degree of the adverb.

> The conference room is *rather small.*
> The case was not presented *too convincingly.*

WORDS USED AS ADJECTIVES AND AS ADVERBS

The same form of some words—*fast, first, ill, last,* and *well,* for example—may be used as an adjective or as an adverb. When such words modify nouns or pronouns, they are adjectives. When they modify verbs, adjectives, or other adverbs, they are adverbs.

> Please notify your supervisor *first. (First* is an adverb modifying the verb *notify.)*
>
> When was the *first* edition published? *(First* is an adjective modifying the noun *edition.)*
>
> Bernice presented her proposal very *well. (Well* is an adverb modifying the verb *presented.)*
>
> George doesn't look *well. (Well* refers to health and functions as an adjective modifying the subject, *George.)*

If the modifier refers to and describes the subject, use an adjective. If it explains the action expressed by a verb, use an adverb.

> Their reaction was *immediate.* (Adjective.)
> They reacted *immediately.* (Adverb.)
> Your description was *accurate.* (Adjective.)
> You described the article *accurately.* (Adverb.)

Adverbs are used when verbs pertaining to sight, sound, touch, taste, and smell express the action of the subject. Adjectives are used when such verbs refer to the condition of the subject.

> The cake tasted *delicious.* (Adjective.)
> We tasted the cake *immediately.* (Adverb.)
> Everything looked *different* to him. (Adjective.)
> He looked at everything *differently.* (Adverb.)

Spot Check 1

Decide which term shown in parentheses is correct; then underline it.

1. Carl said that he feels (good, well) about the settlement.

2. I was sitting (farther, further) from the stage than you were.

3. Some of us were unable to see the performers (clear, clearly).

4. Of the three plans, which one was considered (more, most) favorably?

5. She takes her responsibilities (seriouser, more seriously) than anyone else I know.

6. Everything on the menu sounds (appealing, appealingly) to me.

7. Do you visit the Chicago office (more, most) frequently than Lauren does?

8. Some machines operate more (economical, economically) than others.

9. One or two of the children behaved (bad, badly).

10. The supervisor stared (icy, icily) at the intruder.

11. One of our representatives will call you (short, shortly).

12. The alarm was heard (immediate, immediately).

13. That perfume smells (sweet, sweetly).

14. Some thought the birds were chirping (sweet, sweetly).

15. The stove felt (warm, warmly).

ADVERBS WITH TWO FORMS

Some words have two adverbial forms—one that ends in *ly* and one that does not. The form that does not end in *ly* may also be used as an adjective.

cheap, cheaply	fair, fairly	hard, hardly
direct, directly	deep, deeply	slow, slowly

In some instances, either form of the word may be used; for example:

Would you please drive *slow?* (OR: slowly.)
Why do they walk so *slowly?* (OR: slow.)

In other instances, the choice of form depends on the context in which the word is used. Note the following expressions and the adverb in each.

buy *cheap*	operates *cheaply*
ship *direct*	speak *directly* to
play *fair*	treat *fairly*
go *slow* OR *slowly*	proceed *slowly*
dig *deep*	think *deeply*

THE USE OF ADVERBS

Double Negatives. Do not use two negatives to express a single negative idea: one negative cancels the other and makes the idea positive. Such words as *hardly, only, not, scarcely,* and *never* are negative in meaning and should not be used with other negative words.

INCORRECT:	We *don't* use *none* of their products.
CORRECT:	We *don't* use *any* of their products.
CORRECT:	We *use none* of their products.
INCORRECT:	We *never* hear from them *no* more.
CORRECT:	We *never* hear from them *any* more.
CORRECT:	We *never* hear from them.
INCORRECT:	It *won't* take *but* a few minutes.
CORRECT:	It will take *but* a few minutes.
CORRECT:	It will take *only* a few minutes.
INCORRECT:	We *couldn't hardly* believe our eyes.
CORRECT:	We *could hardly* believe our eyes.

Unnecessary Adverbs. Avoid the use of adverbs that express a meaning already conveyed by the verb.

She has just returned from Hawaii. (NOT: returned back from.)

The members know they must cooperate. (NOT: cooperate together.)

Misplaced Adverbs. Place adverbs as close as possible to the words they modify so that the meaning of the sentence will be unmistakably clear. The adverbs *almost, nearly, scarcely, only,* and *too* require special care in this respect. Note the differences in meaning brought about by changing the position of *nearly* and *too* in the following sentences.

Nearly every driver missed the stop sign.
Every driver *nearly* missed the stop sign.
Most of the sales representatives are young *too.*
Most of the sales representatives are *too* young.
Most of the sales representatives, *too,* are young.
Too, most of the sales representatives are young.

Inappropriate Choice of Adverb. Be especially careful in the use of the adverbs illustrated in the following sentences.

I would *rather* work for you than them. (NOT: sooner.)
She writes *well.* (NOT: good.)
Please send us your payment. (NOT: Kindly.)
We couldn't find the letter *anywhere.* (NOT: anywheres.)
We looked *everywhere.* (NOT: everywheres.)
They are *nowhere* near a settlement. (NOT: nowheres.)

Adverbs Containing *All.* Note the correct spelling of words compounded with the word *all.*

Almost everyone has received a copy.
We were *all most* happy to see you again.
They had *already* paid for their tickets.
The memos are *all ready* to be signed.
Such a gift seems *altogether* inappropriate.
We were *all together* last weekend.
Your answers are *all right.*

Spot Check 2

Decide which term shown in parentheses is correct; then underline it.

1. (Kindly, Please) notify each of the others.

2. Mr. Alioto treats everyone (fair, fairly).

3. We (could, couldn't) hardly see the stage.

4. Do you know where they (went, went to)?

5. They weren't (anywhere, anywheres) near the scene of the accident.

6. Would you (rather, sooner) drive yourself?

7. We were (all ready, already) and waiting for them.

8. The twins are (all most, almost) a year old.

9. I have been looking (everywhere, everywheres) for a replacement.

10. Haven't you (ever, never) won anything?

Study Guide 14

A. Study the following groups of words, noting the difference in meaning between the words in each group. Also note the example sentences.

1. almost   an adverb—nearly
   most   an adjective, an adverb, or a pronoun—nearly all, greatest degree

   It is *almost* time to leave.
   Most cars use unleaded gasoline.
   What is the *most* economical transportation?
   Most of us watch television every day.

2. altogether   an adverb—entirely, wholly
   all together   *all,* a pronoun—every one; *together,* an adverb—in a group

   Their prices are *altogether* too high.
   The regional managers were *all together* in July.

3. farther   an adverb—pertaining to actual distance, more remote
   further   an adverb—additionally, to a greater degree, to a greater extent

   The factory is a few miles *farther* east of here.
   Further, companies have social responsibilities.
   The manager wants to study the proposal *further.*

4. formally   an adverb—in a formal manner
   formerly   an adverb—previously

   The plan was *formally* announced last week.
   The store was *formerly* in the Gleason Mall.

5. maybe   an adverb—perhaps
   may be   a verb phrase

   Maybe you will be able to obtain a refund.
   This *may be* the opportunity of a lifetime.

6. real   an adjective—genuine
   really   an adverb—actually

   Are you certain this is a *real* diamond?
   What do you think their objective *really* is?

7. scarce   an adjective—not plentiful
   scarcely   an adverb—almost not, certainly not, or probably not

   Spare parts for some old equipment are *scarce.*
   There was *scarcely* enough paint to finish this room.

8. sometime   an adverb—at one time, indefinite time
   some time   *some,* an adjective—an indefinite amount or quantity; *time,* a noun—a period of time

   The meeting will be *sometime* next month.
   It will take *some time* to gather that data.

9. sure   an adjective—confident, certain
   surely   an adverb—certainly

   Are you *sure* this is the correct address?
   Surely you can find someone to take your place.

B. In the following sentences, note how changing the position of the adverb changes meaning.

1. *Only* two firms tested the new product. (No other firms tested it.)
   Two firms *only* tested the new product. (They did nothing else.)
   Two firms tested *only* the new product. (They tested no other product.)

   Two firms tested the new product *only.* (They tested no other product.)

2. I cannot type rapidly and accurately *too.*
   I cannot type *too* rapidly and accurately.
   I, *too,* cannot type rapidly and accurately.
   Too, I cannot type rapidly and accurately.

> **ASSIGNMENT: Complete the Unit 14 Worksheet on pages 107–108.**

UNIT 14
Adverbs

WORKSHEET

 A **Which of the forms shown in parentheses is correct? Write it in the space provided.**

1. I hope you will be able to visit our new headquarters (some time, sometime) soon.

1. __sometime__

2. How much (farther, further) will you have to travel each day?

2. __farther__

3. The roof was damaged quite (bad, badly).

3. __badly__

4. (Almost, Most) everyone agrees with you.

4. __Almost__

5. We don't need (any, none) of those items.

5. __any__

6. Is absenteeism (real, really) a major problem in offices?

6. __really__

7. The manager is hardly (ever, never) out of the office.

7. __ever__

8. Which of the three brands is (less, least) expensive?

8. __least__

9. Would you (rather, sooner) leave in the morning than this evening?

9. __rather__

10. Where was he (formally, formerly) employed?

10. __formerly__

11. We think there is scarcely (anything, nothing) left to do.

11. __anything__

12. We are (real, very) sorry about the delay.

12. __very__

13. This machine is (some, somewhat) different from the one I used previously.

13. __somewhat__

14. These shoes are more comfortable than (any, any others) I have ever worn.

14. __any others__

15. Most people take their responsibilities (serious, seriously).

15. __seriously__

16. (Kindly, Please) notify the other members of the committee.

16. __Please__

17. He wishes he had answered some of the questions (different, differently).

17. __differently__

18. We searched (everywhere, everywheres) for the original copy of the contract.

18. __everywhere__

19. Our supplier very (near, nearly) ran out of stock.

19. __nearly__

20. The new cashier has made hardly (any, no) mistakes.

20. __any__

21. The buzzer rang (loud, loudly).

21. __loudly__

22. Both of them felt (bad, badly).

22. __bad__

23. We left as (quick, quickly) as we could.

23. quickly

24. Do you think this jacket fits (good, well)?

24. well

25. When do you expect to (return, return back) to work?

25. return

26. Neither of them had anything (farther, further) to say about the incident.

26. further

27. She responded (cautiouser, more cautiously) than anyone else.

27. more cautiously

28. Everyone invited to the party was asked to dress (casual, casually).

28. casually

29. The storm ended (sudden, suddenly).

29. suddenly

30. Which of the two ads is (more, most) likely to draw a favorable response?

30. more

31. Applicants who appear (confident, confidently) favorably impress us.

31. confident

32. This watch always runs (slow, slowly).

32. slow

33. Did the play end (different, differently) from what you expected?

33. differently

34. The members of the board (meet, meet together) once a month.

34. meet

35. Are these reports (all ready, already) to distribute?

35. all ready

36. (May be, Maybe) we should reconsider their offer.

36. Maybe

37. She said that helping others makes her feel (good, well).

37. good

38. They (sure, surely) were surprised.

38. surely

39. Ted said that he has not been feeling (good, well).

39. well

40. Does your supervisor treat everyone (fair, fairly)?

40. fairly

B Indicate the correct position of each adverb shown in parentheses. In the space provided, write the adverb and the word which should follow it. Note the example.

0. We are ready to submit the report. (almost)

0. almost ready

1. Jane has been interviewed for the job. (only) *(No one else has been interviewed.)*

1. Only Jane

2. Ms. Lange drafted the report yesterday. (only) *(She did nothing but draft the report.)*

2. only drafted

3. The check was mailed two days ago. (only) *(Emphasize the time it was mailed.)*

3. only two

4. Mr. Reeves suggested some changes. (merely) *(He did nothing else.)*

4. merely suggested

5. We arrived late for the meeting. (too) *(The meeting had already ended.)*

5. too late

6. We arrived late for the luncheon. (too) *(Indicate others were late.)*

6. ,too, arrived

7. Margaret reviewed part of the report. (only) *(Not the entire report.)*

7. only part

8. Do you remember making that request? (ever)

8. ever making

9. Everyone is ready. (almost) *(Not every person.)*

9. Almost everyone

10. Lee has an MBA, doesn't she? (too) *(She has another degree.)*

10. too, doesn't

PREPOSITIONS

A **preposition** is a connecting word used before a noun or a pronoun, known as the **object of the preposition,** to show the relationship of that object to some other word in the sentence. Commonly used prepositions include the following:

about	below	in	to
above	beneath	into	toward
across	beside	like	under
after	between	of	underneath
against	by	off	until
among	down	on	up
around	during	over	upon
at	except	past	with
before	for	through	within
behind	from	throughout	without

PREPOSITIONAL PHRASES

A **prepositional phrase** is a group of words consisting of a preposition, a noun or pronoun object, and the modifiers (if any) of the object. Prepositional phrases usually function as adjectives and adverbs.

The meeting *with their attorney* has been postponed. (*With* connects *attorney* to *meeting.* The phrase *with their attorney* functions as an adjective modifying the verbal noun *meeting.*)

Both letters were delivered *to him.* (*To him* functions as an adverb modifying the verb phrase *were delivered.*)

Occasionally, a prepositional phrase may be used as a noun, as in the following sentences.

Before noon is the best time to call the New York office. (*Before noon* functions as a noun; the phrase is the subject of the verb *is.*)

The only way to reach some parts of Alaska is *by plane.* (*By plane* functions as a noun. It further identifies the subject *way* and is the predicate nominative.)

Such expressions as *by means of, in spite of, in addition to,* and *in accordance with* are sometimes considered simple prepositions. Actually, each preposition in these expressions has its own object and is therefore part of a separate prepositional phrase.

The airport remained open *in spite of the heavy snowstorm.* (The object of the preposition *in* is the noun *spite;* the object of the preposition *of* is the noun *snowstorm.*)

We need two copies *in addition to this one. (Addition* is the object of *in; one* is the object of the preposition *to.*)

When *to* is followed by a noun or a pronoun, it is a preposition. However, when *to* is followed by a verb, it is part of an infinitive.

PREPOSITIONAL PHRASE:
Ms. Helson has gone *to Madison.*

PREPOSITIONAL PHRASE:
Did you send a copy *to him?*

INFINITIVE:
Do you plan *to rent* an apartment?

PRONOUNS AS OBJECTS OF PREPOSITIONS

Since some pronouns change form to indicate case, be sure to use the proper form of the pronoun—the objective case—as the object of a preposition. Using the incorrect form of a pronoun is a common error, especially when the preposition has a compound object.

These forms will need to be filled out *by you and him* tomorrow.

Every requisition must be submitted *to her or Mr. Lindsay* for approval.

Employees *like you and them* deserve special and frequent recognition.

What are the names of the two clients *with whom* you had lunch?

If she is not there, please leave a message *with whoever answers the telephone.* (*Whoever* is correct because it is the subject of the verb *answers.* The complete clause—*whoever answers the telephone*—is the object of the preposition *with.*)

When the pronoun is separated from the preposition, it is very easy to use the incorrect form. In such questions as those that follow, *who* is often used in place of *whom* in speech; however, *who* is not considered acceptable in business writing.

Whom are you looking for? *(Whom* is the object of *for.)*

Whom did you speak to? *(Whom* is the object of *to.)*

Spot Check 1

Underline whichever word shown in parentheses correctly completes the sentence.

1. (Who, <u>Whom</u>) did you address the letter to?

2. Were there any messages for Janet or (I, <u>me</u>)?

3. These copies are for (<u>whoever</u>, whomever) needs them.

4. Kevin said that you were planning to go with (<u>us</u>, we).

5. Who was there besides Dave and (<u>her</u>, she)?

6. Mrs. Olivera was sitting two rows behind (<u>us</u>, we) secretaries.

7. Everyone except Irene and (he, <u>him</u>) attended the meeting.

8. (Who, <u>Whom</u>) will you be working with tomorrow?

9. These seats are reserved for you and (<u>me</u>, myself).

10. He said that he ran after (<u>them</u>, they).

IDIOMATIC USE OF PREPOSITIONS

Prepositions are used with other parts of speech in certain idiomatic expressions. If you are not certain about the correct preposition to use in such an expression, consult a dictionary or a handbook on English usage. Note the prepositions used in the following sentences.

All the parts were manufactured *according to* specifications.

Delivery was made *in accordance with* his instructions.

They *agree with* you and him.

I *agree to* the terms stated in your letter.

Most people *agree on* the need to conserve natural resources.

Is postponing the meeting until next Monday *agreeable to* you?

I must *apologize* to both of them.

Did he *apologize for* his rudeness?

When did you *apply for* the job?

You may want to *apply to* some other company.

We usually *buy from* several suppliers. (NOT: buy off OR buy off of.)

She *compared* the temperature in my office *to* that of an oven.

The jurors *compared* one witness's testimony *with* that of another witness.

Our office is *convenient to* public transportation.

Would it be *convenient for* you to meet with us next Friday morning?

Mr. Lawson *departed for* Canada this morning. (NOT: departed to.)

Does your plan *differ from* hers?

We *differ with* them over the procedures that should be followed.

You and I may *differ about* various issues.

Our proposal is *different from* theirs. (NOT: different than.)

In *regard to* the new plan, residents are divided.

They showed little *regard for* our opinions.

A number of prepositions require special attention, including those discussed and illustrated below.

***Among* and *Between*.** Ordinarily, *between* is used when speaking of two persons, things, or groups; *among* is used when speaking of more than two.

The reward should be divided equally *between* you and her.

Our new distribution center will be located *between* Racine and Kenosha.

The proceeds were divided *among* three charitable organizations.

A reprint of the article was circulated *among* the staff.

***Beside* and *Besides*.** *Beside* refers to position or place and means "by the side of; nearby." *Besides* means "in addition to; other than."

The carton was sitting *beside* my desk.

Did anyone *besides* Herman, Mary, and you suggest any changes?

Besides Charles, two other bankers will address the group.

***Except* and *Accept*.** As a preposition, *except* means "excluding; other than." *Accept* is a verb meaning "to receive."

Everyone *except* Margaret attended the seminar.

I *accept* your offer to assist me.

***In, Into,* and *In To*.** *In* indicates being within or moving within the boundaries of a place. *Into* is used with verbs of motion to denote entrance or change of form. When *in* and *to* are written as separate words, *in* may be part of a verb phrase or an adverb and *to* may be part of an infinitive or a preposition.

> Mrs. Rader is *in* the conference room.
>
> The visitors are waiting *in* the lobby.
>
> The visitors have just gone *into* the manager's office.
>
> The play is divided *into* three acts.
>
> Has anyone been *in* to see you this morning? *(In is an adverb; to is part of the infinitive to see.)*
>
> The purse was turned *in* to a security officer. *(In is part of the verb phrase turned in; to is part of the prepositional phrase to a security officer.)*

Like and As. The preposition *like* takes an object; it should not be used as a conjunction to join clauses. If a conjunction is needed, use *as, as if,* or *as though* instead of *like.*

> Your briefcase looks *like* mine.
> I spelled his name exactly *as* he does. (NOT: like.)
> It looks *as if* it may rain. (NOT: like.)

As may also be used as a preposition.

> A car may be used *as* collateral for a loan.
> Patrick has been hired *as* a consultant.

Per, A, and An. The preposition *per* is used before Latin nouns and in such expressions as *55 miles per hour* and *30 miles per gallon.* Whenever possible, use *a* or *an* instead of *per.* Never use *per* to mean "according to" or "in accordance with"; for example, do *not* say "per your instructions."

> Each attendee will receive a *per diem* allowance of $125.
>
> The speed limit within this city is 30 miles *per* hour. (OR: 30 miles an hour.)
>
> They sold their farm for $850 *an* acre. (NOT: per acre.)

To, Too, and Two. *To* may be either a preposition or a part of an infinitive; *too* is an adverb; *two* may be a noun, a pronoun, or an adjective.

PREPOSITION:
To whom did you speak?

PART OF INFINITIVE:
When are they planning *to leave?*

ADVERB:
Do you think their prices are *too* high?

ADJECTIVE:
This file cabinet has *two* empty drawers.

PRONOUN:
We need *two,* I believe.

NOUN:
The number *two* may be written several different ways.

Spot Check 2

Underline whichever word shown in parentheses correctly completes the sentence.

1. Do you buy supplies (from, off) that company?

2. Are your duties different (from, than) the ones you expected to have?

3. What time would be most convenient (for, to) you?

4. Does everyone agree (on, to) the need for greater productivity?

5. She walked through the door and (in, in to, into) her office.

6. Perhaps we should store them (in, in to, into) smaller containers.

7. Please (accept, except) our apologies.

8. The starting salary is $350 (a, per) week.

9. Do you think that salary is (to, too, two) low?

10. Will they divide the reward (between, among) the two of them?

11. The merchandise was shipped (in accordance with, per) their instructions.

12. It looked (as though, like) a hurricane had hit the office.

13. The entertainers left the stage and walked (among, between) the audience.

14. Are the employees divided in (regard, regards) to the new procedures?

15. Has anyone (beside, besides) you and him been asked to work overtime?

SPECIAL SUGGESTIONS

Placement. A preposition ordinarily is placed before its object; however, for emphasis, fluency, or natural order, it may be desirable to place the preposition at the end of the sentence.

> Is that what you asked *for?*
> This is something you can be proud *of.*
> What are you thinking *about?*
> How many can we count *on?*

Essential Prepositions. Do not omit necessary prepositions. Be especially careful when two or more prepositions have the same object, as in the third example that follows.

> *Of* what use is that old machine? (NOT: What use is that old machine?)
>
> What style *of* furniture do you prefer? (NOT: What style furniture do you prefer?)
>
> We have no need *for* or interest *in* a policy of that kind. (NOT: We have no need or interest in a policy of that kind.)

Unnecessary Prepositions. Do not use prepositions unnecessarily. Study the following examples carefully.

> Where are you going next? (NOT: *going to* next?)
>
> Where is Ms. Harris? (NOT: Where is Ms. Harris *at?*)
>
> Some folders fell off the desk. (NOT: fell off *of* the desk.)
>
> We could not help laughing. (NOT: help *from* laughing.)
>
> They will be here at 1 o'clock. OR: They will be here about 1 o'clock. (NOT: They will be here *at about* 1 o'clock.)

Study Guide 15

A. Study the italicized phrases to determine how they are used. Identify the word or words each prepositional phrase modifies.

1. The new warehouse is located *between Rockford and Beloit.*
2. You will find the contract *among those papers.*
3. What country has the highest *per capita* income?
4. Is anyone *besides Dr. Windham* scheduled to speak?
5. We drove *through Salt Lake City* on our way to Phoenix.
6. Everyone *except Nellie* plans to work overtime this week.
7. Linda and Lisa sat *beside each other* at the stockholders' meeting.
8. This copy definitely is different *from the one* you have.
9. They cannot agree *on how much* to increase the sales tax.
10. All pay increases are retroactive *to July 1.*
11. The full amount must be paid *within 10 days.*
12. The new mall will be built *outside the city limits.*
13. Please write your name and address *below hers.*
14. Both of them seem to be *under a great deal of pressure.*
15. Everyone *but him and me* has been asked to sign the petition.
16. Her job requires her to travel *throughout the state.*

B. Some words must be followed by certain prepositions to convey the desired meaning. In the following sentences, note how the meaning changes when the preposition changes.

1. Neither of us is *angry about* what happened. Why are they *angry with* us?
2. Would Monday be more *convenient for* you? The office is *convenient to* a shopping center.
3. The stationery *corresponds to* the sample. Have you *corresponded with* either of them?
4. I may *differ with* him about the changes. We rarely *differ about* ways of reducing expenses. This one *differs* significantly *from* the old one.
5. They should *account for* all contributions. Ms. Devine may have to *account to* Mrs. Diesem.
6. Both of them have *applied to* several companies. Has he *applied for* a marketing position?
7. She seldom *argues with* anyone about anything. He and I *argue about* politics.

> **ASSIGNMENT: Complete the Unit 15 Worksheet on pages 113–114.**

UNIT 15

Prepositions

WORKSHEET

 In the following sentences, draw a line through each unnecessary preposition.

1. I have no idea where they were ~~at~~ yesterday or where they are going ~~to~~ today.

2. If we could open ~~up~~ these windows, we would be able to breathe better.

3. Why did they decide to cancel ~~out~~ at the last minute?

4. We will be returning ~~back~~ to the office ~~at~~ about noon.

5. They thought it would be better for their children if they moved outside ~~of~~ the city.

6. I hope that we will be able to finish ~~up~~ this work before next week.

7. A couple of shelves fell off ~~of~~ the wall because the brackets broke ~~off~~.

8. The ladders were lying ~~up~~ against the wall.

9. Where should I write ~~in~~ my name on this form?

10. If we cross ~~over~~ the street, we will be able to walk in the shade.

 In the following statements, supply any prepositions needed to make the sentences correct. Indicate where the preposition should be inserted, as shown in the example, and write the preposition in the space provided.

0. Was the work done according ∧ specifications? 0. <u>to</u>

1. When was Alice graduated ∧ college? 1. <u>from</u>

2. Were you angry ∧ Ms. Williams? 2. <u>with</u>

3. Is their analysis significantly different ∧ yours? 3. <u>from</u>

4. Do you correspond ∧ either of them frequently? 4. <u>with</u>

5. She looks exactly ∧ her mother. 5. <u>like</u>

6. Is your home convenient ∧ the bus lines? 6. <u>to</u>

7. Do you plan to apply ∧ some other job? 7. <u>for</u>

8. The reduced rate is retroactive ∧ the first of last month. 8. <u>to</u>

9. Is postponing the meeting agreeable ∧ you? 9. <u>to</u>

10. What kind ∧ work interests you most? 10. <u>of</u>

 Examine each italicized prepositional phrase. If it is correct, write *OK*. If it is incorrect, write the preposition that will make it correct.

1. The estate was divided *among the two heirs*. 1. <u>between</u>

2. Isn't the speed limit 65 miles *an hour?*

3. Were you angry *at Don and her* yesterday?

4. I sent an invitation *too every member* of the staff.

5. It depends *up on how much work* we have to do.

6. The driver lost control of the car and ran *in to a tree.*

7. Will it be OK *by you* if we leave later?

8. This computer is different *than that one.*

9. He made several complimentary remarks *to we secretaries.*

10. *Whom* did you wish to speak *to?*

11. We have just entered *in an agreement* with them.

12. She caught *onto the scam* before I did.

13. Why is he always talking *to hisself?*

14. She tells everyone that her niece looks *like she.*

15. Who made the payment is *besides the point.*

16. Was anyone late *beside me?*

17. When did you turn the building pass *into the manager?*

18. We should walk *in the sidewalk* instead of the street.

19. I bought a car *off her* last week.

20. The theft occurred *over the weekend.*

21. Your raise is retroactive *from June 1.*

22. They had no liking *for* or interest *in that suggestion.*

23. The old contract specified interest at the rate of 4 percent *an annum.*

24. The starting salary is $300 *per week.*

25. Everything has been done *accept the final checking.*

2. OK OR per

3. with

4. to

5. upon

6. into

7. with

8. from

9. us secretaries

10. OK

11. into

12. on to

13. himself

14. her

15. beside

16. besides

17. in to

18. on

19. from

20. during

21. to

22. OK

23. per annum OR a year

24. a

25. except

 Write original sentences illustrating the correct use of the following expressions.
(Answers will vary.)

1. agree to

2. agree with

3. apologize for

4. apologize to

5. apply for

6. apply to

7. correspond to

8. correspond with

9. account to

10. account for

1. Did you agree to buying the car from that dealer?

2. Most of us agree with you and George.

3. Did the speaker apologize for arriving late?

4. Both of them should apologize to you.

5. We think you should apply for a position with our company.

6. Does this new directive apply to everyone in the company?

7. The amount received corresponds to the amount promised.

8. How often do you correspond with Ms. Mulholland?

9. We must account to them for the quality of our work.

10. No one was able to account for some of the missing stock.

Conjunctions

CONNECTING WORDS

A *conjunction* connects two or more words, phrases, or clauses, as illustrated in the following sentences.

Ms. Young is efficient *and* cooperative. (*And* connects two adjectives.)

Please ask him *or* her to call me. (*Or* connects two pronouns.)

The work may be done at home *or* in the office. (*Or* connects two prepositional phrases.)

If you are interested in that position *and* if you have the necessary qualifications, you should apply for it. (*And* joins two dependent clauses.)

The meeting was scheduled for this morning, *but* it has been postponed until next Wednesday. (*But* connects two independent clauses—clauses that could stand by themselves as separate sentences.)

Unlike a preposition, which is also a connecting word, a conjunction does not combine with a noun or pronoun object to form a modifying phrase. Also, unlike prepositions, conjunctions may be divided into various classes: *coordinate, correlative,* and *subordinate.* Each of these classes of conjunctions is fully discussed and illustrated here.

COORDINATE CONJUNCTIONS

Coordinate conjunctions are those that connect words, phrases, and clauses of equal grammatical rank and construction. Note the use of *and, but, or,* and *nor* in the following sentences.

The company has offices in Iowa *and* Nebraska. (*And* connects two nouns.)

I was planning to drive to work today, *but* I changed my mind. (*But* connects two independent clauses.)

Would you prefer to buy a car *or* to lease one? (*Or* connects two infinitive phrases.)

The trip was not tiring, *nor* was it boring. (*Nor* connects two independent clauses.)

Use of Coordinate Conjunctions. Coordinate conjunctions must connect elements that are grammatically equal in rank.

INCORRECT: Dale was popular *but* an ineffective manager. (*But* is incorrectly used to connect the adjective *popular* and the noun *manager.*)

CORRECT: Dale was a popular *but* ineffective manager. (*But* is correctly used to connect the adjectives *popular* and *ineffective.*)

Also be sure that the elements joined by a coordinate conjunction are parallel in construction. For example, if one element is an infinitive, the other should be an infinitive; if one is a prepositional phrase, the other should be a prepositional phrase.

INCORRECT: Do you enjoy swimming *or* to ski? (*Or* is incorrectly used to join the gerund *swimming* and the infinitive *to ski.*)

CORRECT: Do you enjoy swimming *or* skiing? (*Or* is correctly used to join the gerunds *swimming* and *skiing.*)

INCORRECT: You will find a laptop computer useful when traveling *and* when you are working at home. (*And* joins a prepositional phrase and a dependent clause.)

CORRECT: You will find a laptop computer useful when you are traveling *and* when you are working at home. (*And* joins two dependent clauses.)

CORRECT: You will find this pocket calculator useful when traveling *and* when working at home. (*And* joins two prepositional phrases.)

However, do not use *and* in place of *to* when an infinitive is required. This incorrect use of *and* frequently occurs when the word immediately preceding it is a verb.

INCORRECT:
Maybe I should try *and* repair it myself.

CORRECT:
Maybe I should try *to* repair it myself.

INCORRECT:
Do you think we should go *and* see them tomorrow?

CORRECT:
Do you think we should go *to* see them tomorrow?

When *but* is used as a preposition, the principles discussed above obviously do not apply.

All the letters *but* this one have been answered.
No one noticed the discrepancy *but* her.

CORRELATIVE CONJUNCTIONS

Correlative conjunctions are coordinate conjunctions used in pairs. The following are commonly used correlative conjunctions. Note that *or* is used with *either* and that *nor* is used with *neither*.

both . . . and
either . . . or
neither . . . nor
not only . . . but also

as . . . as
so . . . as
whether . . . or
whether . . . or not

Both the mayor *and* the governor will attend the ceremony.

We must *either* accept *or* reject their offer without further delay.

Neither she *nor* he was able to meet with us this morning.

You have *not only* the educational qualifications *but also* the practical experience that this job requires.

Please call Mr. Edmonds *as* soon *as* possible.

Use of Correlative Conjunctions. Correlative conjunctions must join elements that are equal in rank and parallel in construction. Consequently, special attention must be given to the connected elements when the parts of the conjunction are far apart.

INCORRECT: We have *neither* ordered desks *nor* chairs for those offices. (This pair of conjunctions joins a verb and a noun.)

CORRECT: We have ordered *neither* desks *nor* chairs for those offices. (The pair of conjunctions joins two nouns.)

INCORRECT: This new machine is *not only* more powerful, *but also* it is less expensive to operate than the old one. (This pair of conjunctions joins an adjective and an independent clause.)

CORRECT: *Not only* is this new machine more powerful, *but also* it is less expensive to operate than the old one. (The pair of conjunctions joins two independent clauses.)

CORRECT: This new machine is *not only* more powerful *but also* less expensive to operate than the old one. (The pair of conjunctions joins two adjectives.)

INCORRECT: The building is *both* modern *and* in a convenient location. (The pair of conjunctions connects an adjective and a prepositional phrase.)

CORRECT: The building is *both* modern *and* conveniently located. (The pair of conjunctions connects an adjective and a participial modifier.)

Although *if* is often used in place of *whether* in highly informal speech and writing, the preferred conjunction is *whether* in an expression such as the one illustrated below.

COLLOQUIAL: Please let me know *if* you will be at the meeting.

PREFERRED: Please let me know whether (OR whether or not) you will be at the meeting.

When *or, nor, either . . . or, neither . . . nor, not only . . . but also,* or *whether . . . or* joins singular subjects, use a singular verb that agrees in person with the subject nearer the verb. Study the following examples carefully.

Neither *she* nor *I am* a member of that organization.

Neither *I* nor *she is* a member of that organization.

Not only *I* but also *each* of them *has* a stake in the outcome.

Not only *each* of them but also *I have* a stake in the outcome.

Does he or *I have* any further obligation to them?

Do I or *anyone else have* any further obligation to them?

The manager wants to know whether *Jane* or *I plan* to attend.

The manager wants to know whether *I* or *Jane plans* to attend.

However, if one of those conjunctions joins a singular subject and a plural subject, use a verb that agrees both in number and in person with the subject nearer the verb. Remember that the pronoun subject *you* always requires a plural verb.

Neither *they* nor *I am planning* to attend.

Neither *I* nor *they are planning* to attend.

Do you or *she* have that responsibility?

Does she or *you* have that responsibility?

I am not sure whether the *chairs* or the *table needs* to be refinished.

I am not sure whether the *table* or the *chairs need* to be refinished.

Ordinarily, subjects joined by *and* or *both . . . and* require a plural verb. However, when *and* joins two singular subjects that name one person or thing, use a singular verb.

She and *I are* members of the committee.

Both *they* and *he have* a responsibility to the company.

Both the *streets* and the *sidewalks need* repairs.

The *vice president* and the *general manager attend* many conventions.

BUT: Our *vice president* and *general manager attends* many conventions.

Franks and *beans is* one of the restaurant's specials on Friday.

BUT: *Franks and beans are served* together in many instances.

SUBORDINATE CONJUNCTIONS

Subordinate conjunctions connect subordinate (dependent) clauses to main clauses. Although a subordinate clause contains a subject and a predicate, it does not make complete sense when it stands by itself; it always functions as an adjective, an adverb, or a noun within a complete sentence. The following are commonly used subordinate conjunctions.

after	before	that	which
although	if	unless	while
because	since	when	where

The car *that* I wanted to buy was too expensive. (*That* connects *I wanted to buy* to the noun *car*. The clause *that I wanted to buy* functions as an adjective.)

Please call me *before* you leave. (*Before* joins *you leave* to the verb *call*. The clause *before you leave* functions as an adverb.)

We have not heard *who* the new manager will be. (*Who the new manager will be* functions as a noun. The entire clause is the direct object of the verb phrase *have heard.)*

Use of Subordinate Conjunctions. Unlike coordinate and correlative conjunctions, subordinate conjunctions do not connect grammatically equal parts of sentences. Thus the previous comments about parallel construction do not apply to the use of subordinate conjunctions.

In many instances, the subordinate conjunction *that* is understood, not stated.

Is this the information *(that)* you need?
Mr. Garcia said *(that)* he applied for the job.

Use *that,* not *when,* to introduce a clause explaining a definite time reference.

It was on Tuesday *that* the merger was announced. (NOT: It was on Tuesday *when* the merger was announced.)

Use *that,* not *where,* to introduce a clause explaining a definite place reference.

Did you read in the newspaper *that* the talks have been called off? (NOT: Did you read in the paper *where* the talks have been called off?)

It was in the first paragraph *that* I noticed the error.

While denotes progressive time, and *when* denotes definite time.

While we were on vacation, several changes were made.

When we returned to the office, we noticed several changes.

Because introduces clauses of reason and is equivalent to *for the reason that.*

They moved to new offices *because* they needed more space.

We arrived an hour late because our flight was delayed in Detroit.

After such words as *reason* or *reason why,* the conjunction *that* should be used rather than *because.*

The reason he was absent was *that* he was ill.
I think the reason why she resigned was *that* she received a better job offer.

When a subordinate conjunction introduces clauses that are widely separated, the conjunction should be repeated.

After the general manager has approved the agreement and *after* the legal department has reviewed and approved it, Ms. Richards will sign it or return it to you for revision.

Do not use *being that* in place of a subordinate conjunction, such as *since.*

Since the premium was not paid on time, the policy lapsed. (NOT: *Being that* the premium was not paid on time, the policy lapsed.)

Such words as *for, since, before,* and *after* may be used as subordinate conjunctions or as prepositions.

PREPOSITION:
Margaret left this message *for* you.

CONJUNCTION:
She left early, *for* she was feeling ill.

PREPOSITION:
We should arrive *before* noon.

CONJUNCTION:
You may get there *before* we do.

PREPOSITION:
I have not heard from them *since* April.

CONJUNCTION:
We have not seen them *since* they were here in April.

In business writing, do not use *like* as a conjunction. Instead, use *as, as if,* or *as though.*

This projector does not work *as* it should. (NOT: This projector does not work *like* it should.)

He and she acted *as though* they were interested in the job. (NOT: He and she acted *like* they were interested in the job.)

The prepositions *except* and *without* cannot be used in place of *unless* to join two clauses. However, they may be used if followed by an object.

We cannot expect to succeed *unless* we diligently apply ourselves. (NOT: *except* or *without.)*

We cannot expect to succeed *without* diligently applying ourselves.

They may decide to leave *without* us.

Bill brought everything he needed to the meeting yesterday afternoon *except* a copy of the contract.

Study Guide 16

A. To make the meaning of a statement absolutely clear, you must use the correct connectives—avoid confusing prepositions with conjunctions. Study the following sentences to note the distinctions that are explained and illustrated.

And expresses addition; *but* expresses opposition and is synonymous with "on the contrary"; *or* indicates an alternative.

1. You have the educational background *and* the experience that this job requires.
2. Ms. Cruz *or* Mr. Richards will make your reservations for you.
3. The meals in that hotel are good *but* expensive.

4. The company offered her a better-paying position, *but* she chose not to accept it.
5. Do you plan to leave on Friday, *or* will you wait until Monday morning?
6. The building has been under construction since last spring, *and* it probably will not be completed until next summer.
7. I ordered a copy of the manual last week, *but* I have not received it.

B. Read the following sentences and explain why the italicized words or expressions are correct and the ones in parentheses are wrong.

1. We are neither present *nor* (or) former members of that organization.
2. Have you heard from either him *or* (nor) her recently?
3. Was it in July or in August *that* (when) we bought this machine?
4. I don't remember reading *that* (where) the company was sold to foreign investors.
5. *Since* (Being that) he had finished his work, he offered to help me.
6. Most people would rather work *than* (then) sit at home.
7. The treasurer was honest, reliable, and *accurate* (an accurate worker).
8. I am sure she did not leave early *without telling someone* (without she told someone).
9. This sofa is so beautifully styled that it looks *as though* (like) it were custom-made.
10. We should replace this machine *unless* (without) we can find someone to repair it quickly and economically.

11. All of us respect Mr. Blake for his ability and *for* his good business judgment (because he has good business judgment).
12. It appears *that* (as) all the banks are closed today.
13. I arranged the furniture *as* (like) she wanted it.
14. It appears *that* (as) the company will have record sales this year.
15. The reason we postponed our trip was *that* (because) rainy weather had been forecast for the whole week.
16. We obviously should try *to* (and) understand their position.
17. Have you heard *whether or not* (if) it is supposed to rain tomorrow?
18. Two customers called you *while* (when) you were away.
19. Did you notice anything different *when* (while) you returned?
20. Those buildings look *as though* (like) they need extensive repairs.

ASSIGNMENT: Complete the Unit 16 Worksheet on pages 119–120; then complete the Part 4 Review on pages 121–122.

UNIT 16

Conjunctions

WORKSHEET

 A **Which conjunction (or other expression) shown in parentheses is correct? Write your answer in the space provided.**

1. (Being that, Since) the printer ribbons were on sale, we bought a dozen.

2. Please do not fold, tear, (nor, or) staple this form.

3. We cannot proceed (unless, without) we have their approval.

4. Did you read (that, where) the savings and loan fiasco will cost taxpayers billions of dollars?

5. They were (either, neither) in Kansas City, Kansas, nor in Kansas City, Missouri.

6. Mr. Harrison is not in the office now, (and, but) we expect him to be here tomorrow.

7. (Both, Either, Neither) they and we have worked hard.

8. You should try (and, to) schedule an appointment to see them Wednesday.

9. (Either, Neither) she or I will collect the data for you.

10. The store opens at either nine (nor, or) ten, I think.

11. Strawberries are plentiful (and, but) quite inexpensive when they are in season.

12. The reason we were late was (because, that) we encountered heavy traffic.

13. The machine runs not only quietly (but, but also) economically.

14. The telephone was ringing (when, while) I entered my office.

15. It was last Tuesday (that, when) she placed the order.

16. I filled out the forms exactly (as, like) I was instructed.

17. Several clients called (when, while) you were in Corvallis last week.

18. I doubt (if, whether) Congress will override the President's veto.

19. They are in their late fifties, but they act (as though, like) they were teenagers.

20. We don't doubt (but what, that) they know exactly what the outcome will be.

1. Since
2. or
3. unless
4. that
5. neither
6. but
7. Both
8. to
9. Either
10. or
11. and
12. that
13. but also
14. when
15. that
16. as
17. while
18. whether
19. as though
20. that

B Underline the incorrect words in the following sentences, and write the correct words in the spaces provided. If a sentence is grammatically correct, examine its meaning and choose a more effective conjunction to relate the ideas to each other. Note the example.

0. The reason we delayed our departure was <u>because</u> it was snowing.
0. _that_

1. He usually finishes his work earlier <u>then</u> I complete my chores.
1. _than_

2. This carpet looks <u>like</u> it has never been cleaned.
2. _as if OR as though_

3. Were you a little nervous <u>when</u> you were speaking?
3. _while_

4. No one can deny <u>but</u> your assessment was correct.
4. _that_

5. I don't buy them <u>without</u> they are on sale.
5. _unless_

6. We wanted to order the deluxe model, <u>and</u> we ordered the standard one instead.
6. _but_

7. The consultants may recommend some changes, <u>and</u> they may suggest that we leave everything as it is.
7. _or_

8. We do not doubt <u>but what</u> they are honest.
8. _that_

9. We had hardly begun <u>than</u> it was time to quit.
9. _when_

10. It was in August <u>when</u> we replaced those two machines.
10. _that_

11. We don't doubt <u>if</u> the deadline will be met.
11. _that_

12. The work will not be completed by the deadline <u>except</u> we work overtime this week.
12. _unless_

13. It looks <u>like</u> it may rain today.
13. _as though_

14. The reason why I was absent was <u>because</u> I was ill.
14. _that_

15. We did not attend the meeting <u>and because</u> we were not invited.
15. _because_

16. Frank does not subscribe to that magazine, <u>or</u> does he plan to.
16. _nor_

17. The manager did not notify <u>neither</u> him or me.
17. _either_

18. Do you plan to invest in either stocks <u>nor</u> bonds?
18. _or_

19. It was almost 10 o'clock <u>that</u> we left.
19. _when_

20. It is doubtful <u>that</u> either of them will be interested in that position.
20. _whether_

C In each of the following sentences, supply the missing correlative conjunction. Insert a caret at the point where the conjunction should appear, and write the appropriate conjunction in the space at the right. Note the example.

0. Mr. Marks would ∧ approve the policy nor discuss it.
0. _neither_

1. Ruth will buy∧ a house or a condominium.
1. _either_

2. I think that∧ he and she are eligible for early retirement.
2. _both_

3. Not only did the merchandise arrive late,∧ it was damaged.
3. _but also_

4. I am not sure∧ we will replace those machines or not.
4. _whether_

5. The replacement part was not∧ expensive as we thought it would be.
5. _so OR as_

PART 4

Other Parts of Speech and Their Usage

REVIEW

In the following sentences, examine the use of adjectives, adverbs, prepositions, and conjunctions. If the sentence is correct, write *OK* in the space provided. If you find an error in usage, underline it and write the necessary correction in the space provided. If a word is missing, place a caret at the point where the word should be inserted and write the word in the space provided. Note the examples.

0. Do you know where she is at? — **0.** is

00. Her report is more ⌃ complete than mine. — **00.** nearly

1. You will need to spend sometime with each of the new employees. — **1.** some time

2. A report must provide up to date information if it is to be as useful as it should be. — **2.** up-to-date

3. We neither heard the commercial on radio or saw the advertisement in the newspaper. — **3.** nor

4. She said she would take her complaint direct to the manager. — **4.** directly

5. What kind a computer do you plan to buy? — **5.** of

6. Would you sooner live in the center of the city than in one of the suburbs? — **6.** rather

7. I think we will be able to hear better if we move more closer to the stage. — **7.** closer

8. There was hardly nothing left for us to do. — **8.** anything

9. Someone turned her purse into one of the security guards. — **9.** in to

10. What is the furthest you have ever driven in one day? — **10.** farthest

11. Should we order some more of them large envelopes? — **11.** those OR these

12. If you were to ask me where they went, I would be unable to tell you. — **12.** OK

13. Neither of them thinks it is to important. — **13.** too

14. The customer didn't want neither Model 100 or Model 250. — **14.** either

15. Chicago is larger than any ⌃ city in Illinois. — **15.** other

16. Both of them worked real hard all morning. — **16.** very

17. This styles of shoes will be very popular. — **17.** These

18. Which of the two routes is more shorter? — **18.** shorter

19. The negotiations seem to be going nowheres. — **19.** nowhere

20. Has anyone written an history of the firm? — **20.** a

21. Do you think this invitation is worded proper?

21. properly

22. If too little people buy tickets, it may be necessary to cancel the dinner.

22. few

23. The pies and other desserts certainly look deliciously.

23. delicious

24. This style is as attractive as, if not more attractive, the other one.

24. than

25. Have the regional managers all ready prepared and submitted their budgets?

25. already

26. She knows most everything there is to know about both of those jobs.

26. almost

27. If the work were divided among you and me, we could finish it today.

27. between

28. She said that she has never felt as good as she has since she had the operation.

28. well

29. He feels like he ought to be given another chance to prove he can do the work properly.

29. as though OR that

30. We read where the hurricane did millions of dollars' worth of damage.

30. that

31. Everybody accept Alvin and me voted in favor of the plan.

31. except

32. Of all the factors to be considered, that one is probably of the lesser significance.

32. least

33. I think they were sitting nearly the edge of the platform.

33. near

34. Frank handled the complaint so smooth that the customer thanked him.

34. smoothly

35. Your proposal will be studied farther.

35. further

36. Do you think they are liable to be disappointed?

36. likely

37. Is there any easy way to make this machine stationery?

37. stationary

38. What is their principle objection to hiring an outside consultant?

38. principal

39. We are willing to meet at whatever time would be most convenient to you.

39. for

40. Jane felt so badly that she could hardly stand up.

40. bad

41. The passed month was a very hectic one for us.

41. past

42. Dividends will be paid biennially—in January and in July.

42. biannually

43. Who is the more popular governor in the country today?

43. most

44. Did you agree to buy a car off him?

44. from

45. This report is different than the one I gave you yesterday.

45. from

46. What style furniture do you prefer?

46. of

47. I did the work per his instructions.

47. in accordance with

48. Did anyone beside you report the error?

48. besides

49. The work was done so careful that it contained no errors.

49. carefully

50. I don't think we need no more of those.

50. any

PART 5

Phrases, Clauses, and Sentences

Before you study Units 17 through 19, complete this survey of phrases, clauses, and sentences. These exercises will help you identify principles that you may wish to give special attention.

· S U R V E Y ·

 Underline all prepositional phrases in the following sentences.

1. A number of customers were waiting for the store to open.
2. Please be sure to sign and date each copy of the agreement.
3. We have not heard from them since they moved to Montana.
4. The car parked beside mine appeared to have a leak in the gas tank.
5. If you leave the film before 10 a.m., you can pick up the prints after 5 p.m.

 Underline all infinitive phrases in the following sentences.

1. To me, neither of them seems too eager to buy another used car.
2. We are expecting him to call us and give us his decision.
3. The next one to be appointed director of marketing probably will be she.
4. I am sorry to have given you the wrong address.
5. We look forward to meeting with you as soon as you return from your trip to Anchorage.

 Underline all gerund phrases in the following sentences.

1. Thank you for sending me a duplicate statement of account.
2. We believe the company will be operating at a profit within a few months.
3. Knowing that household appliances will be on sale, prospective buyers are willing to wait.
4. Being able to get along well with others is important.
5. We appreciate your giving us your wholehearted support.

Underline all participial phrases in the following sentences.

1. Everyone participating in the survey will receive a small gift.
2. One of the bridges built more than 50 years ago has been closed.
3. Thank you for going out of your way to drive me to the airport.
4. Does the post office return mail lacking sufficient postage?
5. His short stories have appeared in several magazines.

 Underline all dependent clauses in the following sentences.

1. The company notified us that Model 40 has been discontinued.
2. What time would be the most convenient for you to meet with us?
3. I prefer to use public transportation because it is convenient and relatively inexpensive.
4. The action was intended to stimulate the economy, and it appears to be working quite well.
5. I do not know when the announcement will be made or who will make it.

 Combine each group of separate sentences into one sentence. Omit and add words as necessary to produce a concise, clear statement.

1. Please call Ms. Walters this morning. Please tell her that the meeting has been postponed.
   Please call Ms. Walters this morning and tell her that the meeting has been postponed.

2. Mr. Ramos was appointed executive vice president. You were on vacation at the time.
   While you were on vacation, Mr. Ramos was appointed executive vice president.

3. These figures seem correct to me. You may wish to have someone else check them.
   These figures seem correct to me, but you may wish to have someone else check them.

4. Enclosed is a copy of the letter. It is dated March 10.
   Enclosed is a copy of the March 10 letter.

5. We visited several cities last week. Grand Rapids was one of them.
   We visited several cities, including Grand Rapids, last week.

Simple Sentences and Phrases

CLASSES OF SENTENCES

On the basis of their purpose or meaning, sentences may be classified as *declarative, interrogative, imperative,* or *exclamatory.*

1. Declarative Sentences. A *declarative sentence* states a fact, an opinion, or a belief and ends with a period. Declarative sentences are the most common.

> The Federal Deposit Insurance Corporation insures individual bank accounts up to $100,000.
>
> More people should exercise their right to vote.

2. Interrogative Sentences. An *interrogative sentence* asks a direct question and ends with a question mark. A *direct question* uses the exact words of the speaker and usually requires a spoken or written response. An *indirect question* does not use the speaker's exact words, and it is part of a sentence.

> What kind of work would you like to do? (Direct question.)
>
> The interviewer asked, "What kind of work would you like to do?" (Direct question.)
>
> The interviewer asked me *what kind of work I would like to do.* (Indirect question.)
>
> Why did the interviewer ask me *what kind of work I would like to do?* (Indirect question within a direct question.)

3. Imperative Sentences. An *imperative sentence* expresses a command, an order, or a request and usually ends with a period. In imperative sentences, the subject *you* is frequently understood rather than stated.

> Do not write below this line. (The subject *you* is understood.)
>
> Please give me your recommendations. (*You* is the understood subject.)
>
> Will you please send us your payment by return mail.

The last example above illustrates an imperative sentence phrased in question form. It is correctly followed by a period because an "action" response—not a spoken or written answer—is required. However, for the sake of courtesy, some writers use a question mark rather than a period after a "polite request" of this type.

4. Exclamatory Sentences. An *exclamatory sentence* expresses strong feeling or emotion and ends with an exclamation point. Exclamatory sentences are not used very often in ordinary business writing, but they arc common in advertising copy, sales letters, and similar promotional materials that are frequently very informal.

> What fantastic bargains these are!
>
> Wait! Don't throw this letter away until you've read it!

Exclamatory sentences often begin with such expressions as *oh, wow, indeed, hey,* and others classified as interjections. An *interjection* is an independent word that frequently stands without any grammatical connection to the sentence that follows it. When used to express strong emotion, interjections are followed by exclamation marks.

> Congratulations! You deserve the promotion!
>
> Wow! That was a terrific speech you gave!

When the interjection is not intended to carry or convey any particularly strong emotion, it is followed by a comma.

> Well, maybe it is a bargain. (Note that no exclamation mark is used after the sentence unless the statement is intended to convey surprise or some other strong emotion.)

Another way of classifying sentences is by structure. By this method, sentences may be classified as *simple, compound, complex,* or *compound-complex.* This unit discusses simple sentences; compound and complex sentences will be presented in Unit 18.

SIMPLE SENTENCES

A *simple sentence* expresses a single thought; it contains one subject and one predicate. As illustrated below, the *simple subject* consists of the word or words that name the person speaking, the person spoken to, or the person or thing spoken about. The *simple predicate* consists of the verb or verb phrase that expresses the action or the state of being of the subject.

> We *have* complete confidence in your ability to do the job.
>
> Please *give* me your answer right away. (The subject *you* is understood.)
>
> The *board of directors met* yesterday afternoon.
> The new *machine will be* available very soon.

A simple sentence may have a *compound subject,* as illustrated below.

> *You, Ms. Saunders,* and *Mr. Pollock* should plan to meet with them next week.
>
> Many *hotels* and *motels* give special discounts to senior citizens.

Similarly, a simple sentence may have a *compound predicate,* that is, more than one verb or verb phrase.

> This catalog *lists* and *describes* all our products and services.
>
> She *has completed* that course and *is planning* to enroll in another one.

A simple sentence may have both a compound subject and a compound predicate.

> *He* and *she read* the letter and *returned* it to me.

The word or words that tell who is speaking, who is spoken to, or who or what is spoken about plus any modifying words or phrases accompanying them make up the **complete subject** of the sentence. The word or words that express the action or state of being of the subject or subjects and any descriptive or completing words or phrases accompanying those verbs or verb phrases make up the **complete predicate.** In each of the following examples, the complete subject is italicized.

> *The program* lasted nearly two hours. (The simple subject is *program;* the simple predicate is *lasted.*)
>
> *A friend of yours* gave me your new address last week. (*Friend* is the simple subject, and *gave* is the simple predicate.)
>
> *The cost of these items* seems reasonable. (The simple subject is *cost;* the simple predicate is *seems.* Note that *reasonable* is a predicate adjective—a word that follows a linking verb and describes the subject.)
>
> *The person in charge of the project* is Lloyd. (The simple subject is *person;* the simple predicate is *is.* Lloyd, which follows the linking verb *is* and further identifies the subject, is a predicate nominative.)
>
> *Dr. Ainsworth, our chief surgeon,* wrote the report. (The simple subject is *Dr. Ainsworth. Chief surgeon* is an appositive; it further identifies Dr. Ainsworth. The simple predicate is *wrote.*)

WORD ORDER OF SENTENCES

The parts of a sentence may be arranged in **normal** or **inverted** word order.

5. Normal Word Order. When the parts of a sentence are arranged in **normal word order,** the complete subject comes before the predicate. Note that the complete subject is shown in italics in these examples:

> *The members of the committee* rejected the proposal. (*Members* is the simple subject.)
>
> *Both applicants* are experienced accountants. (The simple subject is *applicants. Accountants,* which further explains *applicants,* is the predicate nominative.)
>
> *These new machines* are expensive. (*Expensive* is a predicate adjective.)
>
> *Who* will receive the nomination? (The word *who* is the complete subject in this question.)

6. Inverted Word Order. When part or all of the predicate precedes the subject, the sentence is in **inverted word order.** Occasionally a question is in normal word order, but most questions are in inverted word order.

> Is their proposal acceptable to you? (The complete subject is *their proposal.* In normal order, this sentence would be: *Their proposal is acceptable to you?*)
>
> Have you and she been asked to serve on the committee? (The complete subject is *you and she.* In normal word order, this sentence would be: *You and she have been asked to serve on the committee?*)
>
> What types of work have *you* done on a part-time basis? (The complete subject is *you.* In normal word order, this sentence would be: *You have done what types of work on a part-time basis?*)

PHRASES

A **phrase** is a group of words that does not contain a subject or a predicate and that functions as a single part of speech in a sentence or a clause.

7. Prepositional Phrases. A **prepositional phrase** consists of a preposition, its object or objects, and the modifiers (if any) of the object or objects. Although a prepositional phrase usually functions as an adjective or an adverb, it may sometimes function as a noun.

> I have already answered the letter *from Mr. McCoy.* (The prepositional phrase *from Mr. McCoy* functions as an adjective modifying *letter.*)
>
> How long do you plan to stay *in Kenosha?* (The prepositional phrase *in Kenosha* functions as an adverb modifying the infinitive phrase *to stay.*)

From New York to Los Angeles is a long journey. (The two prepositional phrases *from New York* and *to Los Angeles* function together as the noun subject of the verb *is*.)

8. Participial Phrases. A *participial phrase* consists of a participle and its modifiers, a participle and its object, or a participle and its complement. A participial phrase always functions as an adjective modifying a noun or a pronoun. Note the position of each modifying phrase below in relation to the word it modifies.

Buying impulsively, we soon exceeded our budget. (The present participle *buying* and the adverb *impulsively* form a participial phrase modifying the pronoun *we*.)

Having filled out the forms, Pat signed them and sent them on to Miss Quarles. (The present participle *having*, the past participle *filled out,* the modifier *the,* and the noun object *forms* comprise a participial phrase modifying the noun *Pat*.)

Being cautious, the director of marketing gave a conservative estimate of next quarter's sales. (The present participle *being* and its complement, the adjective *cautious,* form a participial phrase modifying the compound noun *director of marketing*.)

The person *handling those accounts* is Mr. Bell. (*Handling those accounts* modifies the noun *person*.)

Delayed an hour, the managers missed their flight connections. (The past participle *delayed,* the modifier *an,* and the noun *hour* form a participial phrase modifying the noun *managers*.)

The reports *written by Grace Sawyer* were excellent. (The participial phrase modifies the noun *reports*.)

9. Gerund Phrases. A *gerund phrase* consists of a gerund (a verb form ending in *ing* that is used as a noun) and its modifiers, a gerund and its object, or a gerund and its complement. A gerund phrase, like a gerund, is always used as a noun. As illustrated below, gerund phrases may function in a variety of ways.

Their talking loudly annoyed other members of the staff. (This gerund phrase functions as the subject of the verb *annoyed*. Note that the gerund *talking* is modified by the possessive pronoun *their,* which functions as an adjective, and the adverb *loudly*.)

Answering customers' inquiries is part of the job. (The gerund *answering,* the modifier *customers',* and the noun *inquiries* form a phrase functioning as the noun subject of the verb *is*.)

Thank you for *sending me the information*. (This gerund phrase functions as the object of the preposition *for*. Note that the gerund *sending* has the direct object *information* and the indirect object *me*.)

One of the receptionist's duties is *answering the telephone*. (The gerund phrase functions as a predicate nominative: it follows the linking verb *is* and renames or further identifies the subject *one*.)

10. Infinitive Phrases. An *infinitive phrase* consists of an infinitive and its modifiers, an infinitive and its subject or subjects, an infinitive and its object or objects, or an infinitive and its complement. As illustrated below, infinitive phrases function as adjectives, adverbs, and nouns.

The orders *to be processed immediately* are on my desk. (This infinitive phrase functions as an adjective modifying the noun *orders*. Note that the infinitive *to be processed* is modified by the adverb *immediately*.)

To avoid heavy traffic, we should leave now. (This infinitive phrase functions as an adverb modifying the verb phrase *should leave;* it tells why. Note that the infinitive *to avoid* has the object *traffic*.)

To be a successful entrepreneur is her ambition. (This infinitive phrase functions as a noun; it is the subject of the verb *is*. Note that *to be* has the complement *entrepreneur*.)

His father would like *him to be an accountant*. (This phrase functions as the direct object of the verb phrase *would like*. Note that *to be* has the subject *him* and the complement *accountant*.)

Your report seems *to be complete and accurate*. (The infinitive phrase functions as a predicate adjective modifying the subject *report*.)

Our goal is *to meet the deadline*. (This infinitive phrase functions as a noun. It follows the linking verb *is* and functions as the predicate nominative, renaming or further identifying the subject, *goal*.)

Anne-Marie seems *to be very happy in her new position at Barnard Associates*. (This long infinitive phrase is the complement of the linking verb *seems*. The entire phrase functions as a predicate adjective—it modifies *Anne-Marie,* the subject.)

11. Absolute Phrases. An *absolute phrase* is a group of words that has no specific relationship to the rest of the sentence. The most common absolute phrase consists of a noun or a pronoun modified by a participle, but prepositional and infinitive phrases may also be independent elements. Absolute phrases are set off by commas.

Everything considered, the conference was very successful. (Absolute participial phrase.)

The flight having been canceled, we returned to the office. (Do not confuse this participial phrase used as an independent element with a participial phrase that modifies a noun or pronoun, such as: *Having been told that our flight was canceled,* we returned to the office.)

As for the others, I am not sure what their plans are. (Absolute prepositional phrase.)

To tell the truth, I would rather work with you. (Absolute infinitive phrase.)

Strictly speaking, the company has no legal or financial responsibility in such situations. (Absolute participial phrase.)

Study Guide 17

A. Study each sentence and determine whether it is declarative, interrogative, imperative, or exclamatory. If necessary, refer to the rules indicated.

1. What is the balance of my account?[2]
2. What a surprise that was![4]
3. The new center will be completed in May.[1]
4. Will you be able to work next weekend?[2]
5. Please review the claim with Mrs. Corbin.[3]
6. Would you please call your secretary.[3]
7. The number of complaints is surprisingly few.[1]
8. The manager wanted to know who authorized the shipment.[1]
9. May we please hear from you within the next ten days.[3]
10. Those prices are unbelievable![4]

B. Study the word order of each of the following sentences. Is it normal, or is it inverted? Refer to the rule indicated if you aren't sure.

1. Who was in charge at that time?[5]
2. Will the construction be completed this fall?[6]
3. Is there an adequate supply for this month?[6]
4. Be sure to bring your cancelled check or receipt with you.[5]
5. To buy a home is one of their goals.[5]

C. Can you identify the kinds of phrases shown in italics in the following sentences? If necessary, refer to the rules indicated.

1. Passengers *needing special assistance* were asked to board first.[8]
2. We need *to order several more copies.*[10]
3. The items *on that shelf* are her property.[7]
4. *As a matter of fact,* the shipment is insured.[11]
5. *Letting them get away with it* would not be the best thing to do.[9]
6. *Everything considered,* the meeting was worthwhile.[11]
7. Who is the attorney *representing the plaintiff?*[8]
8. After *taking the course,* he was able to manage his time better.[9]
9. The insurance adjuster visited the premises *to determine the extent of the damage.*[10]
10. The order *placed on February 12* was canceled a day or two later.[8]
11. A letter *arranged attractively on quality stationery* makes a good impression.[8]
12. *To tell the truth,* some of the parts were not replaced.[11]

ASSIGNMENT: Complete the Unit 17 Worksheet on pages 129–130.

UNIT 17

Simple Sentences and Phrases

WORKSHEET

 A **Combine each group of sentences into one simple sentence. Omit and change words as necessary. Note the example.** (Answers will vary.)

0. California produces citrus crops. Florida produces citrus crops.

California and Florida produce citrus crops.

_____

1. Some cities levy income taxes. Several states levy income taxes.

Some cities and several states levy income taxes.

_____

2. Louis wrote the report. He edited it himself.

Louis wrote and edited the report himself.

_____

3. These letters are not ready to be mailed. Neither are those packages.

Neither these letters nor those packages are ready to be mailed.

_____

4. The company plans to discontinue Model 220. It will replace that machine with Model 300.

The company plans to discontinue Model 220 and to replace it with Model 300.

_____

5. The store offers substantial discounts. The discounts are given to cash customers.

The store offers substantial discounts to cash customers.

_____

6. The visitors are waiting to see the manager. They are from France.

The visitors waiting to see the manager are from France.

_____

7. The defendant met with reporters. They met outside the courtroom.

The defendant met with reporters outside the courtroom.

_____

8. The offices are for rent. They are located on the second floor.

The offices for rent are located on the second floor.

_____

9. The price was $42.50. It was reduced to $34. The reduction was made last Monday.

The price was reduced from $42.50 to $34 last Monday.

10. Ms. Collier answered the reporters' questions. She was representing the company.

Representing the company, Ms. Collier answered the reporters' questions.

B Study the italicized phrase in each of the following sentences. In the space provided, write the type of phrase illustrated: *prepositional, participial, gerund, infinitive,* or *absolute.*

1. The company reimburses its employees *for necessary business expenses.*   **1.** Prepositional

2. The majority of those *polled recently* plan to vote for the incumbent mayor.   **2.** Participial

3. Are you planning *to be on vacation next week?*   **3.** Infinitive

4. After *waiting half an hour,* we decided to leave without them.   **4.** Gerund

5. Sonia worked part-time *to pay part of her college expenses.*   **5.** Infinitive

6. The contestant *submitting the winning entry* will win a trip to Honolulu.   **6.** Participial

7. *Investing for the future* is always a wise thing to do.   **7.** Gerund

8. Merchandise *damaged in transit* may be returned for credit.   **8.** Participial

9. Maintaining and building goodwill is a goal *of every company.*   **9.** Prepositional

10. *Everything considered,* the results of the survey were disappointing.   **10.** Absolute

C For each phrase below, write a simple sentence in which the phrase functions as indicated in parentheses. (Answers will vary.)

1. Using electrical equipment *(adjective)*

Anyone using electrical equipment needs to be careful.

2. To qualify for a better position *(adverb)*

He took the course to qualify for a better position.

3. Increasing productivity *(noun—subject)*

Increasing productivity is one of the company's major goals.

4. To distribute the report *(noun—object of a verb)*

She asked me to distribute the report this afternoon.

5. Repaired last week *(adjective)*

One of the machines repaired last week is out of order again.

CLAUSES

A *clause* is a group of related words that contains a subject and a predicate.

Independent Clauses. An *independent clause* (also referred to as a *main clause* or a *principal clause*) is a group of related words that contains a subject and a predicate, expresses a complete thought, and makes sense when it stands by itself. An independent clause can stand by itself as a simple sentence if it is properly punctuated.

> INDEPENDENT CLAUSE:
> advertising is an important part of marketing
>
> SIMPLE SENTENCE:
> Advertising is an important part of marketing.

Dependent Clauses. A *dependent clause* (also called a *subordinate clause*) contains a subject and a predicate, but the clause does not express a complete thought and cannot stand by itself. Dependent clauses are introduced by relative pronouns (*that, which, who, whom*) and subordinate conjunctions (for example, *although, when, if, because, where, while, after,* and *since*).

> that you may have an opening in your data processing department
> although the price is reasonable

As illustrated below, a dependent clause makes sense only when it is connected to an independent clause.

> Mr. Roland Smythe, one of your employees, recently told me *that you may have an opening in your data processing department.*
> *Although the price is reasonable,* we will be unable to purchase the machine immediately.

COMPOUND SENTENCES

A *compound sentence* consists of two or more independent clauses that express closely related ideas. Each clause could stand alone as a simple sentence.

> The car is nearly five years old, but it is still in good condition. (The simple sentences would be: *The car is nearly five years old. It is still in good condition.*)

The independent clauses of a compound sentence may be joined by a coordinating conjunction (*and, but, or,* or *nor*), correlative conjunctions (for example, *either . . . or* and *not only . . . but also*), or conjunctive adverbs (such as *however, therefore, thus,* or *consequently*).

Note the use of coordinating conjunctions in the following compound sentences. Also note the comment concerning each conjunction.

> I have heard about the article, *but* I have not read it. (Note that *but* introduces a contrasting or opposing thought.)
> Ms. Howard has been offered the position, *and* she most likely will accept it. (*And* introduces an additional thought closely related to the preceding one.)
> You may pay the full amount now, *or* you may pay it in three monthly installments. (*Or* introduces an alternative thought.)
> We did not finish the project today, *nor* will we be able to finish it tomorrow. (*Nor* joins a negative thought to a negative thought. Note that the verb in the first clause is made negative by the adverb *not.* The verb in the clause introduced by *nor* must be positive—*will be*—to avoid a double negative: *nor will we not be able to finish it tomorrow.*)

When a correlative conjunction is used in a compound sentence, each part of the conjunction must be placed at the beginning of its respective clause. Do not insert one part of the conjunction in the middle of one of the clauses.

> *Either* the company did not receive our inquiry, *or* someone chose not to answer it. (NOT: The company *either* did not receive our inquiry, *or* someone chose not to answer it.)
> *Neither* did they offer an apology for the delay, *nor* did we request one. (Since *neither* and *nor* are negative, the verbs are positive: *did offer* and *did request.*)

Correlative conjunctions may be used within a clause, but they should be used only to connect parts of the clause that are parallel in kind as well as in construction.

> The spokesperson *neither* confirmed *nor* denied the reports, but most of us do not believe them. (*Neither* and *nor* connect the verbs *confirmed* and *denied.*)

Either you *or* Ed is likely to be asked to assist them, but neither of you should change your plans at this point. (*Either* and *or* connect the subjects *you* and *Ed.*)

If a conjunctive adverb (sometimes called a *transitional expression*) is used at the beginning of the second clause, a semicolon is used to separate the clauses.

They have not contacted us; *therefore,* we need to call or write them.

Mr. Thomas was entitled to the reward; *however,* he refused it.

In some instances, the clauses of a compound sentence are simply separated by a semicolon.

Managing a department is one thing; managing an entire corporation is another.

I am in favor of the proposal; several others are not.

COMPARISON OF SIMPLE AND COMPOUND SENTENCES

As discussed in Unit 17, a simple sentence may have a compound subject, a compound verb (predicate), or both. Determining that the sentence is actually a compound sentence, not a simple sentence with compound parts, requires that you identify the subject and the verb in each clause. Note these sentences:

Curtains and drapes will be on sale this weekend. (This is a simple sentence with a compound subject: *curtains* and *drapes.*)

Curtains and drapes will be on sale this weekend, but other items will not. (This sentence contains two separate independent clauses connected by the conjunction *but;* therefore, it is a compound sentence.)

She and I found the errors and corrected them immediately. (This is a simple sentence with a compound subject—*she* and *I*—and a compound predicate—*found the errors* and *corrected them immediately.*)

She and I found the errors, and we corrected them immediately. (The first independent clause of this compound sentence contains a compound subject and one predicate; the second clause has one subject and one predicate.)

COMPLEX SENTENCES

If a sentence contains one independent clause and one or more dependent clauses, it is a **complex sentence.** The primary attribute of a complex sentence is that it can show the relative importance of related ideas without the use of several short sentences.

The order has not arrived. We placed it two weeks ago. (Two simple sentences, giving equal importance to both thoughts.)

The order *that we placed two weeks ago* has not arrived. (One complex sentence, giving greater importance to the fact that the order has not arrived.)

When you are ready to apply for a job, I will be happy to arrange an interview for you *if you wish.* (Note that this complex sentence contains two dependent clauses.)

A **compound-complex sentence** consists of two or more independent clauses and one or more dependent clauses.

While we were in Boise, we tried to get in touch with you; however, you were out of the city.

If you would like to attend the seminar, please contact Miss Jenner before Wednesday; otherwise, she will be unable to make all the arrangements *that she must make by Friday.*

FUNCTIONS OF DEPENDENT CLAUSES

Dependent clauses function as adjectives, as adverbs, or as nouns in both complex and compound-complex sentences.

1. Adjective Clauses. A dependent clause that functions as an adjective is usually introduced by a relative pronoun, such as *who, that, which, whoever, whom,* or *whomever.*

The person *who accepts this job* must be willing to relocate. (The dependent clause modifies the subject, *person.*)

The house *that the real estate agent mentioned* is at 444 Warren Avenue.

If an adjective clause is essential to identify or describe the word it modifies, it is a **restrictive clause.** As illustrated in the two sentences above, such a clause is not separated by punctuation from the rest of the sentence.

Some adjective clauses are used merely as additional description or explanation and are not essential to the sense of the sentence. Such a clause is a **nonrestrictive clause,** and it is set off from the rest of the sentence by commas; that is, a comma is used before and after the clause unless it comes immediately before some other mark of punctuation. To test whether the clause is essential, say the sentence without the clause; if the thought is complete, the clause is not essential and is set off by commas.

Edith Weller, *who is manager of the new convention center,* granted the reporter a lengthy interview.

Last week's report, *which was prepared by Charlene Jackson,* indicates a year-to-date gain of approximately 7 percent.

2. Adverbial Clauses. Dependent clauses that function as adverbs are introduced by such subordinate conjunctions as *after, as, as soon as, before, since, if, where, when,* and *while.*

> You should consider the risk involved *before you make such an investment.*
>
> Please have Ms. Pezzutti call me *as soon as she returns to the office.*

If an adverbial clause introduces a main clause, set if off with a comma. If it comes after the main clause, omit the comma unless the adverbial clause is nonrestrictive (unnecessary).

INTRODUCTORY:
After you left yesterday afternoon, his letter of acceptance arrived.

RESTRICTIVE:
His letter of acceptance arrived *after you left yesterday afternoon.*

NONRESTRICTIVE:
His letter of acceptance arrived yesterday afternoon, *after you had decided to appoint someone else.*

3. Noun Clauses. A dependent clause may function as a noun and be the subject, object, or complement of a verb. Such a clause may also be used as the object of a preposition or as an appositive (a word or a group of words that follows a noun or a pronoun and renames or further identifies the noun or pronoun).

SUBJECT OF VERB:
That only two people applied for the job surprised us.

OBJECT OF VERB:
I do not know *when the committee will make its recommendation.*

PREDICATE NOMINATIVE:
One well-known fact is *that an efficient secretary is invaluable.*

APPOSITIVE:
Mr. Robbins' statement, *that I was not interested in your plan,* is not entirely true.

OBJECT OF PREPOSITION:
Please send an invitation to *whomever you wish.*

OBJECT OF INFINITIVE:
We would like to know *who developed the plan.*

Study Guide 18

A. Examine each sentence to determine whether it is simple, compound, complex, or compound-complex in construction.

1. What have been the effects of the collapse of communism and the switch from a state-controlled economy to a free-market economy within the former Union of Soviet Socialist Republics in 1991? *(Simple.)*
2. Have you considered the various employment opportunities that are available in the data processing departments of private companies and government offices? *(Complex.)*
3. The demand for some of our products is seasonal; for example, lawn furniture sells well during the spring and summer. *(Compound.)*
4. Some of our employees work from 8:30 a.m. to 4:30 p.m.; others are on the job from 9 a.m. to 5 p.m. *(Compound.)*
5. I hope that you will be able to give me their current address or to put me in touch with someone who has that information. *(Complex.)*
6. Miss Mendosa suggested that we invite both of them to serve as speakers, and we plan to follow her recommendation. *(Compound-Complex.)*
7. Please do not fold, bend, tear, or staple the enclosed card. *(Simple.)*
8. If you have not already done so, be sure to make your reservations before the end of this week. *(Complex.)*
9. You certainly have earned the promotion! *(Simple.)*
10. Mr. Andrew Rappard and Ms. Carmen Fernandez bought stock in the company when it was selling for less than $20 a share. *(Complex.)*
11. She and I checked them twice. *(Simple.)*
12. Arlene, Marla, and Tom arrived last night and met with us this morning. *(Simple.)*

B. Study each sentence below to determine whether the italicized dependent clause functions as an adjective, an adverb, or a noun. Can you explain why the clause is or is not set off by commas?

1. Anyone *who files his or her tax return after the deadline* may have to pay a penalty.[1]
2. Please call me *when you are ready to leave.*[2]
3. I believe *that the company's headquarters are in Columbus.*[3]
4. Chart 4, *which appears on page 22,* gives a year-by-year summary.[1]
5. Your bid could not be considered *because it was received two days after the deadline.*[2]
6. The contract will be awarded to *whoever submits the lowest bid.*[3]
7. *What the long-range economic effects will be* is anyone's guess.[3]
8. I am enclosing a copy of this new booklet, *which I hope you will find very helpful.*[1]
9. *Before you mail your tax return,* be sure to check all computations carefully.[2]
10. *If you would like to take advantage of this special offer,* simply sign and return the enclosed card.[2]
11. The Festival of States, *which is a very exciting celebration,* is held in St. Petersburg, Florida.[3]
12. Mr. George Brill, *who is a marine biologist,* spoke about the pollution of the oceans.[3]
13. *Whether we will have an exhibit at the convention next year* is something the regional managers will help to decide.[3]
14. Each of us should feel free to share this information with *whoever asks for it.*[3]
15. We do not know *when the maintenance staff will have the machines ready to run.*[3]
16. For the past several weeks Mrs. Thompson has been trying to find a replacement for Terry, a person *whom she regards highly.*[3]

ASSIGNMENT: Complete the Unit 18 Worksheet on pages 135–136.

UNIT 18

Compound and Complex Sentences

WORKSHEET

A Underline the subordinate, or dependent, clauses in the following sentences. Then, in the space provided, write the word *adjective*, *adverb*, or *noun*, to indicate how the clause is used.

1. Several hospitals were sued because they charged outrageous prices for very inexpensive items.
2. The one who recommended the site is Marion Costello, one of our senior vice presidents.
3. That the deadline will be met seems certain.
4. Do you know when the increase will become effective?
5. The changes were made while you were on vacation.
6. The instructions that we were given were rather ambiguous, don't you agree?
7. Please call Miss Richardson after you have discussed the matter with Mr. Quinn.
8. The remodeling project, which began last fall, is expected to cost approximately $150,000.
9. You will need to contact whoever owns the property.
10. One of the machines we recently purchased needs extensive repairs already.

1. Adverb
2. Adjective
3. Noun
4. Noun
5. Adverb
6. Adjective
7. Adverb
8. Adjective
9. Noun
10. Adjective

B Add independent clauses to the following subordinate clauses to make complete sentences. (Answers will vary.)

1. Because the advertisement is attractive, we believe it will draw a very favorable response from customers and prospective customers.

2. If you wish additional information, please do not hesitate to call or write me.

3. When I saw the price, I knew that I had found a real bargain.

4. Whether or not you wish to go, you should respond to the invitation.

5. If Lane's holds a special sale, we should plan to buy some of the products we will be needing later this year.

C   **Add dependent clauses to the following independent clauses.** (Answers will vary.)

1. I hope <u>that you will find an interesting, good-paying job.</u>

2. Please let me know <u>when it would be convenient for you to meet with us.</u>

3. You and I may need to work Saturday <u>if we do not finish this project Friday.</u>

4. This report has made a strong impression on me, <u>although I do not concur with some of the conclusions and</u> <u>recommendations it contains.</u>

5. Ms. Kleinfeld is interested in the position <u>that you told her about last week.</u>

D   **Combine each group of sentences into one compound or complex sentence. Add conjunctions, omit words, change punctuation, and so on, as necessary.** (Answers will vary.)

1. Mr. Jenkins resigned. He was offered a better-paying job.
<u>Mr. Jenkins resigned because he was offered a better-paying job.</u>

2. The company may decide to relocate. It will inform its employees several months in advance of the move.
<u>If the company decides to relocate, it will inform its employees several months in advance of the move.</u>

3. Frank left this morning. He was going to Milwaukee. He was going there to see Dr. Oliver.
<u>Frank, who was going to Milwaukee to see Dr. Oliver, left this morning.</u>

4. Someone will replace Mr. Ellis. We do not know the person's name.
<u>We do not know who will replace Mr. Ellis.</u>

5. Ms. Willis went to Boston. She will address the chamber of commerce.
<u>Ms. Willis went to Boston, where she will address the chamber of commerce.</u>

Effective Sentences and Paragraphs

EFFECTIVE SENTENCES

Effective sentences express ideas clearly and concisely. Thus, although sentences vary widely in construction, all effective sentences have the basic characteristics of unity, coherence, and emphasis.

Unity. When a sentence has the characteristic of *unity,* it expresses one main thought with less important thoughts (if any) clearly subordinate to the principal idea. Compare the different versions of the following example. The principal ideas are italicized.

> *The report,* which was written by Mrs. Martin, *provides a complete summary of the company's finances.*
>
> *The report,* which provides a complete summary of the company's finances, *was written by Mrs. Martin.*
>
> *A complete summary of the company's finances is provided in the report* which was written by Mrs. Martin.
>
> *Mrs. Martin wrote the report* which provides a complete summary of the company's finances.

Note that each version of the sentence discusses the same two ideas: (1) the report provides a complete summary of the company's finances and (2) the report was written by Mrs. Martin. But in two versions, the principal idea is that the report provides a complete summary of the company's finances; in the other two versions, the principal idea is that the report was written by Mrs. Martin.

In the "weak" examples below, both ideas are treated equally. In the "better" examples, it is clear which idea is the principal idea and which is the subordinate one.

WEAK:
Ms. Norris is a well-known economist, and she will speak at the October meeting.

BETTER:
Ms. Norris, a well-known economist, will speak at the October meeting.

WEAK:
More people than ever before will be going to Spain this summer, and we suggest that you make your travel reservations now.

BETTER:
Since more people than ever before will be going to Spain this summer, we suggest that you make your travel reservations now.

Coherence. When a sentence has *coherence,* the parts of the sentence fit together in proper relationships so that there can be no misunderstanding about the intended meaning. To achieve coherence, place modifying adjectives, adverbs, phrases, or clauses near the words they should modify. Note how the italicized modifiers are used both in the incorrect and in the correct sentences in the examples below.

INCORRECT:
The salesclerk showed me several *wool turtleneck men's* sweaters.

CORRECT:
The salesclerk showed me several *men's wool turtleneck* sweaters.

INCORRECT:
Everyone wanted to hear Dr. McInnis talk about the status of women in business *at the convention.*

CORRECT:
Everyone *at the convention* wanted to hear Dr. McInnis talk about the status of women in business.

INCORRECT:
Every one of the supervisors *nearly* agreed with Mr. Framm's decision.

CORRECT:
Nearly every one of the supervisors agreed with Mr. Framm's decision.

INCORRECT:
We will send a copy *when we receive her letter* to the attorneys.

CORRECT:
When we receive her letter, we will send a copy to the attorneys.

When two or more parts of a sentence have the same relation to the main thought, be sure to express those related parts in parallel form.

INCORRECT:
Answering the telephone and *to keep the caller waiting a long time* could result in lost business for a company.

CORRECT:
Answering the telephone and *keeping the caller waiting a long time* could result in lost business for a company.

As the following examples illustrate, illogical comparisons also destroy coherence.

INCORRECT:

Sales in July were higher than *June.*

CORRECT:

Sales in July were higher than *those in June.*

INCORRECT:

Alaska is larger than *any state.*

CORRECT:

Alaska is larger than *any other state.*

Emphasis. Since the most emphatic positions in a sentence are the beginning and the ending, less important details obviously should be positioned in the middle. Compare the following versions of a sentence. Remember that the speaker or the writer must decide what is the most important element of a sentence.

> Because he was unhappy in his work environment, Steve submitted his resignation. (The emphasis in this sentence is on the reason Steve resigned.)
>
> Steve, because he was unhappy in his work environment, submitted his resignation. (The emphasis is now on the person and then the reason.)
>
> Steve submitted his resignation because he was unhappy in his work environment. (The person and the action taken both take precedence over the reason for the action.)

As a general rule, starting a sentence with *there, here,* or *it* weakens the sentence by delaying the naming of the subject. Remember that overuse of any sentence construction may reduce, or even destroy, the effectiveness of a message.

> **WEAK:**
>
> There are several projects that we must finish within the next few days.
>
> **BETTER:**
>
> We must finish several projects within the next few days.

The use of active verbs is generally better than the use of passive verbs. Note that the "doer" is the subject when the verb is active. Also note the difference in the part of the thought that receives the most emphasis in the various versions of the sentence below.

> **PASSIVE:**
>
> Ms. Barnes *was sent* a copy of the August 1 memo by Mr. Brill.
>
> **PASSIVE:**
>
> A copy of the August 1 memo *was sent* to Ms. Barnes by Mr. Brill.
>
> **ACTIVE:**
>
> Mr. Brill *sent* a copy of the August 1 memo to Ms. Barnes.
>
> **ACTIVE:**
>
> Mr. Brill *sent* Ms. Barnes a copy of the August 1 memo.

The use of a passive verb is often preferred when the thought to be expressed is prohibitive or negative in nature, as in the following sentences. Also, as illustrated, the "doer" of the action frequently is not stated.

> Smoking is *prohibited* in this building.
> Shipment of your order *will be delayed* a month.

EFFECTIVE PARAGRAPHS

A paragraph typically consists of a few sentences related to a particular topic or to one aspect of a topic. Thus the subject of the paragraph often appears in a topic sentence placed at the beginning of the paragraph, as in the example below.

> One of the facilities that I would like to recommend for next year's sales conference is Holton House, which is located in Newark. It has just undergone a complete renovation, making it one of the most attractive and well-furnished conference centers in this area, in my opinion. Perhaps most significant of all, its rates are slightly lower than those of other facilities in this area.

For easier reading and greater comprehension, a paragraph generally should contain four or five sentences and occupy eight to ten lines. However, it is not unusual for a paragraph to be either shorter or longer. Most important is that the sentences be arranged so that each sentence proceeds logically from the previous one. Such transitional expressions as *first, next, however, therefore,* and *on the other hand* may be used to help tie the sentences together. Note the example in the second paragraph below.

> Thank you for your invitation to speak at the April 28 meeting of the Youngstown Jaycees. You were most thoughtful to think of me.
>
> I would very much enjoy being with you and the other members of your organization, Ms. Pickens. *However,* I made another commitment several weeks ago to be in Kansas City on April 28.

Further, such transitional expressions may be used effectively to introduce paragraphs—provided that they are used sparingly and logically. Note the use of *further* to link this paragraph to the one above the example. Also note the use of transitional expressions in the following examples.

> Our expenses for the second half of this year are running far ahead of budget. At the same time our sales are at about the same level as last year.
>
> *Consequently,* effective immediately, we must review all travel and other expenses currently budgeted for the remainder of the year and cancel those that are not essential.

Study Guide 19

A. Compare the different versions of each sentence below, noting the change or changes made to improve the sentence.

WEAK:
The building is located in the midtown area, and it is convenient to public transportation, and it is managed by Edwards & Associates.

BETTER:
The building, which is located the midtown area and which is convenient to public transportation, is managed by Edwards & Associates.

INCORRECT:
The rent has not been increased, nor is it not likely to be.

CORRECT:
The rent has not been increased, nor is it likely to be.

INCORRECT:
We need someone with good academic credentials and who has a keen interest in marketing.

CORRECT:
We need someone with good academic credentials and a keen interest in marketing.

CORRECT:
We need someone who has good academic credentials and a keen interest in marketing.

WEAK:
There are several things we must do immediately.

BETTER:
We must do several things immediately.

INCORRECT:
We liked the first car we saw as well, if not better than, any of the others.

CORRECT:
We liked the first car we saw as well as, if not better than, any of the others.

WEAK:
When Margaret talked to Kate about the position, she told her that she definitely was interested in applying for it.

BETTER:
When she talked to Kate about the position, Margaret told her that she definitely was interested in applying for it.

BETTER:
When Margaret talked to her about the position, Kate told her that she definitely was interested in applying for it.

WEAK:
Mrs. Wilson was wearing a dark blue silk dress made by a New York designer at her son's wedding.

BETTER:
At her son's wedding, Mrs. Wilson was wearing a dark blue silk dress made by a New York designer.

INCORRECT:
We need to gather together everything we need.

CORRECT:
We need to gather everything we need.

INCORRECT:
We just paid a great deal of money for that machine, and so we need to take good care of it.

CORRECT:
We just paid a great deal of money for that machine, and we need to take good care of it.

INCORRECT:
I am not sure where they are at today.

CORRECT:
I am not sure where they are today.

B. To develop clear, concise sentences, avoid unnecessary words or language that sounds stilted or affected. Compare the different versions of the sentences below, noting the changes made to provide clarity.

WORDY:
In view of the fact that you and I will be working together on the new budget that the general manager has asked you and me to prepare and that we must submit to him by the first of next month, you and I need to get together right away and get started on it.

BETTER:
Since the general manager has asked us to prepare and submit the new budget by the first of next month, we need to get together to begin working on it immediately.

STILTED:
It is my belief that the remuneration for this specialized position is not equivalent to the remuneration for positions with comparable duties and responsibilities in other departments.

BETTER:
I believe that the salary for this specialized position is not in line with salaries paid for positions with similar duties and responsibilities in other departments.

C. Compare the paragraphs in each of the following groups. Can you explain why the second example in each group is better than the first?

WEAK:

We regret we are unable to grant your request. We are not responsible for merchandise damaged in transit. Neither are we responsible for merchandise lost in transit. The transportation company has that responsibility, and we are willing to supply documents that you may need to substantiate your claim.

BETTER:

We regret that we cannot grant your request, as the transportation company is responsible for merchandise lost or damaged in transit. However, we are willing to supply documents that you may need to substantiate your claim.

WEAK:

I would like to cordially invite you to attend a luncheon, and it will be for Betty Huffman on Friday of next week at the Greenbrier Inn. The purpose of the luncheon is to honor Betty on her tenth anniversary with the company. Let me know whether you can attend, and please do so by next Monday.

BETTER:

You are cordially invited to attend a luncheon for Betty Huffman, who is celebrating her tenth anniversary with the company. The luncheon will be at the Greenbrier Inn on Friday of next week. Please let me know by next Monday whether you will attend.

ASSIGNMENT: Complete the Unit 19 Worksheet on pages 141–142; then complete the Part 5 Review on pages 143–144.

UNIT 19

Effective Sentences and Paragraphs

WORKSHEET

 A   **Rewrite each sentence or group of sentences to provide unity and coherence as well as emphasis on a part of the sentence that you consider important. Add, omit, and change words as necessary to produce one clear, concise statement.** (Answers will vary).

1. I attended Blake College. I majored in accounting. Then I got a job with First Bank and Trust Company.

Before getting a job with First Bank and Trust Company, I attended Blake College, where I majored in accounting.

2. Advances in technology occur almost every day. They create new job opportunities. They affect the lives of all of us.

Advances in technology that create new job opportunities and that affect the lives of all of us occur almost every

day.

3. The basic warranty is good for only 90 days. It provides limited coverage. You should consider the extended plan. It provides nearly complete coverage for six years.

Because the basic warranty provides limited coverage for only 90 days, you should consider the extended plan

which provides nearly complete coverage for six years.

4. The January issue of your magazine was sent to you, and we are at a loss to understand why it has not reached you.

Since your copy of the January issue was sent to you, we do not understand why the magazine has not reached

you.

5. Tom's novel is new. I am certain you will enjoy reading it as much as I did. I am sending you a copy.

Since I am certain you will enjoy reading Tom's new novel as much as I did, I am sending you a copy.

6. I should have bought the other machine. The other machine is faster. It is also easier to operate.

I should have bought the other machine because it is faster and easier to operate.

7. By this plan, you can estimate what your supplies will cost each month, and this will be more satisfactory for you.

Because this plan makes it possible for you to estimate what your supplies will cost each month, you should find it

more satisfactory.

8. Last winter I took a trip to the Caribbean, and two islands particularly interested me. They are Jamaica and St. Thomas.

I found the islands of Jamaica and St. Thomas particularly interesting when I went to the Caribbean last winter.

9. The flag of the United States is called "the Stars and Stripes" or "Old Glory." It contains 50 stars. Hawaii was the last state admitted.

The United States flag, which is called "the Stars and Stripes" or "Old Glory," has contained 50 stars since Hawaii was admitted to the Union.

10. Extra money spent for these chairs is well spent. They are sturdy and well designed. They have foam rubber seats.

These sturdy, well-designed chairs with foam rubber seats are worth the extra money they cost.

11. Companies use many kinds of printed forms. Memos, invoices, and purchase orders are among the many kinds of printed forms that are used.

Companies use many kinds of printed forms, including memos, invoices, and purchase orders.

12. Ms. Olson developed a plan. The plan will save the company money. It reduces the company's mailing and shipping expenses.

Ms. Olson developed a plan that will save the company money by reducing its mailing and shipping expenses.

13. Benjamin Franklin had little formal education. He became one of the best-educated people of his time. He believed the principle that people learn what they teach themselves.

Although Benjamin Franklin had little formal education, he believed that people learn what they teach themselves and became one of the best-educated people of his time.

14. Many new drugs have been developed. They have been tested and found safe under normal conditions. Individual reactions must be studied.

Many new drugs have been developed, tested, and found safe under normal conditions; however, individual reactions to them must be studied.

15. Businesses rely heavily upon computers and other machines. Prospective employees need to know how to use them.

Since businesses rely heavily upon computers and other machines, prospective employees need to know how to use them.

 Select one of the following topics, and write a short paragraph (about five sentences) on it. Remember to arrange the sentences so that each flows smoothly and logically into the next one. Use a separate sheet of paper for this short writing project. (Answers will vary.)

1. Lack of experience can be partly offset by thorough educational training.

2. The ability to write effectively is important in many kinds of work.

3. Listening pays off in the business world.

4. Computers have affected all of us in one way or another.

5. Communicating effectively requires more than using language correctly.

PART 5

Phrases, Clauses, and Sentences

REVIEW

 A **For each phrase below, write a sentence in which the phrase functions as indicated in parentheses. Note the example.** (Answers will vary.)

0. Submitting the lowest bid (Adjective modifying a noun.)

The company submitting the lowest bid may be awarded the contract.

1. Invited to the reception (Adjective modifying a pronoun.)

Everyone invited to the reception has accepted our invitation.

2. Being successful (Noun functioning as the subject of a verb.)

Being successful means different things to different people.

3. To increase productivity (Noun functioning as a predicate nominative.)

One of our goals is to increase productivity.

4. Before April 15 (Adverb modifying a verb or verb phrase.)

Most people file their tax returns before April 15.

5. To be promoted (Adjective modifying either a noun or a pronoun.)

I think you are among those to be promoted.

6. Meeting the deadline (Noun functioning as the object of a preposition)

We need to develop a detailed plan for meeting the deadline.

7. To tell the truth (Absolute phrase preceding an independent clause.)

To tell the truth, the job is more interesting than I thought it would be.

8. Offering next-day delivery service (Adjective modifying a noun.)

What firm offering next-day delivery service do you recommend?

9. To another department (Adverb modifying an infinitive.)

I think he has asked to be transferred to another department.

10. For all new employees (Adjective modifying a noun or a pronoun.)

An orientation program for all new employees will be conducted next Friday.

 Write each of the following groups of sentences as one complex sentence. Insert conjunctions, relative pronouns, and punctuation marks to show the relationship of the thoughts to each other. Make whatever changes in wording or capitalization you consider necessary. Note the example. (Answers will vary.)

0. Four cashiers were hired last week. Business has increased, however, and we are planning to hire two more.

Although four cashiers were hired last week, we are planning to hire two more because business has increased.

1. I called Mr. Hammond yesterday afternoon. He was not in the office.

When I called Mr. Hammond yesterday afternoon, he was not in the office.

2. Mrs. Wilson plans to retire next month. She has been with the company since 1979. She also plans to move to Arizona next month.

Mrs. Wilson, who has been with the company since 1979, plans to retire and move to Arizona next month.

3. The first impression a job applicant makes is very important. That fact is well known.

That the first impression a job applicant makes is very important is a well-known fact.

4. Using the "you approach" makes sense. The effectiveness of a message is ultimately determined by the reader or listener.

Using the "you approach" makes sense because the effectiveness of a message is ultimately determined by the

reader or listener.

5. Ms. Levine is a well-known author and lecturer. She will speak at our marketing conference. Our marketing conference will be in August.

Ms. Levine, who is a well-known author and lecturer, will speak at our marketing conference in August.

PART 6

Capitalization and Number Style

Before you study Units 20 through 22, complete this survey of capitalization and number style. These exercises will help you identify principles that you may wish to give special attention.

SURVEY

 In each of the following sentences, draw three lines under each letter that should be capitalized. If no change in capitalization is necessary, circle the number preceding the sentence. Note the examples.

0. The mayors met with governor hillyer last wednesday.

00. The article was published in June or July of last year.

1. The president of the company, r. j. franklin, was interviewed by one of the reporters representing cnn.

2. At a press conference on the lawn of the white house, the president said that he had discussed the matter with various members of congress.

3. When did former governor Georgeson accept a position with the accounting firm of green & associates?

4. The de Palmas plan to expand their operations in new england this fall.

5. I'm sure, sir, that I had the german measles when I was a child.

6. A group of american, canadian, and mexican investors met with government officials representing countries that are members of the european economic community.

7. Fay used india ink to draw a sketchy map of the canary islands.

8. Did the national association of manufacturers meet in washington state or in washington, d. c.?

9. The company will hold its annual sales conference at the hotel pierre in salt lake city.

10. Be sure to visit the Lincoln memorial, the Ford theater, and the library of Congress while you are in Washington, D.C

11. The panel moderator asked, "do you agree with that assessment of the situation, senator?"

12. Is your new office on north Lincoln boulevard or east Tenth street?

13. "a copy of the article is enclosed," stated the author. "please let me know what you think of it."

14. Do you prefer the site in the western part of the city or the one in the southern part of the county?

15. Edith J. LaCroix, ph. d., was a guest lecturer at one of the universities in the windy city last march.

16. The mayor, Yolanda Amaro, told the members of the city council that she intends to run for reelection.

17. Several firms in the state do business with the department of defense and other federal agencies.

18. She was awarded a bachelor of science degree by the university of north dakota.

19. This week's specials include crisco oil and log cabin syrup.

20. Her question was, why did the government get involved?

21. Please see figure 4 on page 116 of *the communicator's handbook: a guide for writers and speakers.*

22. The announcement was made at 10 a.m., central standard time.

23. "This store," the owner declared, "sells nothing but grade a dairy products."

24. Will there be more states in the union at the beginning of the twenty-first century?

25. Where did you celebrate new year's eve last year?

B **Underline each incorrect number expression in the following sentences, and write the correct expression in the space provided. If no correction is necessary, write *OK*.**

1. That organization has several 100 members.
   1. several hundred

2. Four of the 25 copies were illegible.
   2. twenty-five

3. Their address is as follows: 1,240 Elm Street, Tampa, FL 33618.
   3. 1240

4. The value of the company's assets is between $1 and $1.5 million.
   4. $1 million

5. Please order two rolls of tape and 16 reams of copier paper.
   5. 2

6. We have been at 1 Park Place since 1988.
   6. One

7. The dinner is scheduled for six p.m.
   7. 6 p.m.

8. Let's plan to leave around nine o'clock.
   8. OK

9. The cost of living decreased .3%.
   9. 0.3 percent

10. She joined the company 7/15/90.
    10. July 15, 1990

11. They were married on June 4th of last year.
    11. June 4

12. This coupon is worth 25¢.
    12. 25 cents

13. The price ranges from 90 cents to $1.49.
    13. $.90

14. It isn't worth 2 cents.
    14. two cents

15. This package weighs 16 pounds two ounces.
    15. 2 ounces

16. How would you assess the decade of the '80s?
    16. OK

17. He deposited a 100 dollars in an account that pays 4.5 percent interest.
    17. hundred

18. The company just celebrated its 20th anniversary.
    18. twentieth

19. The office is on East Thirty-Fourth Street.
    19. East 34 OR 34th Street

20. Let's meet at 9 tomorrow a.m.
    20. 9 tomorrow morning OR 9 a.m. tomorrow

21. She paid over $10,000.00 for her car.
    21. $10,000

22. Ed sold 7500 in May and 12,450 in June.
    22. 7,500

23. We have only 2 openings in our 15th Street store.
    23. two

24. This bottle holds 2 and one-half ounces.
    24. 2 1/2 OR 2.5 ounces

25. About 3/4 of the new building has been leased to a large chemical company.
    25. three-fourths

UNIT 20

Capitalization of Names

Business writers sometimes use capitalization solely as an attention-getting device when preparing advertisements, sales letters, and similar materials. Such usage obviously requires exercising good judgment, since the overuse of capitalization distracts the reader's attention from the most important points of a message. For most letters and other kinds of messages, writers generally restrict the use of capitalization to terms that clearly require the special emphasis or significance that capitalization gives them. These are the uses of capitalization presented in Units 20 and 21.

PERSONAL NAMES AND TITLES

1. Complete Names. Always capitalize the name of a person exactly as the owner of the name does. Give particular attention to names containing such prefixes as *da, de, la, Mac, Mc, van,* and *von.* Note the variations in capitalization and spacing in these names, for example:

Rose Mary McDonald	Louis de la Croix
Rosemary MacDonald	Lewis J. de LaCroix
Anne Marie Mac Donald	David C. Delacroix

2. Surnames With Prefixes. If a surname that includes a prefix is used without a first name, initials, or a title, capitalize the prefix—regardless of how the owner of the name writes it.

Henry R. von Hoffman	Mr. von Hoffman
H. R. von Hoffman	Von Hoffman

Do you think that *Von Hoffman* will receive his party's nomination?

Do you think that H. R. von Hoffman will be elected if he receives his party's nomination?

In ordinary business writing, of course, people are seldom referred to by their surnames alone. Most business writers use *Mr., Miss, Ms., Mrs.,* or some other title with surnames and often with complete names.

3. Titles Before Names. Capitalize executive, professional, civic, military, courtesy, religious, and other titles of honor and respect when they appear before the names of persons.

President Donald L. Carlson	Ms. Pauline Pagano
Dr. Annabel J. Diamandis	Sister M. Agnes Moorehead
Governor J. Robert Warren	Reverend Stevens
Lieutenant Karen Olson	Professor Dominguez

However, if the name following the title is in apposition to the title and is set off by commas, do not capitalize the title.

The new *governor,* Enrique Jiminez, won by a landslide.

Our *president,* Ruth Dinsmore, has an MBA from Columbia University.

If a title preceding a name simply designates an occupation, do not capitalize it.

The spokesperson answered all of *reporter* Bill Lane's questions.

The defendant will be represented by *attorney* Shirley Polisky.

4. Titles After Names. Do not capitalize a title after the name of a person unless it is the title of a high-ranking government official, religious dignitary, or other person to whom great respect should be shown.

Ms. Elizabeth Hillyer, *director of marketing,* will chair the meeting.

Was Trygve Lie *Secretary-General of the United Nations* for several years?

5. Titles in Place of Names. Unless it is the title of a high-ranking government official or dignitary used in place of the name of a specific person, do not capitalize a title that stands alone.

The *President* met with the French *ambassador* yesterday. (*President* is always capitalized when it is used to refer to the President of the United States.)

He has been *president* of our company for the past three years.

Ordinarily, capitalize a title that is used in direct address. Common exceptions include *sir, miss,* and *madam.*

Enclosed is the honorarium we discussed, *Professor.*

Thank you, *Doctor,* for your patience.

Yes, *sir,* you will be happy that you took advantage of this offer.

6. Titles With *Ex-, Former, Late,* and *-Elect.* Do not capitalize *ex-, former, late,* or *-elect* when used with a title.

The *late* President Lyndon B. Johnson lived in Texas.
Are you a relative of Senator-*elect* Burnside?

7. Titles in Addresses and Other Parts of Letters. Capitalize all titles in the addresses, salutations, and closings of letters.

Dr. G. L. Harrington   Sincerely yours,
Director of Research
Merritt Laboratories, Inc.
5800 Calloway Street   Lester H. Guthrie
Rego Park, NY 11374   General Manager

Note that only the first word of a complimentary closing and only the important words in titles are capitalized.

Dear Ms. Greene: Sincerely yours,
Dear Sir: President and General Manager
My dear Mr. Burns: Director of Human Resources

Spot Check 1

Draw three short lines under each letter that should be capitalized in each of the following sentences.

1. The president of the company, patrick m. hill, is a retired lieutenant colonel.

2. Do you think von hoffman will be elected mayor?

3. What were the results of the autopsy, doctor?

4. Did former president and mrs. reagan meet the pope?

5. I think, mr. o'Malley, that the receptionist, pat ellis, took the message.

6. Yes, miss, the agreement will be signed by s. l. kaufman, editor in chief.

7. Please use the following closing: very cordially yours, martha d. crowell, vice president and general counsel.

8. Both of us suggested that columnist Mary Hartwig be invited to speak at the next meeting.

9. Didn't mayor-elect Thompson work for your company a few years ago?

10. The restructuring was announced by S. L. Parker, president and chief executive officer.

11. The president probably will support the measure introduced by those senators.

12. In my opinion, Ms. von Fischer should receive the entire staff's wholehearted support.

NAMES OF ORGANIZATIONS AND INSTITUTIONS

8. Complete Names of Companies, Organizations, and Institutions. Capitalize the name of a company, association, church, school, club, or other organization or institution exactly as the organization or institution itself does. Do not capitalize *the* unless it is the first word of the official name.

the Tandy Corporation   Highland Hospital
the American Medical Association Delta Pi Epsilon
The Ohio State University   The Four Seasons

9. Names of Departments and Other Divisions of Organizations. Ordinarily, do not capitalize the name of a department, board, committee, or other part of an organization unless it is part of your own organization. Do not capitalize such names when they are modified by any word other than *the*.

You should discuss the matter with someone in the *Personnel Department*.

Did you talk with anyone else in their *personnel department?*

10. Words Used in Place of Complete Names. Although they may refer to specific organizations, such words as *company, department, association, committee,* and *college* generally should not be capitalized when they are used in place of complete names.

The policy of the *company* is to promote from within.
She is the newest member of the *board*.

Such words and short forms of names *may* be capitalized when you are writing a formal communication and wish to show that you are representing your own organization in some official capacity.

The *Company* will honor its commitment.
I forwarded your application to *Personnel* last week.

If a word used in place of a complete name is modified by any word other than *the,* do not capitalize the word.

Miriam joined our *department* in February.
Does your *company* use electronic mail services?

NAMES OF GOVERNMENT BODIES AND ORGANIZATIONS

11. Complete Names of Government Bodies. Capitalize all important words in the names of government bodies and organizations and their subdivisions.

> Chicago Board of Education United States Army
> the Ninety-ninth Congress the Bush Administration
> Department of the Treasury the United States Senate

12. Short Forms of Names of Government Bodies. Capitalize the short forms of names of government bodies and their major subdivisions.

> Both of them testified before the *Senate*.
> the House the Marines the Administration

13. The Terms *Federal, Government,* and *Federal Government*. Do not capitalize the terms *federal, government,* and *federal government* except when they are part of official names.

> Is it the responsibility of the *federal government?*
> Should such legislation be enacted at the *federal* level?
> Some firms receive many *government* contracts.
> What action will the *Federal Reserve Board* take?

14. The Terms *Union* and *Commonwealth*. Capitalize the words *union* and *commonwealth* when they are used alone to refer to a specific government.

> Does every state in the *Union* impose a sales tax? (*Union* refers to the United States.)
>
> Queen Elizabeth travels throughout the *Commonwealth*. (*Commonwealth* refers to the British Commonwealth.)

Spot Check 2

Draw three short lines under each letter that should be capitalized in each of the following items.

1. Is she a graduate of the university of south florida?

2. A government spokesperson said the department of defense awarded the contract to fairchild electronics corporation.

3. The President's nominee for the supreme court of the united states testified before the senate.

4. Please sign both forms and return them to personnel.

5. Your physician should return the forms to the head of our medical department.

6. Is he a member of the benevolent and protective order of elks?

7. A number of employees belong to that union.

8. The attorney indicated that the decision may be overturned by a federal court.

9. Perhaps we should ask someone at first federal savings and loan association.

10. In addition to Canada, what countries are members of the commonwealth?

11. Were you among those invited to testify before the senate subcommittee last month?

12. I am sure this will be her fourth term as a member of the house of representatives.

CITY, COUNTRY, AND OTHER PLACE NAMES

15. Official Names of Cities, States, and so on. Capitalize the names of towns, cities, states, countries, continents, parks, rivers, oceans, islands, lakes, and so on. When such words as *river, lake, ocean,* and *mountains* are parts of official names, capitalize them. Also capitalize *the* if it is the first word of the official name.

> Birmingham Central Park Lake Ontario
> Arkansas Ohio River Aleutian Islands
> Africa The Dalles Mount Rushmore
> Portugal Indian Ocean Rocky Mountains

16. Imaginative Names of Places. Capitalize imaginative names used in place of official names of specific places.

OFFICIAL NAME	IMAGINATIVE NAME
Dallas	the Big D
Ohio	the Buckeye State
New York City	the Big Apple
Chicago	the Windy City

17. The Word *State*. Capitalize *state* only when it immediately follows the official name of a state or is part of an imaginative name.

> Bill lived in Washington *State* before moving to the *state* of Virginia, the Old Dominion *State*.

18. *City*, *Village*, **and Similar Words.** Do not capitalize *city*, *village*, *county*, or a similar word unless it is part of an official or imaginative name.

Salt Lake City   the Eternal City (Rome)
Westlake Village   Hamilton County

We visited the *city* of Philadelphia, which is the *City of Brotherly Love.*

19. Names of Geographic Regions. Capitalize the names of definite geographic regions and words that designate or describe residents of such regions.

the Far East	the South	Southerner
the Midwest	West Coast	Latin America
Pacific Northwest	New England	Midwesterners

Several government officials toured the *Middle East.*

20. Points of the Compass. Do not capitalize *north, south, east, west,* and other points of the compass when they simply indicate direction or location.

Go *north* on Interstate 95 until you reach Interstate 4; then go *west.*

The office is in the *southeast* part of the city.

21. Names of Streets, Buildings, Monuments, and so on. Capitalize the names of streets, buildings, monuments, and historical sites, including any common-noun elements that are parts of the official names.

Northern Boulevard	East Tenth Street
Park Avenue	Statue of Liberty
Chrysler Building	Independence Hall
Philharmonic Hall	Museum of Modern Art

Spot Check 3

Draw three short lines under each letter that should be capitalized in each of the following items.

1. In what year did the state of alaska become a member of the union?

2. While we were in washington, d.c., we crossed the potomac river and visited arlington national cemetery.

3. LaGuardia airport is located in queens, one of the five boroughs of new york city, the big apple.

4. The statue of liberty is clearly visible from staten island.

5. That tour will take you through the state of utah to the rocky mountains.

6. The company has two branch offices in the northern part of new york state.

7. She is co-owner of the largest automobile dealership in Winnebago county.

8. Their office is at the corner of south first street and northern boulevard.

9. Are you sure that the Williamsons are midwesterners and that the Halls are southerners?

10. The developers plan to build an apartment complex on a bluff overlooking the mississippi river.

11. Everyone visiting the windy city is impressed by sears tower and the merchandise mart.

12. I think avenues run north and south and streets run east and west in that city.

OTHER PROPER NAMES

22. Names of Acts, Laws, Treaties, Documents, and so on. Capitalize the names of acts, laws, treaties, historical documents, and so on. Do not capitalize conjunctions and prepositions of three or fewer letters.

the Declaration of Independence	Bill of Rights
Occupational Safety and Health Act	the Constitution

23. Names of Months, Days of the Week, Holidays, and so on. Capitalize the names of the months, days of the week, holidays, historical periods, and events.

January	Wednesday	World War II
the Dark Ages	the Crusades	Operation Desert Storm
World War II	Labor Day	Mother's Day

24. Names of Seasons, Decades, and Centuries. Do not capitalize the names of the seasons (unless they are personified—given characteristics or attributes of people), centuries, or—with few exceptions—decades.

a winter sport	last summer	twentieth century
the fifties	fall fashions	nineteen hundreds

The oil company's ad mentioned "the icy fingers of Winter."

Were those styles popular during the *Gay Nineties* or during the *Roaring Twenties?*

25. Trademarks, Brand Names, and Market Grades.
Capitalize trademarks, brand names, and terms that designate market grades. A common noun that is used with a term of this type is not ordinarily capitalized.

IBM computers	Ivory soap	Prime beef
Coca-Cola	Grade A eggs	Arrow shirts

Many words formerly used only as trademarks and brand names are now used as general terms and are not capitalized.

aspirin	nylon	mimeograph

26. Words Derived From Proper Nouns.
Ordinarily, capitalize a word that is derived from a proper noun.

Greek sculpture	Colombian coffee	Americanize

However, there are a number of exceptions to this rule, including the following:

india ink	manila folder	pasteurized milk

27. Hyphenated Names.
Capitalize each part of a hyphenated name if each part is ordinarily capitalized when it stands alone.

San Diego-San Francisco flight	Dallas-Fort Worth area
pro-American stance	Spanish-speaking citizens
Ninety-ninth Congress	Pan-American republics

Spot Check 4

Draw three short lines under each letter that should be capitalized in each of the following items.

1. Instead of taking our vacation this summer, why don't we take a week or two near thanksgiving?

2. I used some kleenex to wipe up the india ink that I spilled.

3. I'm sure that chinese restaurant uses dozens of grade a eggs.

4. Was the federal insurance contributions act in effect during the thirties?

5. We spent wednesday and thursday at a resort near the mexican-american border.

6. What merchandise should we feature in our labor day sales ads?

7. The salvage crew recovered various artifacts from a sunken spanish galleon.

8. We may open a distribution center in the racine-kenosha area early next fall.

Study Guide 20

Study the italicized words in the following sentences. If you are unsure why a particular word is or is not capitalized, refer to the rule indicated.

1. Does *former*[6] *Senator*[3] *Arlene M. McConnel*[1] live on *Park Avenue*[21] in *Kansas City*[15,18] and work for *Midwest Industries, Inc.*[8]?

2. The *Secretary of State*[5], officials of the *Department of Defense*[11], and other *government*[13] leaders visited the *Persian Gulf*[15] region during *Operation Desert Shield*[23].

3. Many *federal*[13] agencies have offices in every *state*[17] of the *Union*[14].

4. *Ms. Norma Baker*[1,3], *president*[4] of our *company*[10] lives a few miles *south*[20] of the *city*[18] of *Peoria*[15].

5. This work was done by the *artist*[3] *Van Gogh*[2].

6. The *President*[5] wants the *Senate*[12] to confirm the appointment.

7. Was *nylon*[25] used during the *Roaring Twenties*[23]?

8. A professional *artist*[3], *David Gross,*[1] did the drawing with *india*[26] ink last *February*[23].

9. Most local supermarkets sell *Grade A*[25] eggs, *Parkay*[25] margarine, and hundreds of other items.

10. According to the people in *Personnel*[9], we have two openings for marketing representatives in the *Minneapolis-St. Paul*[27] area.

11. When is *President-elect*[6] *Williams*[3] scheduled to leave for *Africa*[15]?

12. Have you taught in the *Midwest*[19], *Professor*[5]?

13. The contract refers to *Wilson & Company*[8] as "the *Company*[10]."

14. Was the *Declaration of Independence*[22] signed in the *City of Brotherly Love*[16]?

15. Please address the letter as follows:

    Ms. Josephine N. Mendez
    Director of Marketing[7]
    Jameson & Associates
    100 East Weston Street
    Greenville, SC 29615

16. Apples grown in Washington *State*[17] can be found in supermarkets throughout the country.

17. The site most likely to selected for the new office is a few miles *west*[20] of Grand Rapids.

18. The work surely will be completed before this *fall.*[24]

19. We will meet with some *Canadian*[26] investors.

20. The real estate agent told me that the house was built during the *nineteenth century.*[24]

21. Do you think that *ex-Mayor* Burton will join one of the local law firms?

22. How long is the *Golden Gate Bridge*[21]?

23. They work in the *advertising department of the company*[9].

24. You are absolutely right, *miss*[5].

25. Have you met *reporter*[3] Anne Simmons?

ASSIGNMENT: Complete the Unit 20 Worksheet on pages 153–154.

UNIT 20

Capitalization of Names

WORKSHEET

 As you read each sentence below, draw three lines under each letter that should be capitalized. For each sentence that requires no additional capitalization, circle the number preceding the sentence. Note the example.

0. Please meet me at the corner of fifth avenue and 34th street.

1. The flight departed from o'hare international airport in chicago.

2. I believe that the next meeting of the board of directors of the company will be on february 24.

3. Your inquiry has been forwarded to ms. eleanor mason, director of human resources.

4. Plimpton associates, a denver-based company, plans to introduce an updated version of its starwrite software.

5. The federal deposit insurance corporation is an agency of the federal government.

6. The envelope was addressed as follows:

mr. harold b. campbell, jr.

senior vice president

frazer-maslin company, inc.

1000 rush road

stockton, tx 79735

7. We stayed at the jackson inn in johnson city, tennessee.

8. Would you like to be a member of the hudson county board of supervisors?

9. If they were born in the buckeye state, would you consider them easterners or midwesterners?

10. Was queen elizabeth accompanied by prince philip on her recent tour of the commonwealth?

11. Thousands of people have visited the tomb of the late president john fitzgerald kennedy in arlington national cemetery in virginia, the old dominion state.

12. Are you sure they meant washington state, not washington, d. c.?

13. The speaker was columnist william f. buckley.

14. I thought your instructions were to go east for 12 miles and then turn north.

15. Do some of your patients test your patience, doctor?

16. Does the metropolitan museum of art have any of el greco's paintings on display?

17. After colonel sanders retired, he moved to the city of bloomington.

18. Senator-elect blanco expects to be invited to address the members of the national education association.

19. Why did you use a manila folder to make a label for that mason jar, miss?

20. The south is noted for its hospitality.

21. Those who live in this area must pay federal, state, and city income taxes.

22. We bought some polish ham and a bottle of orange juice as well as a dozen grade a eggs.

23. Members of the polar bear club go swimming in icy water during the winter months.

24. How many passengers were on the los angeles-san francisco flight?

25. This building was constructed near the end of the nineteenth century.

26. I believe ybor city is a section of the city of tampa.

27. Stores generally sell only pasteurized grade a milk.

28. The government spokesperson said that the army and navy may participate in joint canadian-american exercises.

29. Please have your doctor complete these forms and return them to our human resources department.

30. A number of people think mayor dukes will win reelection by a landslide.

31. Every member of the association thinks de witt is humorless.

32. It's entirely possible the office will close early the day before thanksgiving.

33. Will that transatlantic flight take us over the canary islands?

34. The federal auditors spent nearly a month going through the first national bank and trust company's records.

35. Will the federal government reimburse the state government under those circumstances?

36. Owning stock in an oil company may take part of the chill away when winter puts its icy hands on your cheeks.

37. Like you, professor, I think the author waxed a bit poetic.

38. Someone said the jaycees would donate a few hundred dollars to the american society for the prevention of cruelty to animals.

39. The president invited the secretary of state and other cabinet members to have breakfast at the white house.

40. Lawton brothers opened a new store across the street from the hotel ashland on northern boulevard.

41. How much would it cost us to rent an ocean-view suite at seaspray resort for a week?

42. Is it possible to see pike's peak from downtown colorado springs?

43. On their way to visit relatives in new england, they stopped in new york city and took the ferry to staten island.

44. The vice president and general manager, herbert stevens, gave the senator a copy of the company's annual report.

45. How many countries are members of the united nations?

46. Please order a supply of nylon ribbons and mimeograph paper.

47. Those looking for the fountain of youth will find it in st. augustine, florida, the oldest city in the country.

48. That deduction is made in accordance with the federal insurance contributions act.

49. The measure has been approved by the house of representatives and the senate.

50. Is a spanish dance company appearing at radio city music hall this fall?

Capitalization—Other Uses

FIRST WORDS

1. Complete Sentences. Always capitalize the first word of a complete sentence.

> *Maybe* this would be a good time to invest in real estate.
>
> *Please* return the enclosed card today.
>
> *What* are their objectives?
>
> *That's* what I thought!

2. Elliptical Expressions. An ***elliptical expression*** is a word or a group of words that is not a grammatically complete sentence but that is used as though it were. Such expressions, which always begin with a capital letter, are not used very often in ordinary business writing.

> Is this a once-in-a-lifetime offer? *Definitely!*
> Who will do the work? *When?*

3. Complete Direct Quotations. Capitalize the first word of a direct quotation that is a complete sentence.

> The interviewer asked, "*When* will you be able to start?"
>
> "*Such* statements have no factual basis," the spokesperson said.

If a direct quotation is interrupted, do not capitalize the first word following the interrupting element unless that word begins a new sentence.

> "*What,*" she asked, "is your career goal?"
>
> "*The* meeting has been canceled," the secretary said.
>
> "*Some* of the committee members won't be back until tomorrow."

4. Incomplete Direct Quotations. If a direct quotation is not a complete sentence, do not capitalize the first word unless it is a proper noun or other word normally capitalized. Note that commas are *not* used to set off an incomplete direct quotation from the rest of the sentence.

> The contract states "payable on or before the first day of each month."
>
> He said "accounting irregularities" resulted in an overstatement of his company's earnings last quarter.

5. Indirect Quotations. Do not capitalize the first word of an indirect quotation. Note that an indirect quotation does not consist of the exact words spoken or written by someone else and is not enclosed in quotation marks.

> The manager asked me *how* much I paid for it. (DIRECT QUOTATION: The manager asked me, "How much did you pay for it?")
>
> I thought you said *you* would accept their offer. (DIRECT QUOTATION: I thought you said, "I will accept their offer.")

6. Independent Questions. Capitalize the first word of an independent question within a sentence. Note the comma before the question.

> The question is, *Can* we meet their deadline?
> The main issue is, *Whom* will such legislation benefit?

7. Statements After a Colon. Capitalize the first word of a sentence following a colon if the sentence states a formal rule, begins a long direct quotation, or requires special emphasis.

> Follow this rule: *Do* not divide a one-syllable word.
>
> Please remember: *No* customer's complaint is trivial.
>
> The catalog states the following: "*Prices* are subject to change without notice."

8. Enumerated Items. Capitalize the first word of each numbered or lettered item displayed on a separate line in a listing of items.

> Please bring the following to the meeting:
>   1. The current procedures manual
>   2. A list of suggested changes

Letters preceding enumerated items are not capitalized. Also note that the first word of a numbered or lettered item *within* a sentence is not capitalized.

> The committee will review and select software for:
>   a. Word processing
>   b. Communications
>
> Be sure to emphasize the following: (a) your experience and (b) your education.

Note that the capitalization of items in outlines and letters preceding them is indicated in Unit 22.

In each of the following sentences, draw three short lines under each letter that should be capitalized.

1. for whom is this copy intended?

2. "which of the applicants," asked the manager, "do you think we should hire?"

3. my first question was, how much will the monthly payments be?

4. we need the following right away:
   1. letterhead stationery
   2. interoffice memo forms

5. she wants to know who will be manager of the Accounting department.

6. please note: the office will close at noon next Friday.

7. remember: to sell John Smith what John Smith buys, you must see John Smith through John Smith's eyes.

8. will both of us attend the cornerstone-laying ceremony? certainly!

9. The agreement clearly states "on the tenth of each month."

10. "if you have any questions," he said, "let me know."

11. She asked, "how much does it cost? will you accept a personal check?"

12. Did you cancel the order? if so, why?

13. Will this offer be repeated? no!

14. For each new product, the chart shows (a) sales for the first quarter of last year, (b) sales for the first quarter of this year, and (c) the percentage of increase or decrease.

15. If either of them asks me, what should I say?

16. Do I know who authorized the payment of that invoice? yes.

LITERARY AND ARTISTIC WORKS

9. Titles of Books, Magazines, and so on. In writing the title of a book, play, magazine, newspaper, report, motion picture, or similar item, always capitalize the first word and the last word. In addition, capitalize all other words in the title except articles, prepositions, and conjunctions that contain three or fewer letters.

> The article appeared in *The Wall Street Journal.*
> It was advertised in *Business Week.*
> Is the correct title of his book *Catcher in the Rye?*
> The article is entitled "For Secretaries Only."
> *Gone With the Wind* is considered a classic.

10. Words Following Dashes and Colons in Titles. Capitalize the first word following a dash or a colon in a title. This rule applies even if the word is an article, a preposition, or a conjunction containing three or fewer letters.

> The article "Exercise–*A* Prescription for Good Health" appeared in last month's issue.
> You will find the book *Personnel Policies: A Guide for Managers* a very useful reference.

11. Use of All-Capital Letters for Titles. It is permissible to write the complete titles of books, magazines, and other publications entirely in capital letters. In ordinary business writing, however, the preferred style is to write titles of complete works in capital and small letters with underscores, which are the equivalent of italics in printed material.

> KEYBOARDING: A SELF-STUDY COURSE
> Sports Illustrated

When they appear in addresses, write titles of publications in capital and small letters without underscores.

> Editor in Chief
> Business Week
> 1221 Avenue of the Americas
> New York, NY 10020

COURSES OF STUDY, SUBJECTS, ACADEMIC DEGREES, INITIALS, AND ABBREVIATIONS

12. Courses of Study and Subjects. Capitalize the names of specific courses of study, but do not capitalize the names of subjects or general areas of study unless they are proper nouns or derivatives of proper nouns.

> Is *Communications 440* devoted to technical report writing?

The company offers evening courses in *conversational Spanish, computer programming, keyboarding,* and *business writing.*

13. Academic Degrees, Initials, and Abbreviations. Always capitalize the principal words in the names of academic degrees following the names of persons.

Mildred M. Noriega, *Doctor of Philosophy*
BUT: She has a *doctor of philosophy* degree.

Also capitalize abbreviations of academic degrees, initials standing for names of people, radio and television station call letters, and most other abbreviations of words that are normally capitalized.

CST *(Central Standard Time)*
Station KADA
Feb. *(February)*
Ed.D. *(Doctor of Education)*
JFK *(John F. Kennedy)*
B.S. *(Bachelor of Science)*
WNBC-TV
EDP *(electronic data processing)*
Washington, DC *(District of Columbia)*
UN *(United Nations)*

TERMS WITH NUMBERS AND LETTERS

14. Terms Preceding Numbers and Letters. Capitalize a term or an abbreviation of a term that is followed by a number or a letter.

Volume IV
Chapter 10
Grade A
Article IX
Part 6
Figure 4
Exhibit B
Table 5
No. 842
Model 400
Style 104B
Flight 32
Fig. 4
Exercise 20
Vol. IV
Illus. D
Diagram 3
Bulletin 24
Chart 10
Section V
Order 5105

EXCEPTIONS: The following terms are exceptions: *line, note, page, paragraph, size,* and *verse.*

The description of the article on *page* 24 indicates that it is available in *size* 12.

Please see *line* 4 of *paragraph* 2.

In the following sentences, draw three lines under each letter or group of letters or words that should be capitalized.

1. The article "on the street today" appeared in *the new york times.*
2. Enclosed is a copy of *stocks: a guide for the small investor.*
3. I plan to take business management 350 and a course in computer programming next term.
4. Paul Richards, ph.d., advised her to work toward an m.b.a.
5. You may need to file schedule d with your form 1040 this year.
6. For a summary of the requirements for a doctor of education degree, see chart 10 on page 36 of the enclosed handbook.
7. Please note that invoice 402 is for volume iv.
8. Have any of the networks televised the old movie *from here to eternity?*
9. Please see figure 4 in chapter 8.
10. The article is entitled "mining stocks—a penny apiece."
11. They will arrive at 7 p.m., cst.
12. I think invoice 2044 should have been for only a dozen size 6 shoes.

Study Guide 21

The italicized terms in the following sentences illustrate the capitalization rules in Unit 21. If you are unsure why a particular term is or is not capitalized, refer to the rule identified by the number following the term.

1. *If*[1] you were to receive such an offer, would you accept it?
2. The question is, *Does*[6] such government-funded research benefit anyone other than those conducting the research?
3. "*Our*[3] new marketing director," Ms. Merola said, "*has*[3] five or six years of experience in field sales."
4. The prospective buyer asked, "*How*[3] long has this house been on the market?"

5. To use Phil's words, this program has "*great*[4] potential in the home computer market."

6. I thought he said *he*[5] would support the plan.

7. Please note: *All*[7] prices quoted here are subject to change without notice.

8. Mail may be divided as follows:
    1. *Incoming*[8]
    2. *Outgoing*[8]
    3. *Interoffice*[8]

9. The article '*Decorating—A Guide for Apartment Dwellers*'[9,10] will appear in the next issue of HOME AND GARDEN MONTHLY[11].

10. Who is the author of *Business Management: The Fundamental Principles*[9,10]?

11. Will Paula Bryant, *Ed.D.*[13], teach *accounting*[12] this fall?

12. She was awarded a *master of science degree*[13] by *NYU*[13].

13. Please see *Figure 4*[14] on *page 220*[14].

14. Will you be under any obligation of any kind? *Absolutely* not![2]

15. Please refer to *Table* 4.[14]

16. Please note that *Style*[14] 20 is not available in *size*[14] 10, Mr. Williamson.

ASSIGNMENT: Complete the Unit 21 Worksheet on pages 159–160.

UNIT 21

Capitalization—Other Uses

WORKSHEET

 In the following sentences, draw three short lines under each letter that should be capitalized. Note that some of the sentences also involve rules presented in Unit 20. If a sentence requires no additional capitalization, circle the number preceding it.

1. is wgn one of the chicago television stations?

2. "my client is eager to resolve the dispute," the attorney stated.

3. The question is, should we continue advertising in that publication?

4. When I saw Everett, he asked, "do you think you will have those revised cost estimates ready for me by next wednesday?"

5. I asked him whether he would be willing to extend the deadline until noon on monday of the following week.

6. "such changes," the speaker declared, "are what caused the company to file for protection under chapter 11 of the bankruptcy laws."

7. "Why would you like to work for allied business machines?" the interviewer asked.

8. I think their president, randolph williams, asked how much longer it would take douglas & associates to complete the audit.

9. Please see table 2 on page 12 of the enclosed brochure.

10. The forms were signed by Grace J. Hollingsworth, ed.d.

11. Please remember: a pronoun must agree with its antecedent in person, number, and gender.

12. The topics to be discussed are (a) tuition refunds and (b) group insurance plans.

13. The theatrical group received a grant from the national endowment for the arts.

14. "In my opinion," the speaker said, "deregulation of the industry has not benefited the general public."

15. The topic is discussed on page 4 of the enclosed pamphlet, which was written by the noted economist, Keith Davis.

16. The group plans to meet with the japanese ambassador as well as with a group of senators and other government officials.

17. The store on eighth street belonged to the de marco family until this fall.

18. How much will it cost you? less than a dollar a week.

19. Have you read Tom Clancy's *the sum of all fears?*

20. Many major cities have a large spanish-speaking population.

B **Review any capitalization rules about which you are uncertain. Then draw three lines under each letter that should be capitalized in the following sentence fragments. Circle the number preceding the item if no additional capitalization is necessary.**

1. At the university of north dakota
2. Along the canadian-american border
3. Five miles south of panama city
4. Draperies made of nylon
5. Along the banks of the ohio river
6. Some black & decker power tools
7. In the twenty-first century
8. Only grade a dairy products
9. Members of the afl-cio
10. In the southeast part of the city
11. By former president gerald ford
12. On new year's day
13. At senator-elect roman's request
14. If the de marco family
15. With our governor, julia ramos,
16. A captain at the united states military academy
17. As indicated previously, sir,
18. While living in washington state
19. In paragraph 4 on page 116
20. These government regulations
21. Speaking from the white house, the president
22. The mayor of the city of san antonio
23. The plan by architect jorge puentes
24. A preview of fall and winter fashions
25. By reading the bill of rights
26. An investigation by the securities and exchange commission
27. Sketches prepared with india ink

28. The items listed on invoice 4046
29. The author of *for whom the bell tolls*
30. A south american delegation
31. During the gay nineties
32. Speaking with a french accent
33. The title of chapter xiv of that book
34. A group of midwesterners
35. Mr. McGuire, vice president and general manager,
36. During operation desert shield
37. A statement by president harold campbell
38. During the late spring and early summer
39. In *effective supervision: a guide for middle managers*
40. The article "tomorrow's technology from today's viewpoint" in *time* magazine
41. During the eighties
42. Every state in the union
43. An exhibition of pre-columbian artifacts
44. After living in the big apple,
45. On the board of the first federal savings and loan association
46. In an advertisement for bayer aspirin
47. On a visit to the middle east
48. At the corner of state street and grand boulevard
49. In the french quarter of new orleans
50. A member of their marketing department

Numbers

The rules presented in this unit reflect current "number style" as it pertains to ordinary business letters, memos, and reports. For the use of numbers in contracts, technical reports, and other special types of communications, you will want to consult a comprehensive writer's handbook or style manual.

GENERAL RULES

1. Numbers *One* Through *Ten*. As a general rule, write the numbers *one* through *ten* in words.

> We may be able to complete the inventory in *one* day.
> I have *nine* or *ten* more letters to answer today.

2. Numbers Over *Ten*. As a general rule, write all numbers over *ten* in figures.

> The company plans to add *11* or *12* marketing representatives to its staff.
> Approximately *150* orders have been received so far.

Many writers omit the comma separating thousands from hundreds in a four-digit number unless the number appears with others requiring the use of a comma. As illustrated below, numbers consisting of five or more digits require a comma to separate hundreds from thousands, thousands from millions, and so on.

> The college expects an enrollment of *1250* full-time students this fall.
> The commissioner of elections said that *9,248* of the *12,656* registered voters cast their ballots last Tuesday.
> This county has a population of *1,011,486*.

NUMBERS IN DATES

3. Month, Day, and Year. When writing a complete date, spell out the month in full, write the day in figures (without the ordinal ending *d, nd, rd, st,* or *th*) followed by a comma, and write the complete year in figures. Unless it appears at the end of the sentence, also use a comma after the year.

> Both of them joined the advertising staff on *September 5, 1991*. (NOT: Sept. 5, 1991; September 5th, 1991; OR 9/5/91.)

On *February 10, 1990,* the company opened a branch office in Cheyenne.

Although most writers write the date in month-day-year sequence, some prefer the day-month-year sequence used by the military services. Note that no commas are used in this style.

> The contract became effective on *1 July 1990*.

4. Month and Day. For a date consisting of the month and day only, spell out the month in full and write the day in figures without an ordinal ending.

> The next payment will be due on *October 12.* (NOT: October 12th.)

5. Day Before Month or Day Alone. When the day comes before the month or stands alone, either write the day in figures with an ordinal ending or write the day in words. Always spell the month in full.

> The lease will expire on the *31st of March*.
> The payment was due on the sixth. (OR: 6th.)
> Will you be available for the meeting on the *21st?* (OR: twenty-first.)

6. Month and Year or Year Alone. Spell out the month in full, and write the complete year in figures. For a date consisting of the month and year only, do not use a comma between them.

> I found a copy of the *June 1990* issue behind one of the cabinets.
> In *1982* we opened a branch office in Milwaukee.

Unless it is class graduation year or a well-known year in history, write a year as a four-digit number.

> In *1990* the company had a hundred employees.
> She was president of the *class of '90*.
> When people talk about the *blizzard of '88,* they mean 1888, not 1988.

NUMBERS IN ADDRESSES

7. House, ZIP Code, and Other Numbers. Always use figures for house, room, apartment, post office box, route, and ZIP Code (including ZIP Plus Four) numbers. *Exception:* The only common exception is the house or building number *One*.

Their new address is as follows: *110* Stuart Avenue, Hartford, Connecticut *06011*.

For additional information, write to Carlson Brothers, *One* Columbus Circle, Suite *500*, Chicago, IL *60610-4268*.

Note that when an address appears within a sentence, some writers spell out the name of the state and others abbreviate it. Also note the use of commas to separate the various parts of an address appearing within a sentence—and the omission of commas in all numbers of four or more digits.

8. Numbers as Street Names. Use words for the numbers *one* through *ten* and use figures for numbers over *ten* when they are used as street names.

Is your office at 500 *Second* Street?
The explosion was at 330 East *14* Street. (OR: 14th.)

As illustrated above, an ordinal ending is not necessary when *East, North,* or a similar word appears between the house number and the street name. However, when *South, West,* or a similar word does not appear between the two numbers, use an ordinal ending with the number used as a street name.

Their office is at 2400 *14th* Street.

Spot Check 1

Underline each incorrectly expressed number or abbreviation in the following sentences. If no correction is necessary, circle the number preceding the sentence.

1. I have met with them 4 or 5 times during the past month.
2. When did they move to 1240 21 Avenue?
3. The reception will be held on June fifth.
4. How much will it cost to send 50 invitations?
5. Construction work began on March 20th of last year.
6. They promised delivery by the 1st of the month.
7. The contract dated Feb. 1st, 1991, may be used as a model.
8. I wish I could find a copy of the August 16, 1991, issue of *Time*.
9. Their headquarters is at Ten East 12 Street.
10. Please send it to 660 5th Avenue, Atlanta, GA 30,303.

11. The building at 1 Davis Circle has fourteen stories.
12. Of the 10,764 responses, 8639 were favorable.
13. She retired from the United States Army on 30 April 1990.
14. Their office is at 1,042 South State Street.

NUMBERS IN EXPRESSIONS OF CLOCK TIME

9. Hour With *a.m.* or *p.m.* Always use figures when expressing clock time with *a.m.* or *p.m.* For time on the hour, omit the colon and zeros (:00) except in tables, agendas, or similar materials in which other times are expressed in hours and minutes.

Your flight will leave at *9:45 a.m.* from LaGuardia Airport.
The office will be open from *8:30 a.m.* to *3 p.m.* tomorrow.

Since *a.m.* indicates morning, never use *a.m.* with *in the morning, this morning,* or some other expression containing the word *morning.* Similarly, do not use *p.m.* with an expression containing the word *afternoon, evening, tonight,* or *night.*

We should arrive at *9:30 a.m.* tomorrow. (NOT: *9:30 a.m.* tomorrow morning.)
It was delivered at *3 p.m.* yesterday. (NOT: 3 p.m. yesterday afternoon.)

Also, do not use *a.m.* as a substitute for *morning* or *p.m.* as a substitute for *afternoon, evening,* or *night.*

The meeting lasted all *morning.* (NOT: all a.m.)
Your attorney called me yesterday *afternoon.* (NOT: yesterday p.m.)

Use the term *noon* or *midnight* without the number *12* unless the time is used with other times expressed in figures.

We left before *noon* and got home around *midnight.*
One flight leaves at *12 noon* and another one at *2:25 p.m.*

10. Hour With *O'Clock.* To express time on the hour with *o'clock,* use either figures or words for the hour. However, use only one style throughout a particular message.

Let's meet in the lobby at *11 o'clock.* (OR: *eleven o'clock,* especially if you wish to be more formal.)
She has a meeting scheduled for *two o'clock.* (OR: *2 o'clock,* especially if you wish to be less formal.)

When used with *o'clock,* time in hours and minutes must be written in words: *quarter past four o'clock, half past two o'clock,* and so on. Consequently, most business writers prefer to write the time in figures with *a.m.* or *p.m.* Never use *a.m.* or *p.m.* with *o'clock,* however.

> Everyone should plan to arrive by *9 a.m.* (OR: 9 o'clock OR: nine o'clock BUT NOT: 9 a.m. o'clock.)
>
> The package arrived at *ten o'clock* this morning. (OR: 10 a.m. today BUT NOT: ten o'clock a.m. OR: ten a.m. o'clock.)

11. Hour or Hour and Minutes Alone. Use either figures (less formal) or words (more formal) to express time without *a.m., p.m.,* or *o'clock.* Avoid mixing the styles within the same message.

> By starting at *9,* we were able to finish early. (OR: nine.)
> Did you take the *five-fifteen* train? (OR: 5:15 train.)
> She is usually here by *8:45.* (OR: eight forty-five.)

SUMS OF MONEY

12. Amounts Over a Dollar. Use figures for amounts of money over a dollar. In a whole-dollar amount, omit the decimal point and zeros (.00) except in a tabulation containing other amounts in dollars and cents.

> If you pay $500 down, your payments will be *$122.75.*
>
> Our first-quarter expenses were as follows:
> | | |
> |---|---|
> | January | $12,735.80 |
> | February | 9,205.00 |
> | March | 7,645.65 |
> | Total | $29,586.45 |

13. Amounts Under a Dollar. Use figures with the word *cents* for an amount under a dollar except in a sentence or a tabulation containing related amounts over a dollar. In the latter case, use the dollar sign and decimal point ($.) before each amount under a dollar.

> That price will give you a profit of *12 cents* on each one.
>
> The parking fee is *$.75* for half an hour and *$7.50* for all day.

If the amount appears in an isolated instance and requires no particular emphasis, write it in words.

> That kind of advice isn't worth *two cents.*

In copy containing several price quotations, use the symbol ¢ with amounts under a dollar unless some of the quotations are a dollar or more.

> Retail prices of *40¢* a dozen for eggs, *85¢* a pound for coffee, and *55¢* a pound for butter are ancient history.

Our survey showed the same item priced at *$1.10, $.98, $.95,* and *$.89* at stores in our neighborhood.

14. Amounts in Millions and Billions. Write round amounts of money in the millions and billions in both figures and words unless they appear with other amounts that must be expressed entirely in figures.

> The company had sales of *$15 million* last year.
>
> One firm reported a profit of *$1,250,000* on sales of *$18,768,975.* (NOT: $1.25 million on sales of $18,768,975.)

In a range of large amounts written with figures and words, repeat the word *million* or *billion* with each amount.

> The value of the contract is between *$1 million* and *$1.75 million.* (NOT: between $1 and $1.75 million.)

15. Indefinite Amounts. Always write an indefinite sum of money in words.

> The loss amounts to *several thousand dollars.* (NOT: several $1,000 OR several 1,000 dollars.)

MEASUREMENTS AND PERCENTAGES

16. Weights and Other Measurements. For weights, quantities, dimensions, temperatures, sizes, distances, and other measurements, use figures.

> The package weighs *4 pounds 6 ounces* (about *2 kilograms*).
> The room is *12 by 18 feet.*
> Each of those plastic bottles holds *2 liters.*

Note that the parts of a measurement or quantity, such as *5 feet 7 inches* or *10 pounds 4 ounces,* are not separated by a comma.

In tabulations and technical writing, the letter *x* is generally used for *by* and such terms as *yards, feet, quarts, meters, kilograms,* and *liters* are usually abbreviated. For ordinary messages, write out such terms in full.

17. Percentages of 1 Percent or Higher. Use figures and the word *percent* for a percentage of 1 percent or higher. In a range of percentages, use the word *percent* after the last figure only.

> About *65 percent* of those polled thought prices would be from *5 to 7½ percent* lower this year. (OR: 5 to 7.5 percent.)

In tabulations and other statistical materials, the symbol % is usually used instead of the word *percent* and it is repeated with each number: *10% to 12.5%.*

18. Percentages Under 1 Percent. For a percentage under 1 percent, either write it partly in words and partly in figures or write it entirely in figures as a decimal amount.

> The prime rate dropped *one-half of 1 percent* last week. (OR: 0.5 percent.)

If you write the percentage as a decimal amount, include the *0* before the decimal point: *0.5 percent* or *0.75 percent,* for example.

19. Percentage Without a Number. Use the word *percentage,* not *percent,* when no number is used.

> A small *percentage* of the questionnaires have been returned.

Spot Check 2

Underline each incorrect expression of a clock time, a sum of money, a measurement, or a percentage.

1. If we sell them for $12.50 each, our profit will be about 8.75%.
2. He is 6 feet, 2 inches tall and weighs 184 lbs.
3. It was nearly ten a.m. when we arrived.
4. The increase amounted to a very small percent.
5. An increase of .75 or 1 percent is significant.
6. The dividends for the first three quarters were $1.25, 90 cents, and $1.05.
7. Perhaps it is worth several 1000 dollars.
8. They may increase the price from $124.95 to $145.00.
9. The bank has assets in excess of $1 billion and liabilities of 600 million dollars.
10. The first meeting will begin at 9:30 a.m. o'clock.
11. Do you expect the meeting to last all a.m.?
12. At 50¢, it is a bargain.

FRACTIONS AND MIXED NUMBERS

20. Fractions Alone. When a fraction stands alone in nontechnical material, write it in words unless the spelled-out form is long and awkward.

> The average price of common stock dropped *three-eighths* of a point.

The length cannot be off more than *³/₃₂* of an inch. (PREFERABLE TO: three thirty-seconds of an inch.)

Always write such expressions as *half a mile* and *quarter of an inch* entirely in words.

> The office is less than *half a mile* from your home. (NOT: ½ a mile.)

> Each hamburger weighed about a *quarter of a pound.*

21. Mixed Numbers. Use figures for a mixed number (a whole number plus a fraction).

> The net weight is *3¾* ounces.
> The door is *2½* feet wide.

AGES AND PERIODS OF TIME

22. Ages in Years, Months, and Days. Use figures for an age expressed in years, months, and days or in any combination of years, months, and days. Do not use commas to separate the parts of the age.

> Their child is *2 years 5 months 14 days* old today.
> He repaid the loan in *3 years 5 months.*

23. Ages in Years Only. Unless it is a significant statistic, write an age given in years only in words.

> Maria was *eighteen* when she started working here.
> Company policy requires executives to retire at *65.*

24. Anniversaries. If an anniversary can be expressed in one or two words, write it in words; otherwise, write it in figures with an ordinal ending.

> They celebrated their *twenty-fifth* wedding anniversary in May.

> The town just celebrated the *150th* anniversary of its founding.

25. Centuries and Decades. Use any of the following styles for centuries and decades:

> 20th century OR twentieth century OR the 1900s OR the nineteen hundreds

> the 1990s OR the nineteen nineties OR the nineties OR the '90s

26. Other Periods of Time. For a period of time that has technical or some other special significance, use figures. Otherwise, use words unless the number requires writing more than two words.

> I was employed by that company for exactly *4 years 7 months.*

> The bank offers fixed-rate mortgages for *15 years* or for *30 years.*

> We will appreciate your paying the balance within *30 days.*

> The usual terms are *2 percent 30 days, net 60 days.*

> The company was founded *148 years* ago. (NOT: one hundred forty-eight.)

The first session started *twenty minutes* late.

We may have to wait *one or two days.*

NUMBERS BEGINNING SENTENCES, RELATED NUMBERS, AND LARGE NUMBERS

27. Numbers Beginning Sentences. Write any number that begins a sentence in words.

Two of the cartons have not been opened.
Two hundred fifty-six signatures appear on the petition.

28. Large Numbers. If a number in the millions or billions can be expressed with a whole number or a whole number plus a simple fraction or decimal, use both figures and words for quick comprehension.

The metropolitan area has a population of over *2 million.*

Exports of corn reached *4¾ million* metric tons. (OR: 4.75 million.)

Otherwise, write the number entirely in figures.

The company manufactured *1,228,750* cars last year.

For a large number at the beginning of a sentence, use as few words as possible: *fourteen hundred ninety-two,* not *one thousand four hundred and ninety-two* or *one thousand four hundred ninety-two,* for example.

29. Related Numbers. Express all related numbers in the same way—either all in figures or all in words. If some of the numbers would ordinarily be written in figures and others in words, write all the related numbers in figures.

Only *two* of the *twelve* offices are vacant. (NOT: Two of the 12.)

This department has *4* secretaries, *12* accountants, and *1* supervisor.

When applying the rule for related numbers, be sure to consider only those numbers that are related.

Each of the *four* cartons should contain *36* tiles and *1* tube of adhesive. (*Four* indicates the number of cartons; *36* and *1* pertain to the contents of the carton.)

When a number appears at the beginning of a sentence and is therefore spelled out, express any number related to it in words.

Eighteen of the *twenty* new employees attended the orientation meeting. (NOT: Eighteen of the 20.)

ADJACENT NUMBERS

30. Adjacent Numbers in Figures or in Words. If two numbers appear together and both are in figures or both are in words, use a comma to separate them. However, do not use a comma between them if one is in figures and the other is in words.

In *1985, 22* employees received awards for their suggestions.

Of the *four, three* are acceptable.

In *1984 two* of the firm's founders retired.

31. Adjacent Numbers With One Part of a Modifier. When two numbers appear together and one is part of a compound modifier, write one in figures and the other in words. Ordinarily, write the first number in words and the second in figures unless the second number would make a much shorter word.

One of the customers paid with *50 one-dollar* bills.

The plan is to construct *two 12-story* apartment buildings on this site.

This building has *six 5-room* apartments. (OR: 6 five-room.)

OTHER NUMBERS

32. Page, Part, Serial, and Similar Numbers. Use figures for page, part, serial, size, model, catalog, and similar numbers.

Model 8 is described on *page 20* of the enclosed catalog.
However, *Style 40* is not available in *size 8.*

33. Indefinite Numbers. Always write indefinite numbers entirely in words. Such numbers often—but not always—contain such words as *a, many, few,* and *several.*

The organizers expect *several thousand* people to attend. (NOT: several 1000.)

This directory lists *hundreds* of Joneses. (NOT: 100s.)

34. Roman Numerals. Roman numerals are seldom used in ordinary business writing. When used in outlines, they are followed by periods. In chapter titles and other divisions of books, they usually are not followed by periods. Note the capitalization of the various parts of the following outline.

   I. Programming Languages
     A. COBOL
     B. BASIC
     C. Pascal
  II. Application Programs
     A. Word processing
     B. Financial spreadsheets
     C. Graphics

You will find that Part B of Chapter VII covers the topic thoroughly.

In the following sentences, underline each error in the expression of numbers. If a sentence requires no change, circle the number preceding it.

1. You may need two four-drawer file cabinets.

2. Only two of the 24 glasses were broken.

3. This office is 12 feet four inches wide.

4. The research project began in the '90s, and it will continue well into the 21st century.

5. This package weighs three and one-half pounds.

6. The couple received fifty twenty-dollar bills on their 20th wedding anniversary.

7. Their daughter is two years, 11 months, three days old.

8. He is only 30, but he looks much older.

9. 150 of the 200 copies have been distributed.

10. The bank reported loan losses of one hundred fifty million dollars.

11. A few 100 firms have filed for protection under Chapter 11.

12. On January 16 12 employees celebrated their 1st anniversary.

13. Each of the 5 thought the order was for 12 reams of stationery and two dozen notepads.

14. They walk 2 or 3 miles almost every day.

15. This container is only ⅔ full.

16. The contents of the report are listed on page iv.

Study Guide 22

The following sentences illustrate the rules for writing numbers presented in Unit 22. If you are unsure why a number is expressed as it is, review the rule indicated.

1. In *February 1992*[6] *two*[30] of the contracts with that firm were canceled.

2. The company will celebrate its *fiftieth*[24] anniversary on *March 20, 1999*[3].

3. We expect to be at your office by *10 o'clock*[10] on the *22nd*[5].

4. *Eighteen*[27] of the *twenty-four*[29] apartments at *One*[7] Temple Terrace were rented on *May 22*[4].

5. The flight lasted *22 days 7 hours 40 minutes*[26].

6. Earnings for the second quarter were *20 cents*[13] a share on sales of *$1.2 million*[28].

7. The price ranges from *$.95* to *$1.20*[13].

8. We have sold *several hundred*[33] at *$1.05*[12] each.

9. The price is between *$3* and *$3.50*[12] a dozen.

10. They sold the house at *1220*[7] *Eighth* Street[8] during the late *eighties*[25].

11. Each carton contains *24 eight-ounce*[31] bottles.

12. We need *22*[2] copies of those *three*[1] memos.

13. The effects of events in the early *1990s*[25] will affect the way we do business well into the *twenty-first century*[25].

14. As indicated on *page 4*[32], the terms are *2 percent*[17] *10 days,* net *30 days*[26].

15. One of the twins is *6 feet 2 inches*[16] tall and weighs *180 pounds*[16].

16. A drop of *0.5 percent*[18] in interest rates would save us *hundreds*[15] of dollars.

17. One of the officers said that a small *percentage*[19] of the loans are at a fixed rate of *7¼ percent*[17].

18. Does it specify *15/16 inch*[20] or *1 5/16 inch*[21]?

19. On her *tenth*[24] employment anniversary she was *32 years 4 months 12 days*[22] old.

20. If we leave at *noon*[11], we should be there before *three*[11].

21. You will find that *Chapter XVI*[34] contains *14 two-color*[31] illustrations.

22. The meeting adjourned at *11:45 a.m.*[9] and resumed at *1 p.m.*[9]

23. Each has projected sales between *$1.25 million* and *$1.5 million*[14] for next year.

24. They hope to own their own company by the time they are *thirty years old*[23].

ASSIGNMENT: Complete the Unit 22 Worksheet on pages 167–168; then complete the Part 6 Review on pages 169–170.

UNIT 22

Numbers

WORKSHEET

 A **Which of the expressions shown in parentheses is correct? Write the answer in the space provided.**

1. Are you looking forward to celebrating December (31st, 31)?

2. He will be on vacation for (10, ten) days.

3. The bonds will mature on (4/16/99, April 16, 1999).

4. Would leaving at 8 (a.m., o'clock a.m.) ensure our arriving on time?

5. It is in accordance with Article (xix, XIX) of the Constitution.

6. Only 2 of the (12, twelve) were acceptable.

7. (20, Twenty) of the shrubs were replaced by the nursery.

8. I thought Lawrence lived at (44, Forty-four) Archer Avenue.

9. The company has a branch office on (1, 1st, First) Avenue.

10. More than ($5,000,000; $5 million) worth of grain was exported last month.

11. Lawrence said the van broke down in front of 124 (20, 20th) Avenue.

12. An increase of (.5, 0.5) percent is most likely.

13. Dr. Sanders would like to meet with you at (nine a.m., 9 a.m.).

14. Only a few (100, hundred) people participated in the survey.

15. About (30%, 30 percent) of the voters cast their ballots in favor of the proposal.

16. I think the new shopping center will be about (½, half) a mile from here.

17. The label states that the net weight is (12½, 12 and one-half) ounces.

18. Nearly (⅔, two-thirds) of the crop has been harvested.

19. We have not heard from them since (June 12th, June 12).

20. Expense reports must be submitted by the (15th, 15) of each month.

21. Today is her (25th, twenty-fifth) employment anniversary.

22. Of the 20, (18, eighteen) are acceptable.

1. 31
2. ten
3. April 16, 1999
4. a.m.
5. XIX
6. 12
7. Twenty
8. 44
9. First
10. $5 million
11. 20th
12. 0.5
13. 9 a.m.
14. hundred
15. 30 percent
16. half
17. 12½
18. two-thirds
19. June 12
20. 15th
21. twenty-fifth
22. 18

23. One of the packages weighs (14 pounds four ounces; 14 pounds, 4 ounces; 14 pounds 4 ounces).

23. <u>14 pounds 4 ounces</u>

24. We bought a (five-gallon, 5-gallon) can of white paint.

24. <u>5-gallon</u>

25. The twins were (17, seventeen) when they began college.

25. <u>seventeen</u>

B Underline each incorrectly expressed number and each incorrect expression related to a number in the sentences below; then write the necessary correction in the space provided. If a sentence requires no correction, write *OK*.

1. Please send me 2 more copies of the booklet.

1. <u>two</u>

2. They will arrive sometime in the p.m.

2. <u>afternoon</u>

3. The store will close early on the 24 of Dec.

3. <u>24th of December</u>

4. Both of them retired when they were 55.

4. <u>fifty-five</u>

5. I have been working for this company exactly six months 18 days.

5. <u>6 months</u>

6. Their baby is exactly 7 months 8 days old.

6. <u>OK</u>

7. The concert will begin at eight o'clock p.m.

7. <u>8 o'clock, eight o'clock OR 8 p.m.</u>

8. Our fiscal year ends June 30th.

8. <u>June 30</u>

9. The metropolitan area has a population of one million two hundred twenty-two thousand five hundred forty.

9. <u>1,222,540</u>

10. Two of the 12 dinner plates were broken.

10. <u>twelve</u>

11. This statement shows payments and charges through 11/30.

11. <u>November 30</u>

12. The new hotel has six two-room suites on each floor.

12. <u>six 2-room OR 6 two-room</u>

13. Several 100 stockholders attended the meeting last year.

13. <u>hundred</u>

14. Its annual sales are between $1 and $1.2 million.

14. <u>$1 million</u>

15. Why not price it at $5.00 instead of $4.99?

15. <u>$5</u>

16. The value of the property has increased about ten percent.

16. <u>10 percent</u>

17. Dewayne usually arrives about 10 minutes early for every meeting.

17. <u>ten</u>

18. About ½ of the work has been completed.

18. <u>one-half</u>

19. The meeting will begin at 9:00 o'clock.

19. <u>9 o'clock</u>

20. We haven't heard from them since the 12th of January.

20. <u>OK</u>

21. Model 60 is listed on page four of the catalog.

21. <u>page 4</u>

22. She retired from the Navy on 31 Jan. 90.

22. <u>31 January 1990</u>

23. The president of the company is a member of the class of 88.

23. <u>class of '88 OR class of 1988</u>

24. Please see Table Two in Appendix A.

24. <u>Table 2</u>

25. Ship it to 9890 North 8th Street.

25. <u>Eighth</u>

NAME _____ DATE _____

PART 6

Capitalization and Number Style

REVIEW

Underline all errors in the use of numbers, expressions related to numbers, and capitalization in the following sentences. Then write the necessary corrections in the spaces provided. If a sentence requires no correction, write *OK*.

1. The article appeared in the 9/91 issue.

2. The convention will be held at 10 Columbus Circle on Monday, Aug. 12th.

3. Several 100 fans were unable to get tickets.

4. Please note the information in table three on page 24.

5. Prices will be as much as ⅕ less during the pre-Easter sale.

6. 40% of the work has been done, Sir.

7. Wasn't the meeting supposed to begin at 10:00 o'clock a.m.?

8. During the 80s, the government deregulated some industries.

9. The president asked the general manager to develop an agenda for the fall meeting.

10. Jan worked on an oil rig in the gulf of mexico for about two years.

11. Their new offices are at 1,660 10th street.

12. Senator-Elect Hamagaki has met with members of the house of representatives.

13. The cost will be somewhere between $2 and $2.5 billion, according to the governor.

14. The unit cost may be as low as 88 cents or as much as $1.02.

15. This package weighs ten pounds five ounces.

16. Some of those touring the new england states were Southerners in their late seventies.

17. The von Hoffman construction company is developing a 100-acre site south of town.

18. Is this item priced only 5¢ over its cost to us?

19. According to a reporter for Station WKPR, the work by the Artist van Gogh sold for $1.5 million.

20. Do you think the library has a copy of the June 1990 issue of *the reader's digest*?

1. September 1991

2. August 12

3. hundred

4. Table 3

5. one-fifth

6. Forty percent; sir

7. 10 o'clock OR 10 a.m.

8. '80s OR eighties

9. OK

10. Gulf of Mexico

11. 1660 Tenth Street

12. Senator-elect; House of Representatives

13. $2 billion

14. $.88

15. 10 pounds 5 ounces

16. New England

17. Von Hoffman Construction Company

18. 5 cents

19. artist Van Gogh

20. The Reader's Digest

21.	You can own a home in starrett city for under $40000.	**21.** Starrett City; $40,000
22.	The proposal was made by the governor of the state of Michigan.	**22.** OK
23.	Let's meet at the corner of 1st street and ocean boulevard.	**23.** First Street; Ocean Boulevard
24.	Is there an american airlines flight in the a.m.?	**24.** American Airlines; morning
25.	The cost of living decreased .5% last month.	**25.** 0.5 percent
26.	About ¾ of those surveyed prefer the Winter months.	**26.** three-fourths; winter
27.	The debates will be televised at eight-thirty p.m.	**27.** 8:30 p.m.
28.	What do you think you will be doing at the end of the first decade of the Twenty-First Century?	**28.** twenty-first century
29.	The president returned to the White House after a weekend in the rockies.	**29.** President; Rockies
30.	Maria hasn't missed a day's work in almost 12 years.	**30.** twelve
31.	They were at the Orange Blossom hotel for the new year's eve celebration.	**31.** Hotel; New Year's Eve
32.	After seeing the statue of liberty, we visited ellis island.	**32.** Statue of Liberty; Ellis Island
33.	The city employs 100s of students during the summer.	**33.** hundreds
34.	Will you be teaching economics 100 next term, Professor?	**34.** Economics 100
35.	The door is 12 feet wide and nine feet high and has six windows.	**35.** 9 feet
36.	The company's training program includes business english and keyboarding courses.	**36.** English
37.	The U.S. chamber of commerce reported a smaller percent of business failures last year.	**37.** Chamber of Commerce; percentage
38.	You will find that information in chapter 3.	**38.** Chapter
39.	Please order 2 bottles of india ink and 12 handbooks, preferably those with the morocco binding.	**39.** OK
40.	She received an honorary Doctor of Philosophy from michigan state university.	**40.** doctor of philosophy; Michigan State University
41.	At the beginning of 1990, two hundred were employed here.	**41.** 200
42.	Your May 10 letter referred to invoice 6606.	**42.** Invoice
43.	There are 15 3-piece suits remaining on that rack.	**43.** three-piece
44.	Part 305 must be exactly two and ⁵⁄₁₆ inches long.	**44.** 2⁵⁄₁₆
45.	The deed to your property on Lake Chelton should be recorded at the orange county courthouse.	**45.** Orange County Courthouse
46.	The 3 republican candidates favor the president's plan.	**46.** three Republican; President's
47.	I think President Marion Nash has done an excellent job.	**47.** OK
48.	The chief executive officer, D. J. Harris, is a trustee of the city's public library.	**48.** OK
49.	I am forwarding your application to personnel today.	**49.** Personnel
50.	They wanted $8876 for one car and $11,375 for the other one.	**50.** $8,876

PART 7

Punctuation

Before studying the principles of punctuation presented in Units 23–31, see how many of the following sentences you can punctuate correctly. Add all necessary periods, commas, quotation marks, and other punctuation marks. Do not make changes in capitalization, spelling, and so on. If the sentence is correct, circle the number preceding it. Note the example sentence, which shows how to use the caret (∧ or ∨) to indicate where a punctuation mark should be inserted when space within the sentence is limited.

SURVEY

0. Miss Pfizer asked, "When will the new equipment be delivered?"

1. When you call him, Margaret, please ask him whether he will be able to meet with us on Monday, July 28.

2. The branch manager of our Freeport office, Ms. Helen Durkin, is looking for an administrative assistant with excellent communication skills.

3. They requested that their April 12 order be shipped cod; therefore, we added the appropriate delivery charges.

4. The three new officers are Willis James, president; Trisha Singleton, vice president; and Felicia Saunders, secretary-treasurer.

5. Lillian Acosta is the person who can help you, Dr. Vicente, and you can contact her at Terwilliger Associates, 6606 Laurelton Drive, Alexandria, VA 22320.

6. Didn't Wilmer say that you and he would like to adopt a baby, Ruth?

7. Dr. French should get the original copy and Miss Bates the duplicate.

8. However important it may be that we buy a new computer, we cannot afford it at this time.

9. The meeting probably will be held in one of the following cities: St. Louis, Lexington, Topeka, or Amarillo.

10. The first article she wrote was entitled "Developing Your Supervisory Skills"; it appeared in the March 5, 1985, issue of *Business World*, a bimonthly magazine.

11. Can we afford to repeat this offer? Unfortunately, no.

12. Sue Ellen Watkins, PhD, is a well-known and highly respected member of numerous professional and civic organizations.

13. Mrs. Saxon, not Ms. Luxton, said that the report contains a few extremely misleading statements.

14. Is it B. J. Hall, Sr.'s plan to retire in January 2000 and return to Wilkes-Barre, where he spent most of his childhood?

15. Kopacs, McBride & Halpern, Inc's president is a member of our board of directors too.

16. First, we'll need to check with Mr. Lane, won't we?

17. Please be sure to notify everyone of the date, time, place, etc.

18. Chart 4 (see page 8) lists our top 20 products and indicates how much revenue each produced last year.

19. Towels, sheets, pillows—all will be available at greatly reduced prices during our Labor Day weekend sale.

20. How can we be sure equipment such as this will increase productivity? is the question we need to answer.

21. In your opinion, should anyone be asked a question such as that?

22. Yes, such a plan is entirely feasible, our architect, E. J. Blake II, stated.

23. Reference materials, for example, dictionaries, writer's handbooks, and directories of various kinds, are indispensable.

24. The question is, What constitutes a reasonable offer?

25. What everyone would like to know is this: Why do so many think that no news is good news?

26. Look! Look! What bargains these are!

27. Brand X, don't you agree, gives a longer-lasting shine than Brand Y?

28. It is available in 9-, 12-, and 15-foot widths.

29. The announcement was made at 8:15 a.m. EST.

30. Weren't NYNEX and some other companies part of AT&T until 1984?

31. The president-elect was the president of the class of '91.

32. Margaret Mitchell's *Gone With the Wind* is still popular.

33. Phyllis, as well as her supervisor, wanted to be sure the information was up to date.

34. These drapes, too, are available in white and green and blue.

35. Facing the east, our manager's office provides a view, a beautiful view, of a lake full of small fishing boats.

36. Plumbers, including apprentices, must know how to "sweat" pipe joints.

37. Thousands of acres of government-owned land were being used by local ranchers.

38. Some forget that the word *misspell* contains two s's.

39. The change, don't you agree, will improve employee morale?

40. However, we may have to reexamine our position later this fall.

41. "When raining cats and dogs, as well as people, like to be inside," the owner of the pet shop said.

42. To avoid costly repairs is one of our objectives.

43. This house has many features that you will like, for example, spacious rooms, an attached garage, and a beautifully landscaped lawn.

44. Their new address is as follows:

    5042 Park Drive

    Belvidere, IL 61008

45. We, being tired and hungry, asked a friendly-looking shopkeeper to tell us how to get to the nearest restaurant serving well-cooked American food.

46. Before the end of this month, we will give you a definite answer.

47. The deadline is June 1, and to finish by then, we will need to work evenings and weekends.

48. The person standing over there is a real estate agent.

49. They own one half of the business, she owns the other half.

50. Were they in Kansas City, Kansas, or in Kansas City, Missouri, last week?

The Period, the Question Mark, and the Exclamation Point

THE PERIOD

The rules presented in this unit concern the use of the period to indicate the end of sentences. Principles covering other uses of the period appear in Unit 24.

1. Declarative Sentences. Use a period at the end of a sentence that expresses a fact, an opinion, a belief, or a possibility.

> The Congress of the United States is divided into the Senate and the House of Representatives.
>
> You are the best-qualified candidate for that position.
>
> We may reach an agreement with them tomorrow.

2. Indirect Questions. Use a period after a statement containing a question that is not stated in the exact words of the person who asked it and that does not require an answer.

> The interviewer asked me when I would be able to start work.
>
> Our supervisor wanted to know who placed the order.

The second sentence above illustrates the importance of punctuation and capitalization in helping a reader accurately interpret the writer's intent. In this sentence, as is often the case in indirect questions, the writer could have presented the statement as one containing a direct quotation.

> Our supervisor wanted to know, "Who placed the order?"

3. Imperative Sentences. Use a period after a sentence that expresses a command or an order.

> File your tax return early, especially if you are due a refund.
>
> Be sure to lock the door when you leave.

If a request phrased as a question requires the reader to respond by acting, not by saying yes or no, use a period after it.

> Would you please cancel my subscription immediately.
>
> May we expect to hear from you within ten days.

For the sake of courtesy and to avoid the appearance of presumptuousness, some writers use a question mark instead of a period after a request phrased as a question.

> Will you please make a copy of the enclosed memo for each member of the committee?

In your own writing, you can avoid having to decide whether to use a period or a question mark after a polite request by simply phrasing the request so that it is clearly either a statement or a question.

> Please reserve a room for me at the Blake Hotel.
>
> Would you be willing to help Tom finish the report this weekend? (By including *be willing to,* the writer gives the reader an opportunity to say no.)
>
> Would it be possible to reschedule the meeting we had planned for this afternoon?

4. Elliptical Expressions. Punctuate an elliptical expression, which is a word or phrase used as a substitute for a complete sentence, just as you would punctuate it if it were a complete sentence.

> Can we afford to miss the deadline? *Unfortunately, no.*
> How much money must you send now? *None.*

Although elliptical expressions appear frequently in advertisements, sales letters, and similar materials, most business writers use them sparingly, if at all, in other types of messages.

THE QUESTION MARK

As indicated in Rule 3, some writers use the question mark at the end of some polite requests. Most often, though, writers use it for the purposes discussed in the following rules.

5. Interrogative Sentences. Use a question mark at the end of a sentence expressing a direct question. As these examples illustrate, *a direct question* requires a written or spoken answer.

> How much should we budget for office equipment next year?
>
> Do you have a copy of the March 15 agreement?

6. Sentences Containing Direct Questions. If a direct question appears within or at the end of a statement, use a question mark at the end of the sentence. Note the use of commas to set off the direct questions in the following sentences.

> You were on vacation last week, *weren't you?*
>
> Their plan will, *do you agree,* reduce costs more than ours?

7. Sentences Containing a Series of Questions.
If a sentence contains a series of questions related to a common subject and verb, use a question mark after each question to achieve the greatest emphasis. Do not capitalize the individual questions unless they begin with words normally capitalized.

> Have you notified Ms. Davis? *Mr. Hill? Mrs. Bell?*
>
> Will the hearings be held in Akron? *in Miami? in Portland?*

8. Independent Question at the Beginning of a Sentence.
An *independent question* is used as part of a sentence, not as a separate sentence. If such a question appears at the beginning of a sentence, use a question mark after it to give it emphasis. Use a period or a question mark, whichever is appropriate, at the end of the complete sentence.

> *What are the common characteristics of business leaders?* is a question these profiles of chief executive officers attempt to answer.
>
> *Has deregulation of the industry produced the intended results?* is your question, isn't it?

Avoid confusing an independent question with an indirect question. Compare the following examples.

> *What should our top priority be?* is the question we must answer first. (Independent question.)
>
> *What our top priority should be* is the question we must answer first. (Indirect question.)

9. Independent Question at the End of a Sentence.
An independent question at the end of a sentence requires a question mark after it to indicate both the end of the question and the end of the sentence. Note that the independent question begins with a capital letter and is preceded by a comma or a colon.

> The question he asked was, *What is the advertising budget for next year?*
>
> What the sales people want to know is this: *When will the upgraded version be available for shipment to customers?*

10. Elliptical Questions.
Use a question mark at the end of an elliptical question (a word or group of words used as though it were a grammatically complete interrogative sentence).

Was the meeting canceled? *When? By whom?*

Some board members opposed the plan. *Which ones? Why?*

11. Statements of Doubtful Accuracy.
To indicate doubt about the accuracy of a word or phrase within a sentence, place a question mark within parentheses immediately after the word or phrase.

> I spoke with *Mr. Burkey(?)* about my account on May 10. (The question mark within parentheses indicates that the writer is not sure of the correct spelling of the name.)
>
> Pat received the special award in *1989(?).* (The writer is not certain of the year. Note the period at the end of the sentence.)

Spot Check 1

Insert the necessary periods and question marks in the following sentences.

1. To whom did you fax the message?
2. Has anyone volunteered for that assignment? If so, who?
3. Be sure to read each question carefully before answering it.
4. Will you please sign and return the enclosed form to me immediately.
5. I think we should find out how much the repairs will cost.
6. Would you handle my mail for me, please?
7. How many copies will we need?
8. When will this special offer expire? On December 31.
9. It was last Thursday, wasn't it, that she called?
10. Do you think Dave will be there? How about Helen?
11. The case is scheduled to go to trial next week, isn't it?
12. His question was this: How much longer can we afford to wait?

THE EXCLAMATION POINT

The exclamation point is seldom used in ordinary business writing. Most commonly, it is used to attract attention and indicate enthusiasm in advertisements as well as in other sales-promotion materials written in an informal style.

12. Exclamatory Statements. Use an exclamation point at the end of a sentence or an expression used as a substitute for a sentence when you wish to indicate surprise, enthusiasm, urgency, or some other strong feeling.

> Don't delay!
> What a surprise!

13. Single Words. An exclamation point may be used after a single word to show strong feeling.

> *Wait!* Don't throw this letter aside!

14. Words Repeated for Emphasis. When a word is repeated for emphasis, an exclamation point may be used after the word each time it is used.

> *Help! Help!* We must liquidate our entire inventory this week!

Insert the necessary exclamation points and other punctuation marks in the following sentences.

1. Congratulations! All of us wish you well in your new assignment.
2. What a beautiful view!
3. Oh, she told me she was considering a job offer from a company in Biloxi.
4. Both of them were present when the announcement was made, weren't they?
5. He is not sure whether or not he will be able to attend the fall meeting.
6. Do we need a dozen extra copies? Probably not.
7. The question is, Will either of them accept an invitation to speak to such a small group?
8. My question is this: How much will it cost?

Study Guide 23

As you read the following sentences, study the uses of the period, the question mark, and the exclamation point. If you are unsure why a particular punctuation mark is used, refer to the rule indicated.

1. The company moved into its new headquarters last spring.[1]
2. Should we trade in the old machines?[5]
3. Congratulations![13] Nothing could please me more than your being appointed manager of the San Francisco office.[1]
4. I spoke with Ms. Carris(?)[11] of your Atlanta office.[1]
5. Sharon wanted to know who authorized the payment to them.[2]
6. Do not write below this line.[3]
7. Were they classmates of yours?[5]
8. You served on that committee last year, didn't you?[6]
9. The next question is as follows: How long should the grace period be?[9]
10. This computer program requires 256K(?)[11] of memory.[1]
11. Who made those changes? When? Why?[5,10]
12. Will new carpeting be installed on each floor? in the lobby? in all offices?[5,7]
13. Which expenses can we reduce further?[8] is the question we need to address next.[1]
14. Taste the difference![12]
15. What a bargain![12]
16. Stop! Stop![14] You can't afford to pass by this once-in-a-lifetime opportunity![12]
17. What do we plan to do about it?[5] At this point, nothing.[4]
18. Return the bottom part of this statement with your check or money order.[3]
19. It was Lloyd Allen, wasn't it, who coined that expression?[6]
20. Maybe we should ask them what changes, if any, should be made.[2]

21. Christopher or Charlene, don't you agree, would be an ideal person for that job?[6]
22. What a terrific idea that is![12]
23. Would you be willing to draft a reply to each of these letters for me?[3, 5]
24. Be sure to notify either Ms. Crawford or Mr. Sherman of any topics that you think should be added to the enclosed draft of the agenda.
25. I asked them what changes they planned to make, but I have heard nothing from either of them.[1]
26. Does that agency sell life insurance? health insurance? automobile insurance?[10]
27. May I help you? is probably the question most shoppers hear most often.[8]
28. The question a number of job applicants have been asked is this: Why do you want to work for our company?[9]
29. It was I, not she, who wanted Marie to reschedule the meeting with Dr. Williamson.[1]
30. I wonder whether we have enough of those.[1]

ASSIGNMENT: Complete the Unit 23 Worksheet on pages 177–178.

UNIT 23

The Period, the Question Mark, and the Exclamation Point

WORKSHEET

 Insert periods, question marks, and exclamation points wherever they are needed in the following sentences.

1. The report indicates that the cost of medical care is far more than many people can afford.

2. Would you like to work for an import-export firm?

3. How long does it take to fly from Boston to Miami? to Seattle? to Denver?

4. What a great idea!

5. When will this new telecommunications equipment be installed? By the end of the second quarter.

6. You are planning to trade in your car, aren't you?

7. Both of them have enough experience, don't they, to perform well in that job assignment?

8. What I would like to know is this: Why was their bid rejected?

9. Mr. Jeffers asked me when the results of the survey would be reported.

10. Incredible! That's what people say when they see our low prices.

11. Just sign the card and drop it in the mail.

12. Is it necessary to risk losing their goodwill? is the first question we should answer.

13. Should other arrangements be made? When? By whom?

14. Should trade restrictions be lifted? Yes, in the opinion of the majority.

15. Would you please write your telephone number and your account number on the face of your check or money order.

16. Friends and relatives should not be given as references when applying for a job, should they?

17. You received a pay increase in June, didn't you, or was it in July?

18. Someone should have asked them what they think about it.

19. Allow three to four weeks for delivery.

20. Did the company declare a dividend for the first quarter? the second quarter?

21. Would you be willing to consider a lower-paying position?

22. Is it a safe investment? was her first question, wasn't it?

23. Hurry! Hurry! Don't miss this once-in-a-lifetime opportunity!

24. We aren't sure how many employees will be interested in taking early retirement.

25. None of those applications have been processed, have they?

Underline the incorrectly capitalized words and the incorrectly expressed numbers in the following sentences; then indicate the necessary corrections in the spaces provided. If a sentence requires no correction, write *OK*.

1. What is the date on invoice 4020?

2. A 100 of those will be needed.

3. The last payment was $225.00.

4. You are entitled to a ten percent discount.

5. I think Size 8 is correct.

6. Sales were up about ⅓ last quarter.

7. They didn't arrive until three p.m.

8. What do you think of the new Fall styles?

9. I think State law requires a 5-cent deposit on each can or bottle of soda.

10. Maybe Mechanic Pat Deeg can repair it.

11. In 1990, two hundred twenty-two employees joined the group insurance plan.

12. Congress passed that bill in the 80s.

13. They spent a week in the virgin islands.

14. It was late in the a.m. when they arrived.

15. The hurricane missed the City of Charleston.

16. He is a member of our Marketing Department.

17. Did you read the article "the role of the small investor"?

18. We believe in a Democratic society.

19. The price ranges from 95¢ to $1.20.

20. The prime rate rose 0.5 percent yesterday.

21. These Venetian blinds are available in all popular sizes up to 60 inches wide.

22. We ran 2 4-color ads last month.

23. He will celebrate his tenth anniversary with the company on February 10th.

24. They have offices at one park avenue.

25. Would you be willing to testify, doctor?

#	Answer
1.	Invoice
2.	hundred
3.	$225
4.	10 percent
5.	size
6.	one-third
7.	3 p.m.
8.	fall
9.	state
10.	mechanic
11.	222
12.	'80s OR 1980s OR eighties
13.	Virgin Islands
14.	morning
15.	city
16.	marketing department
17.	"The Role of the Small Investor"
18.	democratic
19.	$.95
20.	OK
21.	venetian
22.	two
23.	February 10
24.	One Park Avenue
25.	Doctor

UNIT 24

The Period—Other Uses

THE PERIOD WITH ABBREVIATIONS

1. Names and Initials of Persons. Use a period followed by a space after an abbreviation or an initial in the name of a person.

> Robt. J. McFarlane   Lucy R. Carbone   J. T. Houston

If a person's name is represented by initials only, either write the initials with no periods or internal spaces (*JBM*) or write the initials with periods but no internal spaces (*W.A.S.*).

2. Titles Before Names of Persons. Use a period followed by a space after an abbreviation of a title used before the name of a person. Note that *Miss* and *Misses* are not abbreviations and are not followed by a period.

> Mr. Alvin Jacobson Mrs. Barbara Hagner Miss McCoy
> Ms. Lois Painter   Capt. Nora Wilson   Dr. Ellis

Always abbreviate the following titles when they are used before the names of persons. Note that *Mesdames,* the plural of *Mrs.,* is abbreviated *Mmes.*

SINGULAR:	Mr.	Ms.	Dr.	Mrs.
PLURAL:	Messrs.	Mses. OR Mss.	Drs.	Mmes.

Except in addresses and informal messages, such titles as *Governor, General,* and *Captain* are generally written in full. Note that a title should always be written in full if it is used with a last name only. In addition, write the title *Reverend* or *Honorable* in full if it is preceded by the word *the*.

> Will *Governor Alfred Williamson* be present for the ceremony?
> The *Honorable Alice Fredericks* was the judge.
> Did you speak with *Captain Martinez* last week?

3. Seniority Terms. Abbreviate and use a period after *Junior* or *Senior* when it follows the name of a person. Do not use a comma before the abbreviation unless the person to whom the name belongs uses a comma.

> I think *Dr. B. J. Ryder, Jr.,* is the county coroner.
> It is the property of *Mr. and Mrs. Donald Luxton Sr.* (Note that only one period follows an abbreviation at the end of a sentence.)

Note that such terms as *II* and *4th* are not abbreviations and are not followed by a period.

> B. J. Henry II   Wilbur Kelton 2d   Fay L. Dunlop III

4. Academic Degrees and Religious Orders. Use a period after each abbreviated part of the name of an academic degree or religious order, and write the entire abbreviated name without internal spaces. Such names should always be abbreviated when they follow the names of persons; in ordinary business writing, they may also be abbreviated when they stand alone in sentences.

EXCEPTION: *CPA* is written without periods and without internal spaces.

> Joseph R. Burns, Ph.D.   Sister Mary Ann Reed, O.P.
> She has both an *M.B.A.* and a *Ph.D.*

5. Parts of Business Names. Such parts of business names as *Company, Corporation, Incorporated, Limited, Corporation,* and *Brothers* should be abbreviated and followed by a period only when the companies themselves use such abbreviations.

> McGraw-Hill, Inc.   Brown Bros.   Tyne and Co.

Such terms should not be abbreviated when they stand alone in sentences.

> The *company* you should contact is Wilson & Associates, Inc.

6. Entire Names of Firms and Organizations. The entire names of many well-known business firms, government agencies, labor organizations, professional associations, and so on, are often abbreviated. These abbreviations are always written in all-capital letters without periods or spaces.

> IBM UAW CBS NBC ABC FBI AFL-CIO
> UN   AMS ICC NEA RCA YMCA NAACP
> She has been an *IBM* employee for several years.
> The local station is a *CBS* affiliate.

Note that call letters used to identify radio and television stations also are written in capital letters without periods or internal spaces.

> WABC   WNBC-TV   WCBS   WMAQ   WCBS-TV

7. Letter in Place of a Name. Do not use a period after a letter that is used in place of the name of a person, company, or product.

Brand X   Company A   Secretary C   Mr. Z

I think *Brand X* is far better than *Brand Y,* don't you? You will need to ask *Mr. B* first.

8. States and Provinces. When using the two-letter ZIP Code abbreviations of the names of the states, territories, and possessions of the United States and of the provinces of Canada, do not use periods after the letters or leave space between the letters.

AZ (Arizona) CT (Connecticut) NB (New Brunswick)
GA (Georgia) MO (Missouri)   PR (Puerto Rico)

However, write the traditional abbreviations of these names with periods. If the abbreviation consists of capital letters only, use a period after each letter but do not leave a space between the letters.

N.J. (New Jersey)   N.H. (New Hampshire)
N.Y. (New York)   P.E.I. (Prince Edward Island)

However, when an abbreviation representing two or more words consists of both small and capital letters, use a period and a space after each part of the abbreviation.

N. Dak. (North Dakota)   W. Va. (West Virginia)

If the abbreviation consists of a capital letter and one or more small letters, use a period after it.

Ala. (Alabama)   Colo. (Colorado)   Ia. (Iowa)

Unless it appears as part of an address, do not abbreviate the name of a state, territory, or province within a sentence.

After June 1 her address will be 4044 Eighth Avenue, Belvidere, IL 61008.

We drove through *New York* on our way to *South Carolina.*

9. Names of Countries. The names of countries are written and punctuated in the same manner as the traditional abbreviations of states and similar names.

U.S.A. (United States of America)
U.K. (United Kingdom) OR G.B. (Great Britain)
Mex. (Mexico)

The term *United States* is often abbreviated in the names of government bodies and agencies, such as the *U.S. Senate* and the *U.S. Department of Labor.* Generally, though, it and all other place names (except *U.S.S.R.*) are written in full when they are used in sentences.

The *United States* promised technical assistance. Those figures were just released by the *U.S. Department of Labor.*

Spot Check 1

Underline each incorrectly written or incorrectly used abbreviation in each of the following sentences. Then write the necessary correction in the space provided. If no correction is necessary, write *OK*.

1. Do you know Ms Wilford's home address?

   1.   **Ms.**

2. Will B J Hodge, Senior, be there?

   2.   **B. J. Hodge, Sr.,**

3. I think Col. Saunders will retire soon.

   3.   **Colonel**

4. James England, CPA, audited the books.

   4.   **OK**

5. Is Irene M. Forbes, EdD, a member?

   5.   **Ed.D.**

6. We have two new openings in our Colo. office.

   6.   **Colorado**

7. Many foreign corps. have sales offices here.

   7.   **corporations**

8. The US will be represented at the meeting.

   8.   **United States**

9. The address is 312 Inman Road, Tampa, FL 33612.

   9.   **OK**

10. We have received two orders from IBM.

    10.   **OK**

11. Use either of these abbreviations: N.Car. or NC.

    11.   **N. Car.**

12. Is BJR on the staff of A.B.C.?

    12.   **ABC**

13. How many members does the U.S. Senate have?

    13.   **OK**

14. Secretary B expressed a preference for Brand X. computers.

    14.   **Brand X**

15. Had you met Doctor Pat C. Kline previously?

    15.   **Dr.**

10. Terms of Weight and Measurement. In ordinary business writing, both customary and metric terms of weight and measurement are written in full. However, such terms are usually abbreviated in tables, charts, and technical writing.

The abbreviations of most of these terms are written in small letters. Abbreviations of metric terms are always written without periods, and those of customary terms are now commonly written without periods also. If the abbreviation of one or both parts of a term consists of two or more letters (such as *cu* for *cubic,* leave a space between the parts of the abbreviated measurement (such as *cu ft*).

in	(inch OR inches)
ft	(foot OR feet)
oz	(ounce OR ounces)
qt	(quart OR quarts)
mph	(miles per hour)
m	(meter OR meters)
km	(kilometer OR kilometers)
g	(gram OR grams)
L	(liter OR liters)
km/h	(kilometers per hour)
cu in	(cubic inch OR cubic inches)
sq ft	(square foot OR square feet)
cm³	(cubic centimeter OR cubic centimeters)

EXCEPTIONS: Abbreviations of the terms *millimeter, Celsius,* and *Fahrenheit* are commonly used in ordinary business writing.

> This camera requires *35-mm* film.
> The temperature was *9°C* at noon today.
> It was only *48°F* at noon today.

11. Foreign Words and Phrases. Do not use periods with foreign words and phrases that are not abbreviations. Each word, of course, is followed by a space.

ad hoc	in re	a la carte	ad valorem
per diem	ex officio	per capita	per se

The following abbreviations of foreign terms should always be written with periods. Note that no space follows the internal period.

i.e.	(*id est,* meaning "that is")
etc.	(*et cetera,* meaning "and so on")
e.g.	(*exempli gratia,* meaning "for example")

12. *IOU* and *SOS*. These terms are not abbreviations, and they are not written with periods or spaces separating the letters.

13. Shortened Forms of Words. Shortened forms of words such as those listed below are not abbreviations and are not followed by periods.

ad	auto	condo	co-op	math
doc	exam	memo	lab	stereo

Contractions, which are also shortened forms of words or combinations of words, are not followed by periods. The only commonly used contractions in ordinary business writing are those containing verb forms: *let's, can't, should've, won't, they're,* and so on.

14. Terms Used With Dates and Expressions of Time. The following terms are always abbreviated and used with figures: *a.m., p.m., A.D.,* and *B.C.* Note that no space follows the period between the letters. In formal style *A.D.,* the abbreviation of *anno Domini* ("in the year of our Lord"), is written before the year *(A.D. 1988);* in informal style *A.D.* follows the year *(1988 A.D.). B.C.,* meaning "before Christ," is always written after the year: *500 B.C.*

Write abbreviations of time zones in capital letters without periods and without space between the letters. Note that such abbreviations are used with expressions of clock time and enclosed within parentheses or set off with commas.

> His news conference will be broadcast at 8 p.m. *(EST).*
> The game will be telecast at 2:30 p.m., *CST,* I think.
> BUT: All times quoted in this schedule are *Pacific Standard Time.* (NOT: PST.)

Do not abbreviate the names of the days of the week or of months in sentences, datelines of letters and memos, and similar materials. However, it is common practice to use such abbreviations as *Mon.* and *Aug.* in charts, tables, and similar displays.

15. Common Business Expressions. Since some commonly used abbreviations of business terms are written with periods and others are not, you should consult a dictionary or other reference when in doubt. Note that there is no consistent pattern.

COBOL	(Common Business-Oriented Language)
c/o	(care of)
e.o.m.	(end of month)
NA	(not applicable OR not available)
c.o.d. OR COD	(collect [OR cash] on delivery)
FYI	(for your information)
ea.	(each)
f.o.b. OR FOB	(free on board)
misc.	(miscellaneous)
V.P.	(vice president)
PR	(public relations)
AV	(audiovisual)
Enc.	(enclosure)
CEO	(chief executive officer)

Some of these terms are commonly abbreviated within sentences in business letters: *c.o.d., f.o.b.,*

COBOL, BASIC, and abbreviations of other programming languages, for example. The abbreviation *c/o* is used in addresses, and *Enc.* is used for the enclosure notation displayed on letters and memos. Generally, though, the terms are written in full when they appear within sentences except in intracompany correspondence, invoices, and similar materials.

Spot Check 2

Underline each incorrectly written or incorrectly used abbreviation in each of the following sentences. Then write the necessary correction in the space provided. If no correction is necessary, write *OK*.

1. The driveway is 12 ft wide.

   1. _feet_

2. Please specify the date, time, etc.

   2. _OK_

3. Do you have a 35-mm camera?

   3. _OK_

4. We formed an ad. hoc. committee.

   4. _ad hoc_

5. Do you think his I.O.U. is any good?

   5. _IOU_

6. This memo is FYI only.

   6. _OK_

7. Note that all times are CST.

   7. _Central Standard Time_

8. It was 9 pm when we arrived.

   8. _p.m._

9. I saw the ad. in this morning's paper.

   9. _ad_

10. Have you received any cod orders today?

    10. _c.o.d._

11. The monument was built around B.C. 300.

    11. _300 B.C._

12. We reimbursed her for misc. expenses.

    12. _miscellaneous_

13. Use abbreviations in this table, *e.g.,* Nov. and Tues.

    13. _OK_

14. Perhaps we need an int'l trade agreement.

    14. _international_

15. The conference will be held in Feb.

    15. _February_

THE PERIOD WITH NUMBERS

16. Whole Number Plus a Decimal Amount. Use a period as a decimal point to separate a whole number from a decimal amount, as in a number representing dollars and cents. For a whole-dollar amount, omit the decimal point and zeros *(.00)* unless the amount appears in a column of figures containing amounts of dollars and cents.

$125.75 $15   7.25 percent   0.5 percent   16.5%

The machine is used an average of *4.5* hours a day. This sweater was *$45.99* last week, but I paid only *$35* for it this morning.

17. Ordinal Number in Figures. Do not use a period after a number written in figures with an ordinal ending *(st, d, nd, rd, or th).*

1st   21st   2d OR 2nd   3d OR 3rd   10th

Mr. Grant plans to retire on the *15th* of April. There is no bus service on *21st* Street.

THE PERIOD IN OUTLINES, LISTS, AND ELLIPSES

18. Numbers and Letters Preceding Displayed Items. Roman numerals, numbers in arabic figures, and letters appearing before items displayed in outlines and lists are followed by a period unless they are enclosed in parentheses.

I. Business Equipment
  A. Computers
    1. Microcomputers
      a. Features
        (1) Portability
        (2) Cost

19. Displayed Items in Lists and Outlines. Complete sentences displayed as separate items in a list or an outline are followed by a period (or whatever end-of-sentence punctuation mark each sentence requires).

Please note the following:
1. All meetings will be held in Room 1020.
2. The first meeting will begin promptly at 9 a.m.

Similarly, dependent clauses and long phrases displayed as separate items are followed by periods. However, short phrases are not followed by periods unless the phrases are necessary to make an introductory statement grammatically complete.

Please be sure to bring these items:
1. A note pad or notebook
2. Pencils or a pen
BUT: Please be sure to bring:
  1. A note pad or notebook
  2. Pencils or a pen.

20. Ellipses. An *ellipsis,* which normally consists of three periods with a space before and after each of them, may be used to indicate an omission of material or to achieve emphasis in advertising or other special copy. If the ellipsis appears at the end of a sentence, it is followed by a period or whatever other punctuation mark the sentence requires.

> Warm days . . . cool nights . . . ocean breezes . . . await you in this tropical paradise.

> The sentence should read, "Every employee . . . after 10 years of continuous employment."

> Well, as we all know . . . .

Spot Check 3

Underline each error in the following sentences, and write the necessary correction in the space provided. If no correction is necessary, write *OK*.

1. It is due on the 1st. of each month.

    1. <u>first</u>

2. It cost $980, not $890.00.

    2. <u>$890</u>

3. I think Chapter XII. is the one she wrote.

    3. <u>XII</u>

4. Until the next time . . .

    4. <u>. . . .</u>

5. The set includes one of each of the following items:
   1. Sugar bowl
   2. Cream pitcher
   3. Tray

    5. <u>OK</u>

6. Would you please:
   1. Sign and date both copies
   2. Return one copy to me.

    6. <u>copies.</u>

7. The chart in Appendix IX. summarizes our expenses.

    7. <u>IX</u>

8. The nearest hardware store is on 14th Street.

    8. <u>OK</u>

Study Guide 24

Principles of period usage presented in Unit 24 are illustrated in the following sentences. If you are uncertain about a particular use, refer to the rule indicated.

1. Ms.[2] Joy Covey and Dr.[2] Louis J.[1] Anderson visited the headquarters of Lawford Limited[5] on Wednesday,[14] August[14] 22.
2. Lieutenant Holton[2] was interviewed by an NBC[6] reporter this morning.
3. The company[5] may hire Kathryn Foster, Ph.D.,[4] as a consultant.
4. According to Miss[2] Palmer, the balance is $7.50,[16] not $750.[16]
5. Lynn D. Harper, Jr.,[3] is a nephew of the Honorable[2] Grace Harper.
6. While working for the UN,[6] she used this home address: 1440 West 94 Street, New York, NY 10020.[8]
7. Do you think Brand A[7] is good?
8. Please specify the following:
   a. The date
   b. The time
   c. The place[18,19]
9. Please let me know:
   1. How many copies of each handout I should bring.
   2. What time you expect the meeting to end.[18,19]
10. The temperature was only 12°C[10] at 2 p.m.[14]
11. How frequently do you use *ad hoc*[11] or *IOU*[12] in your writing?
12. Most of us use such contractions as *I'll*[13] and *it's*[13] often.
13. Radio contact with the plane was lost at 12:30 a.m. (MST).[14]

14. All prices quoted in this catalog are f.o.b.[15] Philadelphia, Pennsylvania.[8]
15. The 15th[17] of April is the deadline for filing your tax return.
16. As to what the response will be . . .[20]
17. A number of foreign banks have offices in New York City, Miami, and other cities throughout the United States.[9]
18. The memo from President Curtis Benjamin[2] was addressed to all employees of Lambert Industries, Inc.[5]
19. Some of the artifacts date to 300 B.C.[14]; others, to A.D. 200.[14]
20. The employment figures just released by the U.S. Labor Department[9] were the main topic of our phone[13] conversation.
21. Please buy two rolls of 35-mm film.[10]
22. The weight is indicated on this label as 220 g,[10] but I can't[13] read what it is in ounces.[10]
23. Who would have thought . . .?[20]
24. The merchandise was shipped c.o.d.[15]
25. Please confirm the date, time, etc.[11]

ASSIGNMENT: Complete the Unit 24 Worksheet on pages 185–186.

UNIT 24

The Period—Other Uses

WORKSHEET

 A Rewrite each of the following, abbreviating the italicized word or words. Be sure to use the correct capitalization, punctuation, and spacing for each abbreviation.

1. *Mesdame* Brown — 1. Mrs. Brown
2. 24 *degrees Celsius* — 2. 24°C
3. 55 *miles per hour* — 3. 55 mph
4. *February* — 4. Feb.
5. 36 *inches* — 5. 36 in
6. *South Dakota* — 6. S. Dak. OR SD
7. *free on board* — 7. f.o.b. OR FOB
8. *doctor of education* — 8. Ed.D.
9. Dale *Corporation* — 9. Dale Corp.
10. 10 *post meridiem* — 10. 10 p.m.
11. *Robert* Fulton — 11. Robt. Fulton
12. 26 *pounds 4 ounces* — 12. 26 lb 4 oz
13. 36 *millimeters* — 13. 36 mm
14. *Doctor of Medicine* — 14. M.D.
15. *Michigan* — 15. Mich. OR MI
16. *collect on delivery* — 16. c.o.d. OR COD
17. 8 *cubic yards* — 17. 8 cu yd
18. 200 *grams* — 18. 200 g
19. Lyons, *Limited* — 19. Lyons, Ltd.
20. Columbia *University* — 20. Columbia Univ.
21. *For Your Information* — 21. FYI
22. *exempli gratia* — 22. e.g.
23. 1 *gallon* — 23. 1 gal.
24. 2 *meter* — 24. 2 m
25. Lisa Kirk *Junior* — 25. Lisa Kirk Jr.
26. *Saint* Louis — 26. St. Louis
27. *Thursday* — 27. Thurs.
28. *Incorporated* — 28. Inc.
29. 10 *feet* — 29. 10 ft
30. *anno Domini* — 30. A.D.
31. *Doctor* J. Lee — 31. Dr. J. Lee
32. *Enclosure* — 32. Enc.
33. *Governor* — 33. Gov.
34. 9 *ante meridiem* — 34. 9 a.m.
35. Martin *Brothers* — 35. Martin Bros.
36. 1 *inch* — 36. 1 in
37. 1 *kilogram* — 37. 1 kg
38. *Bachelor of Arts* — 38. B.A.
39. Ash *Boulevard* — 39. Ash Blvd.
40. *Mesdames* — 40. Mmes.
41. *miscellaneous* — 41. misc.
42. *et cetera* — 42. etc.
43. *United Nations* — 43. UN
44. Davis *Avenue* — 44. Davis Ave.
45. *in care of* — 45. c/o
46. *Volume* 10 — 46. Vol. 10
47. 5 *liters* — 47. 5 L
48. *pages* 9-11 — 48. pp. 9-11
49. *cubic centimeter* — 49. cm^3
50. *Associated Press* — 50. AP

Insert the necessary periods, question marks, and exclamation points in the following sentences. If an abbreviated term should be written in full, circle it. Note how corrections are indicated in the example sentence. If the sentence is correct as shown, circle the number preceding it.

0. Lorraine M. Young, MD, was on duty (Thurs.) morning, wasn't she?

1. She returned to the (U.S.) after two years of duty in Germany.

2. The oldest city in this country is St. Augustine, (FL)

3. Will John C. Raglan, CPA, be the guest speaker?

4. Will you be able to be with us on the 15th of next month?

(5.) Orville, a graduate of Northwestern, was interviewed for a job with Station WNBC-TV.

6. What a surprise!

7. Therefore, (Chap.) XIX will be of special interest to you.

8. Will the work be completed by the end of (Jan.)?

9. Letters, memos, reports, etc. may be produced easily on a word processor.

10. This invitation should go to the (Hon.) Dwight McPherson.

11. Miss Willis, Ms. McKay, Mrs. Potter, and Mr. Briggs were members of the panel.

12. Is their president meeting with (reps) of the AFL-CIO?

13. Congratulations! All of us are delighted to learn of your promotion.

14. The samples were labeled Brand A, Brand B, etc.

15. We visited Springfield, the capital of (IL)

16. Would you be willing to accept an IOU from either of them?

17. Would you please sign and return the enclosed card immediately.

18. This package weighs 5 (lbs.) 6 (oz.)

(19.) The news conference is scheduled for 8 p.m., EST.

20. Is your (co.) among the Fortune 500?

21. Does this camera require 35-mm film?

22. She joined our accounting (dept.) soon after she was graduated from Rock Valley (Comm. Coll.)

(23.) Both of them now work for IBM.

24. When was he promoted to the rank of (col.)?

25. Many (corps.) have offices in this area.

UNIT 25

The Comma

The comma is used in more different situations than any other punctuation mark. Therefore, Units 25 through 27 present and illustrate principles for using the comma in a variety of common situations.

As you study each principle and the accompanying examples, note that the comma serves one of these basic purposes: Either it separates elements of a sentence, or it sets off words or groups of words. Whichever purpose it serves in a particular situation, the comma signals readers to pause briefly so that they will grasp the intended meaning quickly, easily, and correctly.

WITH DATES

1. Month-Day-Year Date. When the date appears in month-day-year sequence within a sentence, use a comma before and after the year. If the date appears at the end of a sentence, omit the comma after the year and use only the appropriate end-of-sentence punctuation mark.

> A copy of the *September 12, 1985,* agreement is still in the file.
>
> *March 10, 2000,* will mark the firm's one hundredth anniversary.
>
> His résumé indicates that he worked for them from *June 1, 1988,* until *November 1, 1991.*

If the date is displayed by itself, as in the date line of a letter, do not use a comma after the year.

> July 8, 1992   DATE: November 16, 1998

2. Month-Year Date. If the date consists of the month and year only, do not use a comma between the month and the year or after the year.

> Perhaps the library has a copy of the *May 1991* issue.
> The lease will not expire until *January 2000.*

3. Day of Week Plus Month and Day or Month, Day, and Year. Use a comma after the name of the day of the week if it is followed by the month and day or by the month, day, and year. Also use a comma after the month and day or the month and day as well as the year.

> Let's plan to meet on *Tuesday, December 14,* at the Palmer House in Chicago.
>
> Was *Tuesday, September 3, 1991,* her first day with the company?

WITH TITLES, DEGREES, AND SENIORITY TERMS

4. Titles. Always use commas to set off an occupational or other title that follows the name of a person and functions as an appositive. An *appositive* is an expression that further identifies the person.

> Mr. Lance Collier, *associate editor,* suggested changes in the manuscript.
>
> You may wish to contact Henry Harrison, *vice president for marketing.* (No comma is used before the period at the end of the sentence.)

If the title does not function as an appositive, do not use commas to set off the title.

> Is Pat Walton *president-elect* of the association? (When the sentence is changed to normal word order, it becomes clear that *president-elect* functions as a *predicate nominative*—a word that renames the subject of the linking verb *is: Pat Walton is president-elect of the association.*)
>
> Will Victor Diaz, *secretary-treasurer,* be able to attend? (In normal word order, the sentence is: *Victor Diaz, secretary-treasurer, will be able to attend.* Thus it is clear that *secretary-treasurer* is an appositive and is correctly preceded and followed by a comma.)

5. *Jr.* and Other Seniority Terms. When the name of a person includes *Jr., Sr., IV, 4th,* or a similar seniority term, do not use a comma before the seniority term unless you know that the owner of the name prefers to use a comma.

> Mr. Frank L. Walker Sr. Thomas Riley II L. C. Harris 4th
>
> Dr. E. J. Stevens, Jr. (The writer knows that the preference of Dr. Stevens is to use a comma before *Jr.*)

When the name appears within a sentence, do not use a comma after the seniority term unless a comma appears before it.

> Is *Frank L. Walker Sr.* one of the owners?
> Did you invite *Dr. E. J. Stephens, Jr.,* to attend?

Copyright © by Glencoe.

If the seniority term is written as a possessive, do not use a comma after it regardless of whether a comma does or does not appear before it.

What is *Mr. Frank L. Walker Sr.'s* address?

Have you contacted *Dr. E. J. Stephen, Jr.'s* assistant? (Note the comma before—but not after—the possessive *Jr.'s*.)

Never use commas to set off an arabic figure or a roman numeral used as a seniority term, whether it is or is not a possessive.

Perhaps *John Paul Smith II* will contribute to the fund. The call was from *Mrs. R. P. Mailer 4th's* attorney.

6. Academic Degrees and Similar Designations.
Always use a comma between the name of a person and an academic degree, religious order, or similar designation following it.

Francisco Soriano, M.D.   Sister Mary Pauline, O.P.

Within a sentence, also use a comma after such a designation unless the academic degree or other designation is in possessive form.

Did *L. J. Morrison, Ph.D.,* conduct the research?

I thought *Sister Mary Alexius, S.S.N.D.'s* article appeared in the spring issue of the newsletter.

Paul Hellman, Esq.'s office is near the courthouse.

Do not use a title before a name and an academic degree or other designation after the same name that mean the same thing. Use one or the other, never both.

Dr. Susan Farrell OR Susan Farrell, M.D. (NOT: Dr. Susan Farrell, M.D.)

Also, do not use a courtesy title, such as *Ms.* or *Mr.,* and an academic degree, such as *M.D.* or *Ph.D.,* with the same name. Use one title or the other, not both.

Lauren Lindstrom, D.D.S. OR Mrs. Lauren Lindstrom OR Dr. Lauren Lindstrom

7. Titles and Names in Direct Address.
Use a comma before and after a title or a name that is used in direct address. Note that *Doctor, Professor, Lieutenant,* and similar titles should always be written in full (not abbreviated) and capitalized when they are used in direct address.

Thank you, *Jim,* for your invaluable assistance.
We think you are doing an excellent job, *Governor.*
Miss Walters, do you have any suggestions?

Remember that such terms as *miss, sir,* and *madam* are not capitalized when they are used in direct address.

Insert commas wherever they are needed in the following sentences. If the sentence is correct, circle the number preceding it.

1. The cornerstone was laid on April 12, 1990.

2. The agreement dated February 1, 1991, is still in effect.

3. In January 1986 we had only two regional offices.

4. I think it was in May 1991 that we introduced Model 404A.

5. Our first meeting was on Thursday, August 29, 1991, at the Statler Hotel.

6. Please reserve Wednesday, August 15, for a follow-up meeting.

7. If Ryan McBride Jr. cannot accept our invitation, perhaps we should invite Mr. O. J. Taggart, Sr., to chair the panel.

8. What is James Caldwell, Jr.'s official title?

9. Mr. and Mrs. Reynaldo Valdez IV's daughter was in the office yesterday.

10. I think Charlotte Day, M.D., is on the staff of Memorial Hospital.

11. What is the title of Lena Favata, Ph.D.'s new textbook?

12. Maybe Hilda Suarez, advertising manager, would be interested in it.

13. Thank you, sir, for your patience.

14. Was Mr. Ellis chief executive officer in 1990?

15. May I use your name as a reference, Professor?

IN FIRM NAMES, NUMBERS, AND ADDRESSES

8. Names of Firms. Some firms use a comma before *Inc., Limited,* or a similar term at the end of the organization's name; other firms do not use a comma. If the preference of the firm is known, follow the style of the firm; otherwise, do not use a comma before *Inc.* or a similar ending. Do not use a comma after the ending unless a comma is used before it.

Does *Time Inc.* have an office on the Avenue of the Americas?

Will *Blake and Cooke, Limited,* be an exhibitor this year?

If the firm-name ending is written in possessive form, do not use a comma after it—even if a comma is used before the ending.

> We visited *McGraw-Hill, Inc.'s* headquarters in New York.

> Do you have a copy of *Blake and Cooke, Limited's* most recent annual report?

9. Numbers. Use commas to separate thousands from hundreds, millions from thousands, and so on, in whole numbers of four or more digits except in telephone, house or building, page, serial, model, ZIP Code, insurance policy, invoice, charge account, and similar numbers.

$25,420	Invoice 450682	Dayton, OH 45439
page 1022	22,000 acres	8624 First Avenue
(904) 555-1212	$1,574,294	Policy No. 38764230

Unless it is used with other numbers that require the use of a comma, a four-digit number may be written without a comma.

> This order is for *1500* copies.

> About *2,500* of the *42,500* residents were without electricity for a few hours as a result of the storm.

Do not use commas in decimal fractions of four or more digits: *21.4125* or *3.14165,* for example.

When used with *liter, meter,* and other metric terms, numbers of four or more digits are written with a space instead of a comma to separate thousands from hundreds, millions from thousands, and so on.

> 4 220 meters   18 496 kilometers   12 200 kilograms

Note that commas are not used to separate the parts of a single weight or measurement.

> The room is *9 feet 8 inches* wide by *12 feet 4 inches* long.

> This package weighs *6 pounds 7 ounces.*

10. Addresses. Within a sentence, use commas to separate the name of the addressee from the street address, the street address from the city, and the city from the state. Do not use a comma between the state and the ZIP Code, but do use a comma after the ZIP or ZIP Plus Four Code unless it appears at the end of the sentence.

> Sally's home address is 9090 Woodland Hills Drive, Chattanooga, Tennessee 37425, isn't it?

> This bid is from Caldwell Industries, Inc., 4400 Milford Road, Atlanta, GA 30310-6804.

Use commas to set off the name of a state, country, or province that follows the name of a city or county.

> Ms. Caldwell was in Tuscaloosa, *Alabama,* last week.

> The property is in Winnebago County, *Illinois.*

> Who will represent the United States at the meeting in Paris, *France,* next month?

WITH ITEMS IN A SERIES

A *series* consists of three or more words, phrases, or clauses that appear together and have the same function in a sentence.

> The store has a wide selection of *computers, monitors, and printers.* (The three nouns function as objects of the preposition *of.*)

> Should I take one of these capsules *in the morning, at noon,* or at *night?* (These three prepositional phrases function as adverbs modifying the verb *called.*)

> *Jerry, Phyllis,* and *I* signed the petition. (The two nouns and the pronoun are grammatically equal; they make up the compound subject.)

11. Last Two Items Joined by a Conjunction. When three or more items are listed in a series and the last item is preceded by *and, or,* or *nor,* use a comma to separate the items and place a comma before the conjunction preceding the last item.

> Did *you, he, or she* work late last night?

> Do you know *who they are, what they want to discuss, and when they would like to meet with us?*

Do not use a comma after the last item in the series unless the structure of the sentence requires it.

> *Sales personnel, secretaries, and others,* especially those who have frequent contact with customers, should attend this meeting.

12. All Items Joined by Conjunctions. If all the items in a series are joined by *and, or,* or *nor,* do not use commas to separate the items.

> These sweaters are available in *red and green and brown.*

> Neither *you nor he nor I* could have predicted it.

13. *Etc.* or Similar Expression at End of Series. When *etc.* (meaning "and so on"), *and so on,* or a similar expression occurs at the end of a series, use a comma before and, except at the end of a sentence, after the expression. *Note:* Never use *and* or *and so on* with *etc.*

> Please be sure to give the time, date, place, *etc.*

> Towels, sheets, blankets, *etc.,* are on sale this week.

We must collect the data, organize it, *and so on,* by next Friday.

14. Items Joined by an Ampersand. When an ampersand (&) is used to join the parts of a firm name, do not use a comma before the ampersand.

> She has worked as a paralegal for Wilson, Taylor & Dennison.

> Davega, Boynton & Associates submitted the lowest bid.

Spot Check 2

Insert commas wherever they are needed in the following sentences. If a sentence is correct, circle the number preceding it.

1. They bought a 1200-acre ranch near Colorado Springs, Colorado.

2. The park has a number of oak, spruce, and elm trees.

3. Where is Boynton, Inc.'s principal office?

4. Nearly 9800 of the 11,246 registered voters participated in the last election.

5. The name and address of the person to contact is Mr. Carl M. Frye, Walters & Associates, Ltd., 3804 Fifth Avenue, New York, New York 10020.

6. The company manufactures desks, tables, chairs, etc., at its plant in Asheville, North Carolina.

7. We probably will need more knives and forks and spoons.

8. You will find rakes, hoes, shovels, and so on, at our suburban stores.

9. Are those blouses made of silk or nylon or some other kind of material?

10. The assessed value of the property is $42,500.

11. I believe that Donaldson, Devine & Davis will represent the defendant.

WITH ADJECTIVES

15. Coordinate Adjectives. When two or more adjectives that are not joined by *and, or,* or *nor* appear together and separately modify the same noun, use a comma after all but the last adjective before the noun.

> She gave a *complete, accurate* report.

> Everyone appreciates *friendly, helpful, courteous* sales personnel.

To determine whether adjectives are coordinate, substitute *and* for the commas that separate the adjectives. If the meaning remains the same, the adjectives are coordinate.

> Everyone appreciates friendly *and* helpful *and* courteous sales personnel.

Another test to determine whether adjectives are coordinate is to reverse the order of the adjectives. If the meaning remains the same, the adjectives are coordinate.

> Everyone appreciates courteous, friendly, helpful sales personnel.

> Everyone appreciates helpful, courteous, friendly sales personnel.

Note that a comma is not used before *sales;* it is not one of the adjectives (it is part of the compound noun *sales personnel*). Would it make sense to write the sentence as follows?

> Everyone appreciates friendly *and* helpful *and* courteous *and* sales personnel. OR: Everyone appreciates friendly, helpful, *sales,* courteous personnel. (Both tests show that *sales* is not one of the adjectives. Therefore, no comma is used before *sales.*)

16. Adjective Modifying Adjective Plus Noun. Do not use a comma between two adjectives if the first adjective modifies the combined idea of the second adjective plus the noun.

> She is a *popular political* leader.

> Many grocery stores use thousands of *small plastic* bags every day.

> Do you know the name and address of the manufacturer of those *small wooden* benches?

17. Adjectives Out of Normal Order. When adjectives follow the noun they modify, use a comma after the noun and a comma after the last adjective to set off the adjectives.

> The canyon walls, *steep and treacherous,* form a natural boundary for more than 50 miles.

> Their proposal, *sound or unsound,* should be considered carefully.

Note that the punctuation changes when the adjectives are placed in their normal order before the noun they modify.

> The steep and treacherous canyon walls form a natural boundary for more than 50 miles.

Insert the necessary commas in the following sentences. If a sentence is correct, circle the number preceding it.

(1.) There are two large oak trees at the end of the driveway.

2. Dolores gave a short, accurate, interesting description of her duties.

3. The car was found abandoned at the end of a long, narrow alley.

4. These homes, reasonably priced and spacious, should be easy to sell.

(5.) Both of them hope to become famous literary agents.

(6.) It was a short but interesting and informative meeting.

7. An authoritative, up-to-date dictionary is a good investment.

(8.) He was wearing a dark blue suit.

9. That restaurant serves delicious, inexpensive meals.

10. Yesterday was one of those hot, humid summer days.

11. The company, old and reliable, was founded in the late 1900s by the grandparents of the current president and chief executive officer.

Study Guide 25

Note the use of commas in the following sentences. If you are unsure why a comma is— or is not—used in a particular instance, refer to the rule indicated.

1. The May 1, 1991,[1] agreement will remain in effect for several more years.

2. Cooper and Associates was founded in April 1986[2] by James C. Cooper Jr.[5]

3. Please plan to report for work on Monday, July 14,[3] at 8:30 a.m.

4. Mr. R. F. Bowen, manager of information services,[4] spoke first.

5. Wasn't Ms. LaRosa district manager[4] at the time that you were working in the Midwest?

6. Ms. Mary Beth Conway, executive vice president,[4] approved the purchase.

7. I think Mr. and Mrs. Thomas Webber, Jr.'s[5] plan is to buy 1200[9] shares.

8. Angelo Alvarez, Ph.D.,[6] has agreed to serve on the committee.

9. Jean Stevens, CPA's[6] report has not been received, has it?

10. Do you think Harold Robinson IV[5] will join the company?

11. What is the name of Lloyd Poland 2d's[5] most recent novel?

12. Jean Quarles, D.D.S.,[6] has an office at 5660 Third Avenue.[9]

13. We believe, sir,[7] that your analysis is correct.

14. What beginning salary would you expect to receive, Miss Sanchez?[7]

15. We hope, Professor,[7] that you will be able to accept our invitation.

16. You will find all Hill and Colson, Inc.'s[8] prices very reasonable.

17. Paulson Limited[8] occupies most of the floors in this building.

18. Mendez, Olivera & Associates, Inc.,[8] specializes in those products.

19. The firm manufactured 21,250[9] of Model 6060.[9]

20. We drove nearly 2 200 kilometers[9] in three days.

21. Please write to Ms. Carole Vinson, 140 Forrest Boulevard, Huntsville, Alabama 35802,[10] for further information.

22. Please check all names, addresses, etc.,[13] to be sure they are current and accurate.

23. Please proofread all letters, memos, reports, and so on,[13] carefully.

24. He was out of the office on Monday and Wednesday and Friday.[12]

25. Will the convention be held in Boston, Chicago, or Los Angeles?[11]

26. These items should be stored in a cool, dry[15] place.

27. The floors were covered with blue ceramic tiles.[15]

28. We have a complete selection of men's, women's, and children's[15] clothing.

29. Both are well-known public[16] speakers.

30. These containers, inexpensive and biodegradable,[17] will replace those made of styrofoam.

31. Please store them in a cool,[15] dry place.

32. The offices of Burton Inc.[8] are nearby.

33. It weighs 12 pounds 7 ounces.[9]

ASSIGNMENT: Complete the Unit 25 Worksheet on pages 193–194.

UNIT 25

The Comma

WORSHEET

 A **Insert the necessary commas in each of the following sentences. If the sentence is correctly punctuated, circle the number preceding it.**

1. Our copy of the March 1, 1992, agreement cannot be found.

(2.) She will be eligible for retirement in September 2012.

3. Would you be able to meet with us on Tuesday, August 8?

4. On Tuesday, September 3, 1991, she began working for us.

5. Mrs. Lenora Bickford, president and chief executive officer, called a special meeting of the new board of directors.

6. Please be sure to send a copy of your response to Mr. Eugene Chapman, senior systems analyst, before Tuesday, October 14.

(7.) Is Elaine Crawford vice president for public relations?

8. You should notify J. Walter Thomas, Jr., as quickly as possible.

(9.) When does Frank Judson, Sr.'s retirement become effective?

(10.) One of the passengers was carrying a large plastic bag containing a package weighing 15 pounds 11 ounces.

11. We were very appreciative of Lewis Morton, Ph.D's suggestions.

(12.) Mr. and Mrs. W. J. Sloane II sponsored the reception for new employees.

(13.) Did Queen Elizabeth II's husband accompany her on a trip to Canada a few years ago?

14. Teresa Cruz, M.D., writes articles for several well-known professional journals.

15. The group, tired and hungry, were eager to return home.

(16.) I asked Arthur Anderson 5th's assistant to give him the message.

17. Your suggestions make a great deal of sense to me, miss.

18. Thank you, Professor, for providing the information we requested about Miss Arnold.

19. This fabric has a soft, smooth texture.

(20.) Those items were included on Order 1792.

(21.) The trip will cover approximately 1050 miles.

22. Rounded to the nearest dollar, gross sales for the year were $15,468,100.

23. Nearly 1,200 of the 15,000 questionnaires have been returned already.

(24.) When did they move to 4880 Wilshire Boulevard?

25. Their former address was 810 Magnolia Drive, Chattanooga, Tennessee 37424.

26. Is 1224 Sixth Avenue, Belvidere, IL 61008, the correct address?

27. She completed both forms quickly, accurately, and legibly.

28. His new sales territory includes Rock Island, Moline, and Peoria.

(29.) You have a choice of wool or cotton or linen.

30. Newspapers, candy, etc., are available at the stand in the lobby.

31. We should paint the walls, clean the windows, and replace the carpeting.

32. The company offers courses in shorthand, Spanish, accounting, and so on, several times a year.

(33.) Will Jane and Bill and Marie be working with us?

34. Both of them work for the law firm of Jordan, Jordan & Jenkins.

35. The store sells venetian blinds in many different lengths, widths, and colors.

(36.) All members of the panel are highly respected business leaders.

37. Fay is a successful, young sales representative.

38. Your donation, large or small, will be greatly appreciated.

39. Did they move to Columbus, Georgia, or Columbus, Ohio?

(40.) What are the requirements for obtaining a real estate license?

41. We need to obtain new cost estimates before we proceed, Mr. Andrews.

42. Fred Perkins & Associates, Inc., submitted the lowest bid.

43. Dr. Martha Graham, widely known and highly respected, will join the staff of the local junior college.

(44.) Lieutenant Coppola entered the United States Army on 10 March 1988.

45. He gave Lincoln, Nebraska, as his birthplace and April 20, 1974, as his birthdate.

46. Mailing labels, interoffice envelopes, etc., may be obtained from Conrad Baines, assistant to Ms. Richardson.

(47.) We gave her a set of eight stainless steel steak knives.

48. The most recent census indicates that the population of the county is 120,646.

49. We hope it will be a short, mild winter.

50. Fenton's Department Store is having a special sale on many recently discontinued lines of curtains, drapes, and so on.

The Comma (Continued)

WITH REPEATED WORDS AND THE ADVERB *TOO*

1. Repeated Words. When deliberately repeating a word for emphasis, use a comma before the repetition of the word.

> *Many, many* people have visited this resort.
> Your suggestions have been *very, very* helpful.

2. The Adverb *Too*. If the adverb *too* is used in the sense of "also" at the end of a sentence or clause, do not use a comma before it.

> We probably should order some more pens *too.*
> If you would like to invite them *too,* please do.

When the adverb *too* means "also" and appears within a sentence, however, use commas to set it off.

> They, *too,* are planning to lower their prices.
> This order, *too,* requires special attention.

When the adverb *too* is used to mean "greatly" or "excessively," do not set it off with commas.

> One of the drivers was fined for driving *too* fast.
> Some streets are *too* narrow to permit two-way traffic.

WITH CONTRASTING AND INTERRUPTING EXPRESSIONS

3. Contrasting Expressions. Use commas to set off words that express a contrasting thought. Contrasting expressions often begin with *not, but,* and *rather than.*

> Her name is Janine, *not Jeanne.*
> Eileen, *rather than Pauline,* will be in charge.
> He shows up for meetings, *but seldom on time.*

4. Interrupting Expressions. Use commas to set off a word, phrase, or clause that interrupts the thought being expressed and that can be omitted without changing the meaning of the sentence. Such interrupting expressions (sometimes called "parenthetical expressions") include *accordingly, as you know, in fact, of course, in my opinion,* and *no doubt.* Other interrupting expressions may begin with *as well as, in addition to, together with,* and so on.

> The driveway, *as well as the sidewalk,* had to be repaved.
> Any change would, *in my opinion,* be unwise.

CAUTION: Do not use commas to set off an expression that is essential to the meaning of the sentence.

> The vacant position will, *no doubt,* be filled promptly.
> BUT: I have *no doubt* that the vacant position will be filled promptly.
>
> Jean, *as well as Bill,* can prepare those statements.
> BUT: Jean can prepare those statements *as well as Bill.*

WITH APPOSITIVES

5. Restrictive (Essential) Appositives. A *restrictive appositive* renames or further identifies a preceding noun or pronoun and is essential to the meaning of the preceding noun or pronoun. Do not use commas to set off a restrictive appositive.

> Have you seen the play *The Phantom of the Opera?* (*The Phantom of the Opera* is essential to identify which *play.*)
>
> Some forget that there is an *n* in the word *government.* (*Government* is essential to identify which *word.*)

6. Nonrestrictive (Nonessential) Appositives. A *nonrestrictive appositive* is not essential to the meaning of the noun or pronoun preceding it. Use commas to set off such an appositive.

> Hawaii, *the only island state,* is a popular vacation spot.
> Ms. Helms, *the receptionist,* gave me your message.

Spot Check 1

Insert the necessary commas in the following sentences. If a sentence is correct, circle the number preceding it.

1. We have not seen them for a long, long time.

(2.) Their prices are too high.

3. He will be your supervisor too.

4. The lamps, too, are on sale.

5. He was in Kansas City, Kansas, not Kansas City, Missouri.

6. I have no doubt about the outcome.

7. Change, of course, is inevitable.

8. Herman, our Dallas representative, will set up the exhibit.

9. Do you know the poem *Trees?*

10. The word *recommendation* is often misspelled.

11. The company, according to a spokesperson, will not relocate.

12. There has been no change in the opinion of the board members.

13. Please drive very, very carefully.

14. The garage, too, needs a new roof.

15. Surgery, in the opinion of the doctor, will not be necessary.

WITH MODIFYING PHRASES AND CLAUSES

7. Modifying Phrases. When a phrase follows the word it modifies and is not essential to the meaning or clarification of the word it modifies, set the phrase off with commas.

> This company, *presently employing over a thousand workers,* should not be permitted to close.
>
> Jerry, *scheduled to meet with us at three,* notified us that he would be at least an hour late.

However, if the phrase is essential to the meaning or clarification of the word it modifies, do not set the phrase off with commas.

> The site *being considered for the new distribution center* is north of the city.
>
> The flight *scheduled to leave at noon* was the one *canceled at the last minute.*

8. Modifying Clauses. When a modifying clause is not essential to the meaning or clarification of the word it modifies, use commas to set off the clause.

> Mr. Barnes, *who is a graduate of Northern Illinois University,* will join our staff in August.
>
> This new model, *which was introduced in May,* replaces Model 100A.

If the clause is necessary to the meaning or clarification of the word it modifies, do not set it off.

Do you know someone *who has the necessary qualifications for this job?*

Was the person *that you recommended* hired?

WITH AFTERTHOUGHTS AND QUESTIONS ADDED TO STATEMENTS

9. Afterthoughts. Use a comma before an afterthought added at the end of a sentence.

> Taking such a risk would be unwise, *in my opinion.*
> Maurice will take us to the airport, *I think.*

10. Questions Added to Statements. Use commas to set off a direct question (a question requiring a spoken or written answer) within a sentence or at the end of a sentence. A question mark is used at the end of the complete sentence.

> This building has been declared a landmark, *hasn't it?*
> It was Bates & Company, *wasn't it,* that submitted the lowest bid?

Spot Check 2

Insert the necessary commas in the following sentences. If a sentence is correct, circle the number preceding it.

1. Payments and charges made after the 25th of the month will appear on the following month's statement.

2. All mail addressed to Mr. Barrows should be forwarded to his home address.

3. The amount that the jury awarded them seems excessive.

4. The land, being unsuitable for commercial use, will be developed as a park.

5. Their main assembly plant, which is located in Grand Rapids, is being renovated.

6. This bridge, constructed in the early 1900s, is scheduled to be replaced.

7. Such a requirement is unreasonable, isn't it?

8. He was in Cedar Rapids, wasn't he, at that time?

9. We should order two of them, especially if they are on sale now.

10. Our current prices, which became effective the first of last month, are still somewhat lower than those of other firms.

Study Guide 26

A. If you are unsure why commas are—or are not—used in the following sentences, refer to the rules indicated.

1. Those in the medical profession say that the cost of malpractice insurance is very, very[1] high.
2. Maybe new plumbing should be installed in the kitchen too.[2]
3. We cannot afford to be too[2] complacent.
4. Her plan, too,[2] will be considered before a decision is made.
5. I thought it was her recommendation, not his.[3]
6. We liked the location, but not the price,[3] of that house.
7. Mr. Glenn, as well as Mrs. Purcell,[4] has been informed of the changes.
8. Ms. Klein did as well as Miss Colson[4] on that civil service test.
9. The original copy, however,[4] has not been found.
10. The term *go-getter*[5] appropriately describes each of them.
11. Each of the attorneys questioned us prospective jurors.[5]
12. She works for AT&T, a well-known communications firm.[6]
13. One of the consultants, Anne Marie Garcia, was absent.[6]
14. The restaurant owned by Pierre[7] is on 14th Street.
15. Dr. Ainsworth, being very considerate at all times,[7] is highly regarded and respected by the entire community.
16. The speaker that we wanted[8] was unavailable.
17. This medicine, which is extremely potent,[8] should be kept out of the reach of young children.
18. Both of them like winter sports, especially ice-skating and skiing.[9]
19. April 15 is the deadline, isn't it,[10] for filing these tax returns?
20. No decision has been made, has it?[10]
21. I am quite certain that most of them are planning to attend too.[2]
22. Please tell me how you want the work done, and I will proceed accordingly.[4]
23. We use many, many[1] different kinds of printed forms in our offices.
24. The majority of us have noticed that buildings usually do not have a floor with the number 13.[5]
25. Too,[2] some of our customers have suggested that we offer a wider variety of office supplies.
26. Both of those families recently moved here from Chicago, the Windy City.[6]
27. She asked me to tell you that the correct spelling of her name is *Jeri,* not *Jerry*.[3]
28. Which newspaper, in your opinion,[4] is the best-edited one available in this community?
29. Alaska, the last state admitted to the Union,[6] is the largest of the states.
30. Are you sure that his sister Eleanor[5] is planning to apply for the job?
31. One of his cousins, Eduardo Ramirez,[6] has indicated an interest in starting a recycling business.
32. Our records indicate that it is one of the companies that experienced unparalleled domestic and international growth during the period 1980–1990.[5]

B. Although commas and other punctuation marks are of primary concern to most business writers, you undoubtedly will encounter a number of symbols used in various contexts. A few of these symbols and some of their uses are listed below.

1. Asterisk	*		An asterisk is often used after a reference within the text of a document and before a footnote.
2. Diagonal	/		The diagonal (or slash or virgule) is sometimes used to mean "or" in such expressions as *and/or* and *his/her* and to mean "per" in an expression such as *km/hr* (kilometers per hour).
3. "At"	@		The "at" symbol is often used in price quotations; for example, *10 dozen @ $22.50.*

4. Apostrophe   '   An apostrophe is sometimes used with numbers written in figures in technical or statistical materials to mean "minute or minutes" or "foot or feet."

5. Quotation Mark   "   The quotation mark is also frequently used with numbers written in figures in technical or statistical materials to mean "second or seconds" or "inch or inches."

6. Number OR Pound Sign   #   When used before one or more figures, the meaning of the symbol # is "number"; when it follows one or more figures, it means "pound or pounds."

7. Brackets   [ ]   Brackets are commonly used to enclose one or more words within material that is enclosed in parentheses; for example: In his memo Mr. Ames wrote, "The panel members (it was grate [sic] to hear their viewpoints) represented several different organizations."

ASSIGNMENT: Complete the Unit 26 Worksheet on pages 199–200.

UNIT 26

The Comma (Continued)

WORKSHEET

 A **Insert commas wherever they are needed in the following sentences. In some instances, you will need to apply the rules you studied in Unit 25. If a sentence is correctly punctuated, circle the number preceding it.**

1. We still have a long, long way to go.

2. They, too, are planning a short winter vacation.

3. Their approach is much too conservative, in my opinion.

4. She, however, believes the company will resume hiring within the near future.

5. You may be entitled to half of the reward, however.

6. Traffic congestion is a major problem, especially in large metropolitan areas.

7. The merger occurred in 1980, not 1990, if I remember correctly.

8. Grace's opinion, contrary to that of others, is that the operations of the two divisions should be consolidated immediately.

9. A number of companies, both large and small, are struggling to survive in the face of increased foreign competition.

10. Mr. Baker is always trying to drive hard bargains, to take advantage of technicalities, and to force us to carry out contracts that have become disadvantageous to us.

11. Trade expositions, especially those conducted by manufacturers, serve as platforms for launching new products as well as clearinghouses for the announcement of changes in price, design, and style.

12. Many people have learned, to their regret, that the road to riches is not paved with junk bonds.

(13.) The accident occurred on an offshore oil rig in the Gulf of Mexico.

14. This building will house, in addition to a hundred apartments, a recreation center.

15. Election of Paul O'Brien as a vice president of the Brewer Company, a subsidiary of the Preston Corporation, was announced on March 23.

16. Solvency, or the state of being able to pay all debts, is a desirable aim.

17. We have received many, many inquiries about both items advertised in the Sunday, August 8, edition of *The Times*.

18. Hot, humid summer days lead to power outages in some areas.

19. We received a telephone call, not a letter, from our Racine representative this morning.

(20.) Would you please send a photocopy of your October 16 report to Lucy too.

21. The only person who has the authority to make such a major policy decision is, I believe, Mr. Fenton.

22. Harry Helms, his brother-in-law, works for a large firm in San Antonio.

23. We think you will agree that the goal is attainable, however.

(24.) This particular carpeting is available in dark brown and light gray and olive green.

25. Management has indicated that our prices, as well as our costs, will rise slightly during the coming year.

26. Ray Bullard, Mr. Salvatore Minnelli, Jr.'s assistant, may be able to give you that information.

27. I am confident that you, too, will find this offer irresistible.

28. I doubt that they will be too eager to sell the property for less than $85,000, don't you?

29. You will need a valid driver's license, of course.

(30.) The recommendations made by Miss Lerner probably would result in substantial and immediate savings.

31. Pierre Lamont, M.D., in an address at the meeting of the McHenry County Medical Society, talked about the role of the general practitioner.

(32.) There is no doubt about the need for affordable housing.

(33.) We committee members will need more time to study those proposals.

34. Some danger of flooding exists in this area, especially during the spring.

35. Your salary increase will be retroactive to July 1, as a matter of fact.

(36.) The explosion damaged the building next door too.

37. I would take the job, wouldn't you, if it were offered?

38. It was Juan, not John, who authorized the repairs.

39. The company will be represented by Suarez, Suarez & Rivera.

40. Shelton undoubtedly will write to you to confirm the points you, he, and I agreed upon last Thursday.

(41.) The words *principal* and *principle* are among those commonly confused.

42. Interest on the unpaid balance will be charged at the low, low rate of 1.3875 percent a month.

43. The visitors, after waiting nearly an hour, decided to leave.

44. Timothy Wilson, Arlene Daggett, and Ray Hawley III retired in February 1992.

45. We should replace most, if not all, of those heavy metal desks.

(46.) The cold north wind caused temperatures to drop rapidly.

47. Mrs. Stone, together with her husband and children, attended the annual company picnic.

48. The members of the jury, having been sequestered for a week, were eager to return to their homes and their jobs.

49. All of us are looking forward to seeing you on the eighth, Bill.

50. Wilson and Harriman, Inc., was selling pens, notebooks, etc., at unusually low prices last weekend.

The Comma (Concluded)

This unit presents other common uses of the comma that you are likely to encounter in most business writing situations. For assistance in a situation not covered by the principles presented here and in the preceding two units, consult an up-to-date handbook or reference manual for business writers.

BETWEEN INDEPENDENT CLAUSES

As you will remember, a **compound sentence** consists of two or more closely related independent clauses. Each **independent clause** is a group of words that makes complete sense by itself and could stand alone as a separate sentence. For example, the following compound sentence could be divided into two simple sentences:

> The building was scheduled for demolition last year, but it is still standing. (Compound sentence.)

> The building was scheduled for demolition last year. It is still standing. (Two simple sentences.)

A **compound-complex sentence** contains not only two or more independent clauses but also one or more dependent clauses. Each **dependent clause** (or **subordinate clause**) is a group of words that does not make sense by itself, even though it also contains a subject and a predicate. A dependent clause is usually introduced by *as, if, that, which, when,* or a similar word. Note the italicized dependent clauses in the following compound-complex sentence.

> Mr. Larson said *that he would be out of the office two days next week,* but he did not say *where he would be.*

> I asked both of them to help me tomorrow, and they promised *they would.* (Note that the subordinate conjunction *that* is omitted in this example.)

1. In Compound Sentences. When the independent clauses in a compound sentence are joined by the coordinating conjunction *and, but, or,* or *nor,* use a comma before the conjunction that connects them.

> Susan was supposed to drive us to the airport, *but* she was unable to get her car started.

> Ms. Lane may attend the meeting herself, *or* she may ask someone to represent her.

EXCEPTION: If the independent clauses are very short and very closely related, omit the comma before the conjunction that joins them.

> He applied for the job *and* he got it.

If one or both of the independent clauses contain commas, you still may use a comma to separate them unless doing so would make misreading of the sentence likely.

> Your idea is an excellent one, Mark, *and* it deserves everyone's consideration and support.

> If the price of the stock increases, you will make a profit, *but* if it decreases, you will lose more than you invested, Ms. Miller.

If using a comma before the conjunction is likely to cause misreading, a semicolon should be used before the conjunction connecting the independent clauses.

> I will send a copy of the draft to you, Mrs. Acosta; *and* Mr. Day will send you the final version later. (Using a comma instead of a semicolon before *and* could make the reader think that *Mrs. Acosta* is part of a series, not a name in direct address.)

2. In Compound-Complex Sentences. Ordinarily, use a comma before the coordinating conjunction that joins the independent clauses in a compound-complex sentence.

> I called your office immediately after I checked in at the hotel, *but* your secretary said that you would be away until Monday. (Note the dependent clauses *after I checked in at the hotel* and *that you would be away until Monday.*)

> You may obtain a refund immediately, Ms. Compton, *or* you may ask that the amount be credited to your account.

However, if one or both clauses contain commas *and* if misreading would be likely, use a semicolon instead of a comma before the conjunction joining the independent clauses.

> The principal contributors were Mr. Sorenson, Ms. Duke, and Mrs. Georgeson; *and* Miss Romano and I have thanked them for the assistance that they gave us in developing a comprehensive plan.

WITH INTRODUCTORY WORDS, PHRASES, AND CLAUSES

3. Introductory Words. When a word such as one of those listed below introduces a sentence or an independent clause within a sentence, use a comma after it.

accordingly	first	meanwhile	no
besides	further	naturally	obviously
consequently	however	next	otherwise
finally	indeed	nevertheless	therefore

However, no decision has been made.

Otherwise, we will be unable to process your claim properly.

Dr. Morton has another speaking engagement on the 10th; *therefore,* we must try to find someone else.

Yes, you are entitled to three weeks' vacation this year.

Be sure the word is used in an introductory manner, not as a modifier, before you use a comma after it. Note that no comma is used in the following:

However expensive the machine may be, we must buy it.

No amount of money will solve such problems as those.

EXCEPTION: No comma is usually necessary after *thus, hence,* or *then* at the beginning of a sentence or clause.

Then it will be necessary to find some other solution.

The announcement was made at the last meeting; *thus* everyone should have been aware of the change.

4. Introductory Phrases. Use a comma after an **absolute phrase,** which is a phrase that has no grammatical relationship to the rest of the sentence. Such phrases are sometimes called **independent comments** because they reflect the writer's attitude toward the thought expressed by the rest of the sentence.

As a matter of fact, the case was settled out of court.

In reality, the prime rate may not be the lowest rate at which a borrower may obtain money from a bank.

Also use a comma after any introductory phrase that contains a verb or a verb form.

As stated previously, the owners are not interested in selling or leasing the building at this time.

To be perfectly honest, I think it is an excellent opportunity for you.

Following the directions carefully, we assembled the cabinet in less than an hour.

Handled properly, minor disagreements rarely become major disputes.

When preparing tax returns, check all figures and computations carefully. (This prepositional phrase contains the verb form *preparing.*)

If an introductory prepositional phrase is long, use a comma after it. No comma is necessary after a short prepositional phrase unless omitting the comma would cause misreading or misunderstanding or unless the phrase contains a verb form.

By the end of the third quarter, we expect to see a 12 percent reduction in expenses. (Long prepositional phrase.)

By 2000 the company expects to have offices in four or five foreign countries.

For all, time is a valuable commodity. (Omitting the comma could cause misreading.)

When an introductory phrase of any type follows the conjunction joining the independent clauses of a compound or compound-complex sentence, use a comma after—but not before—the introductory phrase.

Sales were right on budget at the end of the first quarter, and *for the first three days of this month,* they are slightly ahead of budget.

We tested the program ourselves for several months, and *to further ensure its acceptability,* we had several outside organizations use it and report their findings to us.

Be careful not to use a comma after a phrase that functions as the subject of a sentence or an independent clause within a compound or a compound-complex sentence.

After a holiday is a good time to shop for bargains.

We process thousands of customers' accounts; therefore, *being able to work well under pressure* is essential in this office.

To establish and maintain a good credit rating is an important goal.

5. Introductory Clauses. Use a comma after a dependent clause that precedes an independent clause. A word such as *although, after, as, before, if, since, unless, until, when, where, whether,* or *while* usually signals such an introductory clause.

As you know, the fare probably will be increased to $1.50 this summer.

If you need additional information, please do not hesitate to call or write me.

This opportunity to win a valuable prize may not be of interest to you, but *before you decide,* read the rest of this letter. (Note that there is no comma before the introductory clause but that a comma does precede the coordinate conjunction *but.*)

Remember that a dependent clause may be used as the subject of a sentence or independent clause and that a single comma should not be used to separate the subject and verb. However, if necessary, two commas may set off a nonessential appositive or other element between the subject and the verb.

When the work will be completed is anyone's guess.

The company, which employs 500 people, has decided to relocate, but *where it will move* has not been announced.

Spot Check 1

Insert the necessary commas in the following sentences. If a sentence is correct, circle the number preceding it.

(1.) They were invited and so was I.

2. The program promises to be an exceptionally good one, and we hope to see you there.

3. The trade deficit, according to recent reports, has declined slightly.

4. I knew that I had met both of them, but to my embarrassment, I could not remember their names.

5. Unfortunately, she will be hospitalized for another week or two.

6. However complex the problem may be, it can be solved.

(7.) The signature is obviously a forgery; thus you will not be liable for the amount charged on that purchase.

8. Yes, you will be required to have a physical examination before you begin work.

9. To obtain your free copy, just sign and return the enclosed card.

10. Having heard the rumor several times, he decided to ask one of the company executives about it.

11. In the spring, rains and melting snow cause flooding in this area.

12. Before the first, glance over this draft so that we can discuss it and make whatever changes may be necessary.

(13.) In the attic is where this belongs, I think.

(14.) After I had mailed the letter was when I remembered that I had forgotten to enclose the check.

15. The changes have not been officially approved, and until they are, we are filling orders at the prices listed in the current catalog.

16. While Mr. Alton was in charge, if I remember correctly, was when the present procedures were adopted.

WITH EXPRESSIONS INTRODUCING EXPLANATIONS, ENUMERATIONS, AND APPOSITIVES

6. *For Example, Namely, That Is,* and Similar Expressions. When *for example, namely, that is,* or a similar expression introduces a nonessential explanation, enumeration, or appositive, use a comma before and after the introductory expression and—except at the end of a sentence—after the explanation, enumeration, or appositive.

By the end of our fiscal year, *that is, June 30,* we hope to have a reorganization plan ready to implement.

Jewelry manufacturers use a variety of metals, *for example,* silver and platinum.

If the explanation, enumeration, or appositive occurs within a sentence and contains commas, however, use a parenthesis or a dash before the introductory expression and after the explanation, enumeration, or appositive. Use a comma after the introductory expression.

Many kinds of wood—*for example, oak, cherry, and mahogany*—are ideal for furniture. (Use dashes for greater emphasis.)

Many kinds of wood *(for example, oak, cherry, and mahogany)* are ideal for furniture. (Use parentheses for less emphasis.)

When *for example, namely,* or *that is* introduces an independent clause in a compound or compound-complex sentence, use a semicolon before the introductory expression and a comma after it.

This company offers its employees unusual benefits; *for example,* it gives its employees completely free medical and dental insurance.

If *for example, namely,* or *that is* introduces one or more clauses, phrases, or words added as an afterthought at the end of a sentence, use a semicolon before and a comma after the introductory expression.

This car has exactly the equipment that I want; *for example,* it has power windows, power locks, and a sunroof.

However, if the explanation is in apposition to the word or phrase immediately before it, use a comma before and after the introductory expression.

> Use a question mark after a direct question, *that is,* a question requiring a spoken or written answer.

7. Such As. Use a comma before—but not after—*such as* when it introduces a nonessential appositive, explanation, or enumeration. Also use a comma after the appositive, explanation, or enumeration except at the end of a sentence.

> Some trees, *such as oaks and elms,* shed their leaves.
> It is available in several color combinations, *such as yellow and brown, blue and white, and red and gray.*

When *such as* introduces an essential appositive, explanation, or enumeration, omit the commas.

> An error *such as that one* is very easy to correct.
> Diseases *such as mumps and smallpox* are rare.

TO INDICATE OMISSIONS

8. Omitted Verbs. When one of the verbs is omitted in a compound sentence, use a comma to indicate the omission. Note that the omission sometimes includes other words closely connected to the verb.

> Ms. Lawrence is president; Mr. Dulles, vice president.
> Part of the order will be shipped in January; the remainder, in April.

Spot Check 2

Insert the necessary commas in the following sentences. If a sentence is correct, circle the number preceding it.

1. The prices of computers such as those are very high.
2. The association has held its convention in cities throughout the country; for example, Boston, Chicago, New Orleans, Los Angeles, and Seattle.
3. Some surnames, such as *Jones* and *Smith,* are very common.
4. Tom is doing graduate work in sociology; Betty, in business administration.

Study Guide 27

If you are unsure why commas are—or are not—used in the following sentences, refer to the rules indicated.

1. John does not belong to that particular organization, nor does he plan to apply for membership within the near future.[1]
2. Please sign the enclosed card and return it without delay.[1]
3. Should we accept the terms they offered, or should we make a counterproposal?[2]
4. Naturally, we would like to get as much on a trade-in as possible.[3]
5. Naturally sweet foods are usually better.[3]
6. To be perfectly honest, I am not interested.[4]
7. Reasonably priced, this new model will be easy to sell.[4]
8. In 1991 the company opened its fiftieth branch.[4]
9. By the end of this year, we expect to recover our investment, and by the end of next year, we should realize a modest profit.[4]
10. When ordering, please specify the method of shipment you prefer.[4]
11. Who will replace her has not been decided.[5]
12. If we can solve the problem, we will, but if we can't, we will try to find someone who can.[5]
13. Two of my coworkers, namely, Irene Esposito and Paul Lin, have each been with the company more than twenty years.[6]
14. The museum's collection includes works by many famous painters; for example, Goya, Rembrandt, and El Greco.[6]
15. Any form of exercise, such as jogging or swimming, is desirable.[7]
16. Stamps such as those are not rare enough to be of much value.[7]
17. Joan will be out of the office Monday; Brenda, Tuesday; and Marsha, Thursday.[8]

ASSIGNMENT: Complete the Unit 27 Worksheet on pages 205–206.

UNIT 27

The Comma (Concluded)

WORKSHEET

A Insert the necessary commas in the following sentences. In doing so, you will need to apply rules presented in Units 25, 26, and 27. If a sentence is correctly punctuated, circle the number preceding it.

1. Set with five huge diamonds, this ring is worth far more than $1,125.

2. Carefully choosing every word, Doris McLain, M.D., briefed the reporters on the results of the laboratory tests.

3. Many tropical fruits, for example, mangos and papayas, can be grown in the Miami, Florida, area.

(4.) We invited them and they accepted.

5. Dr. Kim Wong has become a leader in surgical techniques to correct astigmatism, and she has written several articles about the procedure she uses.

6. This building, which was occupied by a clothing manufacturer until two or three years ago, has been converted into apartments.

7. The committee briefly discussed proposed changes in the retirement plan, but it neither accepted nor rejected any of them, did it?

8. Consequently, banks and other lending institutions are lowering their rates on home mortgages.

(9.) Then Mrs. Hawkins became manager of the payroll section.

10. To tell the truth, I didn't read the contract as carefully as I should have before signing it.

11. Although we would like to buy that house, it costs much, much more than we can afford to pay.

12. Posting job openings at the beginning of each week is a good idea, don't you think?

(13.) In June we will need to review projected expenses for the remainder of the year.

14. Mrs. Grier spoke to Howard about the job; however, he said he would prefer to stay in his present assignment at least one more year.

15. Our sales manager, Frank Ginsberg, has two openings on his staff.

(16.) A requirement such as that one seems unreasonable.

17. The owners permit tenants to have some animals as pets; for example, small dogs, cats, and birds.

18. We will issue the report shortly after the end of our fiscal year, that is, June 30.

19. Ms. Moran is the president-elect of the association; Ms. Stern, the secretary-treasurer.

(20.) Those who drive while under the influence of alcohol risk their lives and the lives of others too.

21. Some sports, such as baseball and football, have become big business.

22. Yes, overnight delivery service is offered by such companies as Interstate Express, National Express, and Continental Express.

23. Our largest customer, namely, Lincolnwood Industries, ordered over $250,000 worth of merchandise last year.

24. An opportunity such as that one doesn't present itself too often.

25. Did the candidates who lost the election continue in politics, or did they choose to pursue other interests?

26. Watered too often, those plants will not survive.

27. He works for a large Midwestern accounting firm; she, a well-known Wall Street investment company.

28. I was not there at the time; thus I am unable to comment on what happened.

29. We prefer to adapt, not adopt, their procedures.

30. However, real gems—such as diamonds, pearls, and rubies—are often difficult to distinguish from synthetic ones.

31. Quality, rather than quantity, is what most people want, in my opinion.

32. However, these asphalt shingles are guaranteed to last 30 years.

33. According to the official, reports of a merger offer have no factual basis whatsoever.

34. If you were in charge of the department, Denise, what changes, if any, would you make first?

35. Working frantically to meet the deadline, Connie made a great many errors.

36. Developing a totally reliable error-analysis routine will be an extremely challenging project for those computer programmers.

37. Further, the company appears to be having a very, very serious cash-flow problem.

38. Consequently, their offer could not be considered.

39. A successful manager obviously has the ability to make sound business decisions.

40. He told me that he would apply for the position; however, I am not sure that he did.

41. In July the polls indicated strong public support for the measure; then in September they began to suggest a change in the public's attitude.

42. Being able to speak and write two or more languages is a valuable asset.

43. Containers such as those should not be used for coffee or tea.

44. A period is used at the end of a declarative sentence, that is, a sentence that expresses a fact or an opinion, for example.

45. On the other hand, gloves are often made of leather and lined with fur.

46. For several days in a row, the temperature was in the 90s.

47. Children's suits, coats, etc., are in a separate department on the second floor.

48. On Thursday and Friday, November 26 and 27, the office will be closed.

49. Will the attorney handling the case be Lee Anne Lawford, D. L. Scott Sr.'s new associate, or someone with more experience than she has?

50. When dried, grapes are raisins and plums are prunes.

Although both the semicolon and the colon appear frequently in letters, memos, and other kinds of messages, neither occurs in very many *different* types of situations. Therefore, correct use of both of these punctuation marks requires learning and applying only a few principles.

Each use of the semicolon and the colon signals a reader to a *partial stop,* not a slight pause (as the comma does) or a full stop (as the period, question mark, or exclamation point generally does). The semicolon always separates elements within a sentence. In the majority of situations, the colon indicates that something follows to explain or complete a statement; in a few instances, however, it simply separates the parts of an expression.

THE SEMICOLON

1. Between Independent Clauses Not Joined by a Conjunction. If the independent clauses in a compound or compound-complex sentence are not joined by *and, or, but,* or *nor,* use a semicolon to separate them.

> In April 1988 Ms. Jasperson was appointed manager of our Concord office; in February 1992 she was appointed national sales manager.

> Most of those who completed the course gave it an excellent rating; a few thought it was not as relevant to their job responsibilities as it could have been.

2. Between Independent Clauses Joined by a Conjunction. If the independent clauses in a sentence are joined by *and, or, but,* or *nor* and if one or both of the clauses are punctuated with commas, use a semicolon instead of a comma to separate the clauses when necessary to prevent misreading.

> Mrs. Stevens will send a copy of the report to you, Mr. Rivers; *and* Mrs. Rodgers, Ms. West, and I will appreciate receiving your comments concerning it. (Using a comma after *Mr. Rivers* might cause misreading.)

In most instances, though, it is not necessary to use a semicolon to separate independent clauses joined by a conjunction—even when both clauses are punctuated with commas.

> We have stores in Princeton, Trenton, and Atlantic City, Mr. Lane, *and* we are planning to open others in Fort Lee, Montclair, and North Bergen. (The use of a comma instead of a semicolon after *Mr. Lane* is not likely to cause misreading.)

3. Before a Transitional Expression (Conjunctive Adverb). Use a semicolon to separate the independent clauses in a compound sentence when the second clause is introduced by a transitional expression (conjunctive adverb). The following words and phrases are among those commonly used as transitional expressions.

accordingly	furthermore	however	hence
consequently	nevertheless	otherwise	thus
in fact	after all	meanwhile	yet

> The building was scheduled to be completed in May; *however,* it was not ready to be occupied until August.

> I thought Mr. Hammond signed the contract; in fact, Mr. Polisky did.

Note that it is not necessary to use a comma after the transitional expressions *hence, thus, then, yet, still,* and *so.* However, other transitional expressions should be followed by a comma.

> Mr. Wilson promised to accept or reject our proposal within a week; *thus* we should receive a letter or a telephone call from him today or tomorrow.

> The plane left about an hour late; *nevertheless,* we arrived about 15 minutes early for our appointment with the group in Marquette.

4. Before *Namely, For Example,* and Similar Expressions. Use a semicolon before and a comma after *namely, for example, for instance, that is,* or a similar expression that introduces a nonessential explanation, enumeration, example, or similar element at the end of a sentence. Note that the first part of the sentence is complete by itself and does not suggest that an explanation, enumeration, or example will follow.

> Some businesses close early on the day before a holiday; *for example,* the Wednesday before Thanksgiving.

> A large number of products are made of aluminum; *for instance,* pans, soda containers, and window frames.

Remember that *namely, that is,* or a similar expression may introduce an appositive at the end of a sentence and require a comma before and after it. Compare the following examples with those above.

> We spent the day walking around The Loop, *that is,* the central business district of Chicago.

> We requested bids from two suppliers, *namely,* Butler Associates and Western Electronics Corporation.

5. Between Items in a Series. Use a semicolon between the items in a series when one or more of the items contain commas.

> This new product is being tested by consumers in Lexington, Kentucky; Tulsa, Oklahoma; and Bangor, Maine.

> Please reserve Monday, June 12; Wednesday, June 21; and Tuesday, June 27 for meetings with the auditors.

Spot Check 1

Insert semicolons and commas where they are needed in the following sentences. If a sentence is correct, circle the number preceding it.

1. Workers have removed all the asbestos; however, they still have not solved the problem of the lead-based paint.

2. Ms. Timms, a well-known attorney, Mr. Willis, an experienced accountant, and I volunteered to serve on the membership committee.

3. Many magazines are available in the library; for example, *Newsweek, Time,* and *Business Week.*

4. Only one person, namely, Beverly Reynolds, knew the answer to his question.

5. John was in Phoenix last week; he will be in Juneau next week.

6. Many kinds of stores sell stationery; for example, drugstores and bookstores.

7. Use a question mark at the end of a direct question; that is, a question phrased in the exact words of the speaker or writer.

8. We checked and double-checked everything; nevertheless, we missed a few misspelled words.

9. The three winners were Jay Gould, Jr., Lavonne Jeffers, and Jerome McKay.

10. Please read the directions on page 1 carefully; then answer all the questions on pages 2 through 4.

THE COLON

6. Before *Namely*, *For Example*, and Similar Expressions. Use a colon before *namely, for example,* or a similar expression that introduces an explanation or example at the end of a sentence when the first part of the sentence suggests that an explanation or example will follow.

> We sell only one brand of shoes: *namely,* Solemates.

As the above example illustrates, using a colon before the introductory expression helps to emphasize the following explanation or example. A comma before such an introductory expression would also be correct if you wished to emphasize the first part of the sentence.

> He spent his entire career with one company: *namely,* Phelps-McLane, Inc.
>
> OR: He spent his entire career with one company, *namely,* Phelps-McLane, Inc.

7. Before a List or an Enumeration. Use a colon after a statement preceding a list or an enumeration. Note that the introductory statement may or may not include *the following, as follows,* or a similar expression to indicate that a list or an enumeration will follow. Also note that the items in a list need not be numbered or displayed on separate lines.

> The three cities being considered are as follows: Eau Claire, Wisconsin; Davenport, Iowa; and Lincoln, Nebraska.

> We plan to open two new distribution centers in Virginia: one in Roanoke and one either in Richmond or in Arlington.

> Please send a copy to each of these representatives:
> Raquel Travolta
> Eduardo Acosta
> Wesley Lindberg

> Please bring these items with you:
> 1. Copies of all correspondence you have had with the complainant.
> 2. Notes concerning any telephone or other conversations between you and the complainant.

When a list or an enumeration and the statement introducing it are interrupted by another sentence, do not use a colon before the list or the enumeration. Note the example at the top of page 209.

The models listed below will be discontinued in March. All remaining stock should be removed from the warehouse during the first week of April.

1. Model 204-B
2. Model 360-C
3. Model 375-D

If a list or an enumeration follows a preposition or a verb, do not use a colon after the preposition or verb unless the items following it are displayed on separate lines.

Please ask each member of your department *to* (1) study the description of each type of medical insurance available, (2) complete the enrollment form, and (3) return the completed form to me by Friday of this week.

Please be sure to ask each of them *to:*

1. Study the agreement carefully.
2. Sign, date, and have witnessed both copies.
3. Return the original copy for our files.

Each of these envelopes *contains* (1) samples of business forms and (2) examples of letterhead designs.

For this meeting, please be sure to *bring:*

1. At least two pens or pencils.
2. A notebook.
3. A list of questions, if any, that you would like answered.

8. Between Independent Clauses.
Use a colon before an independent clause that explains or supplements the preceding independent clause. No conjunction or transitional expression joins the clauses when a colon is used.

The plan you have outlined is very appealing: it provides comprehensive coverage for all members of my family at a reasonable cost.

9. Before a Direct Quotation.
Use a colon before a direct quotation that is introduced by an independent clause, that consists of two or more sentences, or that is set off and displayed separately from the statement introducing it. In such cases, the first word after the colon is always capitalized.

The director of marketing made an optimistic prediction: "By the end of the third quarter, our sales will exceed those for all of last year." (An independent clause introduces the quotation.)

One candidate said: "Most politicians make promises they can't keep. I promise you I won't do that." (The quotation consists of two sentences.)

At a meeting with Mr. Roswell this morning, he told me that one of his college professors gave him this advice:

Take all the time you need to be sure that what you are thinking of doing is something that you truly

want to do. Then if you decide to proceed, get going—and stick with it, even if the going gets a little rough at times. (Note the absence of quotation marks when a long quotation is displayed in this manner.)

10. Between Hours and Minutes.
Use a colon to separate hours from minutes when time is expressed in figures. Do not leave a space before or after the colon.

Our flight left at 11:15 a.m. and arrived at 1:40 p.m.

11. With Salutations and Reference Initials.
Use a colon after the salutation in a business letter and a colon to separate the initials of the writer from those of the typist in the reference initials at the bottom of a letter or memo.

Ladies and Gentlemen:	JWR:LMS
Dear Dr. Hollingsworth:	ENK:mav

Reference initials may be written in arrangements that do not include a colon; for example, *WAS/jbp* or simply *jbp.*

Spot Check 2

Insert colons and other punctuation marks wherever they are needed in the following sentences. Do not make any changes in capitalization. If a sentence is correct, circle the number preceding it.

1. Our office is open from 830 a.m. until 430 p.m.

2. Please be sure to indicate the following date time and place.

3. We noticed one thing about all the applicants all of them seemed highly qualified for the job.

4. I hope one of these dates will be acceptable to you Monday March 12 Wednesday March 21 or Tuesday March 27.

5. Please send a copy of this report to Ms. Crawford, Mr. Dalton, and Miss Evans.

6. There is one thing that I forgot to mention the new model will be available early next month.

Study Guide 28

As you read the following sentences, note the uses of the semicolon and the colon. If you are unsure why a particular punctuation mark is used, refer to the rule indicated.

1. The manufacturer's warranty is good for 90 days;[1] it can be extended for a period of 6 years or 100,000 miles, whichever occurs first.

2. He was scheduled to speak at 10:30[10] a.m.;[3] however, he did not arrive until noon.

3. We have regional service centers in Moline, Illinois;[5] Newark, New Jersey;[5] and San Francisco, California.

4. All of us look forward to seeing you, Roger;[2] and Pat and I hope you will accept our invitation to stay with us.

5. I doubt that she would be interested in that position;[4] that is, I do not believe she would be willing to live out of the country for two or more years.

6. Only one company submitted a bid:[6] namely, Curran & Cooper, Inc.

7. The new members of the advertising staff are as follows:[7] Donald Krebbs, Kathryn Muller, and Wilbur Schmidt.

8. I need three things to finish this job:[7] time, tools, and your help.

9. Let's wait until Monday;[3] then we'll be able to spend all day on that project.

10. When renewing your passport, you should bring the following with you:[7]
    1. Your present passport
    2. Two recent photographs
    3. A completely filled-in application form

11. The ordering procedure has been simplified:[8] one person will order supplies for the entire department.

12. This was Tom's response:[9] "I took the day off because there was an emergency situation in my family, and I simply forgot to call the office."

13. Dr. Young asked:[9] "Does this plan provide adequate protection for our employees? How much does it cost?"

14. One of the economists said:[9] "The economy is on an upswing. Employment is at an all-time high. Personal income continues to rise."

15. Please use one of the following salutations:[7]
    Ladies and Gentlemen:[11]
    Dear Committee Members:[11]

16. Please be sure to invite:[7]
    Mr. and Mrs. Nelson Oakley
    Ms. Rachel Walsh
    Dr. Patricia K. Medina.

ASSIGNMENT: Complete the Unit 28 Worksheet on pages 211–212.

UNIT 28

The Semicolon and the Colon

WORKSHEET

 A **Insert semicolons, colons, and commas as needed in the following sentences. If a sentence is correctly punctuated, circle the number before it.**

1. The amount of the loan was $10,000 the interest rate was 12.5 percent.

2. The meeting is scheduled for June 19 therefore we need to have the report completed and distributed by June 16.

3. Ms. Fairchild hopes Bill will be elected president Cathy vice president and Jane secretary.

4. Shirley prefers Brand A Ed Brand B and I Brand C.

5. There has been a decrease in the prime rate that is the interest rate banks charge their large corporate customers.

6. As others have pointed out the prime rate is not necessarily the lowest interest rate charged by banks instead it is likely to be the base rate.

7. The military action began as Operation Desert Shield it ended as Operation Desert Storm.

8. Tickets are available from the receptionist for the concert on Tuesday evening April 23 Friday evening April 26 and Wednesday evening May 1.

9. Heavy rains delayed work on the project nevertheless the contractors expect to complete it on schedule.

10. Our flight was scheduled to leave at 1115 a.m. however it did not leave until 110 p.m.

11. This policy does not provide complete protection for homeowners for example it excludes sinkhole damage.

12. She is planning on one thing namely owning her own business.

13. The following are the new officers Dolores Edson president Bernie Houston vice president and Howard Costello secretary-treasurer.

14. The two main requirements are education and experience.

15. They plan to spend their vacation as follows one week in Spain one week in Portugal and one week at home.

16. Please be sure to note and remember
    1. The date.
    2. The time.
    3. The place.

17. Some holidays are not celebrated outside the United States for instance Thanksgiving and Independence Day.

18. Please be sure to fax this message to:
    a. Mr. Everett Johnson acting manager of the Pensacola office.
    b. Ms. Genora Nance manager of the Jackson office.

19. These seminars will be held on the following dates. Please plan to attend each of them.

  February 28
  March 10
  March 28
  April 15

20. The telethon was a huge success, it brought in cash donations and pledges totaling over a million dollars.

21. We met our two main goals last month, increased production and reduced expenses.

22. In closing, the speaker said, "You have been a very good audience. I thank you."

23. Judy ended the discussion on a positive note, "We've met every challenge so far, and we can meet this one too."

24. Mr. Gary S. Meyers said:

  Experts stress the importance of establishing a personal relationship with a banker. The usefulness of building credibility for yourself and your ideas cannot be understated. It will go a long way toward getting you the credit you need.

25. Soon after Alice left, Bob called to let me know that she and he will work overtime Thursday and Friday.

26. We must solve the problem, however difficult it may be.

27. Mr. Phelps discussed various trends in advertising, however, he indicated he could not make any long-range predictions regarding them.

28. I thought yesterday was their anniversary, but it is tomorrow.

29. Duane made an interesting observation, "Some people start rumors just to see who spreads them."

30. They have a new address: 2002 Potomac Drive, Washington, DC 20002.

31. Terms such as those we discussed should be acceptable, don't you think?

32. Those who bought computers a few years ago paid much more for them than we who buy them today do.

33. Some groups strongly support the measure, others vociferously oppose it.

34. Try the machine first, then if it meets your needs, buy it.

35. The main topics to be discussed are (1) expenses, (2) schedules, and (3) staff additions.

36. We need more, not less, help in this department.

37. Delivering a speech may take only a few minutes, preparing it, several hours.

38. Sometimes, Jerry, we hire outside consultants, normally, though, we rely on our own staff.

39. Leading is one thing, managing, another.

40. Only two people showed up for the meeting, Jody and Jennifer.

41. The discontinued models are Model 440 and Model 460A.

42. When steamed, Mr. Dennis, these clams are delicious.

43. They were there and so were we.

44. Conservation does more than save for the future, it prevents waste too.

45. It was intended to be a request, but it sounded like a demand.

46. Flight 904, not 409, is the one we were supposed to take.

47. Passengers, too, sometimes become impatient and ill-tempered, according to bus drivers.

48. If so, would you please contact Mr. McGuire by the end of next week.

49. Many, many people collect such things as stamps, coins, salt and pepper shakers, and figurines.

50. I am looking forward to seeing you, Roger and Nancy, as well as the rest of your former coworkers, are too.

The Apostrophe and the Dash

THE APOSTROPHE

As discussed in previous units, the apostrophe is used in forming possessives of most nouns and of certain pronouns. This unit summarizes those uses and introduces others.

1. In Possessives of Nouns. Use an apostrophe when forming either the singular or the plural possessive of a noun.

SINGULAR:	customer's	company's	woman's
PLURAL:	customers'	companies'	women's

We bought several *dollars'* worth of vegetable seeds.
Bennett & Burnett specializes in *children's* clothing.

2. In Possessives of Pronouns. To form the possessive of some indefinite pronouns, use an apostrophe followed by an *s.*

anyone's   everyone's   no one's   somebody's

It has been said that *everyone's* business is *no one's* business.

However, do not use an apostrophe to form the possessive of a personal pronoun; for example, *hers, yours, ours,* and *theirs.*

3. In Plurals of Words Referred to as Words. Use an apostrophe and *s* to form the plural of a word referred to as a word if omitting the apostrophe would cause confusion in reading.

Their proposal contains too many *ifs, ands,* and *buts.* (Omitting the apostrophe does not cause confusion.)

This agreement contains a great many *or's* and *nor's.* (These plural forms are not often used; omitting the apostrophe could cause confusion.)

4. In Plurals of Letters, Figures, and Abbreviations. In general, use an apostrophe and *s* to form the plurals of uncapitalized letters and of uncapitalized abbreviations written with internal periods.

There are two *m's* and one *c* in *recommendation.*
How many *c.o.d.'s* did we receive today?

The plurals of most capital letters and of numbers expressed in figures may be written without an apostrophe; for example:

two Bs   several Js   a few 5s   no 9s
His *4s* and *7s* look very much alike.

For the sake of clarity, however, use an apostrophe to form the plural of the capital letters *A, I, M,* and *U.* (*Note:* For the sake of consistency of style, express related letters in the same manner.)

A's (to avoid confusion with *As*)
I's (to avoid confusion with *Is*)
M's (to avoid confusion with *Ms.*)
U's (to avoid confusion with *Us*)

Those are beautifully scripted *A's.*
As a student, she received mostly *A's* and *B's.* (For consistency of style, both of the plurals are written with an apostrophe.)

5. In Contractions. Use an apostrophe to indicate the omission of one or more letters in a contraction. Also use an apostrophe to indicate the omission of the first two figures in a year date.

aren't (are not)	class of '95	I'm (I am)
it's (it is OR it has)	during the '80s	they're (they are)
nat'l (national)	let's (let us)	you've (you have)

When forming the plural of a contraction, keep the apostrophe in the contraction itself and add an *s*—without an apostrophe before it—at the end of the contraction.

The new manual seems to have a dozen *don'ts* on every page.

Spot Check 1

Insert apostrophes where needed in the following sentences. If a sentence is correct, circle the number preceding it.

1. Is this yours or Pats or someone elses?

2. Each of them is entitled to three weeks paid vacation.

3. We welcome everyones suggestions for improving our products and our services.

4. I believe that his assistants' name is Heather.

5. Have you seen this months' sales report?

6. Dont' forget to dot your *i*s and cross your *t*s!

7. I counted several *I*s and a few *wont*s in that particular message.

8. Are these mens' or womens' jackets?

9. Lets' turn the have-nots into haves.

10. Harrys' comments led me to believe that he thinks everyones' supporting his proposal.

11. Maybe Lee knows whos' been chosen to take her place.

⑫. Representatives from several PTAs were at the school board meeting.

13. That style was fashionable in the '20s.

14. Carlos plans to follow the route of Cortezs' journey sometime next year.

15. Burke Bros.' new office is on the west side of town.

THE DASH

The dash is most often used in place of the comma, parentheses, colon, or semicolon to achieve greater emphasis than those punctuation marks provide. However, the dash is required in some situations. Unless it is required, the dash should be used very sparingly in ordinary business writing.

6. Before a Summarizing Word. Use a dash before *all, these,* or a similar word or expression that summarizes two or more preceding words.

Men, women, children—*all* are welcome at our lodges and resorts.

Tools, lumber—*everything* the do-it-yourself carpenter needs is on sale at Granger's Home Centers.

7. At the End of an Incomplete Statement. Use a dash (or an ellipsis) at the end of an intentionally unfinished statement. An ellipsis consists of three periods, and it may be followed by an end-of-sentence period, question mark, or exclamation point.

As for the others—or As for the others . . . .

8. With Elements Containing Commas. Use dashes to set off a parenthetical (nonessential) element containing commas.

Three staff members—Mark Pascal, Mary Crowell, and Dana Reuss—plan to retire this year.

Items of all kinds—for example, plants, furniture, and tools—can be found at flea markets.

9. With Abrupt Changes in Thought. To set off and emphasize an abrupt change in thought within a sentence, dashes may be used instead of parentheses.

Dave Lynch—I'm sure you remember him very well—resigned in March.

Jack said he was in Portland—Oregon or Maine or some other state, I'm not sure—last week.

10. With Afterthoughts. Use a dash to set off and emphasize an afterthought.

Their cakes are delicious—inexpensive too!

11. Between Independent Clauses. To give special emphasis to the last clause in a compound sentence, a dash may be used instead of a comma or a semicolon between the independent clauses.

Three people are vying for the job—and everyone knows who they are. (The dash replaces a comma.)

Some said it was an interesting meeting—others thought it was too long and rather boring. (The dash replaces a semicolon.)

12. With Explanatory Expressions. To introduce and give special emphasis to an explanatory word, phrase, or clause at the end of a sentence, a dash may be used instead of a colon.

There is one thing that nearly all of us should do more often—exercise.

Mike's plan is an ambitious one—to start as a sales representative and to finish as president of a company.

We found a simple solution to the problem—no one schedules a meeting between 8 a.m. and 9 a.m.

13. With Repetitions and Restatements. To set off and give special emphasis to repetitions and restatements of previous statements within a sentence, use dashes.

I am thankful—very thankful—for your assistance.

Early next month—sometime before the tenth—we need to issue guidelines for conducting employee performance evaluations.

Spot Check 2

Insert dashes wherever they are needed in the following sentences.

1. Towels, sheets, blankets—everything for the bathroom and the bedroom is on sale now at greatly reduced prices.

2. Repairing some of these items,for example, the battery-operated clocks, pocket-sized radios, and pocket calculators,may cost more than replacing them.

3. You bought lunch the last time,I'll buy this time.

4. The grapevine,if you prefer, the rumor mill, seems to be a faster means of communication than electronic mail.

5. We couldn't keep up with the Joneses,or any of our other neighbors.

6. As we've both said before,

7. Some people think there's only one way to do things,their way, of course!

8. Marilyn, Gene, Richard,no one in this department knew anything about it.

9. They have plenty of things to do to keep them busy during the winter months,for example, knitting, crocheting, and quilting.

10. They said they were moving to Alaska,and they are.

Study Guide 29

A. As you read the following sentences, note the uses of apostrophes. If you are unsure of the reason for a particular use, refer to the rule indicated.

1. Wasn't[5] she president of the class of '88?[5]
2. Should I change each of the *we're*s[5] to *we are?*
3. Everyone's[2] job performance is excellent.
4. The name of the joint venture probably will be an acronym formed from the initials of the parent companies'[1] present names.
5. Yes, the word *vacuum* contains two *u's.*[4]
6. Is this yours[2] or hers?[2]
7. These are 7s[4] and those are 1s.[4]
8. We received no c.o.d.'s[4] this week.
9. The plural of the letter *A* is *A's.*[4]
10. Her grades included a few Cs[4] and several Bs.[4]
11. In my opinion, Marie's[1] excuse was a valid one.
12. We need to hear more *whys*[3] before we make up our minds.

13. After checking in the stockroom, I notified the customer that we had no size *13s*[4] in stock.
14. Are any of these letters *yours,*[2] or are they *someone else's?*[2]
15. What was the *employees'*[1]reaction to the *chief executive officer's*[1] announcement?
16. Always be sure to dot your *i's*[4] and cross your *t's.*[4]
17. There are too many *can'ts*[5] and not enough *can's*[3] in this set of rules.
18. This contract certainly is loaded with *therebys*[3] and *therefores.*[3]
19. One of their cars is a *'68,*[5] and it is still in very good condition.
20. I wonder *who's*[5] been appointed manager.

B. As you read the following sentences, note the uses of dashes. If you are unsure of the reason for a particular use, refer to the rule indicated.

1. Now, let's see—[7]
2. This machine—it's about two years old—has more than paid for itself.[9]
3. The Room at the Top—our luxurious rooftop restaurant—offers both private and public dining rooms.[12]
4. Your suggestions will increase productivity—and reduce expenses.[10]
5. The floor is in good condition—the ceiling and walls need repairs.[11]

6. You have excellent—in fact, outstanding—qualifications for this type of work.[13]
7. Jennifer, Kurt, Brenda, Samuel—everyone in the office joins me in wishing you a full and speedy recovery.[6]
8. Some—Steve and I are among them—think the estimate is too conservative.[9]
9. Many vegetables—for example, tomatoes, beans, and carrots—are available at roadside stands as well as in supermarkets.[8]

10. Until the next time—[7]

11. Trucks, cars, motorcycles—all contributed to an enormous traffic jam this morning on the inter-state highway.[6]

12. If any of those rumors are true—[7]

13. Three offices—yours, Nelson's and Becky's—are scheduled to be redecorated next week.[8]

14. Mrs. Ives has the combination to the office safe—and she is the only one who has it.[11]

15. Those are good—and very expensive![10]

ASSIGNMENT: Complete the Unit 29 Worksheet on pages 217–218.

UNIT 29
The Apostrophe and the Dash

WORKSHEET

 A In the space provided, write the contraction of each of the following expressions.

1. would have	1. would've	11. I would	11. I'd			
2. are not	2. aren't	12. might have	12. might've			
3. we would	3. we'd	13. they are	13. they're			
4. I am	4. I'm	14. it has	14. it's			
5. it is	5. it's	15. we are	15. we're			
6. let us	6. let's	16. has not	16. hasn't			
7. will not	7. won't	17. were not	17. weren't			
8. do not	8. don't	18. who is	18. who's			
9. who has	9. who's	19. does not	19. doesn't			
10. cannot	10. can't	20. could have	20. could've			

 B The following sentences contain errors in the formation of possessives and contractions and in the use of possessives. Underline each error; then write the necessary correction in the space provided.

1. After studying everyone's proposals, we've decided to accept <u>her's</u>.   1. hers

2. <u>Lets</u> see how much it's likely to cost before making any commitment to them.   2. Let's

3. She said that she <u>wont</u> know until tomorrow how much the mechanic's bill will be.   3. won't

4. <u>Its</u> less than a week's pay, isn't it?   4. It's

5. We should've checked the <u>tires'</u> pressure before we started on this trip.   5. pressure of the tires

6. I'm not sure <u>whose</u> going and who isn't, are you?   6. who's

7. Are these notes hers, or are they <u>Toms</u>?   7. Tom's

8. The doctor's checking those <u>patients</u> records to be sure that they are complete.   8. patients'

9. The firm's lost <u>it's</u> lease, hasn't it?   9. its

10. <u>Ill</u> answer both of those letters for you if you're too busy with other things.   10. I'll

11. The real estate agent's shown us some houses built in the <u>40s</u>.   11. '40s

12. The coffee's taste is bitter, isn't it? **12.** _taste of the coffee_

13. We'll need several dollar's worth of those. **13.** _dollars'_

14. What is Glen and Iris current home address? **14.** _Iris's_

15. The firm's sales' manager's planning to resign at the end of this month. **15.** _sales_

16. I thought wed never get there, didn't you? **16.** _we'd_

17. Both companies' products compete with our's. **17.** _ours_

18. This two-day sale features womens' shoes. **18.** _women's_

19. Their parent's names are Juanita and Edgar. **19.** _parents'_

20. Jack's memo was full of cant's. **20.** _can'ts_

C Insert the necessary apostrophes and dashes in the following sentences.

1. Many people enjoy watching Macy's Thanksgiving Day parade on television.

2. The mayors' plans for their cities are innovative—to say the least.

3. The commission's report won't be released until the first of next month.

4. That cabinet was a gift from the class of '91, wasn't it?

5. The stockholders' support of the board of directors' action is almost certain.

6. It must have been someone's idea of a practical joke—but no one knows whose.

7. This writer's using so many I's leads me to think he or she's self-centered.

8. Bob's, not Ron's, report was full of *ifs, ands,* and *buts.*

9. Advertising—effective advertising—is essential to a company's successfully marketing its products and services.

10. Aren't there supposed to be two h's in the word *withhold?*

11. These are beautiful capital letters—especially the M's.

12. The candidates—namely, Hillary Hodge, Mary Crowell, and Wesley Lundberg—answered all reporters' questions fully.

13. Wrenches, hammers, pliers—tools of all kinds—should be stored where they're not likely to rust.

14. As to how much time it will take—

15. Some appliances—especially toasters and irons—consume a great deal of electricity.

16. There is one thing everyone likes to hear—his or her name.

17. The offer sounded too good to be true—and it was!

18. There's something every business firm needs—customers.

19. You deserve the award—and I'm sure you'll receive it.

20. It wasn't luck—it was a lot of hard work.

21. Exercise—for example, jogging, swimming, or simply walking—is something most of us need.

22. Now is the time to act—tomorrow may be too late.

23. They seemed to want a week's pay for a day's work.

24. The results were satisfactory—very satisfactory.

25. Each country's leaders expressed interest in holding another conference to discuss trade agreements.

QUOTATION MARKS

Sometimes circumstances require you to use a ***direct quotation,*** that is, a statement consisting of the exact words of another person. More often, though, circumstances permit you to use an ***indirect quotation,*** a statement that does not consist entirely of someone else's exact words. The following principles and examples will help you use quotation marks correctly in these and other situations.

1. With Direct Quotations of Complete Statements. If a direct quotation consists of a complete statement within a sentence, enclose the quoted statement within quotation marks and use commas to set it off from the rest of the sentence.

> Ms. Salsburg said, "I believe further consolidation of our domestic operations would be unwise."

> "We do not plan to write off any foreign loans within the foreseeable future," reported a spokesperson for the bank.

If the quoted statement is interrupted, use commas to set off the interrupting words and enclose both parts of the quotation in quotation marks.

> "Our budget," the governor reported, "is based on a conservative estimate of revenues."

For direct quotations consisting of two uninterrupted statements, use only two quotation marks—one before the first statement and one after the second statement. If the quotation appears at the end of the sentence, use a colon before it.

> Mrs. Lavelle remarked: "We obviously underestimated the demand for the Model 360. At the current rate, we will sell 1200, not 800, this year."

> "Results for the third quarter were better than expected. Everything points toward record earnings for TEC, Inc.," reported financial analyst Lloyd Condon.

If two quoted statements are interrupted, however, enclose each part of the quoted material in quotation marks.

> "We need more information about the market," Miss Wells said. "For that reason, we have hired a research firm."

> "What percentage of the market," asked the marketing director, "does each of our competitors have? How can we increase our share?"

When the direct quotation is introduced by an independent clause, use a colon instead of a comma after the introductory clause.

> Dr. Ashley made this observation: "The new model will be ready to release near the end of this year. For that reason, we will begin promoting it early this fall or late this summer."

If a direct quotation at the beginning of a sentence requires a question mark or an exclamation point after it, do not use a comma to separate the quotation from the rest of the sentence.

> "Do you have any other source of income?" the credit manager asked.

> "Wait a minute!" yelled Dr. Payne. "You need to sign this insurance form before you leave."

As illustrated, the first word of each quoted sentence begins with a capital letter. However, when a quoted sentence is interrupted, the part following the interruption does not begin with a capital letter unless it is a proper noun or other word that is always capitalized.

> "After six months," the interviewer said, "you will be eligible for a salary increase."

2. With Quotations Within Direct Quotations. Use single quotation marks (typewritten apostrophes) to enclose a quotation within a quotation.

> Arlene reported, "I heard Mrs. Helms say, 'The salary of most employees will be increased at least 5 percent.'" (Note that there is no space between the single and double quotation marks ending the quotation.)

3. With Long Direct Quotations. If a quotation consists of two or more paragraphs, use a quotation mark at the beginning of each paragraph and at the end of the last paragraph.

> In the version released to news reporters, Dr. Mark Shearson made the following statement:
> "There is no reason to expect these incentives to diminish. Capital investment remains very strong, and growth in productivity appears to be accelerating.

"Further, deregulation of the economy seems to have produced a renewed sense of opportunity. In electronics and other industries, entrepreneurs are aggressively pursuing the venture capital market and forming new businesses."

Instead of using quotation marks to enclose a long direct quotation, you may display the quoted material by indenting it 5 or 10 spaces from each side margin.

4. With Well-Known Sayings and Proverbs. Do not use quotation marks around well-known sayings or proverbs.

> All of us have heard that an apple a day will keep the doctor away.

5. With Indirect Quotations. Do not use quotation marks to enclose an indirect quotation—a statement not phrased exactly as the speaker or writer expressed it. Such a statement is frequently, but not always, introduced by the word *that*.

> Ann said that she had decided to accept their offer. (Perhaps she actually said, "I have decided to accept their offer.")

In the preceding example, the wording of the statement clearly indicates it is not a direct quotation. Sometimes, though, a statement can be either a direct quotation or an indirect quotation.

> Ms. Moore said the new equipment will be installed next week.
> Ms. Moore said, "The new equipment will be installed next week."

In the above examples, the writer chose to treat Ms. Moore's statement as an indirect quotation in the first version of the sentence and as a direct quotation in the second version.

6. With Terms Following *Marked* and Similar Expressions. Use quotation marks to enclose words or phrases introduced by *marked, labeled, so-called,* and similar expressions.

> It was marked "To be opened by addressee only."
> Both packages should have been labeled "Fragile."

7. With Technical and Trade Terms. When using a technical or trade term in nontechnical writing, enclose the term in quotation marks the first time it appears in the message.

> If you prefer, we could redo pages 8 and 10 with illustrations that "bleed" on both sides. (*Bleed* is a printing and publishing term.)
> Would you like for us to "screen" the type in the heading? (*Screen* is another printing and publishing term.)

8. With Slang and Similar Expressions. When using slang or grammatically incorrect expressions, enclose them in quotation marks to indicate that they are not expressions you normally use in business writing.

> They appeared to be "stressed out" when I saw them.
> All of us feel it "ain't the way to go" in this situation.

9. With Titles of Magazine Articles, Book Chapters, and so on. Use quotation marks around the titles of parts or chapters of books (but not of complete books), short poems, magazine and newspaper articles, lectures, essays, songs and other short musical compositions, radio and television programs, and unpublished manuscripts of books and reports.

> The title of Chapter III is "Etiquette in the Office."
> They were interviewed on "60 Minutes."

10. With Direct Quotations of Portions of Statements. When a direct quotation consists of only a portion of a statement, enclose the quoted words in quotation marks. However, do not use a comma before the quoted words or capitalize the first word of the quotation unless it is a proper noun or other word that is normally capitalized.

> Remember that "the voice with a smile" is important when speaking on the telephone.
> Taking the critics' advice, we went to see "the best musical of the season" last Saturday evening.

Spot Check 1

Insert the necessary quotation marks in the following sentences. If a sentence is correct, circle the number preceding it.

1. "Will it make a significant difference?" he asked.
2. "When," the manager asked, "will they arrive?"
3. Mrs. Molloy said, "Yes, these figures are correct."
4. Jim said, Mr. Lee replied, "Their account is delinquent."
5. Obviously, all that glitters is not gold.
6. Maurice said that he planned to leave early today.
7. The envelope was marked "To be opened by addressee only."
8. I told him we don't need any more, but he wouldn't listen.

9. I found the article "Productivity Plus" quite interesting, too.

10. "The allegations are untrue," Mr. Helms said. "I have no further comment concerning them."

11. One of the candidates was described as "a loose cannon."

QUOTATION MARKS WITH OTHER PUNCTUATION MARKS

When using quotation marks with other punctuation marks, make sure that the punctuation marks are written in the proper sequence.

11. With a Comma or a Period. Always place a comma or a period before a closing quotation mark.

"Until recently," she said, "I would have said it was impossible."

12. With a Semicolon or a Colon. Always place a semicolon or a colon outside a closing quotation mark.

Note the discussion of the following in Chapter 2, "Financial Formulas": return on investment and price-earnings ratio.

He was supposed to lead the audience in singing "The Star Spangled Banner"; however, he had laryngitis and was unable to attend the ceremony.

13. With a Question Mark or an Exclamation Point. If the quotation itself is a question or an exclamatory statement, place a question mark or an exclamation point inside the closing quotation mark.

"That's wonderful news!" exclaimed Mrs. Potter.

"Is Good Enough OK?" was the title of Mr. Stein's manuscript.

If the question mark or exclamation point does not apply to the quotation itself, place the question mark or exclamation point after the closing quotation mark.

Let's stop playing "telephone tag"!

Did Jack say, "Let's not waste our time trying to reinvent the wheel"?

If the question mark or exclamation point applies to both the quotation and the sentence as a whole, place the question mark or exclamation point before the closing quotation mark.

The interviewer asked me, "What is your long-range career goal?"

Keep yelling "Fire!"

14. With Parentheses. If the quoted material is a parenthetical expression, place the quotation marks inside the parentheses. Otherwise, place the quotation marks outside the parentheses.

The title of his address ("Climbing the Corporate Ladder") seems appropriate.

The directions clearly state, "Type or clearly print in ink all information below (do not use pencil)."

UNDERSCORES

The use of underscores in typewritten material is equivalent to the use of italics in printed material.

15. With Foreign Expressions. Underscore a foreign term or expression that is not considered part of the English language. To determine whether a particular expression should be underscored, consult a writer's handbook or a dictionary. If the term appears in the main listing of a dictionary, it is not necessary to underscore it.

Perhaps that comment was merely a lapsus linguae, that is, a slip of the tongue.

16. Words Referred to as Words. Underscore a word referred to as a word. If the word is accompanied by a definition, enclose the definition in quotation marks. In material that is typeset, words used as words appear in italic type.

While talking about the office furniture, Bess used the word *ergonomic* a dozen times.
The term *palindrome* means "a word, verse, sentence, or number that reads the same backward or forward."

17. With Titles of Books and Other Items. Underscore the titles of complete books, magazines, newspapers, pamphlets, long poems, motion pictures, plays, operas, and similar items published as separate works. Also underscore the titles of paintings and pieces of sculpture.

He is a reporter for *The New York Times*.
The title of his book is *The Gregg Reference Manual*.

Another way to display titles, especially in advertisements and other promotional materials, is to type or print them in all-capital letters.

If you're like most people, you'll find BUSINESS WEEK an invaluable source of in-depth information.

Do not underscore the title of a magazine or newspaper when it is used as part of an address in a letter or on an envelope.

Engineering and Mining Journal
1221 Avenue of the Americas
New York, NY 10020

18. With Other Words and Expressions. Underscore any word or expression that you wish to give special emphasis. However, remember that overuse of this technique is self-defeating.

All of us think *you* deserve the award this year.

Spot Check 2

Insert underscores and quotation marks where needed in the following sentences.

1. Some people confuse the word principle with principal.

2. Do you have the latest issue of Sports Illustrated?

3. The ballet critics raved about the dancers who performed the pas de deux.

4. The word empathy means the capacity for participation in another's feelings or ideas, according to one dictionary.

5. In my opinion, it don't make no difference.

6. Please try to eliminate all the widows in these proofs.

7. One of the critics said the play was another one of those comédie larmoyante.

Study Guide 30

Study the use of quotation marks and italics (the equivalent of typewritten underscores) in the following sentences. For help in understanding their use, refer to the rules indicated.

1. "It will be an uphill battle," the candidate said, "but I am confident that I will win it."[1,11]

2. Mr. Bell said, "We need to conduct a study."[1,11]

3. "What is your interpretation of the second paragraph?" Jean asked.[1,13]

4. Darlene said, "The package was marked 'Fragile.' "[1,2,6,11]

5. Dr. Peterson said: "The next meeting will be on May 4. Lucy LaVelle, publisher of *The Capron Courier,* will be our guest speaker."[1,11,17]

6. Our discussion leader said:

   Currently, if your account is an IRA or Keogh, you can withdraw the funds under certain conditions. Before doing so, however, you should consult a tax expert.[3]

7. We know from experience that all that glitters is not gold.[4]

8. One said she would like to see the manager.[5]

9. The editor noticed several "widows" in the first few galleys.[7]

10. We think "them ain't the right parts" for these machines.[8]

11. Some said the plan was "dead in the water."[10,11]

12. I have read the article "Excesses of the '80s"; however, I haven't seen any of the other articles you mentioned.[9,12]

13. The following topics are discussed in Chapter 8, "Popular Investments": stocks, bonds, and real estate.[9,12]

14. Should this memo be stamped "Confidential"?[6,13]

15. Those chasing the thief were yelling "Stop!"[10,13]

16. His usual advice is to "take it easy"![4,13]

17. Her memo includes this statement: "There has been no consistent pattern for the past few years (see Table 3 on page 12)."[1,14]

18. Please note that this is the *tentative* plan.[18]

19. Is *mortgagee* the right term in this instance?[16]

20. Some people would consider it a *faux pas.*[15]

21. Table 8 ("Population Projections") is on page 36.[9,14]

ASSIGNMENT: Complete the Unit 30 Worksheet on pages 223–224.

UNIT 30

Quotation Marks and Underscores

WORKSHEET

 Insert the necessary underscores, quotation marks, commas, periods, and other punctuation marks in the following sentences. Do not add or change capitalization. If the sentence is correct, circle the number preceding it.

1. "I would take that comment," he said, "cum grano salis."

2. "Should I treat this information as confidential?" Ms. Wilkerson asked.

3. I told the interviewer I would not be interested in relocating.

4. Miss Kraft remarked, "Our company's policy is to promote from within. Every manager is expected to adhere to it."

5. "When was Ms. Grant's letter received," asked Mrs. Parsons, "and when did you answer it?"

6. Jack reported, "One of the speakers said that they should be labeled 'couch potatoes.'"

7. The professor said cum grano salis means "with a grain of salt."

8. Her article offers this advice to shoppers:

    Be observant and beware of substitutions. Get what you pay for, not a lower grade of merchandise or a smaller package. Inspect your purchases before you leave the store.

9. As our boss frequently says, you can lead a horse to water, but you can't make it drink

10. Did Roy say, "I'm sorry, Mr. James, but I won't be able to work Saturday morning"?

11. Someone on the second floor was yelling "Fire!"

12. The plumber will have to "sweat" this pipe joint.

13. One or two stores in that mall are likely to go "belly up."

14. I enjoy watching the TV program "60 Minutes"; however, I haven't been able to watch it lately.

15. The following stores sell reproductions of Rodin's The Thinker: Hollandale's and Lehman-Norcross.

16. Did you read the article "My Day on the Farm" in this morning's Daily Reporter?

17. "That's preposterous!" the lawyer exclaimed.

18. Perhaps reluctant would be a more appropriate term.

19. The postscript indicated they were still planning to be open for business by the middle of next month.

20. They seem to have no intention of changing their modus operandi.

Rewrite each of the following sentences. If the sentence is an indirect quotation, change it to a direct quotation. If the sentence is a direct quotation, change it to an indirect quotation. Change the wording, capitalization, and so on, as necessary. Note the example.

0. The credit manager asked me whether I had notified Mrs. Campos.

The credit manager asked me, "Have you notified Mrs. Campos?"

1. The director of marketing reported that sales for the third quarter were 15 percent ahead of budget.

The director of marketing reported, "Sales for the third quarter were 15 percent ahead of budget."

2. Mr. Alberts asked me, "Would you be willing to work with me on this project?"

Mr. Alberts asked me whether I would be willing to work with him on this project.

3. The company is considering several sites. A decision will be made within the next week or two, according to Kathryn McCoy, a company spokesperson.

"The company is considering several sites. A decision will be made within the next week or two," advised Kathryn McCoy, a company spokesperson.

4. Dr. Rydell's instructions were to review the draft of the questionnaire and give him my suggestions for improving it.

Dr. Rydell's instructions were, "Review the draft of the questionnaire and give me your suggestions for improving it."

5. Mr. Fawcett said, "I was quite certain that the price quoted in the ad was inaccurate."

Mr. Fawcett said he was quite certain that the price quoted in the ad was inaccurate.

6. Fern said, "Many people have asked us to share the results of this survey with them."

Fern said that many people have asked us to share the results of this survey with them.

7. "All I know about it," Mayor Hardy said, "is what I read in this morning's *Times*."

Mayor Hardy said all he knew about it was what he read in this morning's *Times*.

8. According to Jeanne, Bob said, "The receptionist is supposed to issue a pass to each visitor."

According to Jeanne, Bob said that the receptionist is supposed to issue a pass to each visitor.

9. Lyle told me that I should have marked the package "Fragile."

Lyle told me, "You should have marked the package 'Fragile.' "

10. Mr. Wilford asked, "Who designed our new letterhead stationery?"

Mr. Wilford asked who designed our new letterhead stationery.

The Hyphen and Parentheses

THE HYPHEN

Although many compound terms require using the hyphen, there is no consistent pattern for doing so. Some compounds always require a hyphen; for example, *cross-reference* and *co-owner*. Others always require the use of a space, not a hyphen, between the parts of the expression; for example, *work force* and *time sheet*. Still others do not involve using either a hyphen or a space between the parts of the compound; for example, *landscape* and *postmark*. In a number of situations, how the particular compound functions as a part of speech dictates how to write it correctly; *run down* (as a verb), *run-down* (as an adjective), or *rundown* (as a noun), for example.

Although you may use a computer or a word processor with a software program for checking the spelling of compounds and other words, you obviously must rely on your own knowledge and judgment in many instances. If you have any doubt, your first step should be to consult a regular desk dictionary. Then if the word is not listed, apply the general guidelines presented in this unit and in various handbooks and manuals for writers.

Another common use of the hyphen occurs in dividing words. Principles pertaining to this topic will be discussed in Unit 32.

THE HYPHEN IN COMPOUND ADJECTIVES

A ***compound adjective*** consists of two or more words that act together as a one-thought modifier. Although the dictionary lists many compound adjectives, it would be impossible for any dictionary to include all of them. Like other writers, you will construct many of the compound adjectives that you use. In doing so, you should follow these general rules unless there is a special rule covering the particular situation.

1. Compound Adjective Before a Noun. When two or more words form a one-thought modifier and *precede* the noun they modify, use a hyphen between the words in the compound adjective.

What we need most is a *long-term* commitment from them.

We may have another *out-of-stock* situation on our hands.

Remember to hyphenate only the words that form the one-thought modifier.

We need *up-to-date* sales figures for this report. (*Sales* is part of the compound noun *sales figures,* not the one-thought modifier.)

Some banks offer *low-cost* auto loans. (*Auto* is part of the compound noun *auto loans,* not the one-thought modifier.)

2. Compound Adjective After a Noun. When two or more words form a one-thought modifier and *follow* the noun they modify, do *not* use a hyphen between the words in the compound adjective.

Are these cost estimates *up to date?* BUT: Are these *up-to-date* cost estimates?

Those puzzles are *easy to solve.* BUT: Those are *easy-to-solve* puzzles.

However, note that some expressions retain one-thought force and require the use of the hyphen to tie them together—even when they follow the nouns they modify. The words in such a one-thought modifier are frequently out of their normal order (*hard-hitting* instead of *hitting hard)* or are in some shortened or otherwise altered form (*duty-free* instead of *free of duty.)*

You can buy some items that are *duty-free* at some airports.

The news commentator's remarks were *hard-hitting.*

SPECIAL RULES

3. Compound Nouns as Modifiers. When a compound noun consisting of two or more separately written words is used as a modifier, do *not* use a hyphen between the parts of the compound.

The booklet contains two copies of each *income tax* form.

Several *nursing home* operators testified at the hearings last week.

Jeanne has a *District of Columbia* sticker on her car.

We recently hired two *junior college* graduates.

If the compound noun is always written with a hyphen, retain the hyphen when the compound is used as a modifier.

Each of those entries should have a *cross-reference*. (*Cross-reference* is used as a noun.)

Please check all *cross-reference* notations carefully. (*Cross-reference* is used as an adjective.)

When two or more separate nouns are used as a one-thought modifier, use a hyphen between the nouns but not between the parts of each noun.

They decided to take the *New York-Chicago-San Francisco* flight.

We stayed at a motel near the *South Carolina-Georgia* border.

This is an introductory course in *hotel-motel* management.

4. Adverbs Ending in *ly* Plus Participles. Do not hyphenate a modifying expression consisting of an adverb ending in *ly* plus a present participle (a verb form ending in *ing*) or a past participle (a verb form that generally ends in *ed*).

Few people like to be near a *constantly ringing* telephone. (Adverb plus present participle.)

Some were selling trinkets to tourists at *highly inflated* prices. (Adverb plus past participle.)

The speaker used several *professionally made* slides to illustrate various points. (Adverb plus past participle.)

The aisle was littered with *recently broken* dishes. (Adverb plus past participle.)

Remember that some words ending in *ly* are adjectives, not adverbs. When an adjective ending in *ly* and a present or past participle are used as a compound modifier, use a hyphen in the modifier whether it appears before or after the noun.

The wax left an *oily-looking* film on the furniture.

Mrs. Ellingson certainly is *friendly-mannered*.

5. Other Adverbs Plus Participles. If a modifying expression consists of an adverb that does not end in *ly* plus a present or past participle, use a hyphen between the words if the modifier appears before the noun.

Jorge is a *well-known* architect in the Miami area.
BUT: Jorge is an architect *well known* in the Miami area.

What can we do about *ever-increasing* costs? BUT: What can we do about costs that are *ever increasing?*

BUT: It has been a *very exciting* day.

6. Independent Adjectives. Do not use a hyphen between two or more independent adjectives preceding a noun.

They were wearing *blue suede* jackets.

The *little red brick* schoolhouse is now a museum.

7. Numbers Plus Other Words. When a number expressed in either figures or words is used with another word to form a compound modifier before a noun, use a hyphen between the number and the other word.

I just wrote Janice a *two-page* memo.

The company plans to build a *16-story* office building.

EXCEPTION: When a number and the word *percent* are used as a one-thought modifier, do not use a hyphen between them.

You may be entitled to a *10 percent* discount.

8. Adjectives With a Common Element. When two or more one-thought adjectives have a common element, omit the common element from all but the last adjective and use a "suspended" hyphen with each preceding adjective.

It is packaged in *1-, 5-,* and *10-pound* quantities.

His report summarizes various *short-* and *long-range* capital requirements.

Spot Check 1

Insert hyphens to join the parts of the one-thought modifiers in the following sentences. If a sentence is correct, circle the number preceding it.

(1.) Do you have a life insurance policy?

(2.) The company has two New York affiliates.

3. Which airlines serve the Miami-Fort Lauderdale area?

4. Some areas have experienced a summer-long drought.

(5.) The house has a recently remodeled kitchen.

6. Most banks offer 15-and 30-year mortgages.

7. Have you ever driven the wrong way on a one-way street?

8. This carpeting is available in 9-and 12-foot widths.

9. It was an awe-inspiring sight.

10. We ordered a dozen small plastic wastebaskets.

11. Many people are complaining about outrageously high medical costs.

12. Do retailers look for friendly-mannered sales personnel?

13. It is advisable to use a quick-drying paint.

14. The company anticipates a 10 percent increase.

15. The witness gave a highly unlikely account of the incident.

16. The chef's secret turned out to be a lemon-lime concoction.

17. What is the trade-in value of this truck?

18. Who won the cross-country event?

19. The land is government-owned.

20. These are old-fashioned oatmeal cookies.

THE HYPHEN IN COMPOUND NOUNS AND VERBS

9. Compound Nouns. As the following examples illustrate, there is no consistent pattern for writing compound nouns. Some are written with a hyphen, some are written with a space between the parts of the compound, and some are written solid.

bankbook	free-fall	postmaster
bank note	free trade	post office
callback	freeway	trademark
call box	halftime	trade name
call-up	half-truth	trade-off

If at least one of the words that make up a compound noun is not a noun, hyphenate the parts of the compound.

Would you be willing to serve as a *go-between?*

A *know-it-all* is unlikely to be very popular.

The reception gave everyone a chance to meet the *higher-ups.*

When two separate nouns identify one person or thing with two different positions or functions, hyphenate them.

Kevin has been elected *secretary-treasurer.*

Pat made the arrangements for the *dinner-dance* at the Biltmore.

If a compound noun consists of a noun plus a present participle, write the compound as two separate words without a hyphen unless the dictionary shows the particular compound written some other way.

cost accounting	decision making	profit sharing
problem solving	word processing	price cutting

10. Compound Verbs. Compound verbs, like compound nouns, are written in different ways. Again, consult the dictionary when you are unsure of a particular compound.

air-condition	back away	shortchange
airlift	backfire	short-circuit

Which company will *air-condition* our offices?
The engine *backfired* twice and then stopped.
Both banks *wrote off* a number of loans.

THE HYPHEN WITH PREFIXES AND SUFFIXES

11. Most Prefixes and Suffixes. As a general rule, do not use a hyphen when the first part of a word is a prefix or when the last part of a word is a suffix.

biannual	overtake	worthless
illogical	semimonthly	youthful
inconvenient	businesslike	clearness
noncommittal	friendship	entertainment

12. *Self, Ex,* and *Elect.* Use a hyphen with the prefix *self,* the prefix *ex* when it means "former," and the suffix *elect* when it is used as part of a title.

self-assurance	ex-champion	mayor-elect
self-confidence	ex-mayor	president-elect
self-reliant	ex-treasurer	senator-elect

Selfsame, selfish, selfless, and other combinations of the word *self* and a suffix are written without a hyphen.

Neither of them can be accused of *selfishness.*

Lynn became president on Monday, and Tom resigned the *selfsame* day.

13. Prefix Plus Capitalized Word. When adding a prefix to a word that begins with a capital letter, use a hyphen after the prefix.

all-American	mid-August	pro-Irish
pre-Christmas	trans-Siberian	non-European

14. To Separate Identical Letters. If the addition of a prefix or a suffix results in a sequence of two *a*'s, two *i*'s, or three identical consonants, use a hyphen after the prefix or before the suffix.

bell-like	shell-less	semi-independent
semi-invalid	shell-like	ultra-ambitious

15. To Distinguish Different Meanings. To distinguish words that have the same spelling and the same pronunciation but different meanings, use a hyphen after the prefix.

recover (to regain)   re-cover (to cover again)
reform (to correct)   re-form (to form again)
remark (to comment)   re-mark (to mark again)

Spot Check 2

Insert hyphens wherever they are needed in the following sentences. If a sentence is correct, circle the number preceding it.

1. Local newspapers have published several write-ups about her.

2. Which branch office serves the mid-Atlantic states?

3. He seems to view himself as a power broker.

4. Who will be the new secretary-treasurer?

5. Some establishments near the base are off-limits to military personnel.

6. Do you think the salesclerk unintentionally shortchanged me?

7. The ex-governor spoke with self-assurance.

8. Both of the former republics are semi-independent.

9. This is an ultra-ambitious plan for increasing sales.

10. The attorney encouraged them to enter into a premarital agreement.

11. Both accident victims are in a semi-invalid state, but they are expected to recover completely.

12. All these price tags have been re-marked.

THE HYPHEN IN SPELLED-OUT NUMBERS AND FRACTIONS

16. Numbers Under 100. When writing the compound numbers between 20 and 100 in words, use a hyphen.

twenty-one   forty-four   ninety-nine

Note that this rule also applies when writing these numbers as ordinal numbers.

twenty-first   forty-second   ninety-ninth

17. Numbers Over 100. When writing numbers over 100 in words, do not use a hyphen before or after such words as *hundred* and *thousand*.

one hundred thirty-two   two thousand fourteen
six million five hundred thousand eight hundred fifty-six

18. Fractions. When a fraction is written in words, use a hyphen to separate the numerator from the denominator unless either or both parts of the fraction already contain a hyphen.

one-tenth   three-quarters   five thirty-seconds
thirty-five sixty-fourths

If a spelled-out fraction is used as an adjective before a noun, use a hyphen between the parts of the fraction.

The Williams family has a *one-third* interest in the corporation.

The amendment was approved by a *three-fourths* majority.

Do not use a hyphen when a fraction is used in a construction like the following one:

One half of the order was shipped in June; the *other half,* in July.

19. Round and Indefinite Numbers. Do not use a hyphen in a round number that is expressed in words. Also do not use a hyphen in an indefinite number, which is always expressed in words.

one hundred   two thousand   many hundreds
five million   several hundred   a few thousand

20. Range of Numbers. The hyphen may be used in place of the word *to* between numbers representing a continuous sequence.

Please note the article on pages 128-132.
Note that this conference is scheduled for April 16-18.

PARENTHESES

In addition to having some uses of their own, parentheses are often used in place of commas or dashes to set off supplementary or explanatory matter that is not essential to the grammatical completeness of a sentence. Unlike dashes, parentheses de-emphasize; like dashes, however, parentheses should be used sparingly.

21. Parentheses Instead of Commas or Dashes. To give the least emphasis to an explanatory or interrupting element that is not essential to the grammatical completeness of a sentence, use parentheses instead of commas or dashes to set off the explanatory or interrupting element.

> Part of the work (about a third) has been completed.
>
> Some analysts (one of them is Dr. Riley, a former employee of the firm) think the company will seek a merger partner.

As illustrated by the last example above, a sentence that is enclosed in parentheses within another sentence does not begin with a capital letter unless the first word is one that would always be capitalized. Also, a sentence enclosed in parentheses within another sentence does not end with a period before the closing parenthesis. However, a question mark or an exclamation point may be used at the end of such a sentence if (1) the question mark or exclamation point applies only to the parenthetical sentence and (2) the sentence in which the parenthetical sentence appears ends with a different punctuation mark.

> Ms. Shirley Kramer (you remember her, don't you?) gave an excellent presentation. (Note the question mark before the closing parenthesis and the period at the end of the complete sentence.)
>
> Is the site still available (and what is the name and address of the owner or agent), or has it already been sold? (No question mark is used before the closing parenthesis because the complete sentence ends with a question mark.)

If a sentence that is enclosed in parentheses appears outside another sentence, the first word is capitalized and the appropriate end punctuation mark is placed before the closing parenthesis.

> The next meeting will be held on June 10. (It was originally scheduled for June 3.)
>
> Michael Lamont has been named president and chief executive officer. (Isn't he a son or grandson of the founder?)

22. With Figures and Letters in Enumerations. Use parentheses to enclose figures or letters preceding enumerated items in a sentence.

> Customer complaints often pertain to (1) delivery service, (2) billing, or (3) follow-up service.
>
> Contingency plans include the following: (a) delaying purchases of equipment, (b) freezing requisitions for new and replacement personnel, and (c) canceling all but essential employee travel.

23. With Doubtful Statements. Use a question mark enclosed in parentheses to indicate that the accuracy of a name, date, or similar detail is in doubt. Note that no space appears before the opening parenthesis and the term preceding it.

> I spoke with Mr. Mateus(?), a member of your credit department, last Tuesday morning.
>
> That model was discontinued in 1988(?).

24. With Dates. Use parentheses to set off dates that indicate the years of a person's life or the time of an event.

> In our first year (1990), our sales were only $122,500.
>
> John F. Kennedy (1917-1963) served as President of the United States from 1961 to 1963.

25. With Numbers in Legal Documents. Numbers in legal documents are usually stated both in words and in figures. In such cases, the number in figures is usually enclosed in parentheses.

> The sum of twenty-five hundred dollars ($2500) shall be paid to the seller within thirty (30) days of the date of this agreement.

Spot Check 3

Insert the necessary hyphens and parentheses in the following sentences. If other punctuation marks are needed before closing parentheses, add them also. If a sentence is correct, circle the number preceding it.

1. They are celebrating their twenty-fifth wedding anniversary.

2. Thirty-two of the apartments have been rented.

3. One thousand forty-six members voted.

4. About three-fourths of the votes have been counted.

5. One sixty-fourth of an inch is the specified tolerance, isn't it?

6. If they own one half of the company, who owns the other half?

7. Please refer to the chart on pages 10-11.

8. Service to a few hundred homes was briefly interrupted yesterday.

9. I think there are three hundred signatures on the petition.

10. I will be on vacation during the period June 28-July 12.

11. Dissident stockholders (approximately 50) challenged the board's decision.

12. Marie Olivera (she retired last February, didn't she) may be interested in working with you on that project.

13. Archibald Donaldson (everyone calls him Archie) is on the committee.

14. Isn't the tenth of next month (will you be available) the date tentatively set for the seminar?

15. Lenders are interested in (1) character, (2) capital, and (3) capacity.

16. The school was named for Booker Taliaferro Washington (1856-1915).

17. The amount of ten thousand dollars ($10,000) shall be due and payable within sixty (60) days.

18. You may need to file the long form (Form 1040).

Study Guide 31

A. Study the following list of expressions. Can you explain why hyphens are used in some but not in others? If not, refer to the rules indicated.

1. a well-known brand[1,5]
2. industry is state-regulated[2]
3. Dallas-Fort Worth area[3]
4. a real estate agency[3]
5. a small brown envelope[6]
6. a 15 percent reduction[7]
7. 8- and 12-ounce containers[7,8]
8. as the owner-manager[9]
9. wore hand-me-downs[9]
10. good at problem solving[9]
11. may trade in her car[10]
12. is self-confident[12]

13. with Senator-elect Hill[12]
14. wall-less work areas[14]
15. my re-marking the tags[15]
16. lawn is well kept[2]
17. a junior college graduate[3]
18. clearly stated opinion[4]
19. perfume was sweet-smelling[2]
20. a two-page letter[7]
21. a 12-foot board[7]
22. as a down payment[9]
23. engaged in double-talk[9]
24. are semi-independent[14]

25. bimonthly reports[11]
26. for selfish reasons[12]
27. to the ex-mayor[12]
28. is very pro-American[13]
29. a storewide clearance[11]
30. twenty-nine days[16]
31. on the twenty-second[16]
32. one thousand two hundred[17]
33. a one-fourth interest[18]
34. one half is; the other half is not[18]
35. three hundred copies[19]
36. see pages 28-34[20]

B. As you read the following sentences, note the use of parentheses. Can you explain each of the uses illustrated? If necessary, refer to the rules indicated.

1. This network will electronically link most of our regional offices (see page 14 of the enclosed directory).[21]

2. Table 6 (see page 8) shows estimated costs and projected sales for products scheduled to be developed during the first quarter.[21]

3. I am sure the number of applicants (12) was rather disappointing.[21]

4. Mrs. Rachel Jeffers (didn't you recommend her to our general manager as a prospective consultant?) will be available to work with you and me next Tuesday.[21]

5. Larry Kirkland (to no one's surprise!) has accepted their offer.[21]

6. Have bids (or are they requests for proposals) been solicited?[21]

7. The reorganization will become effective March 1. (A copy of the new organization chart is attached.)[21]

8. I am enclosing a photocopy of (1) the charge slip, (2) the credit slip, and (3) your most recent statement of my account.[22]

9. Fred Shaeffer(?) outlined the group's opposition to the plan.[23]

10. Leslie M. Washburn (1898-1982) founded the company in 1936.[24]

11. The final installment shall be four hundred thirty-two dollars ($432).[25]

ASSIGNMENT: Complete the Unit 31 Worksheet on pages 231–232 and the Part 7 Review on pages 233–234.

UNIT 31

The Hyphen and Parentheses

WORKSHEET

 A For each of the following sentences that contains an incorrectly written compound word, underline the incorrectly written compound and write it correctly in the space provided. For each sentence that is correct, write *OK*.

1. They are co-producers, according to a network spokesperson.
2. I do not recollect trying to recollect those accounts.
3. We re-marked the merchandise in the stock room.
4. The supermarket gave its employees a retro-active pay increase.
5. They were self confident at the outset.
6. Someone put a flash light in the cornerstone.
7. We stopped for ice cream at a drive in.
8. There is a grand father clock near the staircase.
9. Don't over estimate its value as a timepiece.
10. Some self employed people keep time sheets.
11. He fell overboard while paddling a rowboat.
12. Some object to bill boards along interstate highways.
13. I studied cost-accounting in junior college.
14. The coowners are bilingual.
15. Elsie got one-half of the award, and Clyde got the other half.
16. A draw bridge has many drawbacks.
17. The apartments in this coop have walk-in closets.
18. She is a co-operative coauthor.
19. We had some falllike days in midsummer.
20. The eyewitness was unable to identify any one in the lineup.
21. We expect them to recover by mid-week.
22. They were so home sick they couldn't concentrate on their homework.
23. There was a large turn out for the ballgame.
24. She works as a free lance photographer in the summertime.
25. The sales clerk forgot to give me a sales check.

1. coproducers
2. re-collect
3. stockroom
4. retroactive
5. self-confident
6. flashlight
7. drive-in
8. grandfather
9. overestimate
10. self-employed
11. OK
12. billboards
13. cost accounting
14. co-owners
15. one half
16. drawbridge
17. co-op
18. cooperative
19. fall-like
20. anyone
21. midweek
22. homesick
23. turnout
24. free-lance
25. salesclerk

Insert the necessary hyphens and parentheses in the following sentences. If a sentence is punctuated correctly, circle the number preceding it.

1. This carpeting is available in 9-, 12-, and 15-foot widths.

2. Twenty-two people have signed up for the August 20-22 bus trip to Myrtle Beach.

3. This easy-to-use software (it is being tested now) should be available by mid-June.

4. It is well known that Louis Pasteur (1822-1895) is the person for whom the process of pasteurization is named.

5. The senator-elect called for (1) a reduction in government spending and (2) a corresponding reduction in federal income taxes.

6. According to Sam Willett, Loreen (?) Wolfson indicated that she would like to be considered for the position of secretary-treasurer.

7. The principal plus interest shall be payable in twelve (12) equal installments of three hundred eighty-five dollars ($385).

8. As a full-time employee, you will receive low-cost medical insurance and various company-paid benefits. (See Chapter 4 of your employee handbook for complete details.)

9. Phyllis Morrison (wasn't she on the program last year?) is a former officer of our association.

10. Do you think Myrtle Maitland (is she still a member of your staff) would be willing to serve on this committee too?

11. Our medium-range plan calls for a modest 6 percent increase in each of the New England districts.

12. The real estate developers hope to attract low-, middle-, and high-income families to this new subdivision.

13. The co-owners of the 12-story apartment building reported that all the asbestos has been removed and that a new air-conditioning system will be installed within the near future.

14. Members of the founder's family own approximately one-third of the firm's common stock.

15. An unusually soft-spoken collector called me about my overdue account and told me that I might be able to arrange a 30-day extension if I would stop in to discuss the matter with the credit department manager.

16. The friendly-looking flight attendants served us some highly seasoned roast beef sandwiches on the Chicago-Kansas City flight.

17. Several stores in the midtown area offer brand-name merchandise at greatly reduced prices during their Columbus Day sales.

18. They appeared to be self-appointed spokespersons, and most of the group gave them short shrift.

19. Whether they are old-fashioned or not, our customers demonstrate a clear-cut preference for freshly baked apple pies.

20. As a final touch, they added one day- and one night-blooming water lily to the small pond in the middle of the backyard.

21. Managers, secretaries, and others have expressed an interest in a short keyboarding course designed specifically for microcomputer operators.

22. To obtain complete, up-to-date data, we must conduct a large-scale survey of those in the hotel-motel industry.

23. This floor wax is easy to apply, and it is quick-drying and long-lasting.

24. Two of the officeholders made some off-the-record comments.

25. Some well-known and highly respected economists said that double-digit inflation is a thing of the past.

PART 7

Punctuation

Insert whatever additional punctuation marks are needed in the following sentences. If a sentence is shown punctuated correctly, circle the number preceding it. Where necessary, use carets (∧∨) to indicate the placement of punctuation marks.

REVIEW

1. Many, many people have used this quick-drying latex paint, and I'm confident that you will be pleased with it too.

2. The owner-manager of the store reported a 12 percent increase in sales of our household appliances during the 90-day period ending June 30.

3. Both applicants' answers to Mr. Morgan's questions indicated that they were highly qualified for entry-level positions in the data processing department.

4. Would you be interested in an accounting, a marketing, or an advertising position with that firm, Pat?

5. The company will be celebrating the seventy-fifth anniversary of its founding on August 1, 2000, won't it, Ms. Gomez?

6. The question is this: Is a recount of the stock absolutely necessary?

7. Leading business consultants agree, is one thing, managing, another.

8. "When debugged," the programmer said, "this word processing-graphics-financial spreadsheet package will take a large share of the market within a 6- to 12-month period."

9. Should we have next year's marketing conference in Chicago? in Miami? in Los Angeles?

10. Jody Mapes, PhD, has written several articles for our local newspaper, The Clinton Herald.

11. From 8:30 a.m. to 2 p.m. on Saturday, November 24, Mike, Mary, and I were working on the agenda for the national sales meeting.

12. Carla, did you read the article "At Your Leisure" in the March 10 issue of the magazine Touring the USA?

13. Peter replied, Paul said, "This is a labor-management issue."

14. Tables, chairs, lamps—all are available at rock-bottom prices during our Columbus Day sale.

15. We received 1,220 responses from the 12,500 customers surveyed in December 1992, and we believe that the questionnaire used in that survey (see Appendix B on pages 119–124) can be updated and used in the forthcoming survey.

16. One speaker said business decisions affect everyone in one way or another.

17. All rivers, lakes, etc., should be—but aren't—pollution-free.

18. The US Postal Service handles millions of letters, catalogs, packages, and so on, every day.

19. For further information, write to us at 8608 Fallsburg Road, Pueblo, Colorado 81005, at any time.

20. I think Wilma J Jenkins MD's office is in the northeast not southwest part of town.

21. To think otherwise probably would be a mistake to say the least sir.

22. The question is What should we do to eliminate such bottlenecks as those?

23. A few years ago (five or six) we thought of buying a two-bedroom coop apartment but for various reasons we changed our minds and are still renting a small studio apartment.

24. In 1992 578 employees belonged to the credit union today however nearly two-thirds of our 1250 member work force belong.

25. Refreshments for example coffee milk jelly-filled doughnuts and cupcakes may entice more people to attend our next one-day workshop.

26. How old-fashioned! Benny exclaimed. That style must be from the '50s maybe the '40s!

27. Tired of trying to find a place to park Miss Jeffreys decided she would forgo eating at a downtown restaurant and go to a drive-in instead.

28. This report provides up-to-date accurate information.

29. Everybody knows too many cooks spoil the broth.

30. The person we should ask don't you agree is P A Kern III?

31. The package labeled Fragile is from Ashe Gray & Thomas Inc of Morristown New Jersey.

32. Our supermarkets sell Grade A dairy products too.

33. It seems that I wrote the word too when I should have written to.

34. Are you sure eg means for example and ie means that is?

35. Before I forget it please bring the following plastic cups paper plates knives forks and spoons.

36. She was in such a hurry she forgot to dot her i's and cross her t's.

37. Ms. Wilder speaking to the senator-elect said Those people are pro-American and they are counting on our continued support.

38. Leslie M. Greenburg, Sr.'s family owns one half of the company's outstanding stock and a hundred or so others own the other half.

39. Do you think such investments should be tax-exempt?

40. However these need to be rechecked (1) the battery (2) the fuel pump and (3) the transmission.

41. I am sure that you too will want to hear Mr. Barry Albright president and chief executive officer outline the company's long-range plans.

42. Margaret together with Mrs. Saunders went to the airport to meet the former mayor Lynn O'Donnell.

43. Buildings such as those should be condemned.

44. Frozen foods such as corn and peas should not be thawed and then refrozen in my opinion.

45. Some locally grown vegetables are plentiful now for example sweet corn and tomatoes.

46. There is no one answer to a question such as that is there?

47. Current plans are to release the new model in mid-September.

48. Would you please let me know what you think of this plan.

49. However expensive such insurance may be we need it.

50. Although we wish we could we cannot repeat this once-in-a-lifetime offer.

PART 8

Words and Word References

Before you study Units 32–35, complete this survey of words and word usage. These exercises will help you identify principles that you may wish to give special attention.

SURVEY

A No more than two letters are missing in any word below. Insert the missing letter or letters in each word. If no letter is missing, circle the number preceding the word.

1. sincer _e_ ly	14. promis _so_ ry	27. priv _i_ lege	(40.) oil ____ y
2. debat _a_ ble	15. anniuers _a_ ry	28. bound _a_ ry	41. effic _ie_ nt
3. omit _t_ ed	16. refin _e_ ry	29. quan _t_ ity	(42.) tru ____ ly
4. cat _e_ gory	17. Feb _ru_ ary	(30.) mis ____ take	43. in _t_ erest
5. proc _e_ dure	18. oc _c_ asion	(31.) mis ____ hap	44. ach _ie_ ve
6. valu _a_ ble	19. manag _e_ able	32. vis _i_ ble	45. li _c_ ense
7. sep _a_ rate	20. person _n_ el	33. all _i_ es	46. def _i_ nite
8. chall _e_ nge	(21.) ful ____ filled	34. proce _e_ d	(47.) ath ____ lete
(9.) judg ____ ment	22. veg _e_ table	35. w _ei_ ght	48. su _r_ prise
10. il _l_ ogical	(23.) rec ____ ommend	36. rec _ei_ pt	(49.) issu ____ ing
11. We _d_ nesday	24. cer _e_ mony	37. lib _r_ ary	50. mis _s_ pell
(12.) advis ____ or	25. profit _a_ ble	38. rel _y_ ing	
13. mor _t_ gage	26. commit _t_ ee	39. fr _ei_ ght	

B Rewrite each of the following words, inserting a hyphen wherever the word may be divided correctly.

1. commitment	1. com-mit-ment	6. referred	6. re-ferred
2. importance	2. im-por-tance	7. reference	7. ref-er-ence
3. production	3. pro-duc-tion	8. illegal	8. il-le-gal
4. wholesale	4. whole-sale	9. imaginative	9. imag-i-na-tive
5. performance	5. per-for-mance	10. successful	10. suc-cess-ful

C Note the italicized word in each phrase below. Which of the four words at the right of the phrase has the same or nearly the same meaning as the italicized word? Underline the word you select.

1. an *audacious* person	insolvent	creative	loud	adventurous
2. a *reciprocal* agreement	one-sided	enforceable	mutual	illegal
3. *ambiguous* answers	lengthy	courteous	precise	unclear
4. a *futile* effort	silly	intensive	vein	ineffective
5. a *nominal* charge	known	fair	slight	excessive
6. *extraneous* data	additional	essential	vital	irrelevant
7. a *fortuitous* event	predicted	accidental	odd	productive
8. a *lucrative* business	profitable	unethical	illegal	attractive
9. *relevant* consideration	pointless	essential	family	pertinent
10. a *prolific* writer	imaginative	professional	lively	productive

D Underline the word at the right of each sentence that is completely or almost completely opposite in meaning to the italicized word.

1. They were a *boisterous* group.	quiet	feminine	childish
2. The meaning is rather *obscure.*	hidden	doubtful	obvious
3. We think their proposal is *definitive.*	vague	tentative	precise
4. Both firms are *solvent.*	solid	bankrupt	profitable
5. It was a *figurative* description.	literal	shapeless	numeric
6. We were *oblivious* to the noise outside.	fearful	aware	near
7. What a *hackneyed* expression!	vulgar	ordinary	original
8. She made some *impromptu* remarks.	quick	memorized	unrehearsed
9. We think we made a *prudent* decision.	foolish	indiscreet	moral
10. Why would anyone *malign* them?	warp	straighten	compliment

E In each of the following sentences, which word in parentheses is correct? Write your answer in the space provided.

1. Their (moral, morale) is excellent.

2. She had apple pie for (desert, dessert).

3. I (appraised, apprised) them of my progress.

4. He seems rather (callous, callus).

5. The (coroner, corner) performed an autopsy.

6. Fay was (cited, sighted, sited) for bravery.

7. A settlement seems (eminent, imminent).

8. It was enough to try one's (patience, patients).

9. Nothing seems to (phase, faze) them.

10. They climbed to the (peak, peek).

1. morale
2. dessert
3. apprised
4. callous
5. coroner
6. cited
7. imminent
8. patience
9. faze
10. peak

REFERENCE BOOKS

Everyone who works with words—including those who use computers and word processors equipped with spelling, word division, and other programs—frequently refers to a variety of printed reference materials. If you are like most people, the more experience you gain in writing and speaking, the more you will use the dictionary and other reference materials.

The Dictionary. The dictionary is, of course, the most essential of all references for both speakers and writers. Here is a list of some dictionaries that are widely used in business offices as well as in homes, libraries, schools, and colleges:

> *Webster's Third New International Dictionary* (Unabridged), Merriam-Webster Inc., Springfield, Massachusetts.

> *Webster's Ninth New Collegiate Dictionary* (Abridged), Merriam-Webster Inc., Springfield, Massachusetts.

> *Funk & Wagnall's New Standard Dictionary of the English Language* (Unabridged), Funk & Wagnalls Publishing Company, New York.

> *Funk & Wagnall's New Desk Standard Dictionary* (Abridged), Funk & Wagnalls Publishing Company, New York.

> *The American Heritage Dictionary of the English Language,* American Heritage Publishing Co., Inc., and Houghton Mifflin Company, Boston.

> *The Random House College Dictionary,* Random House, Inc., New York.

The first step in getting the most out of a dictionary is to become acquainted with the extent and variety of information it contains. Scan the table of contents and read the explanatory notes in the front of the dictionary. These notes explain the pronunciation and other symbols and the abbreviations used in word entries. Learn to use the thumb index (if your dictionary has one) and the guide words at the top of the page so that you can locate words quickly. Look up a few words, noting all the types of information given for each and the sequence in which the information is given. A good dictionary will give you invaluable assistance in resolving questions or problems concerning the following:

1. Spelling
2. Syllabication
3. Pronunciation
4. Parts of speech
5. Meanings of words, prefixes, and suffixes
6. Derivation of words
7. Plural forms of nouns
8. Parts of verbs
9. Foreign words and phrases
10. Abbreviations
11. Proofreaders' marks
12. Biographical data
13. Geographical data (in the "Gazetteer" section)
14. Basic spelling, punctuation, and other rules

The variety and extent of information will, of course, vary from one dictionary to another. In addition, the preferred spellings of some words, the substance of some punctuation rules, and so on, differ from one to another. Thus you will want to choose and use the dictionary that best suits your needs.

Spot Check 1

Using your own dictionary or one recommended by your instructor, find the answer to each of the following questions. Write your answer in the space provided, and give the page number or numbers on which you found the answer. (Note: Answers shown here are from *Webster's Ninth New Collegiate Dictionary*.)

1. What other spelling, if any, would be acceptable for the word *judgment?*
   judgement (page 653)

2. What are the guide words on the page where you found the answer to the first question?
   Jubal and *juice* (page 653)

3. If a word has more than one acceptable spelling, what words or symbols are used between the various spellings and what do those words or symbols mean?

or means equal variants; *also* means the spelling after *also* is a secondary variant (page 11)

4. What is the first syllable of the word *progress* when it is used as a noun? as a verb?

prog—as a noun; pro—as a verb (page 940)

5. Which syllable is stressed more when *progress* is pronounced as a noun? as a verb? Show the symbol used to indicate the particular syllable by placing it with the syllable.

'prog—as a noun; 'gress—as a verb (page 940)

6. From what language is the word *miscellaneous* derived? What is the word in that language?

Latin—*miscellaneus* (page 758)

7. What synonyms, if any, are listed for the adjective *grand?*

magnificent, imposing, stately, majestic, grandiose (page 531)

8. What does the verb *fluctuate* mean?

"to ebb and flow in waves; to shift back and forth uncertainly; to cause to fluctuate" (page 475)

9. What principal parts of the verb *speak* are shown?

spoke, spoken, and speaking (page 1131)

10. In what states is there a city named *Albany?*

Georgia, New York, and Oregon (page 1434)

11. Who was John Logie Baird? In what year was he born? In what year did he die?

Scottish inventor—the father of television; 1888; 1946 (page 1394)

12. If a word has more than one meaning, are the meanings listed in historical order, that is, from earliest to most recent? If not, how are they arranged?

Yes (page 19)

13. For what is *MICR* the abbreviation?

magnetic ink character recognition (page 1380)

14. What does the Latin phrase *tempus fugit* mean? On what objects does it frequently appear?

"time flies"—on some clocks (page 1389)

15. What do the mathematical symbols < and > mean?

the symbol < means "less than"; the symbol > means "greater than" (page 1535)

The Thesaurus. Unlike a dictionary, which lists words followed by their meanings, a thesaurus provides two kinds of listings: the first, or main, section is a listing of ideas; the second is a listing of words cross-referenced by number to the ideas in the first section. Thus if you know the idea you want to express but can't think of the right word, you can use the thesaurus to help you find the word. The best-known reference of this type is *Roget's International Thesaurus* (Thomas Y. Crowell Company, Inc., New York).

Style Manual or Writer's Handbook. A good style manual or writer's handbook provides a wealth of information concerning punctuation, capitalization, number usage, abbreviations, manuscript typing, letter preparation, English grammar and word usage, etc. The following are references of this type:

The Gregg Reference Manual, Glencoe Division of Macmillan/McGraw-Hill School Publishing Company, Columbus, Ohio
Writer's Guide and Index to English, Scott, Foresman and Company, Chicago

WORD DIVISION

Whether you use a computer, a word processor, or a typewriter to prepare letters, memos, and other materials, you will want to keep the right margin as nearly even as possible or, in some instances, to "justify" the copy, which means to create a perfectly even right margin. To achieve such a right margin, you very likely will need to divide words at the end of some lines. In doing so, you should:

• Keep word division to a minimum. Divided words reduce fluency in reading and, in unjustified material, can sometimes give the right margin a ragged appearance.

- Avoid ending more than two consecutive lines with a divided word. Remember that automatic word division programs for word processors and other equipment typically are considerably less than 100 percent accurate. Only you have the ability to decide, for example, whether the word *record* functions as a verb that needs to be divided *re- cord* or as a noun or an adjective that needs to be divided *rec- ord.*

- Follow the accepted rules of word division, consulting a dictionary when necessary to determine the correct syllabication of a word. Be sure to check the part-of-speech label or labels following the word in question: the syllabication may differ, depending on how a particular word is used. Also remember that not all the divisions shown in a dictionary may be acceptable in typewritten or printed copy.

Basic Rules. The following rules should always be observed when dividing words in business communications. Dictionaries may not agree on the syllabication of a few words. Please note that the words used to illustrate these rules are divided in accordance with the syllabication shown in *Webster's Ninth New Collegiate Dictionary* (Merriam-Webster Inc., Springfield, Massachusetts).

1. Divide a word only between syllables. If you are uncertain of the syllabication of a word, consult the dictionary.

2. Never divide a one-syllable word, regardless of its length. Remember that adding *ed* to a word does not always increase the number of syllables in the word.

bleached	made	pleased	shopped	thought
cleared	marked	praised	switched	through

3. Never divide after a one-letter syllable at the beginning of a word or before a one-letter syllable at the end of a word. Note the italicized syllables in the following examples.

*a*mount	cutler*y*	fol*i*o	*i*temize	stere*o*
*a*rena	enumerate	*i*deals	omit*s*	*u*nite
criteri*a*	evolved	*i*dentify	opinion	*u*niversal

4. Never divide a word unless you can leave a syllable of at least two letters at the end of the line and carry over to the next line a syllable of at least three characters (three letters or two letters followed by a punctuation mark).

ac- tive	build- er,	em- ployed	lead- er;
as- sign	de- scribe	im- pact	north- ern
brief- ly.	do- ing	in- crease	un- like

5. Never divide an abbreviation.

admin.	COBOL	EPCOT	NASA	UNESCO
AT&T	c.o.d.	FDIC	Ph.D.	U.S.A.

6. Never divide a contraction.

aren't	isn't	she'll	they're	would've
couldn't	o'clock	shouldn't	we've	you're

Spot Check 2

For each of the following words, insert a hyphen wherever the word can correctly be divided. Use a caret (^) to indicate where the hyphen should be inserted. If a word should not or cannot be divided, circle the number preceding it.

1. stopped
2. agreed
3. ill^ness
4. ra^dio
5. branch^es,
6. do^ing
7. amount
8. ad^mire
9. cleared
10. pre^fer
11. f.o.b.
12. they'll
13. watched
14. faul^ty
15. obey
16. brush^es;
17. pro^vide
18. U.S.S.R.
19. on^ly.
20. match^es;
21. clothes

Preferred Rules. When the space remaining at the end of a line permits you to choose the point at which to divide a word, follow the preferred word division rules that appear below.

7. Divide after a prefix or before a suffix.

il- legal	bi- weekly	tri- colored
un- written	ir- responsible	non- exempt
rais- ing	read- ers	count- less
pay- ment	peril- ous	sharp- ness

8. When a word contains double consonants, divide between the two consonants.

paral- lel	col- lateral	dif- ficult
refer- ring	mis- sion	ship- ping

   This rule does not apply if the root word ends in a double consonant.

call- ing	guess- ing	staff- ing

9. When a single one-letter syllable occurs within a word, divide after that syllable.

cata- lyst   cate- gory   divi- dend
apolo- gize   regu- lar   medi- cine

10. Divide after a prefix or before a suffix, not within the prefix or the suffix.

intra- state   *retro*- active   *anti*- trust
desir- *able*   convert- *ible*   alphabet- *ical*

11. When two separately sounded vowels appear together, divide between them.

radi- ation   cre- ative   soci- eties
vi- olation   virtu- oso   seri- als

12. Divide a hyphenated compound word after the hyphen.

go- ahead   self- analysis   forty- two
twenty- fifth   shell- less   co- owner

13. Divide compound words written solid between the elements of the compound.

news- papers   basket- ball   silver- ware
over- burden   under- written   post- graduate

14. Do not divide proper nouns unless it is absolutely necessary to do so.

William Oklahoma Shreveport European American

15. Do not separate titles, initials, or abbreviations for seniority terms or academic degrees from the names with which they appear. For example, do not write *Mr.* or *Ms.* at the end of a line and the name of the person at the beginning of the next line.

16. Do not divide a number written in figures unless it is absolutely necessary to do so. A very long number may be divided after a comma: 24,500,-000.

17. Do not divide at the end of the first line or the last full line in a paragraph.

18. Do not divide the last word in a paragraph.

19. Do not divide the last word on a page.

20. Do not divide at the end of more than two consecutive lines.

Study Guide 32

A. If you do not know why the following terms should not be divided, refer to Rules 1-6.

1. acute[3]
2. haven't[6]
3. FDIC[5]
4. shortly[4]
5. thrifty[3]
6. trio[3]
7. erase[3]
8. oily[3]
9. NASA[5]
10. shiny[3]
11. eject[3]
12. Ed.D.[5]
13. ASPCA[5]
14. U.S.A.[5]
15. mailed[1]
16. unite[3]
17. approx.[5]
18. really[4]
19. aren't[6]
20. they'll[6]
21. thought[1]
22. shouldn't[6]
23. UNESCO[5]
24. planned[1]
25. stretched[1]

B. Dividing words into syllables is helpful in spelling and pronouncing them correctly. Study the following words, which are divided into syllables as shown in the dictionary.

1. ad-ja-cent
2. anx-ious
3. bank-rupt-cy
4. be-liev-able
5. com-pen-sa-tion
6. com-pa-ra-ble
7. com-par-i-son
8. con-tes-tant
9. de-ci-sion
10. de-scrip-tion
11. es-ti-mate
12. fi-nance
13. gov-ern-ment
14. im-pres-sive
15. ju-di-cious
16. knowl-edge
17. lin-ear
18. man-age-able
19. nui-sance
20. opin-ion
21. pre-ferred
22. pref-er-ence
23. re-fer-ring
24. ref-er-ence
25. ser-vice-able
26. te-dious-ness
27. va-lid-i-ty
28. wor-ri-some
29. ver-sa-tile
30. val-i-dat-ed

C. As you study each group of words, note the spelling, part of speech, and meaning of each word. Also note that carefully pronouncing some words that have nearly the same pronunciation will help avoid confusing them.

1. accept   *verb:* to receive
    except   *verb:* to exclude; *preposition:* with the exclusion of; *conjunction:* unless, only

2. adapt   *verb:* to adjust or modify
    adept   *adjective:* proficient or skillful
    adopt   *verb:* to take by choice

3. advice   *noun:* recommendation or suggestion
    advise   *verb:* to recommend or to suggest

4. affect   *verb:* to influence or to pretend or feign
    effect   *verb:* to bring about or to achieve; *noun:* a result or an outcome

5. all ready   *adjective phrase:* entirely prepared
    already   *adverb:* before some definite time

6. all together   *adjective phrase:* assembled or collected in one place or in one group
    altogether   *adverb:* entirely, completely, or wholly

7. amount   *noun:* the total quantity or sum; *verb:* to add up to or to be equivalent to
    number   *noun:* a collection of separate units counted individually

8. every day   *adverbial or noun phrase:* each day
    everyday   *adjective:* ordinary

9. real   *adjective:* genuine, actual, or true
    really   *adverb:* actually or truly

10. sure   *adjective:* certain, confident, or positive
    surely   *adverb:* certainly, confidently, or positively
    very   *adverb:* exceedingly or truly

D. Study the words in the following sentences and note how they are used. The meaning of each word is given in parentheses.

1. This letter will *confirm* my telephone order of October 10. (Ratify, corroborate.)

2. *Depletion* of our capital will result in *bankruptcy*. (Lessening; failure or inability to pay just debts.)

3. Total figures on employment tend to *obscure* these local situations. (Hide.)

4. The speaker explained that progress is being made toward an *equitable* tax program. (Just, fair to all.)

5. Our *ultimate* purpose is the *extensive* enlargement of our present facilities. (Final; broad.)

6. Will the company *defray* the expenses of the trip? (Pay.)

7. What could be more *pertinent* than the data Jim submitted? (Related to the matter in hand, relevant.)

8. This agreement should speed *consummation* of the reorganization plan. (Completion.)

9. The *consumption* of petroleum products is still increasing, isn't it? (Use.)

10. The vote was so close that neither candidate would *concede* defeat. (Admit.)

11. *Eliminating* the oil companies, which had *phenomenal* sales, the decline in profits from last year amounted to 14 percent. (Excluding; extraordinary.)

12. Do *predictions* encourage the belief that by fall the *postponed* boom will develop? (Forecasts; delayed.)

13. It is clear, in *retrospect,* that our *optimism* was based on faulty reading of economic signs. (Meditation on the past; hopeful view.)

14. We have recently announced several changes in our *reorganization* plan designed to provide greater *participation* for holders of *preferred stock.* (Reconstruction; sharing, as in profits; shares entitling the holder to receive dividends before holders of common stock.)

15. Review of this court decision must be given *precedence;* it sets several *precedents* affecting many of our cases. (Priority; rules or examples justifying similar occurrences.)

16. The *agenda* has been agreed upon except for one item on it. (List of things to be done or discussed.)

17. In these days of intensely *competitive* operation, no retailer could long survive if he or she *countenanced* waste and extravagance in his or her business. (Pertaining to rivalry; approved.)

18. The *consignee* reported that the goods had been received. (The person to whom goods are shipped.)

19. Unless you call for the freight by June 10, you must pay *demurrage.* (Payment for such delay.)

20. The *vouchers* must be kept for checking by the auditor. (Receipts of payment.)

21. Orders in some *categories* have been affected adversely. (Classes, lists.)

22. The government imposes *excise taxes* on many articles, such as tobacco and liquor. (Taxes on the manufacture or sale of articles within the country.)

23. The committee requested an *appropriation* of $15,000 for further research. (Sum of money formally set aside for a special use.)

24. The auditor found a *discrepancy* in the firm's accounts. (Disagreement, difference)

25. *Substantial* operating economies should be put into effect at once. (Large.)

ASSIGNMENT: Complete the Unit 32 Worksheet on pages 243–244.

UNIT 32

Reference Books and Word Division

WORKSHEET

 A **Using your dictionary, find the answers to the following questions; then write them in the space provided.**

1. How long is the Mississippi River?

2. The English name of this Italian city is Florence. What is the Italian name?

3. What does the Latin expression *novus ordo seclorum* mean, and where does it appear as a motto?

4. How many kilometers are there in 1 mile?

5. In what year did the noun *double-dealing* first appear in written English?

1. 2470 miles/3975 km (p. 1482)

2. Firenze (p. 1458)

3. "a new cycle of the ages"; on the Great Seal of the U.S. (p. 1388)

4. 1.609 (p. 1338)

5. 1529 (p. 377)

 B **For each of the following terms and expressions, insert a caret (^) at the end of each syllable except a one-letter syllable at the beginning or the end of a word.**

1. iden^ti^ty
2. par^al^lel
3. pref^er^ence
4. con^cen^trate
5. streamlined
6. with^holding
7. de^ferred
8. oc^cur^rence
9. knowl^edge
10. rec^om^men^da^tion
11. re^con^struct
12. men^tioned
13. sep^a^rate
14. fi^nan^cial
15. sub^mit^ted
16. ob^li^ga^tion
17. me^dia
18. en^cour^age^ment
19. co^in^ci^dence
20. com^pa^ra^ble

 C **Which word in parentheses correctly completes each of the following sentences? Write your answer in the space provided.**

1. All are in favor (accept, except) him.

2. Maybe we should (accept, except) her offer.

3. Which job offer do you plan to (accept, except)?

4. He was (accepted, excepted) from attending.

5. Please (accept, except) my apology.

6. Yes, we are (accepting, excepting) all bids.

7. Everyone (accept, except) Nick was there.

8. She is (adapt, adept, adopt) at speaking.

9. We may (adapt, adept, adopt) it to our needs.

10. They may (adapt, adept, adopt) a child.

11. I will (adapt, adopt) his plan as it is.

1. except
2. accept
3. accept
4. excepted
5. accept
6. accepting
7. except
8. adept
9. adapt
10. adopt
11. adopt

12. Is this medicine (affective, effective)?

13. Some (affect, effect) a British accent.

14. You are an (affective, effective) manager.

15. The change won't (affect, effect) us.

16. I used a small (amount, number) of molasses.

17. A large (amount, number) of people attended.

18. They made (an amount, a number) of loans.

19. His goals aren't (all together, altogether) clear.

20. The correspondence is (all together, altogether) in one folder.

21. The copies are (all ready, already) for you.

22. I have (all ready, already) notified them.

23. What (advice, advise) would you offer?

24. He should seek legal (advice, advise).

25. I hope you will (advice, advise) me.

26. We do our best (every day, everyday).

27. They were out of the office (every day, everyday) last week.

28. Reading the newspaper is part of my (every day, everyday) routine.

29. The prospects (sure, surely) look good, don't they?

30. The incumbent governor seems (sure, surely) of reelection.

31. It was (sure, very) good to see them.

32. Winning (sure, surely) is important to them.

33. Is he (real, really) certain it is correct?

34. We use (real, really) vanilla flavoring.

35. She was (real, really) disappointed.

36. They (real, really) are expensive.

37. They have three (adapted, adopted) children.

38. He seems quite (sure, surely) of himself.

39. The play was (adapted, adopted) for TV.

40. They (sure, surely) know the difference.

41. Both are (sure, surely, very) attractive.

42. It was (real, really) easy for them to do.

43. Some people seem (adapt, adept) at lying.

44. The bank (accepted, excepted) both checks.

45. We found them to be (all right, alright).

46. It seems (all together, altogether) appropriate.

47. We were (all together, altogether) in May.

48. Nothing seems to (affect, effect) them.

49. Their mannerisms seem (affected, effected).

50. They (sure, surely) were surprised.

12.	effective
13.	affect
14.	effective
15.	affect
16.	amount
17.	number
18.	a number
19.	altogether
20.	all together
21.	all ready
22.	already
23.	advice
24.	advice
25.	advise
26.	every day
27.	every day
28.	everyday
29.	surely
30.	sure
31.	very
32.	surely
33.	really
34.	real
35.	really
36.	really
37.	adopted
38.	sure
39.	adapted
40.	surely
41.	very
42.	really
43.	adept
44.	accepted
45.	all right
46.	altogether
47.	all together
48.	affect
49.	affected
50.	surely

Spelling—Words With Prefixes and Suffixes

SUGGESTIONS FOR IMPROVING SPELLING SKILL

Using word processing software that includes a dictionary component is an extremely quick and easy way to check the spelling of words. If the program is unable to match a word that you use with one in the dictionary, it will pinpoint the word. However, you, not the computer or the word processor, will need to decide whether the word is the proper one and whether it is spelled correctly. Also, whether you have an "electronic assistant" or not, various circumstances will make it necessary for you to handle all aspects of writing, including ensuring correct spelling, yourself.

Some fortunate people are very adept at spelling; others must work fairly hard to learn to spell words correctly. If you are among those who need help with spelling, you may find these suggestions helpful:

1. Look at any troublesome word very closely and carefully.

2. Pronounce the word accurately, noting the letters and syllables. Sometimes, incorrect spelling is the result of incorrect pronunciation; for example, omitting the *n* before the *m* in *government*.

3. Write the word several times. For particularly difficult words, try pronouncing them syllable by syllable as you write them.

4. Learn the spelling and meanings of prefixes, as in these words: *misstated, disappoint,* and *illegal.*

5. Learn the spelling and meanings of suffixes, as in these words: *evenness, helpful,* and *especially.*

6. Think what the word as a whole means to avoid confusing it with another word that may sound the same or nearly the same, such as *accept* and *except, principal* and *principle,* or *accede* and *exceed.*

7. As you read books, magazines, and other materials, pause when you come across a word that is unfamiliar or that you know causes you difficulty. Study its spelling and try to determine its meaning from the context in which it is used.

8. Develop the "dictionary habit"—there is no substitute for it in learning to spell correctly.

WORDS WITH PREFIXES

A **prefix** consists of one or more letters added to the beginning of a word. Adding a prefix to a word obviously changes the form of the word and modifies its meaning; for example, attaching the prefix *ab-* to the word *normal* produces the word *abnormal.* Most prefixes were originally prepositions or adverbs and were derived from Greek, Latin, or Old English.

A thorough knowledge of prefixes will help you to divide words correctly (or to know whether the division made by a software program is correct), since one logical place to divide is after a prefix (as indicated in Unit 32). Further, knowledge of prefixes will also help you to spell words correctly and to understand their meanings. For example, anyone who knows that *dis-* and *mis-* are prefixes would picture them added to such words as *appear* and *spell* and write *disappear* (not *dissappear*) and *misspell* (not *mispell*). Also, anyone who knows the meaning of the prefixes *inter-* and *intra-* would be highly unlikely to confuse the words *interstate* and *intrastate.*

The following is a list of some commonly used prefixes and their meanings. Note that the list is not complete, nor does it necessarily give all the meanings of each prefix.

ab-	from, away, off, away from, not
ante-	before, in front of, prior to
anti-	opposite, against
bi-	two, twice, doubly
co- and *com-*	with, together
contra- and *counter-*	against

de-	from, down, away
dis-	oppose, exclude, expel, deprive, not
e- and *ex-*	out of, without, former
extra-	additional, outside, beyond
fore-	before, earlier, in front of
il-, im-, in-, and *ir-*	not, in, into, within, toward
inter-	among, between
intra-	within, inside
meta-	among, with, after
mis-	not, lack of, bad or badly, wrong or wrongly
mon- and *mono-*	one
non-	not, unimportant, lacking
post-	after, later
pre-	before
pro-	before, in front of, for, in behalf of, in place of, favoring
re-	again, back, backward
semi-	half, partly, to some extent
sub-	below, beneath, lower, under
super-	above, over, extra, superior
trans-	across, beyond, over, through
un-	not, reverse, free from

With relatively few exceptions, prefixes are simply added to words without any changes in spelling. However, it is sometimes necessary to use a hyphen after a prefix added to a word beginning with a capital letter or, in a few instances, to distinguish words that otherwise could easily be confused; for example, *re-cover* and *recover* or *re-collect* and *recollect*.

Spot Check 1

Add the prefix to the word indicated, and write the resulting word in the space provided. Use your dictionary if necessary.

1. ante + date   antedate
2. anti + British   anti-British
3. bi + annual   biannual
4. co + sponsor   cosponsor
5. co + author   coauthor
6. de + mystify   demystify
7. il + logical   illogical
8. sub + contract   subcontract
9. pro + American   pro-American
10. re + enter   reenter

11. inter + branch   interbranch
12. intra + state   intrastate

WORDS WITH SUFFIXES

A *suffix* is one or more letters added to the end of a word. Adding a suffix changes the meaning of the base word and often the part of speech of the base word. Note the following examples of derivatives of base, or root, words formed by adding various commonly used suffixes.

SUFFIX	BASE (ROOT) WORD	DERIVATIVE
-able	pay (noun, verb)	payable (adjective)
-dom	free (adjective)	freedom (noun)
-ed	value (noun, verb)	valued (verb)
-ible	flex (verb)	flexible (adjective)
-ic	base (noun, verb)	basic (adjective)
-ing	call (noun, verb)	calling (noun, verb)
-less	hope (noun, verb)	hopeless (adjective)
-ly	casual (adjective)	casually (adverb)
-ship	friend (noun)	friendship (noun)
-sion	intrude (verb)	intrusion (noun)
-ty	entire (adjective)	entirety (noun)
-wise	clock (noun, verb)	clockwise (adverb)

The following rules will help you correctly spell many words when adding suffixes. However, remember that there are many exceptions to these (and most other) rules. In this unit—and throughout this book—no attempt has been made to indicate all the exceptions to rules or to show all acceptable spellings of various words.

Words Ending With a Consonant. Rules 1 and 2 describe the situations in which the final consonant of a word generally should be doubled before adding a suffix.

1. If a one-syllable word ends with a single consonant preceded by a single vowel, double the final consonant if the suffix being added begins with a vowel.

ta*g*	ge*t*	wi*n*	sho*p*	ru*n*
tag*g*ed	get*t*ing	win*n*able	shop*p*er	run*n*ing

Note that a final *w, x,* or *y* is not doubled.

show	tax	pay	flaw	wax
showing	taxable	paying	flawed	waxed

2. If a word of two or more syllables (a) is accented on the last syllable and (b) ends with a single consonant preceded by a single vowel, double the final consonant if the suffix begins with a vowel.

disba*r*	rebe*l*	begi*n*	allo*t*	recu*r*
disbar*r*ed	rebel*l*ion	begin*n*er	allot*t*ed	recur*r*ing

Again, do not double a final *w, x,* or *y.*

allow	annex	obey	affix	destroy
allowance	annexed	obeying	affixed	destroying

Rules 3 through 6 define situations in which the final consonant of a word generally should not be doubled.

3. When a word of more than one syllable (a) is not accented on the last syllable and (b) ends with a single consonant preceded by a single vowel, do not double the final consonant when adding a suffix beginning with a vowel.

tim*id*	diff*er*	depos*it*	hon*or*	bon*us*
tim*id*ity	diff*er*ent	depos*it*or	hon*or*able	bon*us*es

A number of words of this type have an equally acceptable alternate spelling in which the final consonant is doubled.

canc*el*	benef*it*	tot*al*
canc*el*ed OR	benef*it*ing OR	tot*al*ed OR
canc*el*led	benef*it*ting	tot*al*led

4. When adding a suffix beginning with a vowel, do not double the final consonant if the accented syllable of the word thus formed differs from the accented syllable of the base, or root, word.

fatal	refer	confer	prefer
fatality	reference	conference	preferable

5. When the final consonant of a word is preceded by two vowels, do not double the final consonant when adding a suffix.

retail	contain	exclaim	amateur
retailing	container	exclaimed	amateurish

Note that derivatives of the word *equip* are exceptions to this rule, and all of them are frequently used.

equipped	equipping	BUT: equipage

If a word ends in *n* preceded by either one or two vowels or by a consonant, retain the *n* when adding the suffix *ness.*

plain	open	vain	modern
plainness	openness	vainness	modernness

6. When a word ends with more than one consonant, do not double the final consonant.

start	conform	concern	return
starting	conformity	concerning	returnable

Words ending in a double consonant generally keep both consonants before a suffix.

access	install	possess	ebb
accessible	installation	possessive	ebbing

When adding the suffix *ly* to a word ending in *ll,* drop one *l.* However, when adding *less* or *like* to a word ending in *ll,* retain the *ll* and insert a hyphen before the suffix.

full	frill	bell	shell	doll
fully	frilly	bell-like	shell-less	doll-like

Spot Check 2

In the space provided, write the word formed by adding the suffix indicated.

1. scrap + ed	1.	scrapped
2. commit + ing	2.	committing
3. casual + ly	3.	casually
4. fulfill + ing	4.	fulfilling
5. confer + ence	5.	conference
6. will + less	6.	will-less
7. uniform + ity	7.	uniformity
8. refer + al	8.	referral
9. allow + able	9.	allowable
10. relax + ation	10.	relaxation
11. employ + er	11.	employer
12. shrub + ery	12.	shrubbery
13. confess + ion	13.	confession
14. comfort + able	14.	comfortable
15. govern + ment	15.	government
16. drag + ed	16.	dragged
17. reveal + ing	17.	revealing
18. joy + ous	18.	joyous
19. relay + ing	19.	relaying
20. confidential + ly	20.	confidentially
21. rigid + ity	21.	rigidity
22. claim + ant	22.	claimant
23. slip + age	23.	slippage
24. relax + ing	24.	relaxing
25. defer + ed	25.	deferred

26. complex + ity	26.	complexity	
27. ship + ing	27.	shipping	
28. offer + ing	28.	offering	
29. rebel + ion	29.	rebellion	
30. quit + ing	30.	quitting	

Words Ending in Silent E.

The next four rules provide guidance for adding suffixes to words ending in silent *e*.

7. If a word ends in a softly pronounced *ce* or *ge*, retain the *e* when adding the suffix *able* or *ous*.

notice	trace	manage	courage
notic*e*able	trac*e*able	manag*e*able	courag*e*ous

8. When adding a suffix beginning with a consonant to a word ending in silent *e*, retain the silent *e*.

grate	sincere	base	late	nine
grat*e*ful	sincer*e*ly	bas*e*ment	lat*e*ness	nin*e*ty

Note that a number of commonly used words are exceptions to this rule. These exceptions include:

judge	true	whole	due	argue
judgment	truly	wholly	duly	argument

9. When adding a suffix beginning with a vowel to a word ending in silent *e*, ordinarily drop the final *e*.

advise	desire	use	arrive	realize
advisory	desirable	usable	arrival	realizing

The following are some common exceptions to this rule. Also note that words ending in *ee* retain the two letters.

mile	dye	age	agree	free
mileage	dyeing	ageing	agreeable	freeing

10. If a word ends in *ie*, change the *ie* to *y* before adding *ing*.

lie	tie	die	vie
lying	tying OR tieing	dying	vying

Words Ending in Y.

Here are two rules pertaining to words that end in *y*.

11. If a word ends with a *y* preceded by a consonant, change the *y* to *i* before adding a suffix. **EXCEPTION:** If the suffix begins with *i*, do not change the *y* to *i*.

easy	heavy	rely	ordinary	deny
eas*i*est	heav*i*est	rel*i*able	ordinar*i*ly	den*i*al

EXCEPTIONS:

deny	supply	remedy	dry
deny*ing*	supply*ing*	remedy*ing*	dry*ing*

12. If a word ends with a *y* preceded by a vowel, retain the *y* when adding a suffix.

delay	journey	employ	buy
dela*y*ed	journe*y*ed	emplo*y*able	bu*y*ing

Common exceptions include the following:

day	pay	say	lay	gay
daily	paid	said	laid	gaiety

Spot Check 3

In the space provided, write the word formed by adding the suffix indicated.

1. reduce + ing	reducing	
2. barrage + ing	barraging	
3. confuse + ion	confusion	
4. reply + ed	replied	
5. notice + able	noticeable	
6. store + age	storage	
7. untie + ing	untying OR untieing	
8. decay + ing	decaying	
9. enforce + ment	enforcement	
10. repay + ed	repaid	
11. mile + stone	milestone	
12. comply + ance	compliance	
13. sense + ible	sensible	
14. employ + er	employer	
15. confuse + ing	confusing	
16. differ + ence	difference	
17. refer + al	referral	
18. charge + able	chargeable	
19. amaze + ment	amazement	
20. seize + ure	seizure	
21. replace + able	replaceable	
22. size + able	sizable OR sizeable	
23. move + able	movable OR moveable	
24. lazy + ness	laziness	
25. stay + ed	stayed	

Study Guide 33

A. Each word below illustrates one of the spelling rules presented in this unit or a common exception to one. If you do not recall the rule involved, refer to the rule indicated.

1. absorbent[6]
2. allies[11]
3. allotted[2]
4. allowance[2]
5. annexes[2]
6. barred[1]
7. belying[10]
8. changeable[7]
9. closing[9]
10. conveyance[12]
11. deference[4]
12. detained[5]
13. dying[10]
14. dropped[1]
15. encouragement[8]
16. enthusiasm[9]
17. entries[11]
18. equipped[5]
19. fatality[4]
20. foreclosure[9]
21. forfeited[5]
22. foundation[6]
23. griping[9]
24. gripping[1]
25. impression[6]
26. inference[4]
27. justifiable[11]
28. leveled[3]
29. lower[1]
30. meanness[5]
31. occurrence[2]
32. preferential[2]
33. traceable[7]
34. truly[8]
35. wall-less[6]

B. Examine the following words, giving particular attention to the italicized letter in each word. Note that the italicized letter is not doubled.

1. a*l*most
2. a*l*ready
3. a*l*though
4. a*l*together
5. a*l*ways
6. appare*l*
7. auxi*l*iary
8. carefu*l*
9. disappoint
10. e*m*inent
11. forgetfu*l*
12. gratefu*l*
13. handfu*l*
14. i*m*itate
15. i*n*oculate
16. mindfu*l*
17. mistaken
18. plentifu*l*
19. we*l*fare
20. wishfu*l*

C. The following are among the most commonly misspelled words in business writing. To determine how many of them you can spell correctly, have someone dictate them to you; then concentrate on those you misspelled.

acquire	amendment	bargain	cabinet
adequate	analysis	basically	calendar
adjustment	anticipate	beneficial	campaign
administrative	anxious	beneficiary	catalog
advertisement	arrangement	brochure	census
advertising	article	budget	certificate
agenda	ascertain	bulletin	choice
alignment	bankruptcy	bureau	column

comparison	fundamental	neighborhood	response
competitive	furniture	nevertheless	responsibility
complete	grateful	occurring	retroactive
concern	handled	organization	salable
confidential	hardware	original	salary
congratulate	hazard	option	satisfactorily
consensus	hoping	output	schedule
consequence	identical	outstanding	separate
controversy	immediately	pamphlet	shortage
courtesy	inasmuch as	partial	significant
cycle	incidentally	participate	similar
defense	incurred	particularly	specialty
deficiency	indebtedness	patronage	statement
definite	independence	permanent	statistics
definitely	independent	permitted	stockholder
delegate	influential	petroleum	straight
develop	initial	phase	strictly
development	inquiry	photostat	subscriber
director	installment	physician	substantial
document	interest	pleasant	superintendent
economical	interpret	pleasure	supervisor
ecstasy	issuing	positive	theory
electronic	journal	practical	throughout
eliminate	knowledge	practically	transit
emphasis	language	practice	undoubtedly
enclose	length	premium	unfortunately
endeavor	liaison	previous	unique
endorsement	license	probably	until
enthusiastic	magazine	professor	usually
envelope	magnetic	purchase	vacancies
equipment	magnificent	quantity	various
especially	management	questionnaire	vehicle
establish	manufacturer	really	vendor
excessive	mathematics	receive	vicinity
expedite	maximum	recently	vocational
expense	medical	reconcile	volume
expensive	memorandum	referring	voluntary
external	meticulous	reimburse	waiver
extremely	minimum	remember	warehouse
facilities	mortgage	renewal	wholesale
familiarize	negative	representative	worthwhile
financial	negotiate	requirement	yield

ASSIGNMENT: Complete the Unit 33 Worksheet on pages 251–252.

UNIT 33

Spelling—Words With Prefixes and Suffixes

WORKSHEET

A In the space provided, insert the missing letter needed to complete the word. If no letter is missing, circle the number preceding the word.

1. mis _s_ tated
2. equip _p_ ed
(3.) tru ____ ly
4. tax _a_ ble
(5.) oil ____ y
6. courag _e_ ous
7. refer _r_ ed

8. slip _p_ ing
(9.) judg ____ ing
10. sincer _e_ ly
(11.) nin ____ th
12. sol _e_ ly
(13.) ful ____ fill

(14.) dis ____ avow
15. nin _e_ ty
(16.) us ____ able
(17.) locat ____ ion
18. rel _i_ able
19. us _e_ ful

(20.) total ____ ed
21. instal _l_ ing
22. saf _e_ ty
(23.) whol ____ ly
(24.) dis ____ allow
25. careful _l_ y

B Only one word in each of the following lines of words is misspelled. Underline that word and write it correctly in the space provided.

1. managerial   <u>managment</u>   manageable   managing   manager
2. dissatisfied   misspell   misstated   <u>dissapoint</u>   missent
3. dairies   stories   <u>attornies</u>   juries   duties
4. <u>differred</u>   referred   preferred   deferred   conferred
5. <u>employe</u>   employer   lessee   lessor   trainee

1. _management_
2. _disappoint_
3. _attorneys_
4. _differed_
5. _employee_

C As you read each of the following sentences, note the words in parentheses. Using the context in which the word is used as a guide, select the word that correctly completes the sentence and write it in the space provided.

1. The instructions are stated (explicitly, implicitly) in this booklet.
2. It has been difficult to (elicit, illicit) a response from them.
3. This may give you some (incite, insight) as to what they are thinking.
4. The solution to the problem has (deluded, eluded) us so far.
5. Automation has (displaced, misplaced) some workers in those industries.

1. _explicitly_
2. _elicit_
3. _insight_
4. _eluded_
5. _displaced_

D Examine the prefixes above each group of words. Select the correct prefix to combine with each word and write it in the space provided.

ante-, anti-	for-, fore-	pre-, pro-	en-, in-
1. _anti_ social	6. _fore_ tell	11. _pro_ ceed	16. _en_ compass
2. _ante_ date	7. _fore_ close	12. _pro_ long	17. _en_ acted
3. _anti_ trust	8. _for_ give	13. _pre_ view	18. _in_ road
4. _ante_ room	9. _fore_ gone	14. _pre_ cede	19. _en_ list
5. _anti_ dote	10. _fore_ cast	15. _pro_ voke	20. _en_ trust

E Choose the correct suffix for each of the following words. In the space provided, write the derivative formed by adding the suffix.

1. remit + ance/ence	remittance	6. occur + ance/ence	occurrence
2. force + able/ible	forcible	7. advise + able/ible	advisable
3. exist + ance/ence	existence	8. charge + able/ible	chargeable
4. clear + ance/ence	clearance	9. differ + ance/ence	difference
5. allow + able/ible	allowable	10. rely + able/ible	reliable

F Match each of the following words with its appropriate definition by writing the letter preceding the word in the space in front of its definition.

a. annuity
b. beneficiary
c. claimant
d. clientele
e. concurrent
f. feasible
g. mandate
h. subsidiary
i. expropriate
j. authorize
k. compromise
l. divulge
m. capitulate
n. appropriation
o. concession
p. malign
q. residual
r. realty
s. exonerate
t. fallacious

_d_ 1. Group of customers or patrons
_c_ 2. One who asserts a right or title
_k_ 3. Settle through mutual concessions
_i_ 4. Deprive of possession
_h_ 5. Company controlled by another
_e_ 6. Taking place at the same time
_j_ 7. Empower; invest with authority
_n_ 8. Funds set aside for some purpose
_l_ 9. Reveal
_o_ 10. Acknowledgment or admission

_q_ 11. The remainder
_t_ 12. Deceptive or misleading
_f_ 13. Capable of being done
_a_ 14. Annual allowance or income
_b_ 15. Receiver of proceeds
_g_ 16. Authoritative command
_s_ 17. Clear from blame
_r_ 18. Real estate
_p_ 19. Defame
_m_ 20. Yield or acquiesce

UNIT 34

Choice of Words

THE RIGHT WORDS

Whether speaking or writing to inform, to persuade, to request, or to accept, your ability to choose the right words to express your thoughts is important.

What are the "right words"? First of all, they are the words that will mean exactly what you want them to mean to your listener or reader. Thus it is important to remember that words have not only specific meanings but also suggested or implied meanings, which may vary from one person to another. For example, consider the actual and emotional meanings of the words *cheap, shoddy, shabby, inexpensive,* and other terms that can be used with the same general meaning as *cheap*. To refer to something as being *cheap* obviously can mean different things to different people; for example, "That's a *cheap* dress" may produce very different emotional reactions among people, depending on the connotation *cheap* has to each of them.

Whenever possible, you should use words that have positive and pleasant connotations. It is, of course, preferable to use common words—words that your listener or reader will recognize immediately and understand easily and correctly.

This unit will alert you to types of words that successful business writers generally avoid. These same types of expressions should also generally be avoided in business speech.

REDUNDANT EXPRESSIONS

A ***redundant expression*** consists of two or more words that mean the same thing or that overlap in meaning. Here are a few such expressions:

NOT:	It is the *customary practice* of the industry.
BUT:	It is the *practice* (or *custom*) of the industry.
NOT:	The staff must *cooperate together*.
BUT:	The staff must *cooperate* (or *work together*).
NOT:	No one has *ever* found the answer yet.
BUT:	No one has *ever* found the answer. OR: No one has found the answer *yet*.

TRITE EXPRESSIONS

A ***trite expression*** is one that has been used by so many people so often that it does little more than reflect the writer's mental laziness or lack of originality. Such expressions are not good business English.

TRITE:	We would like to thank you for . . .
BETTER:	Thank you for . . .
TRITE:	Please be informed that there are . . .
BETTER:	There are . . .
TRITE:	Enclosed please find . . .
BETTER:	Enclosed is . . .
TRITE:	At an early date . . .
BETTER:	Soon (or name the date) . . .

COLLOQUIALISMS

Such colloquial, or informal conversational, expressions as *side with* and *bank on* are usually considered too informal for use in most business writing. In a letter, for example, *agree with* is preferable to *side with* and *depend on* is more appropriate than *bank on.*

Most business writers agree that such contractions as *aren't, won't,* and *we're* are acceptable in all but the most formal business correspondence. However, neither contractions nor such shortened forms of words as *ad, exam,* and *phone* should be overused.

SLANG AND VULGARISMS

No one questions the effectiveness of slang in informal oral communication. It is sometimes used very effectively in advertising copy and sales-promotion letters. However, a particular slang expression is typically short-lived and imprecise in meaning. The best policy is to avoid using slang in ordinary business writing. At one time or another, the following were fairly widely used slang expressions. Do you recognize them? Do you know what they mean?

It's one of my "hang-ups."
The situation was "hairy" for a while.

AFFECTED EXPRESSIONS

Having an extensive English vocabulary and knowing one or more foreign languages are highly desirable and admirable achievements. However, the successful business writer doesn't flaunt such language knowledge when writing to the average person. Specifically, avoid using unusual words, uncommon foreign words and phrases, technical terms, professional jargon, and similar expressions unless the reader or listener is as familiar with them as you are. There are many ways of saying the same thing. In general, if a word helps to get your message across without attracting attention to itself as a word, it is "the right word."

Study Guide 34

A. Study the following words and expressions to avoid using them incorrectly. Note that the word or expression in dark type is the *correct or preferred* one.

1. *allow* for **think**
2. *as per your order* for **in accordance with**
3. *bank on* for **rely on** or **depend on**
4. *beg to differ* for **differ**
5. *both alike* for **alike** or **the same**
6. *bound to* for **determined to** or **certain to**
7. *calculate* for **expect** or **plan**
8. *claim* for **assert** or **maintain**
9. *communication* for **letter**
10. *consensus of opinion* for **consensus**
11. *considerable number* or *amount* for **large number** or **amount**
12. *couple of* for **two of**
13. *deal* for **transaction**
14. *depot* for **station**
15. *Enclosed, please find* for **Enclosed**
16. *final upshot* for **outcome**
17. *first began* for **began**
18. *fix* for **plight** or **bad condition**
19. *fix up* for **repair** or **mend**
20. *foot the bill* for **pay the bill**
21. *have got* for **have** or **have gotten**
22. *help* for **employees**
23. *in back of* for **behind** or **in the rear of**
24. *inside of* for **in** or **within**
25. *kindly* for **please**
26. *locate* for **settle**
27. *no other alternative* for **no alternative**
28. *past history* for **past** or **history**
29. *prior to* for **before**
30. *size up* for **judge** or **estimate**
31. *subsequent to* for **after**
32. *up to now* for **previously** or **until now**

B. Note the spelling and the meaning of the italicized words in the following phrases.

1. The *fiscal* year (Financial.)
2. To *negotiate* a loan (Arrange.)
3. In *collective* bargaining (Joint.)
4. By *disseminating* the information (Spreading widely.)
5. *Dexterity* in using tools (Skill.)
6. The *productivity* of the soil (Fertility.)
7. An *ambiguous* statement (Unclear.)
8. His *effusive* apology (Unduly demonstrative; gushy.)
9. A *bilateral* trade agreement (Between two.)
10. An *integral* part (Essential.)
11. All *superfluous* words (Unnecessary.)
12. The *intricate* wiring (Complicated.)
13. A *rational* decision (Reasonable.)
14. *Ingenious* people (Clever; skillful in constructing or contriving.)
15. *Innumerable* changes (Countless.)
16. The *devaluation* of the currency (Lowering of the legal value.)
17. The *diversity* of opinions (Variety.)
18. The value of the stock *fluctuates* (Changes.)
19. A *tentative* settlement (Temporary; provisional.)
20. To *divest* its holdings (Transfer the ownership.)

ASSIGNMENT: Complete the Unit 34 Worksheet on pages 255–256.

UNIT 34

Choice of Words

WORKSHEET

 A In the space provided, write an acceptable substitute for the italicized expression in each sentence.

1. The new owners plan to *fix up* the building.

2. It was done *prior to* March of last year.

3. We prefer to *size up* the situation ourselves.

4. In some respects, you and she are *both alike*.

5. *Kindly* notify each member of your staff.

6. He *claims* that he was not responsible.

7. When do you *allow* the work will be done?

8. I have forwarded your *communication* to our customer services department.

9. *As per* your order, we are shipping the goods by express.

10. The *final upshot* of the meeting was that nothing will be done about it.

11. We *have got* at least a dozen of those.

12. They were sitting *in back of* us.

13. Someone else will have *to foot* the bill.

14. The members must *cooperate together*.

15. She is *bound* to find out sooner or later.

16. What do you *calculate* his response will be?

17. This company pays its *help* far more than the minimum wage.

18. Can we can *bank on* them to assist us?

19. We expect them *inside of* an hour.

20. Do you know whether anyone has *ever* determined the cause of the shortage *yet*?

21. Harry always *sides with* George.

22. We need *a couple* more laser printers.

23. Who's *running* the department while Miss Cambridge is on vacation?

24. They *have got* to be done immediately.

1. repair

2. before

3. judge

4. alike

5. Please

6. maintains

7. think

8. letter

9. In accordance with

10. outcome

11. have

12. behind

13. to pay

14. cooperate

15. determined OR certain

16. think

17. employees

18. depend on

19. within

20. ever OR yet

21. agrees with

22. two

23. managing

24. have

25. The *consensus of opinion* was that we should survey prospective customers in the Midwest.

26. It seems that we have *no other alternative*.

27. How would you *size up* their chances of winning?

28. Desks, tables, *and etc.,* are on the third floor.

29. We have no doubt *but what* your request will be granted.

30. I arrived late *on account* of the heavy traffic.

31. The new logo is a *round circle* with initials in it.

32. *Subsequent to* January 30, applications will not be accepted.

33. The manager won't *stand for* anyone's being late.

34. I thought the hearings were *over and done with*.

35. *Up to this writing,* there has been no change in the unit price.

36. The meeting ended *at about* noon.

37. Your office will be *opposite to* mine.

38. What happened yesterday is *past history*.

39. We were *quite* sorry you could not be there.

40. That has not been our *past experience*.

41. This service is provided *free of charge* to subscribers.

42. We expect to recover part of the loss *inside of* a year.

43. If the strike continues, we may find ourselves in a *real fix*.

44. Do you think that *deal* will go through?

45. They spend a lot of time *in front of the boob tube*.

46. Again, please *refer back* to the chart on page 26.

47. With respect to sales of this new model, what is your *guesstimate* for next year?

48. The exhibit was a *flop* last year.

49. Where are you *going to* next year?

50. Maybe we shouldn't *turn down* their offer.

25. consensus

26. no alternative

27. judge OR estimate

28. and OR etc.

29. that

30. because

31. circle

32. After

33. tolerate

34. over

35. Until now

36. at OR about

37. opposite

38. history

39. very

40. experience

41. free

42. within

43. difficult situation

44. transaction

45. watching television

46. refer

47. estimate

48. failure OR disappointment

49. going

50. reject

B. **Match each of the following words with its appropriate definition by writing the letter that identifies the word in the space following the definition.**

a. arduous   **c.** dynamic   **e.** emulate   **g.** facilitate   **i.** erroneous
b. exonerate   **d.** disperse   **f.** impede   **h.** exorbitant   **j.** surmount

1. break up; scatter   **1.** d   **6.** absolve; justify   **6.** b

2. active; forceful   **2.** c   **7.** imitate   **7.** e

3. incorrect   **3.** i   **8.** make easier or faster **8.** g

4. excessive   **4.** h   **9.** hinder; interfere   **9.** f

5. difficult; hard   **5.** a   **10.** overcome   **10.** j

Synonyms, Antonyms, and Soundalikes

SYNONYMS

A **synonym** is a word that has the same or almost the same meaning as another word. Synonyms, however, often differ in their accepted usage or in their implied meaning. For instance, examine the word *old* and its synonyms: *aged, ancient, antique, elderly, obsolete, senile, venerable.* Several of the words obviously are not interchangeable: it would be absurd to say that a clock is *elderly,* a grandparent is *antique,* a machine is *senile,* or a tree is *obsolete.*

Consider the distinctions in the following groups of synonyms as given in *Webster's Ninth New Collegiate Dictionary* for the words *famous* and *renew.*

fa·mous \'fā-məs\ *adj* [ME, fr. MF *fameux*, fr. L *famosus*, fr. *fama* fame] (14c) **1 a** : widely known **b** : honored for achievement **2** : EXCELLENT, FIRST-RATE ⟨∼ weather for a walk⟩ — **fa·mous·ness** *n*
syn FAMOUS, RENOWNED, CELEBRATED, NOTED, NOTORIOUS, DISTINGUISHED, EMINENT, ILLUSTRIOUS mean known far and wide. FAMOUS implies little more than the fact of being, sometimes briefly, widely and popularly known; RENOWNED implies more glory and acclamation, CELEBRATED more notice and attention esp. in print; NOTED suggests well-deserved public attention; NOTORIOUS frequently adds to FAMOUS an implication of questionableness or evil; DISTINGUISHED implies acknowledged excellence or superiority; EMINENT implies even greater conspicuousness for outstanding quality or character; ILLUSTRIOUS stresses enduring honor and glory attached to a deed or person.

re·new \ri-'n(y)ü\ *vt* (14c) **1** : to make like new : restore to freshness, vigor, or perfection ⟨as we ∼ our strength in sleep⟩ **2** : to make new spiritually : REGENERATE **3 a** : to restore to existence : REVIVE **b** : to make extensive changes in : REBUILD **4** : to do again : REPEAT **5** : to begin again : RESUME **6** : REPLACE, REPLENISH ⟨∼ water in a tank⟩ **7 a** : to grant or obtain an extension of or on **b** : to grant or obtain an extension on the loan of ⟨∼ a library book⟩ ∼ *vi* **1** : to become new or as new **2** : to begin again : RESUME **3** : to make a renewal (as of a lease) — **re·new·er** *n*
syn RENEW, RESTORE, REFRESH, RENOVATE, REJUVENATE mean to make like new. RENEW implies so extensive a remaking that what had become faded or disintegrated now seems like new ⟨efforts to *renew* a failing marriage⟩ RESTORE implies a return to an original state after depletion or loss ⟨*restored* a fine piece of furniture⟩ REFRESH implies the supplying of something necessary to restore lost strength, animation, or power ⟨lunch *refreshed* my energy⟩ RENOVATE suggests a renewing by cleansing, repairing, or rebuilding ⟨the apartment has been entirely *renovated*⟩ REJUVENATE suggests the restoration of youthful vigor, powers, and appearance ⟨the change in jobs *rejuvenated* her spirits⟩

A knowledge of synonyms will help you avoid repeating the same word over and over. Also, it will help you express the exact shade of meaning that you wish to convey. A thesaurus, such as *Roget's International Thesaurus, Fourth Edition* (Thomas Y. Crowell Company, New York, 1977), or *Webster's Collegiate Thesaurus* (Merriam-Webster Inc., Springfield, Massachusetts, 1976) will help you choose the right word.

*By permission. From *Webster's Ninth New Collegiate Dictionary* © 1991 by Merriam-Webster Inc., publisher of the Merriam-Webster ® Dictionaries.

Spot Check 1

Use a synonym for the italicized word in each of the following sentences. Write the word you choose in the space provided. Use your dictionary or a thesaurus if you wish. (Answers will vary.)

1. None of the tasks were *hard.*
2. She rarely *gripes* about anything.
3. Please *retain* a copy for your files.
4. I *meant* to call you earlier.
5. Who can *foretell* the future?
6. He wants an *approximation* of its cost.
7. When will you *finish* your review?
8. The draft contains several *mistakes.*
9. Would you be willing to *counsel* them?
10. She plans to sell her car after she *fixes* it.

1. difficult
2. complains
3. keep
4. intended
5. predict
6. estimate
7. complete
8. errors
9. advise
10. repairs

ANTONYMS

Antonyms are words that are opposite in meaning. Again, your dictionary or a thesaurus will help you select the appropriate antonyms for words.

buy - sell	arrive - leave	false - true
dull - sharp	empty - full	first - last
smooth - rough	large - small	

Note how the following sentence can be improved by using antonyms instead of repeating the same words.

Unlike the earlier model, which was *complex* and *slow,* the Bx-7 is neither *complex* nor *slow.*

Unlike the earlier model, which was *complex* and *slow,* the Bx-7 is *simple* and *fast.*

Spot Check 2

For each sentence below, replace the italicized word with an antonym. Write the word you select in the space provided. (Answers will vary.)

1. I have *more* work to do than either of them.
2. This cloth has a *rough* texture.
3. When do you think they will *arrive?*
4. The bank should *reject* my application.
5. The wedding guests dressed *formally.*
6. Nick and Nellie were *married* last week.
7. Autumn *precedes* summer.
8. Fewer than a dozen runners *started* the race.
9. The display includes some *natural* plants.
10. Some drivers are more *careless* than others.
11. We arrived *late.*
12. You will find the work *difficult.*

1. less
2. smooth
3. leave
4. approve
5. casually
6. divorced
7. follows
8. finished
9. artificial
10. careful
11. early
12. easy

SOUNDALIKES

Many words have the same or nearly the same pronunciation but different origins, meanings, and spellings; for example:

access, excess	coarse, course
altar, alter	formally, formerly
affect, effect	overdo, overdue
addition, edition	principal, principle
cite, sight, site	waist, waste

Your writing obviously will reflect your knowledge of soundalike words. Notice how the italicized words in the following sentences give each sentence a particular meaning.

Dr. Lyman *formally* announced Ms. Morris's appointment to the commission. (In a formal manner.)

Dr. Lyman *formerly* announced Ms. Morris's appointment to the commission. (Previously.)

Spot Check 3

Which of the words shown in parentheses correctly completes the sentence? Write your answer in the space provided.

1. Your bank card makes it easy to (access, excess) your account.
2. A tailor may (altar, alter) the coat for you.
3. What will be the (affect, effect) of the change?
4. Were you at the construction (cite, sight, site)?
5. The drapes are made of (coarse, course) material.
6. The Longs (formally, formerly) lived in Boise.

1. access
2. alter
3. effect
4. site
5. coarse
6. formerly

7. The payment is nearly a month (overdo, overdue).

7. _____overdue_____

8. Each payment reduces the (principal, principle).

8. _____principal_____

9. We still (waist, waste) a variety of natural resources.

9. _____waste_____

10. A new (addition, edition) will be out in March.

10. _____edition_____

Study Guide 35

A. Study the following words to note the difference in meaning between those in each group.

1.	apology	An acknowledgment which implies that one has been, at least apparently, in the wrong.
	excuse	Reason, explanation, or justification for failing to do something.
2.	assistance	Aid; help.
	assistants	Helpers.
3.	biannual	Twice a year.
	biennial	Once every two years.
4.	client	One who obtains professional advice or services.
	clientele	A group of clients; clients collectively.
5.	comprehensible	Intelligible; understandable.
	comprehensive	Inclusive; extensive; of wide range.
6.	partner	A joint owner of a business; an associate.
	colleague	An associate in a profession, a civil office, or an employment situation.
7.	party	A group of persons. In law, *party* may mean a person; in ordinary business writing, it is incorrect to use it to refer to one person.
	person	A human being; a particular individual.
8.	practicable	Refers to things only. Possible, workable; capable of being done.
	practical	Refers to persons or things. Not theoretical or idealistic; useful; capable of being put to use.
9.	receipt	A written acknowledgment of things received.
	recipe	A formula for mixing ingredients, especially for cooking.
10.	statue	A solid image or likeness.
	stature	Natural height, especially of human beings.
	statute	An established ordinance or decree.

B. In each sentence, the italicized word or phrase—not the one at the end of the sentence—is the one that should be used.

1. We could not find a replacement *anywhere*. (NOT: anywheres.)

2. *Because* I was ill, I could not attend the meeting. (NOT: Being that.)

3. He will be unable to keep his *appointment* with you next Monday because he has a speaking *engagement*. (NOT: date.)

4. We have no doubt *that* the deadline will be met. (NOT: but what.)

5. Miss Miles *graduated from* (OR: *was graduated from*) Santa Fe Community College last year. (NOT: graduated Santa Fe Community College, high school, and so on.)

6. The materials are *free*. (NOT: free of charge.)

7. *Regardless* of what you may have heard, we are not going out of business. (NOT: Irregardless. This expression is not accepted as standard English.)

8. *Fewer* people attended this year than last year. (NOT: Less.)

9. *Incidentally,* have you heard from him recently? (NOT: Incidently. This expression is not accepted as standard English.)

10. Both of them were *rather* disappointed. (NOT: kind of.)

11. It was *not nearly* enough food for a hundred people. (NOT: nowhere near.)

12. This discussion seems to be going *nowhere.* (NOT: nowheres.)

13. I would *rather* go with them than stay here. (NOT: sooner.)

14. We should *try to* meet with them. (NOT: try and.)

15. What *kind of* offer did they make? (NOT: kind of an.)

16. The *reason that* the bank is closed today is that it is a holiday. (NOT: reason because.)

17. The situation seems *rather* serious. (NOT: kind of.)

18. The office is a long *way* from the center of town. (NOT: ways.)

19. *Anyway,* we can do nothing about the situation. (NOT: Anyways.)

C. Study the following pairs of words. If you are unsure how they differ in meaning, consult your dictionary.

1. credible, creditable
2. distinct, distinctive
3. genial, congenial
4. incident, instance
5. leave, let

6. liable, likely
7. lose, loose
8. percent, percentage
9. physical, fiscal
10. precede, proceed

11. respective, respectful
12. serial, cereal
13. stationary, stationery
14. thorough, through
15. tortuous, torturous

D. Study the following sentences and note how the words are used. The meaning of each italicized word is given in parentheses.

1. The spokesperson would not *confirm* reports of merger discussions. (Ratify, corroborate.)

2. Many are concerned about the *depletion* of our natural resources. (Lessening.)

3. Their statements obviously *obscure* some of their difficulties. (Hide.)

4. Is the settlement *equitable*? (Just, fair to all.)

5. Our *ultimate* goal is to lessen the trade gap between them and us. (Final; broad.)

6. The board decided to *defer* making its decision public. (Postpone; delay.)

7. What could be more *pertinent* than the data Jim submitted? (Relevant.)

8. We *misconstrued* what they said. (Incorrectly understood.)

9. Our *consumption* of foreign oil increases the trade deficit. (Use.)

10. Neither would *concede* defeat. (Admit.)

11. The company's *phenomenal* growth pleased stockholders. (Extraordinary.)

12. We should offer the speaker an *honorarium.* (Payment to someone who does not charge a fee.)

13. It is clear, in *retrospect,* that we were too optimistic. (Meditation on the past.)

14. No one has been able to *ascertain* the reason for the delay. (Determine.)

15. The company pays its employees *biweekly.* (Every two weeks.)

16. Please arrange the correspondence *chronologically.* (By date.)

17. *Divulging* trade secrets is sometimes cited as the reason for an employee's dismissal. (Revealing.)

18. The *consignee* reported that the merchandise has been received. (One to whom something is shipped.)

19. It seems to be a *unilateral* decision. (One-sided.)

20. Did the auditors find any *discrepancy* in the bank's records? (Difference; disagreement.)

ASSIGNMENT: Complete the Unit 35 Worksheet on pages 261–262; then complete the Part 8 Review on pages 263–264.

UNIT 35

Synonyms, Antonyms, and Soundalikes

WORKSHEET

A Match each of the following words with its appropriate definition by writing the letter that identifies the word in the space following the definition.

a. pertinent   e. minimize   i. subsidiary   m. discrete   q. perspective
b. conglomerate   f. surplus   j. appraise   n. waive   r. appreciate
c. autonomous   g. arraignment   k. dubious   o. peruse   s. recur
d. beneficiary   h. liable   l. prevalent   p. impede   t. align

1. Take one side or the other.   1. __t__
2. Doubtful or questionable.   2. __k__
3. Independent.   3. __c__
4. Make less in some way.   4. __e__
5. Happen again.   5. __s__
6. One who receives something.   6. __d__
7. Firm owning many businesses.   7. __b__
8. Amount over that needed.   8. __f__
9. Determine value or worth.   9. __j__
10. Relinquish a right.   10. __n__

11. Appropriate to the occasion.   11. __a__
12. Point of view.   12. __q__
13. Study or examine.   13. __o__
14. Firm owned by another firm.   14. __i__
15. Slow down or block.   15. __p__
16. Hearing on a charge.   16. __g__
17. Responsible for something.   17. __h__
18. Separate or distinct.   18. __m__
19. Dominant or widespread.   19. __l__
20. Increase in value.   20. __r__

B For each of the following groups of words, select the word that is *opposite* in meaning to the italicized word and write it in the space provided.

1. *ambiguous*	vague	clear	obscure	large	1.	clear
2. *wholly*	sacred	entirely	partly	irreligious	2.	partly
3. *solemn*	holy	quite	staid	frivolous	3.	frivolous
4. *circuitous*	circular	oval	direct	electrical	4.	direct
5. *erratic*	wrong	correct	consistent	questionable	5.	consistent
6. *illegible*	provable	readable	qualified	competent	6.	readable
7. *insidious*	harmless	sinful	residual	malignant	7.	harmless
8. *pacify*	placate	calm	disturb	destroy	8.	disturb
9. *implicit*	stated	involved	known	understood	9.	stated
10. *pertinent*	unusable	deniable	unworkable	irrelevant	10.	irrelevant

In each of the following sentences, decide which word in parentheses correctly completes the sentence; then write the word in the space provided.

1. The final payment is (overdo, overdue).

2. Does the city (council, counsel) meet daily?

3. Their departure is (eminent, imminent).

4. We tried to (elicit, illicit) a response.

5. Who will attend (beside, besides) you and him?

6. Nothing seems to (faze, phase) them.

7. Who designed the new (stationary, stationery)?

8. We were stranded in the (desert, dessert).

9. I am one of her (assistance, assistants).

10. Their voyages to outerspace made them (famous, notorious).

11. How much (capital, capitol) will we need?

12. Some voters arrived before the (poles, polls) were open.

13. His attitude seems very (callous, callus).

14. When does their (fiscal, physical) year begin?

15. The tailor was unable to (altar, alter) the wedding gown.

16. Who untied the (chord, cord)?

17. Those jars contain (currant, current) jelly.

18. What is the (fair, fare) from here to Memphis?

19. The staff's (moral, morale) is unusually high.

20. No one wants the governor to declare (marital, marshal, martial) law.

21. I won't (medal, meddle) in their business.

22. We could hear bells (pealing, peeling) in the distance.

23. Peggy is the (sole, soul) beneficiary.

24. This substance is (insoluble, unsolvable).

25. Both of them are rather (vain, vane, vein).

1. overdue

2. council

3. imminent

4. elicit

5. besides

6. faze

7. stationery

8. desert

9. assistants

10. famous

11. capital

12. polls

13. callous

14. fiscal

15. alter

16. cord

17. currant

18. fare

19. morale

20. martial

21. meddle

22. pealing

23. sole

24. insoluble

25. vain

PART 8

Words and Word References

REVIEW

 A Each sentence contains an error in spelling, word choice, or word usage. Underline the error and then write the necessary correction in the space provided.

1. One of the attorneys was <u>disbared</u>.
2. Do you think either of these is <u>useable</u>?
3. We were impressed by the <u>moderness</u> of their facilities.
4. Competition is unlikely to <u>lesson</u>.
5. The third item should <u>proceed</u> the first one.
6. Some commuters think the <u>fair</u> is too high.
7. We <u>sincerly</u> hope they are correctable.
8. We must repair it, <u>irregardless</u> of the cost.
9. The other <u>rout</u> runs parallel to Elm Street.
10. Of <u>coarse</u>, we should hire a consultant.
11. Did they hire her as a news <u>corespondent</u>?
12. A small <u>percent</u> of them are opposed to it.
13. They do not want to <u>loose</u> their credibility.
14. We should <u>leave</u> her redesign our stationery.
15. Various taxes are <u>witheld</u> every payday.
16. His <u>knowlege</u> of the business is impressive.
17. The forecaster said it is <u>liable</u> to rain.
18. We treat our clientele <u>respectively</u>.
19. This policy provides <u>comprehensible</u> coverage.
20. I would <u>sooner</u> work than sit around all day.
21. I sincerely regret the letter was <u>mislayed</u>.
22. Please state the length, width, and <u>heighth</u>.
23. It will be on the last <u>Wensday</u> of February.
24. Roger seemed embarrassed by the <u>announcment</u>.
25. Both are <u>imminent</u> psychologists.
26. Mr. Lee's handwriting is <u>allmost</u> illegible.

1. _disbarred_
2. _usable_
3. _modernness_
4. _lessen_
5. _precede_
6. _fare_
7. _sincerely_
8. _regardless_
9. _route_
10. _course_
11. _correspondent_
12. _percentage_
13. _lose_
14. _let_
15. _withheld_
16. _knowledge_
17. _likely_
18. _respectfully_
19. _comprehensive_
20. _rather_
21. _mislaid_
22. _height_
23. _Wednesday_
24. _announcement_
25. _eminent_
26. _almost_

27. The comments were not wholly complimentary.

27. ___wholly___

28. When will the merger be formerly announced?

28. ___formally___

29. Exercise improves one's fiscal condition.

29. ___physical___

30. Some people are reluctant to bear their emotions in public.

30. ___bare___

31. The attorneys cited several precedence.

31. ___precedents___

32. Your canceled check will serve as a recipe.

32. ___receipt___

33. Your local libary should have a copy of this directory.

33. ___library___

34. The city council approved the proposed ordnance.

34. ___ordinance___

35. The drawer contains broshures and pamphlets.

35. ___brochures___

36. It will enhance their profesional stature.

36. ___professional___

37. She allowed nothing to impeed her progress.

37. ___impede___

38. Their acheivments are truly outstanding.

38. ___achievements___

39. If you invent a better mousetrap, you will become notorious too.

39. ___famous___

40. Many attend conventions to become acquainted with their professional partners.

40. ___colleagues___

41. Incidentally, are you going anywheres next summer?

41. ___anywhere___

42. Our supervisor gave us very implicit instructions.

42. ___explicit___

43. Those two models are both alike in many respects, aren't they?

43. ___alike___

44. Mr. Davis is likely to disallow those requests for reimbursment.

44. ___reimbursement___

45. How many copys of the questionnaire were distributed?

45. ___copies___

46. We beleive an announcement of the winners is imminent.

46. ___believe___

47. It seems that the flue epidemic has run its course.

47. ___flu___

48. The procedures are apt to be changed at any time.

48. ___likely___

49. Their volumn of business is nowhere near what we thought.

49. ___volume___

50. The United States and Mexico signed a unilateral trade agreement.

50. ___bilateral___

B Underline the incorrectly spelled word in each numbered line, and write it correctly in the space provided. If all the words in a line are spelled correctly, write *OK*.

1. supervisory	proceedure	programmed	conference	1.	procedure
2. suddenness	oilly	gradually	economical	2.	oily
3. impressive	relieved	aluminum	managment	3.	management
4. acknowledge	athlete	library	priviledge	4.	privilege
5. prominence	irrelevant	existence	reference	5.	OK
6. disappear	witness	vacuum	parallell	6.	parallel
7. auxiliary	ordnary	territory	visible	7.	ordinary
8. petroleum	language	saleable	license	8.	OK
9. requirement	seperate	statistics	volume	9.	separate
10. incurred	minimum	reimburse	noticable	10.	noticeable

INDEX

Instructor's Overview

OVERVIEW OF THE PROGRAM

Objective. The main objective of the Eighth Edition of *Modern Business English* is to help the college student acquire a thorough understanding of the basic principles of grammar, usage, and style as they pertain to business communication and to develop proficiency in applying them. Thus the program provides practical, up-to-date coverage of the parts of speech; phrases, clauses, and sentences; capitalization, punctuation, abbreviation, and number style; word choice, spelling, and other aspects of English usage.

Instructor's Edition. This special edition of the *Modern Business English* program contains:

- A complete, full-size copy of the student's edition of the text-workbook materials, which end on page 268. The major difference is that the answers to the Part Surveys, Spot Checks within the Units, Unit Worksheets, and Part Reviews appear only in this Instructor's Edition.

- Test masters, facsimile keys to the tests, enrichment exercises, and other materials appearing on this and the following pages.

Student's Edition. The student's text-workbook materials are organized into 8 parts, which are divided into 35 units. At the suggestion of instructors using the previous edition, this Eighth Edition:

- Presents all the materials (with the exception of the tests, of course) in the sequence in which the student uses them.

- Provides more application exercises, primarily through the addition of more Spot Checks and the lengthening of others. These, of course, are in addition to the Part Surveys, Unit Worksheets, and Part Reviews.

- Reduces still further the number of practice exercises with multiple correct answers. Realistically, however, it is important to note that some exercises involving punctuation, spelling, and so on, as well as the elementary composition exercises in

Units 17–19, have more than one acceptable solution.

INSTRUCTIONAL PATTERN

The instructional pattern and the program materials for implementing it are briefly discussed below.

1. General Pretest and Individual Analysis. To give you and your students a general indication of their language knowledge and usage skills, you may wish to duplicate and administer the four-page course inventory (the printed master appears on pages I-37–I-40 of this Instructor's Edition) at the outset of the course. Also, to enable each student to derive the greatest benefit from the pretest, duplicate the course inventory analysis form (see pages I-41–I-44 for the printed master) and have each student complete it. Emphasize that the purpose of the inventory is to help the student focus his or her study and that the results of the test will not be used for grading purposes. Since the test obviously does not cover every principle of grammar, usage, and style that the student should know (and that the text-workbook presents), every score needs to be interpreted accordingly.

2. Part Pretest. Each of the eight parts of the text-workbook opens with a survey—a pretest that appears in the student's materials and that covers the principles presented in the units contained in the particular part. Like the general pretest (course inventory), each of these part surveys should be scored but not used for grading purposes. In discussing the results of a survey with the students, encourage each student to study the items he or she answered incorrectly and to find the solution to each problem area when studying the principles presented in the corresponding units.

3. Unit Study and Practice. Each unit is largely self-instructional, for every principle is fully illustrated and explained. Further, almost all units contain a Spot-Check exercise after each few principles so that the student can immediately apply them. As students will quickly realize, they can easily complete any exercise by immediately reviewing the preceding few principles and examples; therefore, the keys to the Spot Checks appear only in this Instructor's Edition.

4. Unit Summary. The Study Guide at the end of each unit uses example applications to summarize the principles covered in the particular unit. Studying these examples and referring to the rules indicated by the superior figures will further ensure the student's thorough understanding of the principles and successful application of them in the unit Worksheet.

5. Unit Exercise. The Worksheet at the end of each unit gives the student an uncoached opportunity to apply the principles presented, illustrated, applied, and reviewed within the unit. As noted previously, the key to each Worksheet appears only in this Instructor's Edition.

6. Part Review. Each of the eight parts of the program ends with a Part Review exercise that gives the student an opportunity to apply principles presented in the units comprising the part. This review obviously does not cover all principles covered in the units or in the end-of-part test; therefore, you may wish to use it as a basis for a comprehensive oral or written review that focuses on specific problems of students.

7. Part Posttest. Each part of the program ends with an objective test. The printed masters of these tests appear on pages I-45–I-60 of this Instructor's Edition. The facsimile keys to these tests appear on pages I-17–I-32.

8. General Posttest. The four-page final test on pages I-61–I-64 of this Instructor's Edition closely parallels the general pretest designed for use at the outset of the course.

ENRICHMENT EXERCISES

The spelling, grammar, and other supplementary exercises on pages I-7–I-12 of this Instructor's Edition may be used as oral or written activities at various points during the course. Where applicable, answers to the exercises are underlined.

The spelling list contains 300 words, with the 50 words in each column arranged in 5-word groups. Thus you will find it easy to make up a number of short exercises by selecting 5-word groups from different columns as well as 5-word groups within a particular column.

If you choose to present the grammar and other exercises orally, you may wish to read some of the items with the incorrect answer and others with the correct answer and have students indicate only the necessary correction (or *OK* if no correction is needed).

CHECKING AND GRADING

For your convenience, this Instructor's Edition provides the keys to the Spot Checks, Surveys, Worksheets, and Reviews on a full-size, page-for-page replica of the student's text-workbook. Should you wish to have students check some of the exercises themselves, you may wish to photocopy the appropriate pages and place them in a binder that you can make available to the students on an "as needed" basis under your supervision.

Spot Checks. These exercises, which appear within most of the units, should be checked and discussed with students as part of your normal presentation of the unit. Although students will have little or no difficulty completing these exercises correctly, it is important to confirm the correctness of all responses immediately to ensure that students do not reinforce incorrect interpretations of principles when they complete the worksheets. We recommend that none of these activities be graded.

Course Inventory and Part Surveys. These exercises are intended to help you assess your students' general level of skill before they study and apply principles of grammar, usage, and style and to help your students focus their study on specific problem areas. We suggest that you not grade any of these materials. Reproducing and using the Course Inventory Analysis Form on pages I-41–I-44 of this Instructor's Edition will reinforce your discussion of the purpose and use of the course inventory and of all the part-opening Surveys. All of these activities should be checked (by the students themselves, if you prefer) and discussed immediately after the students have completed them.

Worksheets and Reviews. The Worksheets and Reviews also should be checked and discussed with students, since you probably will want to rely heavily on the Worksheets for course-grading purposes. Since the main purpose of the Reviews is to help students confirm their understanding of the principles presented in a set of related units before taking an end-of-part test, you may wish to use them for discussion purposes only.

End-of-Part Tests. The end-of-part tests contained in this Instructor's Edition may be reproduced in their present form or modified in any way you wish. The student's performance on each of these tests (or similar ones that you prepare) should, of course, be considered in determining his or her final course grade.

Final Test. The four-page final test on pages I-61–I-64, either in its present form or in some modified form, will help you and your students assess their overall mastery of principles presented and applied in the course. As you will notice, the items in this test closely parallel those in the course inventory.

REFERENCE MATERIALS

Students should be aware of the various types of reference materials and word processing programs used by employees at all levels in business offices and elsewhere. To the greatest extent possible, students should have access to—and be required to use—such materials as a continuing part of this course.

Word Processing Programs. If the equipment and the software are available, students should receive at least some hands-on experience in using text-editing software with automatic spelling and word-division programs. Personal computers, dedicated word processors, electronic typewriters—all are standard equipment in all kinds and sizes of business offices, and students—regardless of the jobs for which they are preparing—should be familiar with, if not proficient in using, such equipment and software.

Dictionaries. Each student should have his or her personal copy of a dictionary. In addition, an unabridged dictionary should be available in the classroom. The Merriam-Webster dictionaries listed below were used as the authorities for spelling, word division, and so on, in the preparation of this edition of *Modern Business English*.

- *Webster's Ninth New Collegiate Dictionary,* Merriam-Webster Inc., Springfield, Massachusetts.
- *Webster's Third New International Dictionary,* Merriam-Webster Inc., Springfield, Massachusetts.

Other widely used dictionaries include the following:

- *The American Heritage Dictionary of the English Language,* American Heritage Publishing Co., Inc., and Houghton Mifflin Company, Boston.
- *Funk & Wagnalls Standard College Dictionary,* Funk & Wagnalls Publishing Company, New York.
- *The Random House Dictionary of the English Language,* Random House, Inc., New York.
- *Webster's New World Dictionary of the American Language,* William Collins + World Publishing Co., Inc., Cleveland.

Other References. The principles of grammar, usage, and style presented in *Modern Business English* are in general agreement with those in the following widely used manual:

- Sabin, William A., *The Gregg Reference Manual,* 7th ed., Glencoe Division, Macmillan/McGraw-Hill School Publishing Company, Columbus, Ohio, 1992.

Other widely used grammar and style references include those listed below.

- Bernstein, Theodore M., *The Careful Writer: A Modern Guide to English Usage,* Atheneum, New York.
- Fowler, H. W., *A Dictionary of Modern English Usage,* Oxford University Press, New York.
- *A Manual of Style,* The University of Chicago Press, Chicago.
- Perrin, Porter G., *Writer's Guide and Index to English,* Scott, Foresman and Company, Chicago.

Course Activities and Schedule

The chart on the following pages lists all the text-workbook and test activities provided in the *Modern Business English* program. In planning your course activities and schedule, we suggest that you:

1. Review the activities, which are listed in the suggested usage sequence. Decide which of them, if any, you wish to combine, to assign exclusively for independent study and completion outside class,

or to omit entirely. The easiest way to do this is to write a code number or letter in the box containing the statement of the activity (for example, *C* for combine; *I* for independent study; *O* for omit).

2. List on a separate sheet any reinforcement or enrichment activities you may wish to incorporate.

3. Combine the two lists of activities into one master list.

Hour	Activities and References*
	Course Inventory (I-37–I-40) and Course Inventory Analysis (I-41–I-44)
	Part 1 Survey: Nouns and Noun Usage (TW 1–2)
	Unit 1 and Study Guide: Nouns—Plural Forms (TW 3–6); Worksheet (TW 7–8)
	Unit 2 and Study Guide: Compound and Other Nouns—Plural Forms (TW 9–14); Worksheet (TW 15–16)
	Unit 3 and Study Guide: Nouns—Possessive Case (TW 17–20); Worksheet (TW 21–22)
	Part 1 Review: Nouns and Noun Usage (TW 23–24)
	Part 1 Test: Nouns and Noun Usage (I-45–I-46)
	Part 2 Survey: Pronouns and Pronoun Usage (TW 25–26)
	Unit 4 and Study Guide: Personal Pronouns–Nominative and Objective Case (TW 27–32); Worksheet (TW 33–34)
	Unit 5 and Study Guide: Personal Pronouns—Possessive Case and Compound Forms (TW 35–38); Worksheet (TW 39–40)
	Unit 6 and Study Guide: Indefinite Pronouns (TW 41–44); Worksheet (TW 45–46)
	Unit 7 and Study Guide: Relative and Interrogative Pronouns (TW 47–50); Worksheet (TW 51–52)
	Part 2 Review: Pronouns and Pronoun Usage (TW 53–54)
	Part 2 Test: Pronouns and Pronoun Usage (I-47–I-48)
	Part 3 Survey: Verbs and Verb Usage (TW 55–56)
	Unit 8 and Study Guide: Forms of Verbs (TW 57–62); Worksheet (TW 63–64)
	Unit 9 and Study Guide: Tenses of Verbs (TW 65–70); Worksheet (TW 71–72)

*I-page references indicate pages that appear in the Instructor's Edition only; TW references indicate pages that appear in both the Instructor's Edition and the student's text-workbook.

Hour	Activities and References*
	Unit 10 and Study Guide: Agreement of Subject and Verb (TW 73–76); Worksheet (TW 77–78)
	Unit 11 and Study Guide: Agreement of Subject and Verb (Continued) (TW 79–82); Worksheet (TW 83–84)
	Unit 12 and Study Guide: Verbals (TW 85–88); Worksheet (TW 89–90)
	Part 3 Review: Verbs and Verb Usage (TW 91–92)
	Part 3 Test: Verbs and Verb Usage (I-49–I-50)
	Part 4 Survey: Other Parts of Speech and Their Usage (TW 93–94)
	Unit 13 and Study Guide: Adjectives (TW 95–100); Worksheet (TW 101–102)
	Unit 14 and Study Guide: Adverbs (TW 103–106); Worksheet (TW 107–108)
	Unit 15 and Study Guide: Prepositions (TW 109–112); Worksheet (TW 113–114)
	Unit 16 and Study Guide: Conjunctions (TW 115–118); Worksheet (TW 119–120)
	Part 4 Review: Other Parts of Speech and Their Usage (TW 121–122)
	Part 4 Test: Other Parts of Speech and Their Usage (I-51–I-52)
	Part 5 Survey: Phrases, Clauses, and Sentences (TW 123–124)
	Unit 17 and Study Guide: Simple Sentences and Phrases (TW 125–128); Worksheet (TW 129–130)
	Unit 18 and Study Guide: Compound and Complex Sentences (TW 131–134); Worksheet (TW 135–136)
	Unit 19 and Study Guide: Effective Sentences and Paragraphs (TW 137–140); Worksheet (TW 141–142)
	Part 5 Review: Phrases, Clauses, and Sentences (TW 143–144)
	Part 5 Test: Phrases, Clauses, and Sentences (I-53–I-54)
	Part 6 Survey: Capitalization and Number Style (TW 145–146)
	Unit 20 and Study Guide: Capitalization of Names (TW 147–152); Worksheet (TW 153–154)
	Unit 21 and Study Guide: Capitalization—Other Uses (TW 155–158); Worksheet (TW 159–160)
	Unit 22 and Study Guide: Numbers (TW 161–166); Worksheet (TW 167–168)
	Part 6 Review: Capitalization and Number Style (TW 169–170)
	Part 6 Test: Capitalization and Number Style (I-55–I-56)
	Part 7 Survey: Punctuation (TW 171–172)
	Unit 23 and Study Guide: The Period, the Question Mark, and the Exclamation Point (TW 173–176); Worksheet (TW 177–178)
	Unit 24 and Study Guide: The Period—Other Uses (TW 179–184); Worksheet (TW 185–186)
	Unit 25 and Study Guide: The Comma (TW 187–192); Worksheet (TW 193–194)

*I-page references indicate pages that appear in the Instructor's Edition only; TW references indicate pages that appear in both the Instructor's Edition and the student's text-workbook.

Hour	Activities and References*
	Unit 26 and Study Guide: The Comma (Continued) (TW 195–198); Worksheet (TW 199–200)
	Unit 27 and Study Guide: The Comma (Concluded) (TW 201–204); Worksheet (TW 205–206)
	Unit 28 and Study Guide: The Semicolon and the Colon (TW 207–210); Worksheet (TW 211–212)
	Unit 29 and Study Guide: The Apostrophe and the Dash (TW 213–216); Worksheet (TW 217–218)
	Unit 30 and Study Guide: Quotation Marks and Underscores (TW 219–222); Worksheet (TW 223–224)
	Unit 31 and Study Guide: The Hyphen and Parentheses (TW 225–230); Worksheet (TW 231–232)
	Part 7 Review: Punctuation (TW 233–234)
	Part 7 Test: Punctuation (I-57–I-58)
	Part 8 Survey: Words and Word References (TW 235–236)
	Unit 32 and Study Guide: Reference Books and Word Division (TW 237–242); Worksheet (TW 243–244)
	Unit 33 and Study Guide: Spelling–Words With Prefixes and Suffixes (TW 245–250); Worksheet (TW 251–252)
	Unit 34 and Study Guide: Choice of Words (TW 253–254); Worksheet (TW 255–256)
	Unit 35 and Study Guide: Synonyms, Antonyms, and Soundalikes (TW 257–260); Worksheet (TW 261–262)
	Part 8 Review: Words and Word References (TW 263–264)
	Part 8 Test: Words and Word References (I-59–I-60)
	Final Test (I-61–I-64)

*I-page references indicate pages that appear in the Instructor's Edition only; TW references indicate pages that appear in both the Instructor's Edition and the student's text-workbook.

I-6 Instructor's Overview

Copyright © by Glencoe.

Supplementary Exercises

WORD CHOICE AND SPELLING

The sentences in Exercises 1 and 2 require the student to choose and correctly spell the right word from those that have the same or nearly the same pronunciation but different spellings and meanings. Each exercise may be divided into several short exercises and administered orally, in which case it is suggested that you (1) pronounce the word that the student is to write; (2) read the sentence, emphasizing the particular word; and (3) repeat the word. Note that the correct answers are underlined.

EXERCISE 1

1. The seventh (addition, edition) of the manual is available in the bookstore.
2. We must check these figures in (addition, edition) to those.
3. One of the buildings has a weather (vain, vane, vein) on the roof.
4. Neither he nor she is a (vain, vane, vein) person.
5. The doctor said that a small (vain, wave, vein) had ruptured.
6. Nothing seems to (faze, phase) either of them.
7. The first (faze, phase) of the project has been completed.
8. Will you (pleas, please) notify each of them.
9. We should not ignore anyone's (pleas, please) for assistance.
10. A few members of the audience seemed to be (board, bored).
11. She had been a member of the (board, bored) for two years.
12. The last payment was a few days (overdo, overdue).
13. Be careful not to (overdo, overdue) strenuous exercises.
14. The prices of some products (vary, very) from one store to another.
15. They appear to be (vary, very) happy.
16. The firm is studying methods of recycling (waist, waste) products.
17. These trousers were made for someone with a small (waist, waste).
18. Perhaps we should (review, revue) the terms of the agreement.
19. We attended a musical (review, revue) at a local theater.
20. Do you think the manager will read the memo (allowed, aloud)?
21. Smoking is not (allowed, aloud) in many offices.
22. Should such materials be stored in (metal, mettle) containers?
23. It is a situation that would test anyone's (metal, mettle).
24. Each of them was awarded a (medal, meddle) for distinguished service.
25. We refuse to (medal, meddle) in matters that do not concern us.

26. Would you like pie or cake for (desert, **dessert**)?

27. Some tourists were stranded in the middle of the (**desert**, dessert).

28. Whom do you consider your closest (**confidant**, confident)?

29. We are (confidant, **confident**) that they will endorse our plan.

30. There is an emergency exit at the end of each (**aisle**, isle).

31. The group spent a few days on an (aisle, **isle**) in the middle of the ocean.

32. The bride and groom stood before the (**altar**, alter).

33. Perhaps it would be wise to (altar, **alter**) our approach.

34. Mosquito (**bites**, bytes) are irritating.

35. The storage capacity of computer diskettes is measured in (bites, **bytes**).

36. Some cars have a (**dual**, duel) exhaust system.

37. They were engaged in some sort of verbal (dual, **duel**).

38. Have you ever eaten (**currant**, current) jelly?

39. Please be sure to use the (currant, **current**) data.

40. Which should be painted first, the walls or the (**ceiling**, sealing)?

41. They were (ceiling, **sealing**) the packages with tape.

42. The patient was in a (**coma**, comma) for two days.

43. Should I use a (coma, **comma**) or a semicolon?

44. The defendant was released on (**bail**, bale).

45. A (bail, **bale**) of hay fell off the wagon.

46. I'm not sure whether he (**chews**, choose, chose) tobacco or gum.

47. Which of them did you (chews, **choose**, chose)?

48. We (chews, choose, **chose**) to attend the afternoon session.

49. Only a musician would know whether it was the right (**chord**, cord).

50. This telephone (chord, **cord**) is too short.

EXERCISE 2

1. Only those who have a password have (**access**, excess) to those files.

2. Why do people travel with (access, **excess**) baggage?

3. How much does a half-page (**ad**, add) cost?

4. Don't forget to (ad, **add**) the sales tax.

5. We may need to make some other (arraignment, **arrangement**) with them.

6. Two attorneys were present at the (**arraignment**, arrangement) of those accused of the crime.

7. Does she plan to wear her mother's (**bridal**, bridle) gown?

8. They are certain to (bridal, **bridle**) at that suggestion.

9. The (**attendance**, attendants) at this year's meeting was larger than we expected.

10. One of the (attendance, **attendants**) will park your car.

11. We very much appreciate the (**assistance**, assistants) you gave us.

12. The clinic employs two or three dental (assistance, **assistants**).

13. Perhaps we should take a much (bolder, boulder) approach.

14. One lane of traffic was blocked by a (bolder, boulder).

15. Their attitude was rather (callous, callus).

16. He has a (callous, callus) on his left hand.

17. The (census, senses) showed an increase in the population.

18. Tangible things can be perceived by one or more of the (census, senses).

19. What kind of breakfast (cereal, serial) do you prefer?

20. Please be sure to check the (cereal, serial) number.

21. The plane (flew, flu, flue) at a very high altitude.

22. Health officials reported a (flew, flu, flue) epidemic.

23. Smoke was billowing from the (flew, flu, flue).

24. Swiss cheese is (holey, holy, holly, wholly).

25. Many people consider such places to be (holey, holy, holly, wholly).

26. Some wreaths are made of (holey, holy, holly, wholly).

27. The report appears to be (holey, holy, holly, wholly) correct.

28. You should not be (billed, build) for purchases you did not make.

29. Where do they plan to (billed, build) the new warehouse?

30. Do you think they will consider (lightening, lightning) our workload?

31. One of the trees was struck by (lightening, lightning).

32. We filled the (pail, pale) with water.

33. She was wearing a (pail, pale) blue dress.

34. I need a (pair, pare, pear) of scissors.

35. What can we do to (pair, pare, pear) expenses?

36. The birds built a nest in the (pair, pare, pear) tree.

37. The summer is our (peak, peek, pique) season.

38. We don't want anyone to get a (peak, peek, pique) at these plans.

39. Such a statement may (peak, peek, pique) their interest.

40. For (instance, instants), you may want to consider a modeling career.

41. It took only a few (instance, instants) to determine the source of the problem.

42. When did they apply for the (loan, lone)?

43. A (loan, lone) thief may have committed the crime.

44. That will not (lessen, lesson) their chances of success.

45. That experience taught us a valuable (lessen, lesson).

46. Some merchandise must be (packed, pact) very carefully.

47. What are the key provisions of the (packed, pact)?

48. I'm not sure whether the ground was damp from (dew, do, due) or from rain.

49. Is there anything else we should (dew, do, due)?

50. The payment was made before it was (dew, do, due).

GRAMMAR AND USAGE

The following exercises may be given orally or reproduced and distributed to students for extra practice in applying various principles of grammar and usage. Exercise 3 requires students to select verbs that agree with their subjects. Exercise 4 gives extra practice in using the correct forms and tenses of verbs. In all exercises, the correct answers are underlined.

EXERCISE 3

1. Each of the claims (was, were) settled out of court.

2. There (has, have) been very few complaints about it.

3. When (was, were) those decisions made?

4. (Do, Does) each of you have a copy of the manual?

5. The majority of our personnel (belong, belongs) to that organization.

6. Where (was, were) you planning to stay?

7. Much of the work (remain, remains) to be done.

8. The news of their promotions (please, pleases) us very much.

9. Neither they nor I (use, uses) that machine very often.

10. A number of companies (exhibit, exhibits) their products at this convention.

11. The number of satisfied customers (continue, continues) to grow.

12. We, as well as he, (know, knows) what the outcome is likely to be.

13. Jean is one of the members who (plan, plans) to attend.

14. Either you or I (am, are, is) likely to be asked to help them.

15. Pat and Fay (work, works) well together.

16. Neither the receptionist nor any of the secretaries (know, knows) who left the message.

17. The secretary and the treasurer (give, gives) reports at those meetings.

18. Twelve ounces (are, is) all this container will hold.

19. The members of the committee seldom (disagree, disagrees) with the rest of us.

20. Colorado Springs (attract, attracts) many tourists.

21. The owner and manager (work, works) late every day.

22. She, together with two partners, (conduct, conducts) seminars for many firms.

23. Several secretaries, as well as the manager, (subscribe, subscribes) to that magazine.

24. Settling disputes (require, requires) tact and patience.

25. The proceeds usually (amount, amounts) to $500 or less.

26. (Hasn't, Haven't) both of those copies been signed?

27. Many a passenger (has, have) misread the schedule.

28. Every man, woman, and child (need, needs) medical insurance.

29. Drinking and driving (doesn't, don't) pay.

30. The paintings, which were donated by Dr. Farnsworth, (are, is) priceless.

31. Such phenomena as he reported (occur, occurs) frequently.

32. (Do, Does) Roger and you share an office?

33. He is the only one of them who (need, needs) our assistance.

34. None of the apartments in this building (appeal, appeals) to him or her.

35. What their reactions will be (remain, remains) to be seen.

EXERCISE 4

1. I would have gone if I (had known, knew) you would be there too.

2. She sometimes wishes she (was, were) someone else.

3. The company (should have, should of) notified each of us.

4. No one had ever (saw, seen) them until this morning.

5. I am certain that Sharon (did, done) most of the work herself.

6. As we entered the office, the telephone (rang, rung).

7. The sweater must have (shrank, shrunk) when I washed it.

8. This suit can be (wore, worn) for business or pleasure.

9. For the first year or two, the company (grew, growed) rapidly.

10. We (are, have been) at this location for nearly five years.

11. Both of them (ran, run) for reelection last fall.

12. It must have (taken, took) several hours to write that letter.

13. No policy is (written, wrote) in stone.

14. Had the meeting (began, begun) when you arrived?

15. The papers were (laying, lying) on your desk when I saw them.

16. Where should I (set, sit) this carton?

17. Taxes may (raise, rise) again this year.

18. The water level has (risen, rose) during the past two days.

19. We should (set, sit) closer to the exit.

20. If I (was, were) you, I would accept the invitation.

21. Both of them were completely (wore, worn) out.

22. I was standing at the corner when a car (came, comes) up on the sidewalk.

23. Have you ever (ridden, rode) a horse in Central Park?

24. They should have (showed, shown) us how to operate the machine.

25. We probably should have (knowed, known) better.

SPELLING

Each column on the next page contains 50 words representing such common spelling problems as *ei* and *ie* combinations, one or more pairs of doubled letters, and *ant* and *ent* endings.

accelerate	acceptable	accompany	accuracy	accordance	adhere
acceptance	accommodate	achievement	across	adequate	advise
accessible	acknowledge	acquire	admission	advisable	aggravate
accessory	acquaintance	admissible	advertise	agreeable	apologize
accidentally	adjoining	allowance	analyze	anxious	appreciable
adjacent	adjustment	amateur	appearance	applicable	bargain
allege	advisory	anticipate	around	appropriate	committee
alignment	allocate	appraisal	article	approximate	comparison
analyze	amendment	brochure	believable	ascertain	conscientious
apparatus	apparent	cancellation	budget	association	controversy
applicable	appointment	catalog	certificate	correlation	coordinate
arbitration	assistant	chargeable	consensus	column	coordination
artery	attention	competent	consistent	compromise	counterfeit
auxiliary	authorize	congratulate	decision	consequence	delegate
available	beliefs	conversion	deficiency	definite	discernible
basically	beneficial	criticize	delivery	destination	distribution
cabinet	bribery	deductible	description	disguise	endorsement
commission	campaign	defendant	emphasis	drudgery	enterprise
competitive	collectible	defense	emphasize	endeavor	envelope
conceivable	concede	desirable	excessive	exceeded	grateful
convenience	concession	difference	exercise	expedite	height
courtesy	confidential	directory	expedient	extension	inasmuch as
develop	cycle	eliminate	experience	flexible	interest
enthusiastic	economical	especially	feasible	furniture	irresistible
excusable	efficient	existence	forfeit	incidentally	jeopardize
exorbitant	envelop	February	fundamental	installment	knowledgeable
explanation	excellence	financial	hesitant	itemize	license
extremely	familiarize	foreign	immediately	laboratory	mortgage
franchise	hoping	freight	inquiry	liaison	necessary
grievance	inevitable	identical	inventory	library	neighborhood
hazard	influential	initial	itinerary	leisure	occasion
incurred	installation	intention	length	meticulous	participant
interpret	issuing	justifiable	likable	occupation	preference
magnificent	management	language	maintenance	occurrence	previous
manageable	negotiate	maximum	miscellaneous	pamphlet	proceeded
modernize	noticeable	original	negotiation	permission	prominent
negative	organize	penalize	option	practical	recommendation
negligible	paralyze	permanent	positive	precedent	reimburse
omission	participate	possible	preferable	recognize	remittance
partial	permissible	precede	realize	reconcile	responsibility
probably	possession	receive	recede	regrettable	satisfactory
recurrence	quantity	relieve	recently	relevant	significant
remember	reference	representative	responsible	requirement	specialize
repetition	renewal	specification	schedule	seize	sufficient
salable	requisition	stabilize	sensitive	separate	theory
similar	supervise	succeed	serviceable	substantial	threshold
throughout	undoubtedly	surprise	supersede	tremendous	valuable
vacuum	verifiable	unique	until	usually	various
vehicle	Wednesday	variety	volume	visible	veteran
withhold	yield	vicinity	voluntary	volunteer	worthwhile

Modern Business English

COURSE INVENTORY

Underline each error in the following sentences, and write the necessary correction in the space provided. If a sentence requires no correction, write *OK*. Note the example.

0. Each of our marketing representatives submit daily reports.
0. submits

1. I wish the guarantee was good for a year instead of 90 days, don't you?
1. were

2. That contract already has several addendums.
2. addenda

3. The next board of directors' meeting is scheduled for the 10th of next month.
3. directors

4. We would of attended the conference if we had been invited.
4. (would) have (attended)

5. I think they may be willing to consider some other site.
5. OK

6. You and I will have to complete the project ourselfs.
6. ourselves

7. Has some of the documents been misplaced?
7. Have (been misplaced)

8. Do you think hunting and fishing are more enjoyable than to play tennis.
8. playing (tennis)

9. She hardly never misses a deadline.
9. ever

10. The situation doesn't look as badly to us as it did a few days ago.
10. bad

11. Neither of us knows who they are planning to appoint as her successor.
11. whom

12. Until today we were unaware of him asking for a transfer.
12. his

13. Do you know where Janice went to yesterday afternoon?
13. went (OMIT to)

14. Has anyone else in the office ever spoke to you about it?
14. (Has) spoken

15. I think most everybody in this department has a copy of the manual.
15. almost

16. Don't you think we should try and find a solution to the problem?
16. (should try) to (find)

17. Perhaps those assignments will be given to you and myself.
17. me

18. We were supposed to have left yesterday.
18. to leave

19. Of the many articles she has written, this one is better.
19. best

20. Pat is the one whom we hope will be appointed director of marketing.
20. who

21. Many a car, van, and truck have been ticketed for illegal parking.
21. has (been ticketed)

22. The spokesperson would neither confirm or deny that the company was seeking a merger partner.
22. nor

23. Mr. Wilson requested that we leave nothing laying on the window-sills.

23. lying

24. Helen thinks that you may want she to be your assistant.

24. her

25. What is the current price of a ounce of gold?

25. an

26. Bill is working with us for the past year, and we are very pleased with his work.

26. has been working

27. Both of their son-in-laws are CPAs.

27. sons-in-law

28. When I saw her, she was going in her office.

28. into

29. It is possible that they and we view the situation quite different.

29. differently

30. Which of those kind of containers should we use?

30. (those) kinds

31. How many attornies are there in your firm's legal department?

31. attorneys

32. As soon as possible, please let Fay or I know where you will be staying.

32. me

33. After you have been with the company eight years, you will be eligible for four weeks vacation.

33. (four) weeks'

34. A number of items is out of stock.

34. are

35. Marie Ashner is Al's and Ann's supervisor.

35. Al (and Ann's)

36. There has been only two bids received so far.

36. have (been)

37. The manager, as well as all the branch managers, are studying the proposals.

37. is (studying)

38. What is the company doing to reduce it's operating expenses?

38. its

39. You have more retailing experience than him.

39. he

40. We received less responses than we expected.

40. fewer

41. The new model does not seem to be much different than the old one.

41. (different) from

42. Do you think someone of those would be more appropriate?

42. some one

43. Chicago is larger than any city in Illinois.

43. (any) other (city)

44. Twelve ounces are all this cup will hold.

44. is

45. Margaret is the one who's signature is missing.

45. whose

46. Some of the tomatoes is too ripe to ship.

46. are

47. To our surprise, the errors had all ready been corrected.

47. already

48. Don't you agree that all of we employees deserve a merit increase?

48. us

49. One or two of the others arrived more later than we did.

49. later

50. The photocopier is only one of the machines that needs to be repaired.

50. need

Insert the necessary periods, commas, and other punctuation marks in the following sentences. Draw three lines under each letter or group of letters that should be capitalized. If a sentence is correct as it is shown, circle the number preceding it. Note the example.

0. "Do you agree," the manager asked, "that we should meet with them next Friday?"

1. "Finding a convenient place to park," Mr. Edwards said, "is very difficult in this area, and it's quite expensive too."

2. Wasn't mayor-elect Fulton operating a delivery service in the Dallas–Fort Worth area before he entered politics?

3. Managers, secretaries, accountants—all business employees should, in my opinion, read the article "Golden Parachutes with a Silver Lining" in the March 12 issue of *business for today,* a weekly news magazine with articles on a wide variety of topics.

4. Both of us are planning to attend the meeting in San Antonio, Texas, this fall; however, we probably will not attend any other conventions this year.

5. "Both announcements were prepared Wednesday and released Thursday morning," Ray Stone said.

6. Some cities have large parades on Columbus Day, New Year's day, and other holidays.

7. Carefully tailored clothing for men, women, and children is available in a wide range of ready-to-wear sizes in most large department stores.

8. Therefore, we should ask them what the final bill will be.

9. If Miss Sterling is interested in working for our company, Bob, please tell her that we have several openings in New England.

10. Burton, Burton & Bartow, a public relations firm, has entered into an agreement with Richardson Bros., according to a joint statement issued by the firms' presidents.

11. The IRS would be especially interested in such things as tax-exempt investments, large charitable contributions, etc., wouldn't it?

12. What I would like to know is this, senator: Do you intend to reenter the law firm you were with previously, or are you seriously thinking of seeking a junior college presidency?

13. We were supposed to meet in his office on Thursday, June 4, but because of illness, I was unable to keep the appointment.

14. They are planning to spend a week or so in Poplar Grove, which is located in Boone County.

15. I am not sure whether they were living in Johnson City or somewhere else in the state of Tennessee before 1988.

16. It most likely was Gary, not Larry or some other member of the company, who said that he would like to work for the Securities and Exchange Commission or some other government agency.

17. "Yes, I definitely prefer brand x," declared one of the interviewees.

18. In 1991 (see the chart on page 8) three products accounted for more than half of our sales.

(19.) Miss McCoy reviewed the manuscript and forwarded it to editor Lou LaBelle.

20. By the end of May of next year, we expect to be in new spacious offices in the Marshall Building at the corner of Tenth Street and Oakland Boulevard.

21. The Granger Corporation as well as Thomas Bros. is planning to open offices in these cities: Springfield, Massachusetts, Albany, New York, and New Orleans, Louisiana.

22. Will you be taking a two- or three-week vacation this year?

23. An executive vice president, Shirley Hendricks, has spoken to representatives of ABC, CNN, and NBC.

24. "What a surprise," exclaimed one of her associates.

25. Mr. Stein is a well-known and highly regarded consultant to many North American companies, and he has done some work for several federal agencies.

C Underline each error in word choice, spelling, number expression, or abbreviation usage in the following sentences, and write the necessary correction in the space provided. If a sentence is correct as it is shown, write *OK*.

1. I received an acknowledgment of my letter on July 21st.

1. _(July) 21_

2. Our records indicate that they were disatisfied with the terms outlined in our May 4, 1992, letter.

2. _dissatisfied_

3. One group of proBritish supporters has its headquarters at One Churchill Plaza.

3. _pro-British_

4. It was around three in the p.m. when I received his call.

4. _afternoon_

5. The Lakeland Corporation is remodeling 2 penthouse apartments in the 18-story building at 30 East Essex Place.

5. _two_

6. We distributed a few 100 copies of that 12-page pamphlet at the convention last week.

6. _(few) hundred_

7. We are experiencing some difficulty in deciding whether moving would be advantagous to us.

7. _advantageous_

8. They are the two principle stockholders.

8. _principal_

9. One of the sights being considered for the new mall is about 12 miles from here.

9. _sites_

10. We obtained a $40,000 loan in 1991 at an interest rate of eight and a quarter percent.

10. _8.25 (percent)_

11. If lightning means anything, it is liable to rain any minute.

11. _likely_

12. Ten of the 15 openings have been filled.

12. _fifteen_

13. The top of one of the credenzas was mared.

13. _marred_

14. This cookbook contains some excellent receipts for berry pies.

14. _recipes_

15. This insecticide should rid your home of flys.

15. _flies_

16. $2,500.00 may be a reasonable price for that piece of equipment.

16. _Twenty-five hundred dollars_

17. The Wells family owns about 1/3 of the firm's common stock.

17. _one-third_

18. They seem unconcerned about the rescheduling of the seminar.

18. _OK_

19. She lived in Madrid for about 2 years.

19. _two_

20. I paid $1.20 for each of them; he paid only 95¢.

20. _$.95_

21. What affect will it have on members of our personnel department?

21. _effect_

22. Recent polls show that a large percent of voters are in favor of the proposal.

22. _percentage_

23. I am planning to take my vacation, but I won't be going anywheres in particular.

23. _anywhere_

24. The room is 12 feet four inches wide.

24. _(12 feet) 4 (inches)_

25. Their office is at 2200 West Twelfth Street.

25. _12 OR 12th_

PART 1 TEST

Nouns and Noun Usage (Units 1–3)

 A In the space provided, write the singular possessive, plural, and plural possessive forms of the following nouns. If possession should be indicated by an *"of"* phrase rather than by the addition of an apostrophe or an apostrophe and *s*, write the appropriate *"of"* phrase.

SINGULAR	SINGULAR POSSESSIVE	PLURAL	PLURAL POSSESSIVE
1. company	company's	companies	companies'
2. owner-manager	owner-manager's	owner-managers	owner-managers'
3. customer	customer's	customers	customers'
4. series	of the series	series	of the series
5. employee	employee's	employees	employees'
6. attorney	attorney's	attorneys	attorneys'
7. shelf	of the shelf	shelves	of the shelves
8. policy	of the policy	policies	of the policies
9. Mr. Walsh *(formal)*	Mr. Walsh's	Messrs. Walsh	Messrs. Walsh's
10. Ms. Cady *(formal)*	Ms. Cady's	Mses. OR Mss. Cady	Mses. OR Mss. Cady's
11. memo	of the memo	memos	of the memos
12. committee	committee's	committees	committees'
13. editor in chief	editor in chief's	editors in chief	editors in chief's
14. child	child's	children	children's
15. witness	witness's	witnesses	witnesses'
16. sheep	sheep's	sheep	sheep's
17. German	German's	Germans	Germans'
18. sales tax	of the sales tax	sales taxes	of the sales taxes
19. crisis	of the crisis	crises	of the crises
20. get-together	of the get-together	get-togethers	of the get-togethers
21. cloth	of the cloth	cloths	of the cloths
22. IOU	of the IOU	IOUs	of the IOUs
23. tomato	of the tomato	tomatoes	of the tomatoes
24. knife	of the knife	knives	of the knives
25. sister-in-law	sister-in-law's	sisters-in-law	sisters-in-law's

The following sentences contain errors in the formation and use of the plural and possessive forms of nouns. Underline each error, and write the necessary correction in the space provided. If no correction is needed, write *OK*.

1. The managers of those stores reported a large number of customers' buying TVs and VCRs.

2. The ambiguity of the contract's terms may lead to several disputes during the '90s.

3. Entries in the indices of publications are usually arranged in alphabetic order.

4. Some employees received substantial bonusses.

5. The jurors' decision indicated that they believed both of the plaintives.

6. Ed and Elaine attended various events for alumna of the local community college.

7. Some industrys produce tons of toxic wastes.

8. We were pleased to learn of B. J. Henry Jr. assuming the presidency of the company.

9. Betty and Bob's positions are comparable in most respects.

10. Field Brother's advertisements appear in both local newspapers.

11. Each of the claims is approximately equal to three week's salary.

12. The presentations stressed the whats and whens, not the whys.

13. Rotting leafs damaged the roofs of both buildings.

14. Which stores offer the widest selections of men and women's clothing?

15. Both of her brother-in-laws are mechanics.

16. Phyllis's and Andy's offices are near Pat.

17. Mrs. Bradford and Young are the principal stockholders.

18. The sale's managers of many firms subscribe to those publications.

19. Does the value of those corporation's assets exceed their liabilities?

20. These articles are of interest to employers' thinking of changing their employee-benefit programs.

21. Many prospective buyers use their present cars and trucks as trade ins.

22. We should order at least 12 dozens of those hanging file folders.

23. The co-owners decided they would accept c.o.d.s.

24. Will the proceed of each of those fund-raising activities go to charitable organizations?

25. The storm did several thousand dollar's worth of damage to those crops of tomatoes and potatoes.

1. customers
2. (terms) of the contract
3. indexes
4. bonuses
5. plaintiffs
6. alumni
7. industries
8. B. J. Henry Jr.'s
9. Betty's (and Bob's)
10. Field Brothers'
11. (three) weeks'
12. OK
13. leaves
14. men's
15. brothers-in-law
16. Pat's
17. Mmes. OR Mesdames
18. sales (managers)
19. corporations'
20. employers
21. trade-ins
22. (12) dozen
23. c.o.d.'s
24. proceeds
25. dollars'

PART 2 TEST

Pronouns and Pronoun Usage (Units 4–7)

 A **Which of the pronouns shown in parentheses correctly completes the sentence? Write your answer in the space provided.**

1. Do you know (who, whom) was responsible?

2. Mr. Weeks would like for you and (I, me, myself) to work this weekend.

3. What would you do if you were (her, she)?

4. Glen and Lois said (their, there, they're) cooperating with the investigators.

5. Do you know (who's, whose) proposal will be accepted?

6. Everyone must do (her, his, her or his, their) share of the work.

7. Perhaps (them, those) are more appropriate.

8. The committee issued (its, their) report yesterday.

9. Will this plan benefit all of (us, we) employees?

10. Our office, (that, which) is located on Booth Boulevard, has been completely remodeled.

11. (Who, Whom) did you invite?

12. I read in the newspaper (that, where) the companies plan to merge.

13. Lee and Irene often help (each other, one another).

14. Tom is often mistaken to be (he, him).

15. Is (any one, anyone) of the proposed sites acceptable to you?

16. The ones most likely to win are you and (them, they).

17. Kirk decided to repair the equipment (himself, hisself).

18. The manager thinks you and (I, me, myself) should attend both meetings.

19. They said nothing about (our, us) having to work overtime last weekend.

20. Neither of the companies raised (its, their) prices.

21. (Some one else, Someone else) must have taken the message.

22. We should solicit several (other's, others') opinions.

23. Which of these folders is (your's, yours)?

24. Few people would have done a better job than (he, him).

1. ___who___

2. ___me___

3. ___she___

4. ___they're___

5. ___whose___

6. ___her or his___

7. ___those___

8. ___its___

9. ___us___

10. ___which___

11. ___Whom___

12. ___that___

13. ___each other___

14. ___he___

15. ___any one___

16. ___they___

17. ___himself___

18. ___I___

19. ___our___

20. ___its___

21. ___Someone else___

22. ___others'___

23. ___yours___

24. ___he___

25. Are Terry and (her, she) going to Columbus with you?

25. <u>she</u>

 B **Underline each error in the use of pronouns in the following sentences, and write the necessary correction in the space provided. If no correction is needed, write *OK*.**

1. I thought it was her, but I wasn't sure.

1. <u>she</u>

2. John said he thinks its his responsibility.

2. <u>it's</u>

3. Whom do you think should be appointed?

3. <u>Who</u>

4. Him and I agree on almost everything.

4. <u>He</u>

5. Most of the staff think that every thing is under control.

5. <u>everything</u>

6. Jeanne said neither of those was her's.

6. <u>hers</u>

7. Martin's is one of those companies who moved into a new mall last month.

7. <u>that</u>

8. It's being overlooked seems unlikely.

8. <u>Its</u>

9. You may invite whoever you wish to attend.

9. <u>whomever</u>

10. They seem to be much busier than us.

10. <u>we</u>

11. The leading candidates are him and her.

11. <u>he and she</u>

12. One of the bridesmaids tripped on their dress.

12. <u>her</u>

13. Did you mistake Bill to be I?

13. <u>me</u>

14. The manager seemed to appreciate us finishing the project ahead of schedule.

14. <u>our</u>

15. Marilyn and myself will make all the changes you requested.

15. <u>I</u>

16. Were you aware of them being asked to serve on the finance committee?

16. <u>their</u>

17. This job requires some one who has a technical background, doesn't it?

17. <u>someone</u>

18. I think everyone else writing is more legible than mine.

18. <u>everyone else's</u>

19. Do you think anyone of those would be acceptable to the others?

19. <u>any one</u>

20. One of the firms plans to build their new distribution center in this area.

20. <u>its</u>

21. Are you sure their going to be there?

21. <u>they're OR they are</u>

22. One of her brothers-in-law submitted their application for that job.

22. <u>his</u>

23. Every manager knows that their success depends upon employees who are competent and dependable.

23. <u>his or her OR her or his</u>

24. Do you know whose going with them?

24. <u>who's</u>

25. Does this list include all the accounts that are overdue?

25. <u>OK</u>

PART 3 TEST

Verbs and Verb Usage (Units 8–12)

 A   **Choose the verb or verb phrase shown in parentheses that correctly completes the sentence, and write your answer in the space provided.**

1. Helen (is, has been) on our staff nearly a year.
2. Larry (said, says) that he drafted the memo himself.
3. (Are, Is) either of those yours?
4. Perhaps we (should have, should of) been more careful.
5. She, as well as the rest of us, (are, is) aware of their plans.
6. (Doesn't, Don't) either of them appeal to you?
7. None of the equipment (need, needs) to be repaired immediately.
8. The folders were (laying, lying) on your desk.
9. If I (was, were) you, I would accept their invitation.
10. Who recommended that the changes (are, be, were) made immediately?
11. The members of the panel (has, have) been selected.
12. By the time we arrived, most of the others had (gone, went) home.
13. It (began, begun) to rain the minute we left the office.
14. Every man, woman, and child (learn, learns) from experience.
15. The president and chief executive officer (was, were) at the conference.
16. One of the topics to be discussed (are, is) productivity.
17. A number of employees in this department (work, works) late almost every day.
18. In this case, there (seem, seems) to be no absolute criteria.
19. I (would attend, would have attended) if it had been possible.
20. Until yesterday, neither of us had ever (driven, drove) such a large truck.
21. Ryan & Associates usually (advertise, advertises) in local newspapers.
22. Nearly one-fourth of the employees (belong, belongs) to more than one professional association.
23. If she (had been, would have been) at the meeting, one of us would have seen her.

1. has been
2. said
3. Is
4. should have (been)
5. is
6. Doesn't (appeal)
7. needs
8. (were) lying
9. were
10. be (made)
11. have (been selected)
12. (had) gone
13. began
14. learns
15. was
16. is
17. work
18. seem
19. would have attended
20. (had) driven
21. advertises
22. belong
23. had been

24. Joyce is one of those who (plan, plans) everything very carefully.

24. _plan_

25. The board of directors (do, does) not agree on that particular issue.

25. _do (agree)_

 B The following sentences contain errors involving verbs, verb phrases, infinitives, participles, and gerunds. Underline each error; then write the necessary correction in the space provided. If no correction is needed, write *OK*.

1. The number of accounts that is delinquent is far fewer than we had expected.

1. _are_

2. Who complained about Jerry taking a day off?

2. _Jerry's_

3. She would have liked to have attended the conference in Phoenix.

3. _to attend_

4. If he would have accepted their offer, he would be much happier.

4. _had accepted_

5. One of us should of notified them yesterday.

5. _should have notified_

6. Louise usually prepares a weekly status report, don't she?

6. _doesn't_

7. The vice president and the general manager endorses our plan.

7. _endorse_

8. There is a number of orders to be processed.

8. _are_

9. She is the only one of them who have volunteered to assist us.

9. _has volunteered_

10. Two months seem a long time to wait for an answer.

10. _seems_

11. The evening news usually include a brief report about the stock market.

11. _includes_

12. One series of games were played in Atlanta.

12. _was played_

13. Some of the members supports such an amendment.

13. _support_

14. Something in those cartons have spilled.

14. _has spilled_

15. Have some of the information been provided?

15. _Has been provided_

16. Every toaster and iron in the store come with a 90-day warranty.

16. _comes_

17. Either you or I are responsible.

17. _am_

18. Neither the door nor the windows was open.

18. _were_

19. Expenses are among the topics on the agenda.

19. _is_

20. Who recommended the requests were approved?

20. _be approved_

21. How many times have you wrote to them?

21. _have (you) written_

22. You will have received a corrected statement of your account within the next few days.

22. _will receive_

23. Next Monday she will be living here a year.

23. _will have been living_

24. We would have been surprised if the plants had growed any taller.

24. _had grown_

25. You, as well as he, knows what the outcome is likely to be.

25. _know_

NAME _____   DATE _____

 Which of the words shown in parentheses is correct? Write your answer in the space provided.

1. You are entitled to a (10 percent, 10-percent) discount.   1. __10 percent__

2. This building is (government owned, government-owned).   2. __government-owned__

3. We may try (and, to) lease more office space.   3. __to__

4. The reason she was absent is (because, that) she was ill.   4. __that__

5. How much (farther, further) will you need to travel each day?   5. __farther__

6. Of the three, which one is (good, better, best)?   6. __best__

7. Was anyone (beside, besides) her given a merit increase?   7. __besides__

8. I doubt that we need (any, no) more of those.   8. __any__

9. He seems to know less about it (than, then) we do.   9. __than__

10. (Almost, Most) everyone has endorsed the new plan.   10. __Almost__

11. It is (liable, likely) to rain later today.   11. __likely__

12. We processed (fewer, less) orders yesterday than we did this   12. __fewer__
    morning.

13. Do you think their prices are (to, too, two) high?   13. __too__

14. Both of you (sure, surely) knew what their response would be.   14. __surely__

15. Helping others makes most people feel (good, well).   15. __good__

16. This is a (real, very) interesting position.   16. __very__

17. California is more populous than (any, any other) state.   17. __any other__

18. Which of (that, them, those) letters needs to be answered?   18. __those__

19. The label had fallen (off, off of) the folder.   19. __off__

20. Everyone was there (accept, except) you.   20. __except__

21. I don't think the situation looks (bad, badly), do you?   21. __bad__

22. The visit ended rather (abrupt, abruptly).   22. __abruptly__

23. I don't know where they were (going, going to), do you?   23. __going__

24. Both critics gave the movie (a, an) excellent review.   24. __an__

25. What (kind of, kind of a) license is needed?   25. __kind of__

The following sentences contain errors involving adjectives, adverbs, prepositions, and conjunctions. Underline each error, and write the necessary correction in the space provided. If no correction is needed, write *OK*.

1. Are these packages already to ship?

2. I think it was in August when we bought this machine.

3. Fay is a officer of the company.

4. Some of their coworkers criticized them for taking their responsibilities so casual.

5. We couldn't hardly hear either of the first two speakers.

6. Perhaps we need to spend sometime with them.

7. Regulators said the arrangement was an elicit one.

8. He said that he hasn't been feeling good for several days.

9. We should not leave early without we notify someone.

10. Something doesn't seem quite right, does it?

11. She got a well-paying job right away.

12. The meeting was scheduled for today, and it was postponed until next week.

13. This machine operates more efficient than either of those.

14. The increase is retroactive from January 1.

15. I am not sure who the principle stockholders are.

16. When does your company's physical year end?

17. This container is fuller than that one.

18. Is this report supposed to be turned into Mr. Wells tomorrow?

19. It looks like we will need to work overtime if we expect to finish this job today.

20. Mr. Morris appeared quite optimistically about the likelihood of an early settlement.

21. They have no interest or need for a larger warehouse at this point.

22. They don't never want to be stranded in such an isolated place again.

23. Wouldn't you sooner work with her than with him?

24. Is this copy different than that one?

25. Nancy spoke criticallier than anyone else.

1. all ready
2. that
3. an
4. casually
5. could hardly hear OR couldn't hear
6. some time
7. illicit
8. well
9. unless
10. OK
11. good-paying
12. but
13. more efficiently
14. retroactive to
15. principal
16. fiscal
17. more nearly full
18. in to
19. as though
20. optimistic
21. interest in
22. ever
23. rather
24. different from
25. more critically

PART 5 TEST

Phrases, Clauses, and Sentences
(Units 17–19)

 Combine each group of sentences below into one unified, coherent sentence that emphasizes the part of the thought that you consider important. Add, omit, and change words as necessary. Note that some of the sentences contain errors. (Answers will vary).

1. A spokesperson for the company made an announcement. The company is combining some of its head-quarters operations. It is also opening two new branch offices.

   A company spokesperson announced that the company is combining some of its headquarters operations and opening two new branch offices.

2. Ms. Moreno has two immediate goals. One of them is to complete work toward a degree in accounting. The other is to obtain a position with a firm in Chicago.

   Ms. Moreno's immediate goals are to complete work toward a degree in accounting and to obtain a position with a firm in Chicago.

3. David Weston worked for Woburn & Company for three years. He was a marketing representative. He will join our staff next week. He will be assistant manager of our marketing department.

   After three years as a marketing representative for Woburn & Company, David Weston will join our staff next week as assistant marketing manager.

4. I was in Lansing last week. I met with Denise Lopez. Denise is one of our consultants.

   While I was in Lansing last week, I met with Denise Lopez, one of our consultants.

5. Dr. Ellis is planning to hold a meeting. He's scheduled it for next Friday morning. He will discuss various changes in employee benefits paid for by the company.

   Dr. Ellis has scheduled a meeting for next Friday morning to discuss various changes in company-paid employee benefits.

 For each of the following phrases, write a short sentence in which the phrase functions as the part of speech indicated in parentheses. (Answers will vary.)

1. In the early fall *(Adverb)*

   Some of our employees prefer to take their vacations in the early fall.

2. Using public transportation *(Noun)*

   Many business and government leaders encourage using public transportation.

3. Bought at special sale prices *(Adjective)*

Some stores do not grant refunds for merchandise bought at special sale prices.

4. To use credit wisely *(Noun)*

One way to save money is to use credit wisely.

5. For new employees *(Adjective)*

The reception for new employees is scheduled for this evening.

C Underline each error in the following sentences, and write the necessary correction in the space provided. If a sentence does not contain an error, write *OK*.

1. There is several letters that need to be answered immediately.

        1. are

2. I would have gone if they would have asked me.

        2. had asked

3. Don't he expect you to call me today?

        3. Doesn't (expect)

4. The report may be a few days' late.

        4. days

5. They maybe here within a few minutes.

        5. may be

6. Do you think we should study their proposal further?

        6. OK

7. In my opinion, everyone must decide for themselves.

        7. herself or himself OR himself or herself

8. They are employees and stockholders to.

        8. too

9. What does the president and the chief executive officer think of your proposal?

        9. do (think)

10. I hope they ask you and myself for our suggestions.

        10. me

11. Oliver took it upon hisself to conduct those negotiations.

        11. himself

12. Neither of the bridegrooms rented their tuxedo.

        12. his

13. We do not want to spend no more than necessary.

        13. any

14. I think that I would of accepted almost any entry-level job.

        14. (would) have (accepted)

15. None of us could have predicted Jack resigning.

        15. Jack's

16. You have more sales experience than me.

        16. I

17. It is a matter of principal as far as they are concerned.

        17. principle

18. Do you think us objecting will make any difference?

        18. our

19. The customers' standing in line didn't notice anything unusual.

        19. customers

20. I thought both machines had been inspected thorough, didn't you?

        20. thoroughly

PART 6 TEST

Capitalization and Number Style
(Units 20–22)

 A Draw three lines under each letter or group of letters that should be capitalized in each of the following sentences. In addition, draw a line under each word or group of words that should be underscored. If a sentence requires no change, circle the number preceding it.

1. Are you sure, may, that one of the shops in lincoln square village sells china?

2. I think marilyn painter said that she would like to work as a teller for the chemical bank and trust company.

3. The publication of a sequel to gone with the wind in the fall of 1991 produced mixed reactions among southerners, northerners, and others.

4. Are you sure that miss green has a bachelor's degree from northwestern university?

5. Lloyd Bates, president and chief executive officer, said, "we have expanded our operations to cover every state in the union. early in the twenty-first century we expect to open offices in europe, asia, and africa."

6. Someone told me that former governor roswell is a graduate of the united states military academy at west point.

7. Will the president's address to a joint session of congress be broadcast by nbc or some other network?

8. Would I want to live on a farm north of the city? maybe.

9. Perhaps you should ask tax consultant Yvonne de la Vega whether you need to file schedule d with your form 1040 this year.

10. Our accounting department compiled the data appearing in table 2 on page 9.

11. If you like polish food, I can give you the name of an excellent restaurant in the windy city.

12. Some coworkers who went camping in the rockies said they took nothing with them but several cans of campbell's soup, a few dozen grade a eggs, and a bottle of bayer aspirin.

13. The article "saving energy: a do-it-yourself guide," which appeared in the spring issue of home and garden quarterly, generated a great deal of interest.

14. Please note: prices quoted are f.o.b. salt lake city and are subject to change without notice.

15. The question is, is it the responsibility of the federal deposit insurance corporation or some other agency of the federal government?

16. Sara Farley, ph.d., was living in new york state before she moved to salt lake city.

17. If you have studied business management, business english, and related subjects, you will want to attend this special seminar.

18. She said she received an a in each of these courses: american history, computer science 200, and spanish 120.

19. "You won't want to miss our fantastic fourth of july celebration," the mayor said.

20. The metropolitan museum of art is exhibiting works by van gogh.

21. Please remember to specify:
   1. <u>the</u> date, time, and place of the meeting.
   2. <u>what</u> materials the attendees will need to bring with them.

22. Is <u>their</u> office located on <u>n</u>orthern <u>b</u>oulevard or on <u>s</u>outh <u>t</u>enth <u>s</u>treet?

23. I suggest, sir, that you ask her whether she prefers to use the title <u>ms.</u>, <u>m</u>iss, or <u>m</u>rs.

24. The ambassador was particularly interested in an exhibit of pre-<u>c</u>olumbian artifacts.

25. They are on <u>f</u>light 200, which is scheduled to arrive at <u>o'h</u>are at 8:45 p.m.

B Underline each error in the expression of numbers and related terms in the following sentences, and write the necessary correction in the space provided. For each sentence that requires no correction, write *OK*.

1. I made a payment of $225 on June <u>10th</u>.
   1. June 10

2. In the early '90s the value of the firm's assets was between <u>$200</u> and $225 million.
   2. $200 million

3. They obtained a $60,000 mortgage at <u>eight and one-half percent</u>.
   3. 8.5 (percent)

4. The room is <u>11 feet, 9 inches</u> by 18 feet.
   4. 11 feet 9 inches

5. She owns <u>one-half</u> of the stock; he owns the other half.
   5. one half

6. The repairs will cost several <u>1,000</u> dollars.
   6. (several) thousand

7. The quarterly dividend has been as low as $.12 and as high as $1.22.
   7. OK

8. Twelve of the <u>36</u> items in that container were damaged.
   8. thirty-six

9. Our new office is at 3260 North <u>4th</u> Street.
   9. Fourth (Street)

10. The letter concerning Invoice 430 was dated <u>4/10/92</u>.
   10. April 10, 1992

11. A large <u>percent</u> of customers buy two or three at a time.
   11. percentage

12. Flight 330 is scheduled to arrive at <u>2 o'clock p.m.</u>
   12. 2 o'clock OR two o'clock OR 2 p.m.

13. Her home address is 3204 Wellington Place, Tampa, Florida <u>33,612.</u>
   13. 33612

14. About <u>¾</u> of the work has been completed.
   14. three-fourths

15. I think she was <u>22</u> last week.
   15. twenty-two

16. I think <u>2</u> requisitions were for 3 dozen notepads and 10 reams of plain paper.
   16. two

17. <u>150</u> questionnaires were mailed the 10th.
   17. One hundred fifty

18. This carton contains <u>24 8-ounce</u> jars.
   18. (24) eight-ounce

19. Table 8 appears in Chapter <u>ix</u>.
   19. (Chapter) IX

20. The company will celebrate its <u>100th</u> anniversary in 2002.
   20. one hundredth

21. Of the 64,200 miles she traveled last year, only <u>4800</u> were by automobile.
   21. 4,800

22. In <u>1991 32</u> new positions were added in the company's Los Angeles office.
   22. 1991, 32

23. The meeting continued most of the <u>a.m.</u>
   23. morning

24. If we sell them for $12.50 each, our profit will be <u>12.6%</u>.
   24. 12.6 percent

25. The daily fluctuation is between <u>.75</u> and 1 percent.
   25. 0.75 (and 1 percent)

PART 7 TEST

Punctuation (Units 23–31)

Insert the necessary commas, periods, quotation marks, underscores, and other punctuation marks in the following sentences. When necessary, use a caret (∧ or ∨) to indicate where a punctuation mark should be inserted. Do not make any changes in capitalization. If a sentence requires no additional punctuation, circle the number preceding it. Note the example.

0. "The meeting should end around 3:30, Ms. Wilson said.

1. I am not certain whether their office is in Columbus, Ohio, or in Columbus, Georgia.

2. Computers, printers, fax machines—all are available at greatly reduced prices at all our stores in the Minneapolis–St. Paul area.

3. His current home address is as follows: 4240 Beloit Road, Rockford, Illinois 61110-7077.

4. What do you think of Russ's handling of the labor-management dispute?

5. According to this prospectus, income from such investments is tax-exempt.

6. Yes, we offer a wide selection of carpeting in 9-12 and 15-foot widths.

7. How long would it take us to drive from here to Chicago? to St. Louis? to Indianapolis?

8. The question is, How long can we afford to wait for them to decide what they want to do?

9. Senator-elect Sue Ames is co-owner of that real estate agency, isn't she?

10. Some people misspell the word parallel by using two l's at the end of the word too.

11. The announcement was made at 8:15 a.m. CST.

12. "What a wonderful surprise!" exclaimed Miss Hardwick.

13. Surprisingly, the month-by-month summary (see Table 2 on page 6) indicates an average gain of 3.2 percent.

14. It was she, not he, who suggested that we should trade in that equipment by mid-September.

15. The manager asked how much longer it would take to finish the project.

16. Mrs. Crawford, our director of marketing, has asked all of the regional managers to update their sales and expense budgets for the third quarter.

17. Many English words, such as macadam and pasteurize, are derived from names of people; others, such as china and damask, are taken from names of places.

18. Would you please notify each member of your staff of these changes.

19. The seminars are tentatively scheduled for Wednesday, May 4, Thursday, May 12, and Tuesday, May 17, Roger.

20. "Will either of those companies, Mr. Winters asked, be invited to bid on this project?"

21. We are very, very fortunate to have Edith McBride, Ph.D., as a member of our staff.

22. Congratulations! All of us are delighted to hear that you have been appointed vice president and general manager of Freiberg, Foley & Burns.

23. Jeff, as well as Maureen, will be at the meeting; however, no one representing our department has been invited.

24. Friends and close relatives, for example, should not be given as references when applying for a job.

25. I thought that Mr. Graham asked why the order was shipped c.o.d.

26. Would you be willing to answer this letter for me?

27. To obtain a free copy, simply sign and return the enclosed card.

28. Some of the positions will be filled in January, others in June or July.

29. Thinking interest rates would drop further, they decided to wait a few more months before applying for a home-improvement loan.

30. The owners permit tenants to have some animals as pets, for example, small dogs, cats, and birds.

31. Normally, the report is issued soon after the end of our fiscal year, that is, June 30.

32. The committee discussed proposed changes in the benefits program, but according to the chairperson, it has no immediate plans to accept or reject any of them.

33. When the next conference will be held has not been announced, has it?

34. A requirement such as that one is, in my opinion, unreasonable.

35. Containers such as those should not be used because they are not biodegradable.

36. Real gems, such as diamonds, pearls, and rubies, are often difficult to distinguish from synthetic ones.

37. The attorney handling the case is R. J. Wheeler, Jr.'s new law partner, Melissa Patterson.

38. According to the official, reports of an impending merger are erroneous.

39. We are confident that you, too, will want to take advantage of this once-in-a-lifetime investment opportunity.

40. One of our customers, namely, Lockwood Industries, bought nearly $7500 worth of merchandise last month.

41. To become the leader in its field is the company's goal.

42. Consequently, banks and others offering charge cards have increased their interest rates.

43. In 1980, 80 percent of those surveyed were in favor of such a plan; in 1990, 68 percent of those who participated in a similar survey thought such a plan was a good idea.

44. The series of articles, which I found very interesting, appeared in The New York Times.

45. After calling Joe, Jack decided that he should summarize their discussion in a memo to the general manager.

46. "At 9 o'clock tomorrow morning," Ms. Hammond said, "we are scheduled to meet with a group of investors."

47. To tell the truth, I made a serious mistake: I should have read the contract very, very carefully before signing it.

48. Do you have a copy of the March 1992 agreement in your files, Henry?

49. He gave Springfield, Illinois, as his birthplace and March 10, 1971, as his birthdate.

50. The company offers evening courses in keyboarding, business writing, and so on, throughout the year.

PART 8 TEST

Words and Word References
(Units 32–35)

 A **Which of the words shown in parentheses correctly completes the sentence? Write your answer in the space provided.**

1. Those two colors are (complementary, complimentary).

2. How would you assess the (moral, morale) of the staff?

3. The recognition you have received is (overdo, overdue).

4. The hotel gave us a tastefully decorated (suit, suite).

5. Thank you for your (assistance, assistants).

6. These have (all ready, already) been checked.

7. What (advice, advise) did you offer them?

8. All have been reviewed (accept, except) this one.

9. How will that (affect, effect) the others?

10. Perhaps it was (all together, altogether) unnecessary.

11. We may be able to (adapt, adept, adopt) their plan to suit our particular needs.

12. They have been here (every day, everyday) this week.

13. The stage play was (adapted, adopted) for TV.

14. A small (amount, number) of accounts are in arrears.

15. They (passed, past) us on the way to work.

16. How do they treat their (employees, help)?

17. I would (rather, sooner) work with you than with anyone else.

18. How much (experience, past experience) do you have?

19. Would you (kindly, please) inform them?

20. (Before, Prior to) joining our company, she worked for The Bates Corporation.

21. In many respects, they are (alike, both alike).

22. I doubt that such a statement would be (comprehensive, comprehensible) to anyone.

23. We should invest in it, (irregardless, regardless) of what the others do.

24. (Incidently, Incidentally), how much will your suggestion save the company?

25. A large (percent, percentage) of the claims were invalid.

1. complementary
2. morale
3. overdue
4. suite
5. assistance
6. already
7. advice
8. except
9. affect
10. altogether
11. adapt
12. every day
13. adapted
14. number
15. passed
16. employees
17. rather
18. experience
19. please
20. Before
21. alike
22. comprehensible
23. regardless
24. Incidentally
25. percentage

In the space provided, write the word formed by adding the suffix or prefix shown in parentheses.

1. care (ful)
2. defer (ed)
3. mar (ed)
4. (re) enter
5. (mis) sent
6. whole (ly)
7. (bi) annual
8. (mid) July
9. (inter) state
10. value (able)

1. careful
2. deferred
3. marred
4. reenter
5. missent
6. wholly
7. biannual
8. mid-July
9. interstate
10. valuable

11. (co) owner
12. appraise (al)
13. deny (ing)
14. (ab) normal
15. (il) logical
16. wall (less)
17. sincere (ity)
18. house (hold)
19. (self) control
20. (dis) allow

11. co-owner
12. appraisal
13. denying
14. abnormal
15. illogical
16. wall-less
17. sincerity
18. household
19. self-control
20. disallow

From the following list of words, select an appropriate synonym for the italicized word in each sentence below. Write the word you select in the space provided.

revealed   position   viewpoint   worthy   hinder   believable   informal   deniable

1. We should try to view the situation from their *perspective*.
2. They were dressed in *casual* attire.
3. Such information should not be *divulged*.
4. We should allow nothing to *impede* our progress.
5. The story did not seem *credible*.

1. viewpoint
2. informal
3. revealed
4. hinder
5. believable

Underline the misspelled word, if any, in each line of words below; then write the word correctly in the space provided. If none of the words in the line are misspelled, write *OK*.

1. differed	referal	preference	conference
2. sincerely	hilly	oilly	usually
3. eighth	ninty	fourteenth	twelfth
4. judgment	judging	managment	managing
5. attorneys	compelled	withheld	embarrased

1. referral
2. oily
3. ninety
4. management
5. embarrassed

Which word shown at the right of the italicized word is opposite in meaning to the italicized word? Write your answer in the space provided.

1. *circuitous*	square	direct	short
2. *potent*	strong	weak	poisonous
3. *chastised*	praised	punished	purified
4. *ambiguous*	vague	clear	petite
5. *complex*	difficult	certain	simple

1. direct
2. weak
3. praised
4. clear
5. simple

FINAL TEST

Modern Business English

 A **Underline each error in the following sentences, and write the necessary correction in the space provided. If a sentence requires no correction, write *OK*. Note the example.**

0. Each of the companies were represented.

1. If you was the general manager, what would you do?

2. Both of the analysises were helpful.

3. They are members of a manufacturers' association.

4. We should of told you last Friday.

5. Maybe they will accept our offer.

6. Perhaps he has no one to blame but hisself.

7. Do each of the others have a copy?

8. She likes swimming and skiing better than to play tennis.

9. We don't want to order no more like those.

10. This medicine does not taste badly to me.

11. She is the one who we are planning to hire.

12. I doubt that anyone will object to us taking the day off.

13. She doesn't know where he was at yesterday.

14. Has anyone else wrote to you about our discount policy?

15. I believe most everybody agrees with you.

16. We need to try and find a solution quickly.

17. Dr. Collins probably will want you and myself to work this week-end.

18. We wanted to have met with them last week.

19. Which of these four ads is more appealing?

20. Who do you think we should hire?

21. Every man, woman, and child in the area were at the picnic.

22. I am certain that neither the car or the van was parked illegally.

23. They sat the cartons near the door and left.

24. We do not want Ann or he to be disappointed.

25. She is a honorary member of the society.

26. John is living here since last July, and he seems to like this area.

27. Both of their daughter-in-laws are attorneys.

0. ___was (represented)___

1. ___were___

2. ___analyses___

3. ___manufacturers___

4. ___(should) have (told)___

5. ___OK___

6. ___himself___

7. ___Does (have)___

8. ___playing tennis___

9. ___any___

10. ___bad___

11. ___whom___

12. ___our___

13. ___was (OMIT at)___

14. ___(Has) written___

15. ___almost___

16. ___(try) to (find)___

17. ___me___

18. ___to meet___

19. ___most (appealing)___

20. ___Whom___

21. ___was___

22. ___nor___

23. ___set___

24. ___him___

25. ___an___

26. ___has been living___

27. ___daughters-in-law___

28. The driver obviously was not looking when he ran <u>in to</u> the stop sign.

29. I don't write as <u>legible</u> as she does.

30. Do you think <u>these kind</u> of bulbs will last longer?

31. The Walshes and the Rileys are co-owners of two research <u>labora-torys</u>.

32. I hope they will let you or <u>I</u> inspect the premises.

33. When will you be eligible for a <u>three weeks</u> vacation?

34. <u>Was</u> a number of employees ill last week?

35. Are you <u>Russ's</u> and Barbara's supervisor?

36. There <u>has</u> been only two complaints so far.

37. Mrs. Haines, as well as several other experts, <u>have spoke</u> on that topic.

38. The company has made <u>it's</u> position known.

39. Doesn't he have more experience than <u>her</u>?

40. There were <u>less</u> people attending this year than there were last year.

41. This one is quite <u>different than</u> that one.

42. Do you think <u>any one</u> with a master's degree would be interested?

43. Atlanta is larger than <u>any city</u> in Georgia.

44. I think that a hundred pounds <u>are</u> too much for either of them to carry.

45. Do you know <u>whose</u> planning to buy that land?

46. None of the cartons was <u>setting</u> in the hall.

47. They had <u>all ready</u> left when I arrived.

48. Are you certain they're planning to invite <u>we</u> administrative assistants?

49. It takes him <u>more longer</u> to get to work than it takes me.

50. Mine is the only one of the expense reports that <u>were</u> questioned last month.

28.	into
29.	legibly
30.	this (kind) OR (these) kinds
31.	laboratories
32.	me
33.	(three) weeks' OR three-week
34.	Were
35.	Russ (and Barbara's)
36.	have (been)
37.	has spoken
38.	its
39.	she
40.	fewer
41.	(different) from
42.	anyone
43.	(any) other (city)
44.	is
45.	who's
46.	were sitting
47.	already
48.	us
49.	longer (OMIT more)
50.	was (questioned)

 B Insert the necessary periods, commas, and other punctuation marks in the following sentences. Draw three lines under each letter or group of letters that should be capitalized. If a sentence is correct as it is shown, circle the number preceding it. Note the example.

0. "How many citizens of our state, governor burnside asked, do you think will support such a tax-abatement plan?"

1. "To improve our competitive position, dr. stone said, is our objective, and we've made significant progress toward achieving it."

2. Doesn't ex-senator walton have an interest in some firms in the new jersey-pennsylvania area?

3. Secretaries, accountants, managers, everyone will, I believe, be interested in the article planning for tomorrow in the july issue of *investment weekly*, one of our new magazines of special interest.

4. We undoubtedly will have an exhibit at the trade fair in green bay, wisconsin next spring, however, I am less certain about our participation in other meetings.

5. The order was placed on monday and received on thursday, carol conway said.

6. Our special sales on columbus day, independence day, and other holidays are very, very popular.

7. Many retailers offer stoves, refrigerators, and other household appliances at greatly reduced prices during their once-a-year clearance sales.

8. Nevertheless, both of them would like to know more about the position.

9. When you see miss cook, Cindy, be sure to ask her about the changes in the west coast office.

10. Sanford, Baker & Adams, a local law firm, will represent several Lane Bros. officers named in the suit brought by one of the company's largest clients.

11. The irs may raise a number of questions about such things as interest-free loans, large charitable contributions, etc., don't you think?

12. My next question is this, mayor: Do you plan to seek reelection, or do you plan to enter the real estate business?

13. I called her on Thursday, June 14, but according to my notes, she was not in the office.

14. We are planning to drive to overland park, which is located in johnson county.

15. Did they have an office in Salt Lake city or somewhere else in the state of Utah at that time?

16. It was Floyd, not Lloyd, who said that the company was being investigated by the securities and exchange commission or some other government agency.

17. "Well, I certainly hope that you sell nothing but grade a dairy products," one of the customers commented.

18. In 1991 (see the chart on page 10) three products accounted for about half of our sales.

19. Ms. Adams read the letter and forwarded it to lawyer Kathleen Kiley.

20. By the first of may of next year, we should be in our spacious, modern headquarters at the corner of oak avenue and broadway.

21. Danforth and Associates, as well as Jackson Inc., has branch offices in these cities: Independence, Missouri; Gary, Indiana; and Oak Park, Illinois.

22. We need to consider the short-and long-term consequences of such actions.

23. One of our senior vice presidents, Bonita Hooper, has agreed to meet with representatives of abc, cbs, and nbc.

24. What a bargain! exclaimed one of the shoppers.

25. Mr. Lopez is a well-known and highly respected member of the Latin American community, and he has served as a consultant to several federal agencies.

C Underline each error in word choice, spelling, number expression, or abbreviation usage in the following sentences, and write the necessary correction in the space provided. If a sentence is correct as it is shown, write *OK*.

1. We placed an order for letterhead stationery on May 10th.

1. May 10

2. Two of the mispelled words in the June 1, 1991, agreement were *accommodate* and *recommend*.

2. misspelled

3. A number of preThanksgiving shoppers watched the parade from the top of One Park Place.

3. pre-Thanksgiving

4. I thought the meeting was to be this a.m.

4. morning

5. We have leased 2 floors of the 12-story office building at 200 West Elm Street.

6. We need a few 100 more of those 16-page pamphlets.

7. An acknowledgment of the agreement would not be inappropriate.

8. I am certain that I paid the bill, but I can't find the recipe.

9. Whom did the authors sight as the source of that information?

10. We were fortunate to obtain a $10,000 loan at 12 and a half percent in 1989.

11. Do you think it's liable to rain today?

12. Of the 12 plates, two were broken.

13. Those lacking proper credentials will be bared from the hearings.

14. Our consultants recommended that we provide our employees more comprehensible medical insurance.

15. After two trys, he decided to give up.

16. $400.00 seems to be a reasonable price for that piece of equipment.

17. About ¾ of the company's common stock is owned by institutional investors.

18. None of our executives have any personal knowledge of any misappropriation of funds.

19. An absence of 3 days obviously requires an explanation.

20. If one store sells this item for 80¢, why should I pay you $1.20 for it?

21. We believe a large amount of people will be interested in those products.

22. Only a small percent think such a zoning ordinance should be adopted.

23. We intend to proceed, irregardless of what any of the others do.

24. This room is 12 feet eight inches long.

25. I thought your office was at 1200 South Twelfth Street.

5. two

6. (few) hundred

7. OK

8. receipt

9. cite

10. 12.5 (percent)

11. likely

12. 2

13. barred

14. comprehensive

15. tries

16. Four hundred dollars

17. three-fourths

18. OK

19. three

20. $.80

21. number

22. percentage

23. regardless

24. (12 feet) 8 (inches)

25. 12 OR 12th

Modern Business English

COURSE INVENTORY

 A **Underline each error in the following sentences, and write the necessary correction in the space provided. If a sentence requires no correction, write *OK*. Note the example.**

0. Each of our marketing representatives <u>submit</u> daily reports.

0. <u>submits</u>

1. I wish the guarantee was good for a year instead of 90 days, don't you?

1. _____

2. That contract already has several addendums.

2. _____

3. The next board of directors' meeting is scheduled for the 10th of next month.

3. _____

4. We would of attended the conference if we had been invited.

4. _____

5. I think they may be willing to consider some other site.

5. _____

6. You and I will have to complete the project ourselfs.

6. _____

7. Has some of the documents been misplaced?

7. _____

8. Do you think hunting and fishing are more enjoyable than to play tennis.

8. _____

9. She hardly never misses a deadline.

9. _____

10. The situation doesn't look as badly to us as it did a few days ago.

10. _____

11. Neither of us knows who they are planning to appoint as her successor.

11. _____

12. Until today we were unaware of him asking for a transfer.

12. _____

13. Do you know where Janice went to yesterday afternoon?

13. _____

14. Has anyone else in the office ever spoke to you about it?

14. _____

15. I think most everybody in this department has a copy of the manual.

15. _____

16. Don't you think we should try and find a solution to the problem?

16. _____

17. Perhaps those assignments will be given to you and myself.

17. _____

18. We were supposed to have left yesterday.

18. _____

19. Of the many articles she has written, this one is better.

19. _____

20. Pat is the one whom we hope will be appointed director of marketing.

20. _____

21. Many a car, van, and truck have been ticketed for illegal parking.

21. _____

22. The spokesperson would neither confirm or deny that the company was seeking a merger partner.

22. _____

23. Mr. Wilson requested that we leave nothing laying on the window-sills.

23. _____

24. Helen thinks that you may want she to be your assistant.

24. _____

25. What is the current price of a ounce of gold?

25. _____

26. Bill is working with us for the past year, and we are very pleased with his work.

26. _____

27. Both of their son-in-laws are CPAs.

27. _____

28. When I saw her, she was going in her office.

28. _____

29. It is possible that they and we view the situation quite different.

29. _____

30. Which of those kind of containers should we use?

30. _____

31. How many attornies are there in your firm's legal department?

31. _____

32. As soon as possible, please let Fay or I know where you will be staying.

32. _____

33. After you have been with the company eight years, you will be eligible for four weeks vacation.

33. _____

34. A number of items is out of stock.

34. _____

35. Marie Ashner is Al's and Ann's supervisor.

35. _____

36. There has been only two bids received so far.

36. _____

37. The manager, as well as all the branch managers, are studying the proposals.

37. _____

38. What is the company doing to reduce it's operating expenses?

38. _____

39. You have more retailing experience than him.

39. _____

40. We received less responses than we expected.

40. _____

41. The new model does not seem to be much different than the old one.

41. _____

42. Do you think someone of those would be more appropriate?

42. _____

43. Chicago is larger than any city in Illinois.

43. _____

44. Twelve ounces are all this cup will hold.

44. _____

45. Margaret is the one who's signature is missing.

45. _____

46. Some of the tomatoes is too ripe to ship.

46. _____

47. To our surprise, the errors had all ready been corrected.

47. _____

48. Don't you agree that all of we employees deserve a merit increase?

48. _____

49. One or two of the others arrived more later than we did.

49. _____

50. The photocopier is only one of the machines that needs to be repaired.

50. _____

B Insert the necessary periods, commas, and other punctuation marks in the following sentences. Draw three lines under each letter or group of letters that should be capitalized. If a sentence is correct as it is shown, circle the number preceding it. Note the example.

0. "Do you agree," the manager asked, "that we should meet with them next friday?"

1. Finding a convenient place to park mr. edwards said is very difficult in this area and its quite expensive too.

2. Wasn't mayor-elect fulton operating a delivery service in the dallas fort worth area before he entered politics

3. Managers secretaries accountants all business employees should in my opinion read the article golden parachutes with a silver lining in the march 12 issue of *business for today,* a weekly news magazine with articles on a wide variety of topics.

4. Both of us are planning to attend the meeting in san antonio texas this fall; however we probably will not attend any other conventions this year.

5. Both announcements were prepared wednesday and released thursday morning ray stone said.

6. Some cities have large parades on columbus day new year's day, and other holidays.

7. Carefully tailored clothing for men women and children is available in a wide range of ready to wear sizes in most large department stores.

8. Therefore we should ask them what the final bill will be

9. If miss sterling is interested in working for our company, bob, please tell her that we have several openings in new england.

10. Burton Burton & Bartow a public relations firm has entered into an agreement with Richardson Bros., according to a joint statement issued by the firms presidents.

11. The irs would be especially interested in such things as tax exempt investments large charitable contributions etc. wouldnt it

12. What I would like to know is this senator Do you intend to reenter the law firm you were with previously or are you seriously thinking of seeking a junior college presidency

13. We were supposed to meet in his office on Thursday June 4 but because of illness I was unable to keep the appointment.

14. They are planning to spend a week or so in poplar grove which is located in boone county.

15. I am not sure whether they were living in Johnson city or somewhere else in the state of Tennessee before 1988.

16. It most likely was Gary not Larry or some other member of the company who said that he would like to work for the securities and exchange commission or some other government agency.

17. Yes I definitely prefer brand x declared one of the interviewees

18. In 1991 see the chart on page 8) three products accounted for more than half of our sales.

19. Miss McCoy reviewed the manuscript and forwarded it to editor Lou LaBelle.

20. By the end of may of next year we expect to be in new spacious offices in the Marshall Building at the corner of tenth street and oakland boulevard.

21. The Granger Corporation as well as Thomas Bros. is planning to open offices in these cities Springfield Massachusetts Albany New York and New Orleans Louisiana.

22. Will you be taking a two or three week vacation this year?

23. An executive vice president Shirley Hendricks has spoken to representatives of abc cnn and nbc.

24. What a surprise exclaimed one of her associates.

25. Mr. Stein is a well known and highly regarded consultant to many North American companies, and he has done some work for several federal agencies.

 Underline each error in word choice, spelling, number expression, or abbreviation usage in the following sentences, and write the necessary correction in the space provided. If a sentence is correct as it is shown, write *OK*.

1. I received an acknowledgment of my letter on July 21st.

1. _____

2. Our records indicate that they were disatisfied with the terms outlined in our May 4, 1992, letter.

2. _____

3. One group of proBritish supporters has its headquarters at One Churchill Plaza.

3. _____

4. It was around three in the p.m. when I received his call.

4. _____

5. The Lakeland Corporation is remodeling 2 penthouse apartments in the 18-story building at 30 East Essex Place.

5. _____

6. We distributed a few 100 copies of that 12-page pamphlet at the convention last week.

6. _____

7. We are experiencing some difficulty in deciding whether moving would be advantagous to us.

7. _____

8. They are the two principle stockholders.

8. _____

9. One of the sights being considered for the new mall is about 12 miles from here.

9. _____

10. We obtained a $40,000 loan in 1991 at an interest rate of eight and a quarter percent.

10. _____

11. If lightning means anything, it is liable to rain any minute.

11. _____

12. Ten of the 15 openings have been filled.

12. _____

13. The top of one of the credenzas was mared.

13. _____

14. This cookbook contains some excellent receipts for berry pies.

14. _____

15. This insecticide should rid your home of flys.

15. _____

16. $2,500.00 may be a reasonable price for that piece of equipment.

16. _____

17. The Wells family owns about 1/3 of the firm's common stock.

17. _____

18. They seem unconcerned about the rescheduling of the seminar.

18. _____

19. She lived in Madrid for about 2 years.

19. _____

20. I paid $1.20 for each of them; he paid only 95¢.

20. _____

21. What affect will it have on members of our personnel department?

21. _____

22. Recent polls show that a large percent of voters are in favor of the proposal.

22. _____

23. I am planning to take my vacation, but I won't be going anywheres in particular.

23. _____

24. The room is 12 feet four inches wide.

24. _____

25. Their office is at 2200 West Twelfth Street.

25. _____

Modern Business English

COURSE INVENTORY ANALYSIS CHART

In the chart below and on the following pages, circle the number of each test item that you answered incorrectly on the Course Inventory. As you study the principles of grammar, usage, and style presented in *Modern Business English,* Eighth Edition, give special attention to those covered under the topic headings indicated for the various text units.

Section A

Test Item	Text Unit	Topic Heading
1	11	14. Subjunctives
2	1	7. Foreign Nouns
3	3	Nouns Providing Description Only
4	9	Errors in Use of Tenses
5	14	5. maybe/may be (Study Guide)
6	5	Compound Personal Pronouns
7	10	4. Verb Followed by a Subject
8	16	Use of Coordinate Conjunctions
9	14	Double Negatives
10	13	Predicate Adjectives
11	7	4. Subject or Object of an Infinitive
12	5	1. Possessive Forms Used as Modifiers
13	15	Unnecessary Prepositions
14	8	Troublesome Verbs
15	14	1. almost/most (Study Guide)
16	16	Use of Coordinate Conjunctions
17	5	Common Usage Errors
18	12	Tenses of Infinitives
19	13	Correct Use of Adjectives
20	7	1. Subject of a Verb
21	10	Singular Subjects Modified by *Every* or a Similar Expression
22	16	Correlative Conjunctions
23	8	Troublesome Verbs
24	4	Pronouns With the Infinitive *To Be;* 6. Subject of an Infinitive
25	13	Articles
26	9	The Present Perfect Progressive Tense
27	2	Compound Nouns Written With Spaces or Hyphens
28	15	*In, Into,* and *In to*
29	14	Function of Adverbs
30	13	Correct Use of Adjectives
31	1	4. Nouns Ending in *Y*
32	4	6. Subject of an Infinitive

Test Item	Text Unit	Topic Heading
33	3	Nouns Naming Inanimate Things
34	11	12. *A Number* and *The Number* as Subjects
35	3	4. Nouns Joined by *and*
36	10	5. Verb Preceded by *There* or *Here*
37	10	3. Subject and Verb Separated by Parenthetical Expression
38	5	Possessive Case of Personal Pronouns
39	4	1. Subject of a Verb
40	13	10. *few/less* (Study Guide)
41	15	Idiomatic Use of Prepositions
42	6	4. Compound Indefinite Pronouns
43	13	Correct Use of Adjectives
44	11	1. Quantities and Amounts
45	7	10. Use as Adjectives
46	11	11. Indefinite Pronouns; Unit 8, Principal Parts of Some Troublesome Verbs
47	14	Adverbs Containing *All*
48	4	5. Object of a Preposition
49	14	Use of *More* or *Less* and *Most* or *Least*
50	11	10. Relative Pronouns

Section B

Test Item	Text Unit	Topic Heading
1	30	1. With Direct Quotations of Complete Statements
	20	3. Titles Before Names
	24	2. Titles Before Names of Persons
	27	2. In Compound-Complex Sentences
	29	5. In Contractions
	30	11. With a Comma or a Period
2	29	5. In Contractions
	20	6. Titles With *Ex-, Former, Late,* and *-Elect.*
	20	15. Official Names of Cities, States, and so on
	31	3. Compound Nouns as Modifiers
	23	5. Interrogative Sentences
3	25	With Items in a Series
	29	6. Before a Summarizing Word
	26	4. Interrupting Expressions
	30	9. With Titles of Magazine Articles, Book Chapters, and so on
	20	23. Names of Months, Days of the Week, Holidays, and so on
	30	17. With Titles of Books and Other Items
	26	6. Nonrestrictive (Nonessential) Appositives
4	20	15. Official Names of Cities, States, and so on
	25	10. Addresses
	28	3. Before a Transitional Expression
5	20	23. Names of Months, Days of the Week, Holidays, and so on
	30	10. With Direct Quotations of Complete Statements
	20	1. Complete Names
6	20	23. Names of Months, Days of the Week, Holidays, and so on
	25	11. Last Two Items Joined by a Conjunction

Test Item	Text Unit	Topic Heading
7	25	11. Last Two Items Joined by a Conjunction
	31	4. Adverbs Ending in *ly* Plus Particples
	31	1. Compound Adjective Before a Noun
8	27	3. Introductory Words
	23	1. Declarative Sentences
9	20	3. Titles Before Names
	25	7. Titles and Names in Direct Address
	20	19. Names of Geographic Regions
10	25	14. Items Joined by an Ampersand
	26	6. Nonrestrictive (Nonessential) Appositives
	29	1. In Possessives of Nouns
11	21	13. Academic Degrees, Initials, and Abbreviations
	31	1. Compound Adjective Before a Noun
	25	13. *Etc.* or Similar Expression at End of Series
	23	6. Sentences Containing Direct Questions
12	25	7. Titles and Names in Direct Address
	20	5. Titles in Place of Names
	28	8. Between Independent Clauses
	27	1. In Compound Sentences
	23	9. Independent Question at the End of a Sentence
13	25	3. Day of Week Plus Month and Day or Month, Day, and Year
	27	1. In Compound Sentences
	27	4. Introductory Phrases
	23	1. Declarative Sentences
14	20	15. Official Names of Cities, States, and so on
	26	8. Modifying Clauses
15	20	18. *City, Village,* and Similar Words.
	20	17. The Word *State*
16	26	3. Contrasting Expressions
	20	11. Complete Names of Government Bodies
17	30	1. With Direct Quotations of Complete Statements
	27	3. Introductory Words
	20	25. Trademarks, Brand Names, and Market Grades
	23	1. Declarative Sentences
18	31	21. Parentheses Instead of Commas or Dashes
19	20	3. Titles Before Names
20	20	23. Names of Months, Days of Week, Holidays, and so on
	27	4. Introductory Phrases
	25	15. Coordinate Adjectives
	20	21. Names of Streets, Buildings, Monuments, and so on
21	26	4. Interrupting Expressions
	28	7. Before a List or an Enumeration
	28	5. Between Items in a Series
	25	10. Addresses
22	31	1. Compound Adjective Before a Noun
	31	8. Adjectives With a Common Element
23	20	3. Titles Before Names
	26	6. Nonrestrictive (Nonessential) Appositives
	21	13. Academic Degrees, Initials, and Abbreviations
	24	6. Entire Names of Firms and Organizations
	25	11. Last Two Items Joined by a Conjunction

Test Item	Text Unit	Topic Heading
24	30	1. With Direct Quotations of Complete Statements
	30	13. With a Question Mark or an Exclamation Point
	23	1. Declarative Sentences
25	31	5. Other Adverbs Plus Participles
	31	3. Compound Nouns as Modifiers
	27	1. In Compound Sentences
	20	13. The Terms *Federal, Government,* and *Federal Government*

Section C

Test Item	Text Unit	Topic Heading
1	22	4. Month and Day
2	33	Words With Prefixes
3	33	Guidelines for Adding Prefixes; Unit 22, Numbers in Addresses
4	22	9. Hour With *a.m.* or *p.m.*
5	22	1. Numbers *One* Through *Ten*
6	22	33. Indefinite Numbers
7	33	Words Ending in Silent *E.* (8)
8	35	Soundalikes
9	35	Soundalikes
10	22	17. Percentages of 1 Percent or Higher
11	35	Study Guide, Section C (6)
12	22	29. Related Numbers
13	33	Words Ending With a Consonant (1)
14	35	Study Guide, Section A (9)
15	33	Words Ending in *Y* (11)
16	22	27. Numbers Beginning Sentences
17	22	20. Fractions Alone
18	33	Words With Prefixes
19	22	26. Other Periods of Time
20	22	13. Amounts Under a Dollar
21	32	Study Guide, Section C (4)
22	22	19. Percentage Without a Number
23	35	Study Guide, Section B (1)
24	22	16. Weights and Other Measurements
25	22	8. Numbers as Street Names

PART 1 TEST

Nouns and Noun Usage (Units 1–3)

 A In the space provided, write the singular possessive, plural, and plural possessive forms of the following nouns. If possession should be indicated by an *"of"* phrase rather than by the addition of an apostrophe or an apostrophe and s, write the appropriate *"of"* phrase.

SINGULAR	SINGULAR POSSESSIVE	PLURAL	PLURAL POSSESSIVE
1. company			
2. owner-manager			
3. customer			
4. series			
5. employee			
6. attorney			
7. shelf			
8. policy			
9. Mr. Walsh *(formal)*			
10. Ms. Cady *(formal)*			
11. memo			
12. committee			
13. editor in chief			
14. child			
15. witness			
16. sheep			
17. German			
18. sales tax			
19. crisis			
20. get-together			
21. cloth			
22. IOU			
23. tomato			
24. knife			
25. sister-in-law			

The following sentences contain errors in the formation and use of the plural and possessive forms of nouns. Underline each error, and write the necessary correction in the space provided. If no correction is needed, write *OK*.

1. The managers of those stores reported a large number of customers' buying TVs and VCRs.

1. _____

2. The ambiguity of the contract's terms may lead to several disputes during the '90s.

2. _____

3. Entries in the indices of publications are usually arranged in alphabetic order.

3. _____

4. Some employees received substantial bonusses.

4. _____

5. The jurors' decision indicated that they believed both of the plaintives.

5. _____

6. Ed and Elaine attended various events for alumna of the local community college.

6. _____

7. Some industrys produce tons of toxic wastes.

7. _____

8. We were pleased to learn of B. J. Henry Jr. assuming the presidency of the company.

8. _____

9. Betty and Bob's positions are comparable in most respects.

9. _____

10. Field Brother's advertisements appear in both local newspapers.

10. _____

11. Each of the claims is approximately equal to three week's salary.

11. _____

12. The presentations stressed the whats and whens, not the whys.

12. _____

13. Rotting leafs damaged the roofs of both buildings.

13. _____

14. Which stores offer the widest selections of men and women's clothing?

14. _____

15. Both of her brother-in-laws are mechanics.

15. _____

16. Phyllis's and Andy's offices are near Pat.

16. _____

17. Mrs. Bradford and Young are the principal stockholders.

17. _____

18. The sale's managers of many firms subscribe to those publications.

18. _____

19. Does the value of those corporation's assets exceed their liabilities?

19. _____

20. These articles are of interest to employers' thinking of changing their employee-benefit programs.

20. _____

21. Many prospective buyers use their present cars and trucks as trade ins.

21. _____

22. We should order at least 12 dozens of those hanging file folders.

22. _____

23. The co-owners decided they would accept c.o.d.s.

23. _____

24. Will the proceed of each of those fund-raising activities go to charitable organizations?

24. _____

25. The storm did several thousand dollar's worth of damage to those crops of tomatoes and potatoes.

25. _____

PART 2 TEST

Pronouns and Pronoun Usage (Units 4–7)

 A Which of the pronouns shown in parentheses correctly completes the sentence? Write your answer in the space provided.

1. Do you know (who, whom) was responsible?

2. Mr. Weeks would like for you and (I, me, myself) to work this weekend.

3. What would you do if you were (her, she)?

4. Glen and Lois said (their, there, they're) cooperating with the investigators.

5. Do you know (who's, whose) proposal will be accepted?

6. Everyone must do (her, his, her or his, their) share of the work.

7. Perhaps (them, those) are more appropriate.

8. The committee issued (its, their) report yesterday.

9. Will this plan benefit all of (us, we) employees?

10. Our office, (that, which) is located on Booth Boulevard, has been completely remodeled.

11. (Who, Whom) did you invite?

12. I read in the newspaper (that, where) the companies plan to merge.

13. Lee and Irene often help (each other, one another).

14. Tom is often mistaken to be (he, him).

15. Is (any one, anyone) of the proposed sites acceptable to you?

16. The ones most likely to win are you and (them, they).

17. Kirk decided to repair the equipment (himself, hisself).

18. The manager thinks you and (I, me, myself) should **attend** both meetings.

19. They said nothing about (our, us) having to work overtime last weekend.

20. Neither of the companies raised (its, their) prices.

21. (Some one else, Someone else) must have taken the message.

22. We should solicit several (other's, others') opinions.

23. Which of these folders is (your's, yours)?

24. Few people would have done a better job than (he, him).

1. _____

2. _____

3. _____

4. _____

5. _____

6. _____

7. _____

8. _____

9. _____

10. _____

11. _____

12. _____

13. _____

14. _____

15. _____

16. _____

17. _____

18. _____

19. _____

20. _____

21. _____

22. _____

23. _____

24. _____

25. Are Terry and (her, she) going to Columbus with you?

25. _____

 B Underline each error in the use of pronouns in the following sentences, and write the necessary correction in the space provided. If no correction is needed, write *OK*.

1. I thought it was her, but I wasn't sure.

1. _____

2. John said he thinks its his responsibility.

2. _____

3. Whom do you think should be appointed?

3. _____

4. Him and I agree on almost everything.

4. _____

5. Most of the staff think that every thing is under control.

5. _____

6. Jeanne said neither of those was her's.

6. _____

7. Martin's is one of those companies who moved into a new mall last month.

7. _____

8. It's being overlooked seems unlikely.

8. _____

9. You may invite whoever you wish to attend.

9. _____

10. They seem to be much busier than us.

10. _____

11. The leading candidates are him and her.

11. _____

12. One of the bridesmaids tripped on their dress.

12. _____

13. Did you mistake Bill to be I?

13. _____

14. The manager seemed to appreciate us finishing the project ahead of schedule.

14. _____

15. Marilyn and myself will make all the changes you requested.

15. _____

16. Were you aware of them being asked to serve on the finance committee?

16. _____

17. This job requires some one who has a technical background, doesn't it?

17. _____

18. I think everyone else writing is more legible than mine.

18. _____

19. Do you think anyone of those would be acceptable to the others?

19. _____

20. One of the firms plans to build their new distribution center in this area.

20. _____

21. Are you sure their going to be there?

21. _____

22. One of her brothers-in-law submitted their application for that job.

22. _____

23. Every manager knows that their success depends upon employees who are competent and dependable.

23. _____

24. Do you know whose going with them?

24. _____

25. Does this list include all the accounts that are overdue?

25. _____

PART 3 TEST

Verbs and Verb Usage (Units 8–12)

 A Choose the verb or verb phrase shown in parentheses that correctly completes the sentence, and write your answer in the space provided.

1. Helen (is, has been) on our staff nearly a year.   1. _____

2. Larry (said, says) that he drafted the memo himself.   2. _____

3. (Are, Is) either of those yours?   3. _____

4. Perhaps we (should have, should of) been more careful.   4. _____

5. She, as well as the rest of us, (are, is) aware of their plans.   5. _____

6. (Doesn't, Don't) either of them appeal to you?   6. _____

7. None of the equipment (need, needs) to be repaired immediately.   7. _____

8. The folders were (laying, lying) on your desk.   8. _____

9. If I (was, were) you, I would accept their invitation.   9. _____

10. Who recommended that the changes (are, be, were) made immediately?   10. _____

11. The members of the panel (has, have) been selected.   11. _____

12. By the time we arrived, most of the others had (gone, went) home.   12. _____

13. It (began, begun) to rain the minute we left the office.   13. _____

14. Every man, woman, and child (learn, learns) from experience.   14. _____

15. The president and chief executive officer (was, were) at the conference. 15. _____

16. One of the topics to be discussed (are, is) productivity.   16. _____

17. A number of employees in this department (work, works) late almost every day. 17. _____

18. In this case, there (seem, seems) to be no absolute criteria.   18. _____

19. I (would attend, would have attended) if it had been possible.   19. _____

20. Until yesterday, neither of us had ever (driven, drove) such a large truck. 20. _____

21. Ryan & Associates usually (advertise, advertises) in local newspapers.   21. _____

22. Nearly one-fourth of the employees (belong, belongs) to more than one professional association. 22. _____

23. If she (had been, would have been) at the meeting, one of us would have seen her. 23. _____

24. Joyce is one of those who (plan, plans) everything very carefully.

24. _____

25. The board of directors (do, does) not agree on that particular issue.

25. _____

B The following sentences contain errors involving verbs, verb phrases, infinitives, participles, and gerunds. Underline each error; then write the necessary correction in the space provided. If no correction is needed, write *OK*.

1. The number of accounts that is delinquent is far fewer than we had expected.

1. _____

2. Who complained about Jerry taking a day off?

2. _____

3. She would have liked to have attended the conference in Phoenix.

3. _____

4. If he would have accepted their offer, he would be much happier.

4. _____

5. One of us should of notified them yesterday.

5. _____

6. Louise usually prepares a weekly status report, don't she?

6. _____

7. The vice president and the general manager endorses our plan.

7. _____

8. There is a number of orders to be processed.

8. _____

9. She is the only one of them who have volunteered to assist us.

9. _____

10. Two months seem a long time to wait for an answer.

10. _____

11. The evening news usually include a brief report about the stock market.

11. _____

12. One series of games were played in Atlanta.

12. _____

13. Some of the members supports such an amendment.

13. _____

14. Something in those cartons have spilled.

14. _____

15. Have some of the information been provided?

15. _____

16. Every toaster and iron in the store come with a 90-day warranty.

16. _____

17. Either you or I are responsible.

17. _____

18. Neither the door nor the windows was open.

18. _____

19. Expenses are among the topics on the agenda.

19. _____

20. Who recommended the requests were approved?

20. _____

21. How many times have you wrote to them?

21. _____

22. You will have received a corrected statement of your account within the next few days.

22. _____

23. Next Monday she will be living here a year.

23. _____

24. We would have been surprised if the plants had growed any taller.

24. _____

25. You, as well as he, knows what the outcome is likely to be.

25. _____

PART 4 TEST

Other Parts of Speech and Their Usage
(Units 13–16)

 A **Which of the words shown in parentheses is correct? Write your answer in the space provided.**

1. You are entitled to a (10 percent, 10-percent) discount.

2. This building is (government owned, government-owned).

3. We may try (and, to) lease more office space.

4. The reason she was absent is (because, that) she was ill.

5. How much (farther, further) will you need to travel each day?

6. Of the three, which one is (good, better, best)?

7. Was anyone (beside, besides) her given a merit increase?

8. I doubt that we need (any, no) more of those.

9. He seems to know less about it (than, then) we do.

10. (Almost, Most) everyone has endorsed the new plan.

11. It is (liable, likely) to rain later today.

12. We processed (fewer, less) orders yesterday than we did this morning.

13. Do you think their prices are (to, too, two) high?

14. Both of you (sure, surely) knew what their response would be.

15. Helping others makes most people feel (good, well).

16. This is a (real, very) interesting position.

17. California is more populous than (any, any other) state.

18. Which of (that, them, those) letters needs to be answered?

19. The label had fallen (off, off of) the folder.

20. Everyone was there (accept, except) you.

21. I don't think the situation looks (bad, badly), do you?

22. The visit ended rather (abrupt, abruptly).

23. I don't know where they were (going, going to), do you?

24. Both critics gave the movie (a, an) excellent review.

25. What (kind of, kind of a) license is needed?

1. _____

2. _____

3. _____

4. _____

5. _____

6. _____

7. _____

8. _____

9. _____

10. _____

11. _____

12. _____

13. _____

14. _____

15. _____

16. _____

17. _____

18. _____

19. _____

20. _____

21. _____

22. _____

23. _____

24. _____

25. _____

The following sentences contain errors involving adjectives, adverbs, prepositions, and conjunctions. Underline each error, and write the necessary correction in the space provided. If no correction is needed, write *OK*.

1. Are these packages already to ship?

2. I think it was in August when we bought this machine.

3. Fay is a officer of the company.

4. Some of their coworkers criticized them for taking their responsibilities so casual.

5. We couldn't hardly hear either of the first two speakers.

6. Perhaps we need to spend sometime with them.

7. Regulators said the arrangement was an elicit one.

8. He said that he hasn't been feeling good for several days.

9. We should not leave early without we notify someone.

10. Something doesn't seem quite right, does it?

11. She got a well-paying job right away.

12. The meeting was scheduled for today, and it was postponed until next week.

13. This machine operates more efficient than either of those.

14. The increase is retroactive from January 1.

15. I am not sure who the principle stockholders are.

16. When does your company's physical year end?

17. This container is fuller than that one.

18. Is this report supposed to be turned into Mr. Wells tomorrow?

19. It looks like we will need to work overtime if we expect to finish this job today.

20. Mr. Morris appeared quite optimistically about the likelihood of an early settlement.

21. They have no interest or need for a larger warehouse at this point.

22. They don't never want to be stranded in such an isolated place again.

23. Wouldn't you sooner work with her than with him?

24. Is this copy different than that one?

25. Nancy spoke criticallier than anyone else.

1. _____

2. _____

3. _____

4. _____

5. _____

6. _____

7. _____

8. _____

9. _____

10. _____

11. _____

12. _____

13. _____

14. _____

15. _____

16. _____

17. _____

18. _____

19. _____

20. _____

21. _____

22. _____

23. _____

24. _____

25. _____

PART 5 TEST

Phrases, Clauses, and Sentences
(Units 17–19)

 Combine each group of sentences below into one unified, coherent sentence that emphasizes the part of the thought that you consider important. Add, omit, and change words as necessary. Note that some of the sentences contain errors.

1. A spokesperson for the company made an announcement. The company is combining some of its head-quarters operations. It is also opening two new branch offices.

_____

_____

2. Ms. Moreno has two immediate goals. One of them is to complete work toward a degree in accounting. The other is to obtain a position with a firm in Chicago.

_____

_____

3. David Weston worked for Woburn & Company for three years. He was a marketing representative. He will join our staff next week. He will be assistant manager of our marketing department.

_____

_____

4. I was in Lansing last week. I met with Denise Lopez. Denise is one of our consultants.

_____

_____

5. Dr. Ellis is planning to hold a meeting. He's scheduled it for next Friday morning. He will discuss various changes in employee benefits paid for by the company.

_____

_____

 For each of the following phrases, write a short sentence in which the phrase functions as the part of speech indicated in parentheses.

1. In the early fall (*Adverb*)

_____

_____

2. Using public transportation (*Noun*)

_____

_____

3. Bought at special sale prices *(Adjective)*

_____

_____

4. To use credit wisely *(Noun)*

_____

_____

5. For new employees *(Adjective)*

_____

_____

C Underline each error in the following sentences, and write the necessary correction in the space provided. If a sentence does not contain an error, write *OK*.

1. There is several letters that need to be answered immediately.　**1.** _____

2. I would have gone if they would have asked me.　**2.** _____

3. Don't he expect you to call me today?　**3.** _____

4. The report may be a few days' late.　**4.** _____

5. They maybe here within a few minutes.　**5.** _____

6. Do you think we should study their proposal further?　**6.** _____

7. In my opinion, everyone must decide for themselves.　**7.** _____

8. They are employees and stockholders to.　**8.** _____

9. What does the president and the chief executive officer think of your proposal?　**9.** _____

10. I hope they ask you and myself for our suggestions.　**10.** _____

11. Oliver took it upon hisself to conduct those negotiations.　**11.** _____

12. Neither of the bridegrooms rented their tuxedo.　**12.** _____

13. We do not want to spend no more than necessary.　**13.** _____

14. I think that I would of accepted almost any entry-level job.　**14.** _____

15. None of us could have predicted Jack resigning.　**15.** _____

16. You have more sales experience than me.　**16.** _____

17. It is a matter of principal as far as they are concerned.　**17.** _____

18. Do you think us objecting will make any difference?　**18.** _____

19. The customers' standing in line didn't notice anything unusual.　**19.** _____

20. I thought both machines had been inspected thorough, didn't you?　**20.** _____

PART 6 TEST

Capitalization and Number Style
(Units 20–22)

 Draw three lines under each letter or group of letters that should be capitalized in each of the following sentences. In addition, draw a line under each word or group of words that should be underscored. If a sentence requires no change, circle the number preceding it.

1. Are you sure, may, that one of the shops in lincoln square village sells china?

2. I think marilyn painter said that she would like to work as a teller for the chemical bank and trust company.

3. The publication of a sequel to gone with the wind in the fall of 1991 produced mixed reactions among southerners, northerners, and others.

4. Are you sure that miss green has a bachelor's degree from northwestern university?

5. Lloyd Bates, president and chief executive officer, said, "we have expanded our operations to cover every state in the union. early in the twenty-first century we expect to open offices in europe, asia, and africa."

6. Someone told me that former governor roswell is a graduate of the united states military academy at west point.

7. Will the president's address to a joint session of congress be broadcast by nbc or some other network?

8. Would I want to live on a farm north of the city? maybe.

9. Perhaps you should ask tax consultant Yvonne de la Vega whether you need to file schedule d with your form 1040 this year.

10. Our accounting department compiled the data appearing in table 2 on page 9.

11. If you like polish food, I can give you the name of an excellent restaurant in the windy city.

12. Some coworkers who went camping in the rockies said they took nothing with them but several cans of campbell's soup, a few dozen grade a eggs, and a bottle of bayer aspirin.

13. The article "saving energy: a do-it-yourself guide," which appeared in the spring issue of home and garden quarterly, generated a great deal of interest.

14. Please note: prices quoted are f.o.b. salt lake city and are subject to change without notice.

15. The question is, is it the responsibility of the federal deposit insurance corporation or some other agency of the federal government?

16. Sara Farley, ph.d., was living in new york state before she moved to salt lake city.

17. If you have studied business management, business english, and related subjects, you will want to attend this special seminar.

18. She said she received an a in each of these courses: american history, computer science 200, and spanish 120.

19. "You won't want to miss our fantastic fourth of july celebration," the mayor said.

20. The metropolitan museum of art is exhibiting works by van gogh.

21. Please remember to specify:
1. the date, time, and place of the meeting.
2. what materials the attendees will need to bring with them.

22. Is their office located on northern boulevard or on south tenth street?

23. I suggest, sir, that you ask her whether she prefers to use the title ms., miss, or mrs.

24. The ambassador was particularly interested in an exhibit of pre-columbian artifacts.

25. They are on flight 200, which is scheduled to arrive at o'hare at 8:45 p.m.

B Underline each error in the expression of numbers and related terms in the following sentences, and write the necessary correction in the space provided. For each sentence that requires no correction, write *OK*.

1. I made a payment of $225 on June 10th.   **1.** _____

2. In the early '90s the value of the firm's assets was between $200 and $225 million.   **2.** _____

3. They obtained a $60,000 mortgage at eight and one-half percent.   **3.** _____

4. The room is 11 feet, 9 inches by 18 feet.   **4.** _____

5. She owns one-half of the stock; he owns the other half.   **5.** _____

6. The repairs will cost several 1,000 dollars.   **6.** _____

7. The quarterly dividend has been as low as $.12 and as high as $1.22.   **7.** _____

8. Twelve of the 36 items in that container were damaged.   **8.** _____

9. Our new office is at 3260 North 4th Street.   **9.** _____

10. The letter concerning Invoice 430 was dated 4/10/92.   **10.** _____

11. A large percent of customers buy two or three at a time.   **11.** _____

12. Flight 330 is scheduled to arrive at 2 o'clock p.m.   **12.** _____

13. Her home address is 3204 Wellington Place, Tampa, Florida 33,612.   **13.** _____

14. About ¾ of the work has been completed.   **14.** _____

15. I think she was 22 last week.   **15.** _____

16. I think 2 requisitions were for 3 dozen notepads and 10 reams of plain paper.   **16.** _____

17. 150 questionnaires were mailed the 10th.   **17.** _____

18. This carton contains 24 8-ounce jars.   **18.** _____

19. Table 8 appears in Chapter ix.   **19.** _____

20. The company will celebrate its 100th anniversary in 2002.   **20.** _____

21. Of the 64,200 miles she traveled last year, only 4800 were by automobile.   **21.** _____

22. In 1991 32 new positions were added in the company's Los Angeles office.   **22.** _____

23. The meeting continued most of the a.m.   **23.** _____

24. If we sell them for $12.50 each, our profit will be 12.6%.   **24.** _____

25. The daily fluctuation is between .75 and 1 percent.   **25.** _____

PART 7 TEST

Punctuation (Units 23–31)

Insert the necessary commas, periods, quotation marks, underscores, and other punctuation marks in the following sentences. When necessary, use a caret ($\wedge$ or $\vee$) to indicate where a punctuation mark should be inserted. Do not make any changes in capitalization. If a sentence requires no additional punctuation, circle the number preceding it. Note the example.

0. "The meeting should end around 3:30, Ms. Wilson said.

1. I am not certain whether their office is in Columbus Ohio or in Columbus Georgia.

2. Computers printers fax machines all are available at greatly reduced prices at all our stores in the Minneapolis St Paul area.

3. His current home address is as follows 4240 Beloit Road Rockford Illinois 61110-7077.

4. What do you think of Russs handling of the labor management dispute

5. According to this prospectus income from such investments is tax exempt.

6. Yes we offer a wide selection of carpeting in 9 12 and 15 foot widths.

7. How long would it take us to drive from here to Chicago to St. Louis to Indianapolis

8. The question is How long can we afford to wait for them to decide what they want to do

9. Senator elect Sue Ames is co-owner of that real estate agency isn't she

10. Some people misspell the word parallel by using two ls at the end of the word too.

11. The announcement was made at 8 15 a m CST.

12. What a wonderful surprise exclaimed Miss Hardwick

13. Surprisingly the month by month summary see Table 2 on page 6 indicates an average gain of 3.2 percent.

14. It was she not he who suggested that we should trade in that equipment by mid September.

15. The manager asked how much longer it would take to finish the project.

16. Mrs. Crawford our director of marketing has asked all of the regional managers to update their sales and expense budgets for the third quarter.

17. Many English words such as macadam and pasteurize are derived from names of people others such as china and damask are taken from names of places.

18. Would you please notify each member of your staff of these changes

19. The seminars are tentatively scheduled for Wednesday May 4 Thursday May 12 and Tuesday May 17 Roger

20. Will either of those companies Mr. Winters asked be invited to bid on this project

21. We are very very fortunate to have Edith McBride Ph D as a member of our staff.

22. Congratulations All of us are delighted to hear that you have been appointed vice president and general manager of Freiberg Foley & Burns.

23. Jeff as well as Maureen will be at the meeting however no one representing our department has been invited.

24. Friends and close relatives for example should not be given as references when applying for a job.

25. I thought that Mr. Graham asked why the order was shipped c o d

26. Would you be willing to answer this letter for me

27. To obtain a free copy simply sign and return the enclosed card.

28. Some of the positions will be filled in January others in June or July.

29. Thinking interest rates would drop further they decided to wait a few more months before applying for a home improvement loan.

30. The owners permit tenants to have some animals as pets for example small dogs cats and birds.

31. Normally the report is issued soon after the end of our fiscal year that is June 30.

32. The committee discussed proposed changes in the benefits program but according to the chairperson it has no immediate plans to accept or reject any of them.

33. When the next conference will be held has not been announced has it

34. A requirement such as that one is in my opinion unreasonable.

35. Containers such as those should not be used because they are not biodegradable.

36. Real gems such as diamonds pearls and rubies are often difficult to distinguish from synthetic ones.

37. The attorney handling the case is R. J. Wheeler, Jr.'s new law partner Melissa Patterson.

38. According to the official reports of an impending merger are erroneous.

39. We are confident that you too will want to take advantage of this once in a lifetime investment opportunity.

40. One of our customers namely Lockwood Industries bought nearly $7500 worth of merchandise last month.

41. To become the leader in its field is the company's goal.

42. Consequently banks and others offering charge cards have increased their interest rates.

43. In 1980 80 percent of those surveyed were in favor of such a plan in 1990 68 percent of those who participated in a similar survey thought such a plan was a good idea.

44. The series of articles which I found very interesting appeared in The New York Times.

45. After calling Joe Jack decided that he should summarize their discussion in a memo to the general manager

46. At 9 o'clock tomorrow morning Ms. Hammond said we are scheduled to meet with a group of investors

47. To tell the truth I made a serious mistake I should have read the contract very very carefully before signing it.

48. Do you have a copy of the March 1992 agreement in your files Henry

49. He gave Springfield Illinois as his birthplace and March 10 1971 as his birthdate.

50. The company offers evening courses in keyboarding business writing and so on throughout the year.

NAME _____ DATE _____

PART 8 TEST

Words and Word References
(Units 32–35)

 A **Which of the words shown in parentheses correctly completes the sentence? Write your answer in the space provided.**

1. Those two colors are (complementary, complimentary). 1. _____

2. How would you assess the (moral, morale) of the staff? 2. _____

3. The recognition you have received is (overdo, overdue). 3. _____

4. The hotel gave us a tastefully decorated (suit, suite). 4. _____

5. Thank you for your (assistance, assistants). 5. _____

6. These have (all ready, already) been checked. 6. _____

7. What (advice, advise) did you offer them? 7. _____

8. All have been reviewed (accept, except) this one. 8. _____

9. How will that (affect, effect) the others? 9. _____

10. Perhaps it was (all together, altogether) unnecessary. 10. _____

11. We may be able to (adapt, adept, adopt) their plan to suit our particular needs. 11. _____

12. They have been here (every day, everyday) this week. 12. _____

13. The stage play was (adapted, adopted) for TV. 13. _____

14. A small (amount, number) of accounts are in arrears. 14. _____

15. They (passed, past) us on the way to work. 15. _____

16. How do they treat their (employees, help)? 16. _____

17. I would (rather, sooner) work with you than with anyone else. 17. _____

18. How much (experience, past experience) do you have? 18. _____

19. Would you (kindly, please) inform them? 19. _____

20. (Before, Prior to) joining our company, she worked for The Bates Corporation. 20. _____

21. In many respects, they are (alike, both alike). 21. _____

22. I doubt that such a statement would be (comprehensive, comprehensible) to anyone. 22. _____

23. We should invest in it, (irregardless, regardless) of what the others do. 23. _____

24. (Incidently, Incidentally), how much will your suggestion save the company? 24. _____

25. A large (percent, percentage) of the claims were invalid. 25. _____

B In the space provided, write the word formed by adding the suffix or prefix shown in parentheses.

1. care (ful)
2. defer (ed)
3. mar (ed)
4. (re) enter
5. (mis) sent
6. whole (ly)
7. (bi) annual
8. (mid) July
9. (inter) state
10. value (able)

1. _____
2. _____
3. _____
4. _____
5. _____
6. _____
7. _____
8. _____
9. _____
10. _____

11. (co) owner
12. appraise (al)
13. deny (ing)
14. (ab) normal
15. (il) logical
16. wall (less)
17. sincere (ity)
18. house (hold)
19. (self) control
20. (dis) allow

11. _____
12. _____
13. _____
14. _____
15. _____
16. _____
17. _____
18. _____
19. _____
20. _____

C From the following list of words, select an appropriate synonym for the italicized word in each sentence below. Write the word you select in the space provided.

revealed   position   viewpoint   worthy   hinder   believable   informal   deniable

1. We should try to view the situation from their *perspective*.
2. They were dressed in *casual* attire.
3. Such information should not be *divulged*.
4. We should allow nothing to *impede* our progress.
5. The story did not seem *credible*.

1. _____
2. _____
3. _____
4. _____
5. _____

D Underline the misspelled word, if any, in each line of words below; then write the word correctly in the space provided. If none of the words in the line are misspelled, write *OK*.

1. differed   referal   preference   conference   1. _____
2. sincerely   hilly   oilly   usually   2. _____
3. eighth   ninty   fourteenth   twelfth   3. _____
4. judgment   judging   managment   managing   4. _____
5. attorneys   compelled   withheld   embarrased   5. _____

E Which word shown at the right of the italicized word is opposite in meaning to the italicized word? Write your answer in the space provided.

1. *circuitous*   square   direct   short   1. _____
2. *potent*   strong   weak   poisonous   2. _____
3. *chastised*   praised   punished   purified   3. _____
4. *ambiguous*   vague   clear   petite   4. _____
5. *complex*   difficult certain   simple   5. _____

A **Underline each error in the following sentences, and write the necessary correction in the space provided. If a sentence requires no correction, write _OK_. Note the example.**

0. Each of the companies were represented.   **0.** was (represented)

1. If you was the general manager, what would you do?   **1.** _____

2. Both of the analysises were helpful.   **2.** _____

3. They are members of a manufacturers' association.   **3.** _____

4. We should of told you last Friday.   **4.** _____

5. Maybe they will accept our offer.   **5.** _____

6. Perhaps he has no one to blame but hisself.   **6.** _____

7. Do each of the others have a copy?   **7.** _____

8. She likes swimming and skiing better than to play tennis.   **8.** _____

9. We don't want to order no more like those.   **9.** _____

10. This medicine does not taste badly to me.   **10.** _____

11. She is the one who we are planning to hire.   **11.** _____

12. I doubt that anyone will object to us taking the day off.   **12.** _____

13. She doesn't know where he was at yesterday.   **13.** _____

14. Has anyone else wrote to you about our discount policy?   **14.** _____

15. I believe most everybody agrees with you.   **15.** _____

16. We need to try and find a solution quickly.   **16.** _____

17. Dr. Collins probably will want you and myself to work this week-end.   **17.** _____

18. We wanted to have met with them last week.   **18.** _____

19. Which of these four ads is more appealing?   **19.** _____

20. Who do you think we should hire?   **20.** _____

21. Every man, woman, and child in the area were at the picnic.   **21.** _____

22. I am certain that neither the car or the van was parked illegally.   **22.** _____

23. They sat the cartons near the door and left.   **23.** _____

24. We do not want Ann or he to be disappointed.   **24.** _____

25. She is a honorary member of the society.   **25.** _____

26. John is living here since last July, and he seems to like this area.   **26.** _____

27. Both of their daughter-in-laws are attorneys.   **27.** _____

28. The driver obviously was not looking when he ran in to the stop sign.

28. _____

29. I don't write as legible as she does.

29. _____

30. Do you think these kind of bulbs will last longer?

30. _____

31. The Walshes and the Rileys are co-owners of two research laboratorys.

31. _____

32. I hope they will let you or I inspect the premises.

32. _____

33. When will you be eligible for a three weeks vacation?

33. _____

34. Was a number of employees ill last week?

34. _____

35. Are you Russ's and Barbara's supervisor?

35. _____

36. There has been only two complaints so far.

36. _____

37. Mrs. Haines, as well as several other experts, have spoke on that topic.

37. _____

38. The company has made it's position known.

38. _____

39. Doesn't he have more experience than her?

39. _____

40. There were less people attending this year than there were last year.

40. _____

41. This one is quite different than that one.

41. _____

42. Do you think any one with a master's degree would be interested?

42. _____

43. Atlanta is larger than any city in Georgia.

43. _____

44. I think that a hundred pounds are too much for either of them to carry.

44. _____

45. Do you know whose planning to buy that land?

45. _____

46. None of the cartons was setting in the hall.

46. _____

47. They had all ready left when I arrived.

47. _____

48. Are you certain they're planning to invite we administrative assistants?

48. _____

49. It takes him more longer to get to work than it takes me.

49. _____

50. Mine is the only one of the expense reports that were questioned last month.

50. _____

 B **Insert the necessary periods, commas, and other punctuation marks in the following sentences. Draw three lines under each letter or group of letters that should be capitalized. If a sentence is correct as it is shown, circle the number preceding it. Note the example.**

0. How many citizens of our state, governor burnside asked, do you think will support such a tax-abatement plan?

1. To improve our competitive position dr stone said is our objective and weve made significant progress toward achieving it

2. Doesnt ex senator walton have an interest in some firms in the new jersey pennsylvania area

3. Secretaries accountants managers everyone will I believe be interested in the article planning for tomorrow in the july issue of *investment weekly* one of our new magazines of special interest.

4. We undoubtedly will have an exhibit at the trade fair in green bay wisconsin next spring however I am less certain about our participation in other meetings.

5. The order was placed on monday and received on thursday carol conway said.

6. Our special sales on columbus day independence day and other holidays are very very popular.

7. Many retailers offer stoves refrigerators and other household appliances at greatly reduced prices during their once a year clearance sales.

8. Nevertheless both of them would like to know more about the position

9. When you see miss cook Cindy be sure to ask her about the changes in the west coast office.

10. Sanford Baker & Adams a local law firm will represent several Lane Bros. officers named in the suit brought by one of the companys largest clients.

11. The irs may raise a number of questions about such things as interest free loans large charitable contributions etc. dont you think

12. My next question is this mayor Do you plan to seek reelection or do you plan to enter the real estate business

13. I called her on Thursday June 14 but according to my notes she was not in the office.

14. We are planning to drive to overland park which is located in johnson county.

15. Did they have an office in Salt Lake city or somewhere else in the state of Utah at that time

16. It was Floyd not Lloyd who said that the company was being investigated by the securities and exchange commission or some other government agency.

17. "Well, I certainly hope that you sell nothing but grade a dairy products," one of the customers commented

18. In 1991 see the chart on page 10 three products accounted for about half of our sales.

19. Ms. Adams read the letter and forwarded it to lawyer Kathleen Kiley.

20. By the first of may of next year we should be in our spacious modern headquarters at the corner of oak avenue and broadway.

21. Danforth and Associates as well as Jackson Inc. has branch offices in these cities Independence Missouri Gary Indiana and Oak Park Illinois.

22. We need to consider the short and long term consequences of such actions.

23. One of our senior vice presidents Bonita Hooper has agreed to meet with representatives of abc cbs and nbc.

24. What a bargain exclaimed one of the shoppers

25. Mr. Lopez is a well known and highly respected member of the Latin American community and he has served as a consultant to several federal agencies.

 C **Underline each error in word choice, spelling, number expression, or abbreviation usage in the following sentences, and write the necessary correction in the space provided. If a sentence is correct as it is shown, write *OK*.**

1. We placed an order for letterhead stationery on May 10th.

    1. _____

2. Two of the mispelled words in the June 1, 1991, agreement were *accommodate* and *recommend*.

    2. _____

3. A number of preThanksgiving shoppers watched the parade from the top of One Park Place.

    3. _____

4. I thought the meeting was to be this a.m.

    4. _____

5. We have leased 2 floors of the 12-story office building at 200 West Elm Street.

6. We need a few 100 more of those 16-page pamphlets.

7. An acknowledgment of the agreement would not be inappropriate.

8. I am certain that I paid the bill, but I can't find the recipe.

9. Whom did the authors sight as the source of that information?

10. We were fortunate to obtain a $10,000 loan at 12 and a half percent in 1989.

11. Do you think it's liable to rain today?

12. Of the 12 plates, two were broken.

13. Those lacking proper credentials will be bared from the hearings.

14. Our consultants recommended that we provide our employees more comprehensible medical insurance.

15. After two trys, he decided to give up.

16. $400.00 seems to be a reasonable price for that piece of equipment.

17. About ¾ of the company's common stock is owned by institutional investors.

18. None of our executives have any personal knowledge of any misappropriation of funds.

19. An absence of 3 days obviously requires an explanation.

20. If one store sells this item for 80¢, why should I pay you $1.20 for it?

21. We believe a large amount of people will be interested in those products.

22. Only a small percent think such a zoning ordinance should be adopted.

23. We intend to proceed, irregardless of what any of the others do.

24. This room is 12 feet eight inches long.

25. I thought your office was at 1200 South Twelfth Street.

5. _____

6. _____

7. _____

8. _____

9. _____

10. _____

11. _____

12. _____

13. _____

14. _____

15. _____

16. _____

17. _____

18. _____

19. _____

20. _____

21. _____

22. _____

23. _____

24. _____

25. _____